Leadership Anatomy

Deconstruct Theories for Victory

Satpreet Singh

(BOOK TITLE GOES HERE)
Copyright © 2023 by Satpreet Singh

All rights reserved. No part of this book may be reproduced or transmitted in any form or by any means without written permission from the author.

ISBN: 978-1-7375532-2-9 (Print)
ISBN: 978-1-7375532-4-3 (E-Book)

LCCN: 2023947647

Printed in the USA by Sikh Reference Library USA

SPECIAL THANKS

To the eternal leader of leaders, Sahib Sri Guru Gobind Singh Ji, whose profound wisdom, and unwavering courage continue to inspire leaders across the ages. His legacy is a testament to the enduring spirit of leadership.

I also extend my heartfelt gratitude to the mother of the Khalsa Panth, Mata Sahib Kaur Ji, whose strength, resilience, and unwavering support have been a guiding force for leaders within the Khalsa community and beyond.

In the earthly realm, I am deeply grateful to my parents, Sardar Tasvir Singh and Sardarni Raj Kaur, for their boundless love, encouragement, and unwavering belief in my journey as a leader and author. Their wisdom and support have been the cornerstone of my endeavors.

To my beloved wife, Rupinder Kaur, your unwavering support, love, and patience have been the driving force behind this endeavor. Her strength and encouragement sustain me in my pursuit of knowledge and leadership.

Satpreet Singh

DEDICATION

With utmost respect and admiration, this book is dedicated to the Leaders of Khalsa Panth, For their unwavering commitment to principles of courage, equality, and justice. Their leadership has been a guiding light, inspiring generations to stand firm in the face of adversity. May their legacy of selfless service and unwavering resolve continue to illuminate the path to victory for all.

TABLE OF CONTENTS

Foreword xxi

Chapter One
Unpacking Leadership Theories 1
    Role of Leadership 1
    Multifaceted Nature 3
    Significance of Understanding 5
    Core Principles 8
    Relevance in Modern Leadership 10
    Need for Deconstruction 12
    How to Deconstruct 14
    Benefits of Deconstruction 17

Chapter Two
The Foundation of Leadership and Theories 23
    Understanding the Historical Roots 24
    Evolution 25
    Leadership in Military and Strategic Context 28
    Philosophical Perspective 31
    Industrial Revolution 35
    Transition From Agrarian to Industrial 37

Scientific Management and Efficiency Driven.........39
Early 20th-Century..41
Connection to Historical Notion...............................44
Influence of Historical Perspective...........................46
Civil Rights Movement and Leadership...................51
Leadership Responses to Social Changes.................54
Lessons from Historical Power Structures................59
Synthesis and Reflection..61
Key Takeaways..66

Chapter 3
Innate Leadership Theories 69
    Understanding Innate Leadership 69
    Significance of Understanding..................................71
    The Great Man Theory..75
        Born Leaders and Natural Abilities 79
        Prominent Historical Leaders 81
        Evaluation and Relevance.................................85
        Implications...89
    Trait Theory 91
        Cardinal Traits 95
        Central Traits 99
        Secondary Traits 101
        Nature Vs. Nurture...105
    Effective Leadership Traits.......................................109
    Cultivating Leadership Traits 112

Chapter Four

Leadership Styles and Approaches 115
    Laissez-Faire Leadership 117
        Origin 119
        Advantages and Disadvantages 121
        When it works 125
        Case Study 129
        Impact on Morale 133
        Minimal Intervention 134
        Strategies for Motivation 136
        Examination of Challenges 140
    Charismatic Leadership 142
        Qualities 144
        Examples 148
        Strategies of Cultivation 150
        Steps for Communication 152
        Examination of Ethical Implications 156
        Potential Downsides 158
    Autocratic Leadership 160
        Key Characteristics 160
        Historical Context 162
        Demanding Situations 168
        Effective Use 170
        Directive Leadership 173
        Adaptive Leadership 175

Chapter Five

Behavior and Interactional Theories 179
    Behavioral Theories 182
    Historical Context 185
    Specific Behaviors 188
    Real World Example 190
    Models 192
    Case Study 198
    Role of Communication 204
    Decision-Making and Problem-Solving 208
    Conflict Resolution and Negotiation 214
    Relationship Leadership 219
    Interpersonal Dynamics 222
    Key Interpersonal Skills 225
    Influence and Persuasion 230
    Analysis of Interpersonal Skills 235
    Compatibility 243
    Emotional Intelligence 248

Chapter Six

Situational and Contextual Theories 255
    Importance 256
    Contingency Theory 260
    Historical Context 262
    Matching Leadership Style 269

Strategies to Assess Situation 271
Case Study 273
Flexibility in Leadership..278
Assess Demand of Different Situations 283
Communication and Feedback...................................289
Situational Leadership and Model 292
Examples...296
Challenges and Criticism 297
Broader Perspective 302
Case Study 308
Continuous Learning...311

Chapter Seven
Transformational and Modern Approaches 317
    Importance 318
    Transformational Leadership.....................................322
        Historical Context 324
        Components 326
        Examples..330
        Impact 332
        Case Study 339
        Analysis of Components.................................342
    Authentic Leadership..359
        Key Principles...360
        Importance 362
        Strategies to Embrace 365

Role of Value 370
Self-Reflection and Growth 374
Strategies for Continuous Growth 376
Authentic Organization Culture 379
Steps for Leaders..382

Chapter Eight
Decision-Making and Influence Theories 385
Importance 387
Vroom's Decision-Making Theory 391
Historical Context 394
Key Concept..396
Symbolic Leadership 397
Examples..399
Variants of Decision-Making..........................401
When and How to Apply Variants..................403
Dynamics of Decision Making 410
Impact of Style...414
Influential Factors 416
Ethical-Decision Making 421
Power and Influence Theory 426
Source of Power..431
Leveraging Source of Power.........................435
Influential Tactics 439
Balancing Power and Responsibility 446
Strategies for Maintaining Balance................449

Developing Influence Skills..................................456

Chapter Nine
LMX and Contextual Approaches 461
   Significance..462
   Dynamics and Individual Interactions 464
   Leader-Member Exchange...466
      Leader-Member Exchange Theory 466
      Managerial Implications 468
      Historical Context 469
      In-Group and Ou-Group Dynamics 473
      Treatment of Team Members................................476
      Implications of Differentiated Team....................479
      Strategies of Positive LMX Relationship 482
      Benefits of High-Quality LMX Relationship 489
      Challenges and Pitfalls..494
      Communication Techniques 498
   Path-Goal Theory..501
      Historical Context 504
      Situational Demand..508
      Clearing the Path..511
      Align Individual and Team Goals........................516
      Case Studies..518
      Impact on Employee Satisfaction 522
      Adaptive Leadership Under Path-Goal Theory ...526

Chapter Ten

Servant and Coaching Leadership 531
    Servant Leadership 536
        Historical Context 538
        Core Principals 542
        Role of empathy and support 546
        Case Study 552
        Analysis of Empathy and Support 554
        Benefits 557
        Positive Organizational Culture 559
        Challenges and Criticism 561
        Strategies for Addressing Challenges 564
        Developing Servant Leadership Skills 567
    Coaching Leadership 570
        Historical Context 573
        Key Principals 574
        Role of Coch Leader 578
        Difference from Traditional Leadership 581
        Techniques and Strategies 584
        Case Study 593
        Examination of Role 596
        Feedback and Accountability 601
        Techniques for Constructive Feedback 604

Chapter Eleven

Leadership Adaptation and Future Trends 607

Critical Need 608
Importance of Aligning Leadership Styles 610
Historical Examples 615
Evolving Global Landscape 617
Challenges and Opportunities 622
Strategies for Leaders 625
Global Trends and Shifts 628
Technology and Digital Leadership 633
Cultural Competency and Diversity 638
Sustainability and Ethical Leadership 644
Leadership Development and Future Trends 648
Prediction of Future Trends 653
Role of Continuous Learning 659

Chapter Twelve

Reflection and Integration 665
    Integration 666
    Role of Integration and Reflection 669
    Identification of Personal Insights 671
    Prompts of Reflection 673
    Ever Evolving Tapestry 676
    Role of Change and Innovation 679
    Leaders Role in Driving Change 681
    Challenges and Opportunities 684
    The Ethical Imperative of Leadership 688
    Integration and Synthesis 693

Creating Personal Leadership Philosophy 696

Appendix One 701

Appendix Two 703

*****

FOREWORD

In the pursuit of victory, leadership stands as the beacon that guides us through the often-turbulent waters of progress and achievement. It is a journey where theory meets practice, where strategies are molded by insight, and where the mastery of leadership is the key to realizing our boldest aspirations.

In "Leadership Anatomy: Deconstruct Theories for Victory," Satpreet Singh, an accomplished organizational leader, entrepreneur, and seasoned researcher with eight copyrights to his name, takes us on an exhilarating expedition through the intricate world of leadership. His wealth of experience and relentless curiosity about the art and science of leadership shine brightly in the pages of this book.

"Leadership Anatomy" is not just a book; it's a roadmap to success. Satpreet has skillfully dissected the diverse theories that underpin leadership, from traditional traits and behaviors to modern paradigms like servant and coaching leadership. With every chapter, he unveils the layers that make up the very fabric of leadership.

What sets this book apart is its unwavering commitment to practicality. Satpreet Singh deftly connects theoretical constructs to real-world scenarios, offering profound insights into how these theories can be brought to life. Through illuminating case studies, actionable examples, and thought-provoking exercises, he empowers readers to not only understand but also apply these theories in their own leadership journeys.

"Leadership Anatomy" is an inclusive guide. Whether you are a seasoned leader looking to refresh your perspective or an emerging leader eager to navigate the intricate landscape of leadership, this book has something invaluable to offer. It nurtures our capacity to adapt, urges us to reflect on our own leadership styles, and fuels our determination to confront the diverse challenges of leadership with grace and ethics.

As you embark on this voyage through the inner workings of leadership theories, under Satpreet Singh's expert guidance, I encourage you to be receptive and curious. The wisdom woven into these pages is not just for the leaders of today but for the architects of the future, those who dream of shaping a world defined by excellence and achievement.

I am honored to commend "Leadership Anatomy: Deconstruct Theories for Victory" to everyone. May this book empower you, as it has empowered countless others, to chart a course toward leadership mastery and, ultimately, the victory everyone seeks.

Rupinder Kaur
President
Sikh Reference Library USA

CHAPTER ONE
Unpacking Leadership Theory Through Deconstruction

In today's rapidly changing world, leadership theories play a crucial role. To understand the field of leadership better, we need to explore the foundational theories that have shaped it over time, starting from early trait theories to contemporary approaches such as adaptive leadership. By comprehending the historical evolution and common threads among these theories, leaders can gain insights into the core principles that underlie effective leadership. In modern leadership, deconstructing theories can help navigate complex situations. By breaking down various theories, leaders can extract practical insights that are directly applicable to real-world challenges. This process is especially relevant given the dynamic challenges organizations face today.

Role of Leadership in Today's Dynamic World

In the rapidly evolving landscape of the 21st century, the role of leadership has taken on unprecedented significance. Organizations across sectors are facing a multitude of challenges, including technological advancements, globalization, economic uncertainty, and shifting workforce dynamics. In this context, effective leadership has emerged as a cornerstone for navigating these challenges and driving organizational success.

Leadership extends far beyond traditional notions of authority and management. Today, leaders are expected to be visionary, adaptable, and empathetic, capable of guiding their teams through ambiguity and change. They are tasked with fostering innovation, cultivating diverse and inclusive workplaces, and maintaining a strong ethical compass amidst complex decision-making.

Navigating Complexity and Uncertainty

The modern world is characterized by volatility, uncertainty, complexity, and ambiguity (VUCA). Rapid technological advancements disrupt industries, consumer preferences shift rapidly, and global events can trigger unexpected changes. In this environment, leaders must possess the ability to steer their organizations through turbulence while maintaining strategic focus.

Inspiring and Mobilizing Teams

Effective leadership is about more than just giving orders; it involves inspiring and mobilizing teams toward a common vision. Leaders must be able to communicate their vision clearly, instill a sense of purpose, and empower their team members to contribute their best efforts. This requires strong communication skills, emotional intelligence, and the capacity to foster a positive and collaborative team culture.

Adapting to Changing Workforce Dynamics

The nature of work itself is transforming, with remote and flexible work arrangements becoming more common. This requires leaders to adapt their management styles and find new ways to engage and motivate team members who may be geographically dispersed.

Ethical and Social Responsibility

Leadership in the modern world extends beyond the boundaries of an organization. Leaders are expected to make ethical decisions that consider not only their organization's success but also the impact on society and the environment. Corporate social responsibility and ethical leadership are integral to building trust and long-term sustainability.

Innovation and Creativity

Innovation is a driving force in modern business, and leaders play a pivotal role in fostering a culture of creativity and innovation within their organizations. They need to encourage experimentation, provide resources for new ideas, and create an environment where calculated risks are embraced.

The Multifaceted Nature of Leadership

Leadership is a dynamic and multi-dimensional concept that encompasses a diverse range of qualities, behaviors, and skills. To fully appreciate the complexity of leadership, it's essential to explore its various facets in detail.

Influential and Visionary

Leaders are visionaries who possess the ability to inspire and motivate others to work towards a common goal. They articulate a clear and compelling vision, outlining a desired future state that resonates with their team members. Through effective communication and charisma, leaders galvanize individuals to contribute their efforts towards the achievement of this shared vision.

Adaptive and Flexible

Effective leadership is not rigid; it adapts to the context and needs of the situation. Leaders understand that different challenges require different approaches. They can transition between different leadership styles, such as transformational, situational, or servant leadership, depending on the circumstances. This adaptability ensures that leaders can respond appropriately to various scenarios, fostering greater effectiveness.

Emotionally Intelligent and Empathetic

Leadership is not just about tasks and strategies; it's also about relationships. Leaders with high emotional intelligence can perceive, understand, and manage their own emotions as well as the emotions of others. They practice empathy, actively listening to their team members' concerns and feedback. This emotional connection cultivates trust and rapport, enabling leaders to build strong, collaborative teams.

Strategic and Forward-Thinking

Leaders operate with a strategic mindset, considering both short-term objectives and long-term goals. They possess the ability to analyze complex situations, anticipate challenges, and make informed decisions that align with the organization's overarching mission. Strategic leaders take a holistic view, ensuring that their actions contribute to the sustainability and growth of the organization.

Collaborative and Team-Oriented

Modern leadership places a strong emphasis on collaboration and teamwork. Leaders who promote a culture of inclusivity and cooperation create an environment where diverse perspectives are valued. They encourage open dialogue, foster a sense of belonging, and facilitate the exchange of ideas. This team-oriented approach leads to higher engagement, innovation, and productivity.

Ethical and Responsible

Ethics are an integral part of effective leadership. Ethical leaders adhere to a set of moral principles, making decisions that are not only in the best interest of the organization but also aligned with broader societal values. They prioritize integrity, honesty, and transparency, setting an example for ethical behavior throughout the organization.

Continuous Learning and Growth

Leadership is a journey of continuous improvement. Effective leaders invest in their personal development, seeking opportunities to enhance their skills and knowledge. They remain curious, staying attuned to emerging trends, technologies, and industry developments. This commitment to growth not only benefits the leader but also contributes to the organization's agility and innovation.

Leadership is a multifaceted concept that encompasses a wide array of attributes and skills. Effective leaders are influencers, visionaries, adaptable, emotionally intelligent, strategic thinkers, collaborators, ethical role models, and lifelong learners. Embracing and embodying these various facets enables leaders to navigate the complexities of the modern world and drive both personal and organizational success.

Significance of Understanding Leadership Theories

Leadership theories serve as a vital framework for comprehending the intricacies of leadership dynamics and practices within organizations. These theories provide valuable insights into how leaders can effectively navigate challenges, foster innovation, and guide their teams toward success. Understanding these theories is crucial for both aspiring and experienced leaders, as they offer a roadmap for making informed decisions and driving organizational growth.

Informing Decision-Making

Leadership theories offer a wealth of knowledge that informs decision-making. By studying these theories, leaders gain a deeper understanding of the principles that underlie effective leadership. They can analyze various situations, assess the needs of their team and organization, and make decisions that align with established best practices.

Tailoring Leadership Approaches

Every organization and team is unique, and effective leaders recognize that a one-size-fits-all approach to leadership may not be suitable. Leadership theories provide a spectrum of approaches, from charismatic leadership to transformational leadership to situational leadership. Armed with this knowledge, leaders can tailor their style to match the specific needs, goals, and challenges of their team and organizational context.

Navigating Complexity

The modern business landscape is marked by complexity, rapid change, and ambiguity. Leadership theories equip leaders with tools to navigate these challenges effectively. For example, situational leadership theories emphasize adapting leadership styles based on the specific situation, allowing leaders to address varying levels of competence and commitment within their team.

Fostering Innovation

Innovation is a cornerstone of organizational success. Leadership theories shed light on how leaders can encourage a culture of innovation within their teams. Transformational leadership, for instance, encourages creativity by inspiring employees to think outside the box and take calculated risks, ultimately driving innovation and adaptability.

Developing High-Performing Teams

Leadership theories offer insights into team dynamics and how leaders can foster collaboration, communication, and engagement. By understanding the factors that contribute to effective teamwork, leaders can create an environment that promotes synergy, shared goals, and high levels of performance.

Enhancing Communication Skills

Effective leadership hinges on strong communication. Leadership theories emphasize the significance of clear and open communication between leaders and their teams. By studying these theories, leaders can refine their communication skills, ensuring that their messages are understood, motivating, and aligned with the organization's vision.

Managing Change

Change is inevitable in today's dynamic world. Leadership theories provide strategies for effectively managing and leading through change. Leaders can draw from change management theories to facilitate smooth transitions, reduce resistance, and maintain team morale during times of transformation.

Cultivating Ethical Leadership

Ethical leadership is crucial for maintaining trust and integrity within an organization. Leadership theories often include discussions on ethical considerations and the importance of principled decision-making. Leaders can use these insights to navigate ethical dilemmas and create a culture of ethical behavior.

Continued Growth and Development

Leadership is a journey of continuous learning. By exploring various leadership theories, leaders can continue their professional development. This ongoing learning helps leaders stay relevant, adapt to new challenges, and refine their leadership skills.

Understanding leadership theories is paramount for effective leadership in today's complex and evolving world. These theories provide a foundation for informed decision-making, the adaptation of leadership styles, the navigation of challenges, and the cultivation of innovation and ethical behavior. By leveraging the insights gained from leadership theories, leaders can steer their organizations toward success while fostering a culture of excellence and growth.

Understanding Leadership's Core Principles

Amid the diverse array of leadership theories that have emerged over time, there exist common threads that weave through the fabric of leadership understanding. These threads reflect the enduring principles that underpin effective leadership, transcending the variations in approaches and perspectives. By exploring these commonalities, we gain insight into the foundational principles that guide leadership in all its forms.

1. **Influence and Inspiration:** Across all theories, leadership is fundamentally about influence and inspiration. Whether it's the visionary charisma of transformational leaders or the empowering support of servant leaders, the ability to inspire and guide individuals toward a shared goal is at the heart of effective leadership. Leaders harness their influence to motivate, guide, and direct the efforts of their teams.

2. **Adaptation to Context:** A prevailing theme is the recognition that leadership is not a static concept. Contingency theories highlighted the significance of adapting leadership approaches to suit the context, while adaptive leadership underscores the need to navigate complexity with flexibility. This principle acknowledges that the effectiveness of leadership strategies depends on the unique circumstances at play.

3. **Focus on Relationships:** Leadership theories consistently emphasize the importance of relationships. Whether it's building emotional connections in transformational leadership or serving the needs of followers in servant leadership, the quality of interactions between leaders and their teams is paramount. Effective leaders foster trust, open communication,

and collaboration, recognizing that strong relationships are the bedrock of a thriving organization.

4. **Ethical and Authentic Behavior:** Ethical conduct is a cornerstone of leadership theories. Authentic leadership emphasizes the alignment of values and actions, while the consideration of ethical dilemmas runs through the fabric of ethical decision-making in all leadership models. Leaders are expected to act with integrity, honesty, and transparency, setting an example for ethical behavior throughout their organization.

5. **Vision and Purpose:** Leadership theories consistently highlight the role of vision and purpose in guiding teams. Whether it's the shared vision of transformational leaders or the alignment of values in authentic leadership, a clear sense of direction and purpose inspires individuals to work cohesively toward a common goal. A compelling vision gives meaning to tasks and fosters a sense of unity.

6. **Continuous Learning and Growth:** Modern leadership approaches, as well as transformational theories, underscore the importance of continuous learning and personal growth. Whether it's the adaptive mindset of adaptive leadership or the pursuit of self-awareness in authentic leadership, effective leaders are committed to their own development. They recognize that leadership is a journey of growth and evolution.

7. **Empowerment and Collaboration:** Empowerment and collaboration are recurring themes in leadership theories. Servant leadership prioritizes the growth and well-being of followers, while adaptive leadership encourages teams to participate in problem-solving. These principles reflect the understanding that effective leaders empower their teams, foster collaboration, and distribute decision-making authority.

While leadership theories may differ in their terminology, frameworks, and emphases, they share these core principles that define effective leadership. By acknowledging these common threads, aspiring and practicing leaders can cultivate a holistic understanding of leadership that transcends theoretical boundaries, enabling them to navigate the complexities of leadership in a dynamic and evolving world.

The Relevance of Theory Deconstruction in Modern Leadership

In an ever-evolving world marked by rapid changes, disruptive technologies, and diverse cultural landscapes, the practice of leadership has transformed into a dynamic and multifaceted endeavor. Amid this evolution, the concept of theory deconstruction has emerged as a valuable tool for leaders seeking to navigate the complexities of modern leadership challenges. By dissecting and analyzing established leadership theories, theory deconstruction equips leaders with the insights needed to adapt and thrive in this shifting landscape.

The Shifting Landscape of Leadership

Modern leadership is characterized by unprecedented challenges, including remote work arrangements, digital transformations, global interconnectedness, and evolving employee expectations. The traditional hierarchical leadership models may no longer suffice in addressing these multifaceted complexities. Leaders are now called upon to possess a holistic understanding of diverse leadership approaches and tailor their strategies to match the unique demands of their organizations and teams.

Unprecedented Challenges

1. **Remote Work and Virtual Teams:** The rise of remote work, accelerated by technological advancements, has

redefined the dynamics of leadership. Leaders are now faced with the task of managing teams spread across different locations, time zones, and cultures. Effective communication, collaboration, and team cohesion become paramount in this scenario.

2. **Digital Transformations:** The digital era has ushered in a wave of transformations across industries. Leaders must navigate the integration of technologies like artificial intelligence, automation, and data analytics into their operations. The ability to leverage these tools while ensuring the human element is not lost becomes a crucial leadership skill.

3. **Global Interconnectedness:** Organizations are operating in an increasingly globalized world, interacting with diverse cultures, markets, and regulatory environments. Leaders must possess cross-cultural competencies and a global mindset to navigate this interconnected landscape successfully.

4. **Evolving Employee Expectations:** The expectations of the modern workforce have evolved. Employees seek purpose, meaningful work, and a healthy work-life balance. Leaders need to create inclusive and supportive environments that prioritize employee well-being, growth, and engagement.

Challenges to Traditional Hierarchical Models

The traditional hierarchical leadership models, characterized by top-down decision-making and rigid structures, are encountering limitations in addressing the multifaceted challenges of the modern era. These models may hinder agility, innovation, and adaptability, which are crucial traits in today's fast-paced environment.

The Holistic Understanding of Diverse Leadership Approaches

To navigate the complexities of the contemporary landscape, leaders must embrace a holistic understanding of diverse leadership approaches. One-size-fits-all solutions are no longer effective. Instead, leaders need to draw insights from a range of theories—such as servant leadership, transformational leadership, authentic leadership, and adaptive leadership—to tailor their strategies based on the unique demands of their organizations and teams.

Tailoring Leadership Strategies

Adapting to contemporary challenges requires leaders to be agile and responsive. Leaders may need to shift their leadership style based on the situation, whether it's fostering collaboration among remote teams, inspiring innovation through a compelling vision, or guiding teams through digital transformations. The ability to assess the context and choose the most suitable leadership approach is a hallmark of effective modern leadership.

The shifting landscape of leadership demands a departure from traditional models and a deep dive into the principles of adaptable, inclusive, and innovative leadership. Leaders must embrace change, cultivate a global perspective, and tailor their strategies to the specific needs of their teams and organizations. By doing so, they can effectively steer their organizations through the complexities of the modern world while empowering their teams to excel in a rapidly changing environment.

The Need for Theory Deconstruction

In response to challenges, the need for a deeper understanding of leadership has become paramount. This is where theory deconstruction comes into play. Theory deconstruction involves dismantling established leadership theories to examine their underlying principles, assumptions, and applications. By delving beyond the surface-level understanding, leaders can extract actionable insights that resonate with the intricacies of contemporary leadership scenarios.

The Limits of Surface-Level Understanding

Surface-level understanding of leadership theories may provide a general overview of principles, but it often falls short of addressing the complexities of real-world leadership scenarios. Leadership in the modern era requires more than a superficial grasp; it necessitates a thorough exploration of the underlying dynamics, assumptions, and applications that shape effective leadership.

Theory Deconstruction

Theory deconstruction involves an in-depth dissection of existing leadership theories to uncover their core principles, hidden assumptions, and practical implications. It's a process of breaking down theories to their essential components and critically examining how these components interact in different contexts. This approach allows leaders to move beyond the "what" of leadership to the "why" and "how," facilitating a deeper understanding of the theories' relevance and applicability.

Unearthing Underlying Principles

At the heart of theory deconstruction lies the quest to unearth the underlying principles that drive effective leadership. Leaders examine the foundational beliefs that guide each theory, shedding light on the reasoning behind certain behaviors, strategies, and approaches. This exploration enables leaders to grasp the theory's essence and apply it more adeptly to the challenges they face.

Challenging Assumptions

Theory deconstruction encourages leaders to challenge assumptions inherent in established theories. By scrutinizing these assumptions, leaders can discern their validity in contemporary contexts and identify areas where adaptation or modification may be necessary. This critical evaluation enables leaders to determine the extent to which a theory aligns with their organization's values, goals, and unique circumstances.

Practical Insights for Modern Leadership

Theory deconstruction yields practical insights that bridge the gap between theory and practice. Leaders gain a comprehensive understanding of how specific leadership approaches translate into tangible actions and outcomes. This deeper comprehension empowers leaders to make informed decisions about which elements of a theory are most relevant to their current challenges and how to integrate them into their leadership strategies.

Aligning with Contemporary Leadership Scenarios

Theory deconstruction equips leaders with a toolkit of adaptable leadership principles that resonate with the intricacies of contemporary leadership scenarios. Rather than adhering rigidly to a single theory, leaders can draw from a spectrum of insights to tailor their strategies to the unique demands of their organizations, teams, and environments.

Theory deconstruction serves as a compass, guiding leaders toward a more profound and nuanced understanding of leadership dynamics. By dissecting established theories, leaders gain the ability to transcend surface-level understanding, extract practical insights, and apply adaptable strategies that align with the complexities of modern leadership. Through theory deconstruction, leaders can be better prepared to navigate the multifaceted landscape of leadership with confidence, agility, and a deep sense of purpose.

How to Deconstruct Leadership Theories

The process of deconstructing leadership theories emerges as a powerful tool. Deconstruction involves a systematic examination of the components that underlie the effectiveness of established leadership theories. By asking critical questions and delving into the nuances of these theories, leaders can uncover practical insights that bridge the gap between theoretical concepts and real-world leadership scenarios.

Scrutinizing Components for Effectiveness

Deconstructing leadership theories requires breaking them down into their constituent parts to discern how these components contribute to the theory's effectiveness. Leaders dissect the theory's core principles, identifying the fundamental tenets that shape its approach to leadership. These principles often serve as the guiding philosophy that informs behaviors, decisions, and strategies.

Asking Critical Questions

Critical questions lie at the heart of theory deconstruction. Leaders inquire deeply into the theory's foundations:

- **Core Principles:** What are the foundational principles that define the theory's approach to leadership? How do these principles drive leadership behaviors and actions?

- **Contextual Interaction:** How do the theory's principles interact with different contexts? How adaptable is the theory to varying situations, cultures, and organizational settings?

- **Practical Implications:** What are the practical implications of the theory for real-world leadership situations? How can its principles be translated into actionable strategies that address contemporary challenges?

Understanding Contextual Interactions

An essential aspect of theory deconstruction is evaluating how a theory's principles interact with different contexts. Leadership is not a one-size-fits-all endeavor; effective leaders adapt their strategies based on the situation. By analyzing how a theory's components respond to different contexts, leaders can better understand its applicability and limitations in diverse scenarios.

Uncovering Practical Implications

Perhaps the most valuable outcome of theory deconstruction is the extraction of practical insights. By scrutinizing how a theory's principles manifest in practice, leaders gain insights into how to implement successful leadership strategies. Deconstruction translates theoretical concepts into actionable steps that resonate with the complexities of real-world leadership challenges.

Informing Successful Leadership Strategies

As leaders engage in theory deconstruction, they gain a richer understanding of the nuances that inform successful leadership strategies. For instance:

- **Servant Leadership:** By deconstructing this theory, leaders might uncover the importance of empowering team members, fostering collaboration, and prioritizing individual growth.

- **Transformational Leadership:** Deconstruction might reveal the power of communicating a compelling vision, creating emotional connections, and inspiring innovation.

- **Adaptive Leadership:** Leaders might discover the significance of flexibility, resilience, and continuous learning in navigating change and ambiguity.

Applying Insights in Leadership Practice

The insights gained through theory deconstruction are not theoretical exercises; they are tools for enhancing leadership practice. Leaders can integrate these insights into their decision-making, communication, team building, and problem-solving strategies. This integration allows leaders to tailor their approach to specific situations, fostering adaptability and effectiveness.

Deconstructing leadership theories empowers leaders to move beyond theoretical abstractions and extract practical wisdom. By dissecting the core principles, exploring contextual interactions, and uncovering practical implications, leaders gain actionable insights that inform successful leadership strategies. Theory deconstruction serves as a bridge between theory and practice, enabling leaders to navigate the complexities of contemporary leadership with a profound understanding of how to inspire, motivate, and guide their teams toward excellence.

Benefits of Theory Deconstruction

The practice of theory deconstruction yields a multitude of advantages for both individual leaders and the organizations they serve. By dismantling established leadership theories and extracting their essential principles, leaders can tap into a rich resource of insights that enhance their effectiveness and drive organizational success.

1. **Enhanced Adaptability:** Theory deconstruction equips leaders with a versatile toolkit of diverse leadership principles that can be adapted to specific situations. In today's fast-paced and ever-changing environment, where challenges are multifaceted and context-dependent, adaptability is paramount. Leaders who can draw from a range of approaches are better prepared to address the unique challenges that arise, ensuring that their strategies remain relevant and effective.
2. **Informed Decision-Making:** Deconstructing theories empowers leaders to make informed decisions that align with the specific needs of their teams and organizations. By gaining a deeper understanding of the principles underlying different leadership theories, leaders can tailor their strategies to match the context. This informed decision-making fosters better outcomes, enhances team morale, and contributes to organizational success.

3. **Increased Innovation:** Synthesizing insights from various theories encourages leaders to think creatively and stimulate innovation within their teams. Theory deconstruction encourages leaders to combine elements from different approaches, sparking fresh perspectives and approaches to complex problems. This infusion of diverse ideas can lead to innovative solutions, process improvements, and novel ways of tackling challenges.
4. **Cultivation of Diverse Leadership Styles:** Theory deconstruction enables leaders to cultivate a leadership style that aligns with their personal strengths, organizational needs, and the demands of the environment. By integrating aspects of different theories, leaders can create a well-rounded approach that resonates with their unique attributes. This not only enhances their authenticity as leaders but also enables them to address a wider range of situations effectively.
5. **Empowerment of Team Members:** As leaders apply insights from theory deconstruction, they empower their team members. By tailoring leadership strategies to the specific needs of individuals, leaders can foster a culture of trust, collaboration, and empowerment. Team members are more likely to excel when they are led by a leader who understands their unique needs and motivators.
6. **Building Strong Organizational Culture:** Theory deconstruction contributes to the cultivation of a strong and cohesive organizational culture. When leaders draw from a diverse range of insights, they can shape a culture that values adaptability, creativity, and collaboration. This shared approach to leadership principles contributes to a unified organizational identity and a positive work environment.
7. **Continuous Learning and Growth:** Theory deconstruction encourages leaders to engage in continuous learning and growth. By actively seeking to understand and apply diverse leadership principles, leaders embark on a journey of self-improvement and development. This commitment to learning

translates into improved leadership skills and a willingness to adapt and evolve as the leadership landscape evolves.

Theory deconstruction is a dynamic and proactive practice that empowers leaders and organizations to thrive in the modern leadership landscape. From enhanced adaptability and informed decision-making to increased innovation and the cultivation of diverse leadership styles, the benefits are wide-ranging and profound. By leveraging the insights gained through theory deconstruction, leaders can effectively navigate challenges, inspire their teams, and contribute to the growth and success of their organizations.

How Theory Deconstruction Enhances Leadership Practices

Theory deconstruction is not a theoretical exercise; it has a tangible impact on leadership practices in real-world scenarios. By integrating insights from different leadership theories, leaders can create innovative approaches that resonate with the unique challenges they face. Let's explore a couple of real-world examples that demonstrate how theory deconstruction enhances leadership practices:

Example 1: Integrating Servant and Adaptive Leadership

Imagine a leader who operates in a highly dynamic industry characterized by rapid technological advancements and constant market shifts. This leader recognizes the need to empower their team members while navigating uncertainty. Through theory deconstruction, they analyze the principles of both servant leadership and adaptive leadership.

- **Servant Leadership Insights:** From servant leadership, the leader draws insights into the importance of putting the needs of their team members first. They focus on fostering a culture of support, growth, and collaboration, empowering team members to contribute their best.

- **Adaptive Leadership Insights:** From adaptive leadership, the leader gains an understanding of the significance of flexibility and resilience. They learn to navigate change by encouraging learning, experimentation, and quick adaptation to shifting circumstances.

Application

This leader creates an environment where team members are supported, valued, and empowered to adapt to change. They prioritize open communication, involve team members in decision-making, and encourage continuous learning. By combining elements of both servant and adaptive leadership, this leader effectively guides their team through the uncertainties of the rapidly changing business landscape.

Example 2: Merging Transformational and Authentic Leadership

Consider a leader responsible for leading a team in a creative industry where innovation and collaboration are paramount. The leader seeks to inspire their team to think outside the box while fostering an environment of authenticity and ethical behavior. Theory deconstruction guides their approach.

- **Transformational Leadership Insights:** From transformational leadership, the leader understands the importance of visionary inspiration. They learn how to create a compelling vision that excites and motivates their team to reach for new heights of creativity and innovation.
- **Authentic Leadership Insights:** From authentic leadership, the leader gains insights into the significance of leading with integrity and transparency. They recognize that by embodying their authentic selves, they can foster trust and open communication within the team.

Application

Drawing from both transformational and authentic leadership, this leader crafts a leadership approach that combines visionary inspiration with ethical behavior. They communicate a captivating vision that aligns with the team's creative aspirations while exemplifying authenticity and ethical decision-making. This approach not only motivates the team but also creates a culture of trust and collaboration.

The examples above illustrate how theory deconstruction enhances leadership practices by allowing leaders to integrate insights from different theories into their approach. By leveraging elements from various leadership paradigms, leaders can tailor their strategies to address the unique challenges of their industries and teams. Theory deconstruction empowers leaders to be agile, innovative, and adaptable in their leadership practices, ultimately driving success and fostering positive organizational cultures.

Theory deconstruction offers a path to effective leadership in the modern world. By dissecting established leadership theories, leaders can extract valuable insights and adapt their strategies to meet the challenges of today's dynamic landscape. This approach empowers leaders to navigate complexity, inspire innovation, and foster a culture of adaptability within their teams and organizations. The journey through the intricacies of leadership theories has brought us to a rich understanding of their evolution, principles, and applications.

*****

CHAPTER TWO
The Foundation of Leadership and Theories

In the grand theater of human progress, leadership takes center stage as a defining force that orchestrates the symphony of success and shapes the destiny of nations, organizations, and societies. The essence of leadership is perennial, guiding individuals and collectives towards shared aspirations, catalyzing transformation, and achieving triumph against the odds. Yet, to navigate the currents of the present and chart a course for the future, we must embark on an expedition into the past, unearthing the historical roots that underlie the tapestry of contemporary leadership theories.

This chapter stands as a threshold to the corridors of leadership wisdom, beckoning us to grasp the profound significance of unearthing the ancestral origins that anchor the theories we scrutinize today. Like a giant redwood, whose towering stature is a testament to its history, the edifices of leadership theory draw sustenance from the yesteryears that birthed them. By unveiling these historical foundations, we gain more than a glimpse into the forces that have sculpted the evolution of these theories; we gain a perspective into the very core of the leadership practices they advocate.

Our journey through time compels us to decipher the intricate relationship between leadership and history—an intricate dance between societal contexts, prevailing ideologies, and human aspirations. From the tribal chieftains of ancient civilizations, entrusted with guiding their communities through the uncharted territories of survival, to the pioneering industrialists of the bygone eras, whose visions propelled entire industries forward—the historical contexts that nurtured these leaders have indelibly marked the principles they espoused.

With this, we embark on our narrative, preceded by a succinct overview of why these historical footprints matter. By unraveling the context in which each leadership theory emerged, we unveil the cognitive sparks that ignited the flame of thought, ultimately giving birth to the diverse array of leadership ideologies we encounter today. Moreover, comprehending these historical underpinnings equips us with a discerning lens to assess the adaptability and pertinence of these theories in our rapidly changing contemporary landscape.

As we set the stage for our odyssey into the evolution of leadership theories, we acknowledge the formidable sway that history wields over the landscape of leadership wisdom. By paying homage to the intellectual and cultural heritage that has paved our intellectual path, we prime ourselves to traverse epochs and schools of thought. Through this pilgrimage, we seek to untangle the intricate threads that compose the rich fabric of leadership theories, thus illuminating a course toward effective leadership amid the flux of a dynamic world.

Understanding the Historical Roots

The historical roots of leadership theories act as a compass that guides our understanding of leadership's essence. In unraveling the trajectories that brought these theories to light, we gain insights into the nuanced interplay between leadership and the backdrop of the times. Just as a tree's growth is influenced by the richness of the soil, it's rooted in. Leadership theories are deeply influenced by the historical, social, and cultural contexts that nurture them.

By tracing the footsteps of leaders who once navigated through uncharted territories, we can comprehend the rationale behind their strategies, decisions, and actions. Historical leadership exemplars become the living embodiments of theory, showcasing the profound impact of different leadership approaches across diverse eras. Understanding the past also equips us with the wisdom to discern which principles have stood the test of time and which have evolved in response to shifting paradigms.

Evolution

The historical influences that have shaped leadership theories act as an invaluable teacher, offering lessons that resonate across time. Just as architects draw inspiration from past structures to build innovative marvels, contemporary leaders can glean insights from the foundational principles that have guided leaders through centuries. By appreciating the evolution of leadership theories, we gain a more holistic understanding of the dynamic nature of leadership.

As we stand on the cusp of exploring the evolution of leadership theories, we are poised to witness how the luminaries of their times forged new paths, grappled with challenges, and harnessed opportunities. These leaders were not bound by our modern context but were pioneers in their own right, crafting methodologies that were responsive to their circumstances. Their stories not only enrich our historical comprehension but also offer timeless lessons that can be adapted to modern scenarios.

By tracing the lineage of leadership theories, we connect the dots between the past and the present, creating a bridge that spans epochs and ideologies. We are invited to observe how leadership practices have morphed, redefined, and reinvigorated themselves, perpetually in conversation with the needs and exigencies of their times.

As we embark on this journey through the annals of leadership history, we unearth insights that resonate across generations, cultivating a deeper appreciation for the art and science of leadership. By unraveling these historical narratives, we uncover the hidden gems that illuminate the path to effective leadership, empowering us to forge ahead with a tapestry of wisdom woven from the threads of time. We venture back to the cradle of civilizations, where leadership ideals were first sculpted in the crucible of early human societies. Ancient civilizations serve as the foundational canvas on which the earliest depictions of leadership were etched. From the wise sages of Mesopotamia to the valorous military leaders of Khalsa Raj and ancient Egypt, these cultures provided a spectrum of leadership models that drew from cultural norms, ethical virtues, and strategic acumen.

Ancient Civilizations and Their Leadership Ideals

In the vast expanse of history, ancient civilizations stand as the bedrock upon which the foundation of leadership ideals was laid. These early societies, characterized by their complex social structures, diverse cultures, and intricate belief systems, nurtured leaders whose legacies continue to resonate across the ages. From the shores of the Indus Valley to the banks of the Nile, leaders emerged as guiding lights, entrusted with the daunting responsibility of steering their communities through the uncharted waters of existence.

A Tapestry of Wisdom, Fairness, and Benevolence

Within the annals of these ancient civilizations, the narratives of leadership are replete with tales of rulers who aspired to govern with wisdom, fairness, and benevolence. These leaders, whether they be Sardars, kings, pharaohs, emperors, or chieftains, were not just temporal figures but were often revered as embodiments of divine authority. Their rule was seen as a harmonious alignment between earthly governance and cosmic order.

Leadership during this epoch was not merely about wielding power; it was about assuming the mantle of responsibility to ensure the well-being and prosperity of the people under their stewardship.

Leaders were expected to possess qualities that mirrored the virtues upheld by their societies. Wisdom, a keen understanding of human nature, and an ability to navigate the complexities of societal dynamics were attributes highly prized in these revered figures.

The Divine Mandate and Cosmic Connection

In many ancient civilizations, leadership was intrinsically intertwined with the divine. Rulers were often regarded as chosen by the gods, bestowed with a divine mandate to uphold justice, maintain order, and protect their domains. This sacred connection between leaders and the divine realm imbued leadership with a profound sense of purpose and responsibility.

For example, in the Khalsa Raj, leaders such as Baba Banda Singh Bahadar and Maharaja Ranjit Singh were seen as guardians of Sikh sovereignty. Their rule was characterized by a strong commitment to justice, equality, and religious freedom. Their leadership ideals were deeply rooted in Sikh principles, and they sought to lead with wisdom and fairness, fostering a sense of unity among diverse communities.

Steering Through the Ebbs and Flows

Leaders in ancient civilizations were not immune to the challenges and complexities of their times. Whether it was navigating through periods of abundance or scarcity, peace or conflict, these leaders were expected to be adaptable and resilient. Their ability to guide their communities through times of uncertainty showcased their leadership acumen and the extent of their commitment to their people's well-being.

The sagas of ancient leaders reveal their capacity to inspire loyalty, mobilize resources, and make difficult decisions that shaped the destinies of their realms. Their stories remind us that leadership, even in times of antiquity, was a dynamic and multidimensional endeavor that demanded a delicate balance of authority, empathy, and strategic foresight.

Echoes Through the Corridors of History

The ideals of leadership that emerged in ancient civilizations have cast a long shadow on the evolution of leadership theories. The reverence for wisdom, the pursuit of fairness, and the ethos of benevolence—all hallmarks of leadership in these times—have resonated through the corridors of history, leaving an indelible mark on subsequent generations of leaders.

From Hammurabi's Code in Mesopotamia to the principles of Dharma in ancient India, these foundational leadership ideals have transcended time and cultural boundaries. In the Khalsa Raj, the legacy of leaders like Maharaja Ranjit Singh exemplified the enduring impact of ancient leadership virtues, as they drew inspiration from historical examples to forge a sense of unity and justice within their communities.

The sagas of leadership in ancient civilizations illuminate a profound truth: the essence of effective leadership is not confined by the boundaries of time but is a universal and timeless endeavor. Leaders of antiquity set the stage for the leadership principles that would continue to shape societies for millennia to come. Their commitment to wisdom, fairness, and benevolence has become a beacon that guides modern leaders in navigating the complexities of our contemporary world, reminding us that the echoes of the past continue to resonate in our present and future pursuits of leadership excellence.

Leadership in Military and Strategic Contexts

Amidst the tapestry of history, a distinct form of leadership emerged in the crucible of military and strategic contexts. In parallel with the rise of early civilizations, the annals of history are adorned with accounts of commanders and generals whose tactical brilliance shaped the outcomes of battles and conquests. These leaders navigated the tumultuous landscapes of warfare, where every decision and maneuver held the potential to reshape empires and alter the course of history. Their leadership was a symphony of courage, strategic insight, and the ability to galvanize loyalty in the face of unparalleled adversity.

Khalsa Fauj: A Saga of Military Leadership

The story of the Khalsa Fauj—a martial community that emerged during the late 17th century within the Sikh tradition—adds a vivid hue to the narrative of military leadership. In a time of political upheaval and oppression, the Khalsa Fauj's leaders exemplified the art of military leadership that had resonated through history.

Courage: The Bedrock of Military Leadership

Leadership in military and strategic contexts is anchored in courage—the audacity to face the unknown and lead troops into the heat of battle. Ancient commanders and generals, like leaders of the Khalsa Fauj, understood that courage was not just a personal attribute but a quality that could inspire and embolden their troops. Leaders who embodied courage led by example, proving to be a rallying point even in the bleakest moments.

Strategic Acumen: The Art of Warfare

In the realm of military leadership, strategic acumen is the compass that guides leaders through the intricate dance of warfare. Ancient tacticians and modern commanders alike share the ability to analyze terrain, assess the enemy's strengths and weaknesses, and craft strategies that can turn the tide of battle. The ability to anticipate the opponent's moves, like the leaders of the Khalsa Fauj, marked the distinction between mere commanders and true strategic visionaries.

Inspiring Loyalty in Adversity

Leadership in military contexts is not just about strategy; it's about the ability to inspire unwavering loyalty even in the harshest of circumstances. Ancient generals and leaders of the Khalsa Fauj knew that trust and loyalty were currency on the battlefield. By forging deep bonds with their troops and cultivating a sense of camaraderie, these leaders ensured that their soldiers would fight not just for victory but for the honor of their leader.

The Khalsa Fauj and Leadership Excellence

The leaders of the Khalsa Fauj, including Guru Gobind Singh and his successors, embodied the quintessence of military leadership. In the face of overwhelming odds, they exemplified the qualities of courage, strategic brilliance, and the ability to inspire fierce loyalty. Their leadership transformed a community into a disciplined and resolute force, capable of defending their faith and ideals against formidable adversaries.

Legacy Across Millennia

The echoes of military leadership resonate through the annals of time, connecting the great commanders of ancient civilizations with the leaders of the Khalsa Fauj and beyond. The valor of Alexander the Great, the wisdom of Sun Tzu, and the audacity of Maharaja Ranjit Singh all find common ground in their mastery of military leadership.

Leadership in military and strategic contexts is an intricate symphony, where courage, strategic insight, and the power to inspire coalesce to shape destinies. From ancient generals to the leaders of the Khalsa Fauj, the legacy of military leadership endures as a testament to the indomitable spirit of leaders who face the crucible of warfare. Through their stories, we glean timeless lessons on leadership's transformative power, its ability to forge unity amidst chaos, and its capacity to transcend epochs, cultures, and the ebb and flow of history.

Philosophical Perspectives on Leadership Qualities

As the tapestry of human thought evolved, so too did the exploration of leadership in the realms of philosophy. Philosophers of antiquity embarked on a journey of introspection, probing the essence of leadership and the qualities that defined an exemplary leader. This philosophical exploration transcended time, leaving behind a legacy that continues to illuminate the path of leadership in modern times.

The Quest for Virtue and Wisdom

In the annals of philosophical thought, leadership became a subject of contemplation for thinkers across cultures and epochs. These thinkers, whether in ancient Greece, China, India, or in the heart of Punjab, shared a common pursuit: to unravel the qualities that set leaders apart and define their virtuous essence. In their discussions, virtues such as wisdom, integrity, and moral courage emerged as the cornerstones of exemplary leadership.

Wisdom

Wisdom, often celebrated as the pinnacle of human virtue, was recognized as a guiding light for leaders. Philosophers like Confucius emphasized the importance of sagacity—the ability to make sound judgments and decisions based on deep understanding and experience. Just as the fertile fields of Punjab yield abundance, wisdom cultivated by leaders was seen as the foundation upon which leadership could stand resolute.

Integrity

In the tapestry of leadership, integrity emerged as an unshakable principle. Philosophers across cultures underscored the significance of ethical conduct and honesty. Just as the rivers of Punjab flow with unyielding integrity, leaders were expected to be steadfast in their adherence to truth, justice, and honor. A leader's actions, guided by unwavering integrity, were believed to inspire trust and foster a sense of moral coherence within a community.

Moral Courage

Philosophers recognized that leadership often demanded moral courage—the strength to stand up for one's convictions, even in the face of opposition. The valor and resilience akin to historical struggles were mirrored in the moral courage leaders were expected to possess. The ability to champion justice, even when it meant confronting adversity, was a hallmark of true leadership.

A Bridge Between Ancient Wisdom and Modern Leadership

When intertwined with Punjab's rich cultural tapestry, the philosophical contemplations of antiquity forged a bridge between ancient wisdom and modern leadership paradigms. Leaders who embrace qualities like wisdom, integrity, and moral courage are following a tradition that draws strength from the very soul of Punjab. Just as ancient philosophers sought the highest virtues in leadership, contemporary leaders who tread the path of virtue carry forward the legacy of ethical leadership, echoing the resilience of spirit.

Leadership Beyond Strategy

The philosophical exploration of leadership qualities transcends the tactical aspects of leadership. While strategy and decision-making hold their place, the focus on virtues speaks to the inner landscape of a leader's character. Historical landscapes are marked by vibrant diversity, the ancient thinkers recognized that leadership is not solely about achieving objectives; it's about fostering harmony, guiding with ethical principles, and inspiring collective progress.

The philosophical perspectives on leadership qualities, when viewed through the lens of heritage, continue to resonate as a tapestry woven with the threads of wisdom, integrity, and moral courage. These attributes, championed by ancient thinkers and embodied in the spirit of Punjab, transcend the boundaries of time and culture, providing a timeless compass for leadership excellence.

The discourse on leadership virtues is a reminder that leadership is not merely about guiding outcomes; it's about nurturing the human spirit, upholding moral principles, and leaving a legacy that reverberates through history.

Medieval and Renaissance Leadership Concepts

Within the grand tapestry of leadership evolution, the medieval and Renaissance periods emerge as intricate threads, weaving a complex narrative of shifting paradigms and evolving philosophies. These eras were marked by the dominance of feudal systems and monarchical rule, where leadership was inextricably intertwined with notions of nobility and lineage. The historical backdrop of these times set the stage for the gradual emergence of early leadership writings, a turning point that saw the systematic articulation of ideas about effective governance and rule.

Feudal Systems and the Portrait of Authority

The medieval era, the cultural landscapes of the time, saw the rise of feudal systems—a social hierarchy where power flowed from the top down. Within this system, leaders held dominion over territories, exercising authority and control. Kings and nobles commanded respect and allegiance, contributing to the prevailing order. Leadership often followed lines of birthright, as noble families wielded hereditary power. This hierarchical structure defined the social order and cast its influence on all facets of life.

Monarchical Rule and the Weight of Sovereignty

The Renaissance brought a new flourish to the canvas of leadership. Monarchies rose to prominence, shaping the contours of leadership. Kings and queens held sway not just in governance but in matters of culture, art, and identity. Just as leaders of the time sought to preserve and propagate their ideals, monarchs of the Renaissance assumed roles as cultural custodians, defining the ethos of their times through their patronage.

Emergence of Early Leadership Writings

Amidst the Renaissance's intellectual revival, early writings on leadership began to illuminate the corridors of thought. Philosophers, scholars, and leaders alike embarked on a journey to systematically articulate their ideas about leadership. The writings of Kavi Santokh Singh, Rattan Singh Bhangu, Machiavelli, Erasmus, and their contemporaries resonated with the principles that governed leadership strategies and the symbiotic relationship between rulers and the ruled.

A Turning Point in Leadership Discourse

The rise of early leadership writings marked a pivotal turning point in the discourse of leadership. Philosophers grappled with questions about the nature of authority, the responsibilities of leaders, and the delicate balance between power and moral duty. This period highlights the universal nature of leadership challenges and inquiries.

Legacy in Modern Leadership

The concepts that unfolded during the medieval and Renaissance periods continue to cast their shadow upon modern leadership paradigms. The interplay between authority and ethics remains relevant in contemporary discussions. The intricate dance between leadership and societal structures serves as a reminder that the evolution of leadership is deeply intertwined with historical and cultural contexts.

The medieval and Renaissance periods stand as pivotal chapters in the ongoing story of leadership. The hierarchical structures, philosophical musings, and shifting paradigms of these eras shaped the discourse on leadership principles. As we reflect upon these historical epochs, we are reminded that leadership is a dynamic journey that transcends time and culture, weaving together the legacies of the past with the aspirations of the future. Just as history's lessons endure, so too do the insights from these periods continue to guide and inspire leaders in the present day.

Industrial Revolution

The dawn of the Industrial Revolution heralded a seismic shift in the very fabric of societies, reshaping the landscape of leadership theories. As agrarian societies metamorphosed into industrial economies, the dynamics of leadership underwent profound transformations, mirroring the sweeping changes that marked this era. At the heart of this transformation was the emergence of scientific management—a guiding philosophy that championed efficiency, standardization, and hierarchical control.

The Genesis of Transformation

The Industrial Revolution, akin to a powerful force reshaping landscapes, brought forth the mechanization of industries, urbanization, and a shift from craft-based production to mass manufacturing. As traditional roles and structures crumbled in the face of change, leadership found itself at a crossroads. In context, this was an era of upheaval, like the trials that shaped its history.

Scientific Management

As industries grew in scale and complexity, the need for efficiency became paramount. Frederick Taylor's principles of scientific management emerged as a guiding light. Taylor's approach, the pursuit of progress during turbulent times, emphasized the meticulous analysis of work processes, leading to standardized procedures and enhanced productivity. This heralded a new era in leadership—one where the management of resources and tasks took center stage.

Efficiency and Standardization

Scientific management, with its focus on optimizing efficiency, mirrored resilience in adapting to changing circumstances. Communities persevered through transformation, industries sought to maximize output by minimizing waste, reducing costs, and streamlining operations. Leaders became conductors of a well-orchestrated symphony of tasks, ensuring that every element contributed to the larger production process.

Hierarchical Control and Oversight

In an era marked by industrial expansion, leadership took on a new hue. Hierarchical control, akin to the structured systems of authority in history, became a linchpin of industrial leadership. Clear lines of command ensured that tasks were executed with precision, reflecting the synchronized efforts of communities during trying times. Managers became the architects of efficiency, orchestrating a workforce engaged in specialized tasks.

The Human Element

While scientific management celebrated efficiency, it sometimes neglected the human aspect of work. Historical periods faced challenges of their own, this approach raised concerns about employee well-being and job satisfaction. Critics noted that the rigid focus on efficiency could overshadow the intrinsic value of human engagement and creativity. Leadership, in the context of the Industrial Revolution, was thus tasked with harmonizing efficiency with a sense of purpose.

Legacy and Modern Leadership

The legacy of the Industrial Revolution's impact on leadership persists in modern management practices. The principles of efficiency, standardization, and hierarchical control remain relevant, though tempered by a growing emphasis on human-centric leadership. Heritage endures in its diverse cultural expressions, the evolution of leadership theories during the Industrial Revolution continues to influence contemporary leadership paradigms.

The Industrial Revolution marked a monumental epoch in the journey of leadership theories. The rise of scientific management mirrored Punjab's ability to navigate transformations, adapting to change with resilience. The emphasis on efficiency, standardization, and hierarchical control laid the foundation for modern leadership practices. As we reflect on this era, we are reminded that leadership, like Punjab's history, is a story of adaptability, innovation, and the dynamic interplay between tradition and progress.

Transition from Agrarian to Industrial Societies

The annals of history bear witness to the profound transition from agrarian to industrial societies—an epochal shift that reshaped the very foundations of human existence. In this transformative journey, leadership emerged as a linchpin, evolving to meet the demands of a new era. As the landscapes of rural life gave way to the mechanical rhythms of factories, a new breed of leadership was called upon—one capable of navigating the complexities of large-scale production and workforce management. This transition ushered in a pivotal chapter in the story of leadership, where leaders faced the challenge of optimizing resources and systems to achieve unprecedented levels of productivity.

The Agrarian Tapestry Unravels

The transition from agrarian to industrial societies mirrored the evolution of historical phases, marked by shifts in socioeconomic structures and cultural paradigms. History bore witness to transformation, societies around the world underwent a metamorphosis as mechanization and urbanization replaced agrarian ways of life. The idyllic scenes of rural farming were replaced by the hum of machines and the rhythm of factories—a new dawn characterized by innovation and expansion.

The Leadership Imperative

In this era of transformation, leadership was thrust onto a new stage of complexity and challenge. The leaders of yesteryears, who guided agricultural communities, found themselves navigating uncharted waters. The demands of industrialization necessitated a fresh approach—one that encompassed not only strategic decision-making but also the intricacies of managing vast workforces, optimizing production processes, and maintaining synergy among the various cogs of the industrial machine.

Navigating Complexity

Leaders found themselves at the helm of industrial juggernauts, steering organizations through the intricate labyrinth of large-scale production. As the shift to factories and production lines unfolded, leaders had to optimize resource allocation, streamline processes, and ensure the seamless coordination of tasks. Diverse communities coalesced during times of change, industrial leaders fostered collaboration and interdependence among workers to ensure productivity and progress.

From Farm to Factory

The transition to industrial societies marked a paradigm shift in leadership. Leaders were now tasked with orchestrating not only the cultivation of crops but also the orchestration of industrial workflows. This new breed of leadership, mirroring ability to adapt and thrive, embodied adaptability, innovation, and the ability to harness technological advancements for collective progress.

Optimizing Resources for Productivity

Leaders grappled with the challenge of optimizing resources to achieve unprecedented levels of productivity—a challenge that resonates with history of resourceful resilience. Efficient allocation of labor, materials, and technologies became paramount, aligning with the essence of communities coming together to thrive in the face of change. As the demands of the industrial age grew, leaders rose to the occasion, seeking innovative solutions to maximize output.

Legacy in Contemporary Leadership

The transition from agrarian to industrial societies forged a blueprint for contemporary leadership. The ability to navigate complexity, optimize resources, and foster collaboration remains central to modern leadership paradigms. heritage endures in its traditions and expressions, the legacy of this transition endures in the skills and approaches leaders employ to navigate the intricacies of today's rapidly evolving world.

The transition from agrarian to industrial societies stands as a testament to humanity's capacity for transformation. Leadership, mirroring the adaptive spirit of Punjab's history, evolved to meet the challenges of a new era. As leaders guided their organizations through the uncharted waters of industrialization, they left an indelible mark on the leadership narrative—one that continues to shape the way leaders navigate complexity, optimize resources, and lead their teams toward shared goals. history is a story of resilience and progress, so too is the story of leadership in the face of transition and transformation.

Scientific Management and Efficiency-Driven Leadership

The annals of leadership history saw the emergence of a paradigm that revolutionized the way organizations functioned—scientific management. Spearheaded by leaders like Frederick Taylor, this approach marked a turning point in how efficiency and precision were prioritized in the realm of leadership. Taylor's principles aimed to streamline processes, maximize output, and eliminate waste, setting the stage for a more systematic and results-oriented approach to leadership that mirrored the spirit of progress seen in history.

The Birth of Scientific Management

The dawn of the 20th century witnessed a rapidly changing world. As industries expanded and complexities grew, the need for a more efficient and structured approach to leadership became evident. Frederick Taylor, an engineer, introduced the principles of scientific management, placing emphasis on data-driven decision-making, standardized processes, and the meticulous study of work methods.

Efficiency as the Guiding Star

Scientific management elevated efficiency to a new pedestal, mirroring the industrious spirit that defined growth. Leaders were tasked with overseeing processes that minimized waste and optimize productivity. Taylor's methods sought to maximize output by ensuring that tasks were executed with utmost efficiency and precision, resonating with ethos of resourcefulness and innovation.

Streamlining Processes for Optimal Results

Taylor's principles introduced a systematic approach to leadership, communities found ways to adapt and thrive amidst change. Work processes were analyzed, optimized, and standardized to ensure consistent performance. This approach, like ability to find harmony amid diversity, sought to create a harmonious symphony of tasks that contributed to the overall success of the organization.

Eliminating Waste and Redundancy

Efficiency-driven leadership under the banner of scientific management aimed to eliminate waste, and communities making the most of available resources. Taylor's ideas emphasized minimizing idle time, reducing unnecessary steps, and maximizing the use of resources. Leaders, like the stewards of progress, were tasked with ensuring that every element of the organization worked in unison, without redundancies.

Impact on Modern Leadership

The legacy of scientific management endures in modern leadership practices, history continues to influence its culture. The emphasis on efficiency, data-driven decision-making, and process optimization remains relevant in today's complex and fast-paced world. Leaders continue to strive for precision and productivity, leveraging Taylor's principles to guide their organizations toward excellence.

Balancing Efficiency and Human Factors

While scientific management celebrated efficiency, it also raised questions about the human element, akin to focusing on community and human values. Critics noted that an overemphasis on efficiency could neglect the well-being and satisfaction of employees. Leaders, as stewards of their teams, had to navigate the delicate balance between efficiency-driven processes and nurturing a positive work environment.

Scientific management ushered in an era of efficiency-driven leadership, revolutionizing the way organizations operated. Leaders like Frederick Taylor carved a path that mirrored history of resourceful adaptation, where progress was shaped by innovation and precision. The principles of scientific management continue to influence modern leadership, emphasizing the importance of efficiency, precision, and the dynamic interplay between process optimization and the human element. history shapes its present, so too do the principles of scientific management shape the way leaders navigate the complexities of contemporary organizational landscapes.

Early 20th-Century Trait Theories

In the early 20th century, a new chapter unfolded in the realm of leadership theories—one that turned the spotlight onto the innate qualities that define effective leaders. This era witnessed the rise of trait theories, a paradigm that sought to decipher the intrinsic attributes that set leaders apart. These theories marked a departure from earlier approaches that focused on external behaviors, instead delving into the foundational characteristics that predisposed individuals to excel in leadership roles. This exploration of inherent traits drew a significant connection to historical notions of character and virtue, bridging the gap between past ideals and the evolving landscape of leadership understanding. In this exploration, we delve into the realm of early 20th-century trait theories, examining their focus on inherent leadership qualities and their profound connection to the historical legacy of character and virtue.

The Paradigm Shift to Inherent Qualities

In the 20th century, a paradigm shift in leadership theories occurred, redirecting the focus towards the inherent qualities that underlie effective leadership. This marked a departure from previous theories that emphasized observable behaviors and actions.

Rise of Trait Theories

Trait theories gained prominence during this era by proposing that certain inherent attributes distinguish individuals with a natural propensity for excelling in leadership roles. This represented a shift from theories that heavily emphasized external actions and situational factors, instead highlighting the personal characteristics that set successful leaders apart.

Universal Traits in a Diverse Landscape

Scholars and researchers aimed to identify traits that transcended industries, cultures, and contexts, similar to the timeless virtues celebrated in history. Through studies, assessments, and observations, they aimed to isolate key attributes that consistently emerged among effective leaders.

Complex Interplay of Traits and Dynamics

The emphasis on inherent leadership qualities recognized the intricate interplay between intrinsic traits and external dynamics. While situational factors and behaviors were acknowledged, the emphasis on innate qualities underscored their significant contribution to a leader's effectiveness.

Influence on Leadership Development

As the century progressed, the exploration of inherent leadership qualities continued to shape leadership development programs, organizational training, and the identification of potential leaders. Trait theories laid a foundation for understanding leadership.

Echoing Historical Significance

The focus on inherent leadership qualities echoed the historical importance of virtuous character in leadership. Just as historical leaders were admired for their qualities, 20th-century leaders were assessed for attributes that contributed to their effectiveness.

Shaping Contemporary Leadership

The 20th century's emphasis on inherent qualities left a lasting impact on contemporary leadership theories and practices. This shift opened doors to exploring the unique attributes that define leaders, contributing to the ever-evolving tapestry of leadership understanding.

The 20th century marked a significant turning point in leadership theories, with a pronounced focus on inherent leadership qualities. This shift introduced a new dimension to understanding effective leadership, resonating with the historical significance of virtuous character. Trait theories added depth to the exploration of leadership attributes, influencing the ongoing evolution of leadership concepts as the world continued to evolve.

Connection to Historical Notions of Character and Virtue

The 20th century witnessed a convergence between contemporary leadership theories and historical notions of character and virtue, creating a bridge between the past and the evolving landscape of leadership understanding. As leadership theories evolved, there emerged a distinct recognition of the significance of character and virtue in shaping effective leaders, echoing the enduring legacy of these concepts throughout history.

Character as the Foundation

In the 20th century, scholars and thinkers began to draw connections between effective leadership and the foundational qualities of character. Just as historical leaders were admired for their virtuous conduct, contemporary leadership theories started to emphasize the importance of attributes such as integrity, honesty, and moral courage. This resonance between historical ideals and modern theories reflected an understanding that character serves as the bedrock of exceptional leadership.

Virtue in Action

The alignment between historical notions of virtue and 20th-century leadership theories was particularly evident in the emphasis on virtuous behavior and ethical decision-making. history celebrated leaders who upheld moral virtues, leadership theories of this era recognized that leaders who demonstrated virtues such as empathy, fairness, and compassion were better equipped to inspire and guide their teams.

Ethical Leadership Amid Complexity

The 20th century was marked by complex societal shifts, technological advancements, and globalization—changes that mirrored the evolving landscapes of history. In the midst of this complexity, the connection to historical notions of virtue gained renewed significance. Leaders faced challenges that demanded ethical decision-making, drawing parallels to the historical leaders who navigated moral dilemmas with wisdom and integrity.

A Reflection of Cultural Heritage

Cultural expressions are shaped by its history, the connection to historical notions of character and virtue underscored the enduring influence of cultural heritage on leadership theories. This connection was a testament to the timeless wisdom embedded in historical practices, guiding leaders in the 20th century toward values that were deeply rooted in virtuous conduct.

Balancing Virtue and Pragmatism

The 20th century's alignment with historical virtues didn't occur in isolation. Leaders and scholars recognized the need to strike a balance between virtuous ideals and pragmatic leadership approaches. Just as historical leaders navigated the complexities of their times while upholding virtues, 20th-century leaders sought to integrate ethical principles into their leadership styles while adapting to the ever-changing modern landscape.

Guiding Leadership Practices

The connection to historical notions of character and virtue provided a moral compass for leaders in the 20th century. The influence of these concepts permeated leadership development programs, training, and organizational values. Leaders were reminded of the enduring importance of leading with integrity, drawing inspiration from the historical leaders who paved the way.

The 20th century's alignment with historical notions of character and virtue marked a harmonious blending of the past with contemporary leadership thought. history shaped its cultural practices, the connection to historical virtues guided leaders toward ethical conduct and principled decision-making. This connection, in the midst of evolving challenges, served as a timeless reminder that effective leadership is rooted in character and virtue, echoing the wisdom of historical leaders who paved the way for a virtuous leadership legacy.

The Influence of Historical Perspectives on Modern Leadership

The study of leadership is a journey through time, a tapestry woven from the threads of history, culture, and human progress. history has forged its cultural heritage, so too has the passage of time left an indelible mark on the understanding of leadership. The influence of historical perspectives on modern leadership is a testament to the intricate interplay between past experiences and contemporary challenges. In exploring this dynamic relationship, we embark on a journey that navigates the impact of historical events and eras on the evolution of leadership theories and practices.

World Wars and Situational Leadership

The tumultuous landscapes of the world wars cast a stark light on the notion of leadership's adaptability. As the world grappled with unprecedented challenges, leaders were confronted with the imperatives of situational leadership—adjusting their approaches to address the unique needs of each moment. The echoes of history, where leaders navigated diverse contexts, resonated in this era as leaders were compelled to shift their strategies in response to the changing tides of conflict.

Contingency Theories and Adaptability

Contingency theories emerged as a response to the complex, ever-shifting realities of leadership. Like the dynamic historical phases, where adaptation was key to survival, leaders in the modern era were required to tailor their approaches to fit the circumstances at hand. These theories recognized that leadership effectiveness hinged on the ability to flexibly adapt strategies and behaviors to the specific demands of a given situation.

Evolving Leadership Landscapes and the Birth of Contingency Theories

In the ever-evolving tapestry of leadership thought, the 20th century witnessed the emergence of contingency theories—a response to the intricate and unpredictable realities of leadership in dynamic environments. history was marked by diverse phases and ever-shifting landscapes, leaders in the modern era grappled with the complexities of a rapidly changing world. Contingency theories recognized that a one-size-fits-all approach to leadership was insufficient in navigating these diverse and shifting contexts.

Adaptation as a Survival Imperative

History is replete with examples of leaders adapting to the demands of different epochs, mirroring the core tenet of contingency theories. Just as survival in historical phases required leaders to embrace adaptation, so too did leaders in the modern era recognize that adaptability was paramount for success. Theories like these acknowledged that the effectiveness of leadership hinged on the ability to flexibly adjust strategies, behaviors, and decision-making approaches to align with the specific demands of a given situation.

Tailoring Leadership Approaches

Contingency theories encouraged leaders to tailor their leadership approaches to the unique circumstances they faced. This recognition mirrored the way historical leaders tailored their strategies to the prevailing environment. In the modern era, leaders understood that what worked in one situation might not work in another. They embraced the idea that leadership was not a static set of skills, but a dynamic set of principles that could be adapted to the nuances of each context.

Adaptable Strategies for Diverse Realities

Leaders in the 20th century recognized that different situations demanded different strategies. Contingency theories encouraged leaders to assess the factors at play—such as the nature of the task, the characteristics of the team, and the context of the organization—and choose the most suitable leadership style. This adaptable approach resonated with Punjab's history, where leaders navigated changing landscapes by understanding and adapting to local conditions.

Navigating Unpredictable Terrain

Historical leaders faced uncertain environments, modern leaders confronted unpredictable economic, technological, and social shifts. Contingency theories offered a framework that acknowledged the uncertainty of leadership contexts, highlighting the need for leaders to be versatile and responsive. By embracing adaptability, leaders prepared themselves to navigate the unexpected and seize opportunities amidst the challenges.

Legacy in Modern Leadership

The legacy of contingency theories endures in modern leadership practices. Leaders recognize that adapting their strategies to fit the ever-changing landscape is a crucial skill. historical phases shaped the region's cultural evolution, contingency theories reshaped the understanding of effective leadership. The ability to be flexible, to assess and adapt, is now a hallmark of successful leaders, illustrating the lasting influence of contingency theories on the ever-evolving canvas of leadership thought.

Contingency theories emerged as a beacon of guidance in the dynamic and uncertain landscapes of leadership. History highlighted the importance of adaptation, these theories acknowledged that leaders needed to tailor their approaches to fit the unique demands of each situation. The ever-changing contexts of leadership, both in Punjab's historical phases and in the modern era, remind us of the enduring relevance of adaptability—an indispensable trait for leaders seeking to thrive amidst the challenges and opportunities of their times.

Leadership Responses to Volatile Historical Contexts

As history's tempests raged, leaders emerged who exhibited resilience and foresight. history witnessed leaders steering through uncertainty, modern leaders were tasked with providing stable guidance during times of volatility. The influence of historical contexts propelled leaders to anticipate challenges and chart paths forward that considered the lessons of the past while addressing the complexities of the present.

Historical Tempests and Resilient Leaders

Amidst history's tempestuous moments, leaders emerged who demonstrated remarkable resilience and foresight. history saw leaders navigating through periods of uncertainty, modern leaders were thrust into volatile historical contexts that demanded steady guidance. These eras of turbulence and transformation called for leadership responses that could not only weather the storm but also steer the course toward calmer waters.

Charting Paths Through Uncertainty

Punjab's history is marked by leaders who successfully navigated through uncertain phases, often facing unprecedented challenges. The modern era echoed this narrative as leaders found themselves contending with the unpredictable currents of economic shifts, technological advances, and social upheavals. Like their historical counterparts, modern leaders were called upon to provide direction and stability amidst the chaos, their actions guided by a deep understanding of historical lessons.

Anticipating Challenges Through Historical Lens

leaders drew insights from their history, modern leaders were driven to anticipate challenges by understanding the nuances of their historical contexts. The influence of historical events provided a lens through which leaders could foresee potential pitfalls and vulnerabilities. By drawing from the past, leaders gained a heightened awareness of how the actions taken in turbulent times could impact the future trajectory of their organizations and communities.

Balancing Past Wisdom with Present Complexity

Modern leaders were tasked with striking a balance between the wisdom of the past and the intricacies of the present. The lessons of history served as a compass, guiding leaders to navigate the complexities of rapidly changing landscapes. The ability to interpret and apply historical lessons equipped leaders with a unique advantage—an advantage that allowed them to lead with a sense of purpose and strategic vision.

Foresight as a Guiding Star

In historical phases, leaders were lauded for their ability to foresee challenges and respond with foresight. The same principle applied to modern leaders, who utilized their understanding of historical contexts to anticipate disruptions and upheavals. Foresight became a guiding star, illuminating the path forward and helping leaders make decisions that balanced immediate needs with long-term sustainability.

Lessons Learned and Applied

The influence of historical contexts was palpable in the leadership responses to volatility. historical lessons informed its cultural practices, modern leaders used historical insights to design resilient strategies and contingency plans. By leveraging historical parallels, leaders could address crises with a comprehensive perspective, considering the lessons of the past as they crafted effective responses to the challenges of the present.

Legacy of Navigating Turbulence

The legacy of leadership responses to volatile historical contexts endures as a testament to the enduring influence of history on leadership. historical leaders left an impact on the region's cultural evolution, modern leaders shaped their organizations and communities by drawing from historical insights. The ability to navigate turbulence with foresight remains a hallmark of effective leadership, bridging the gap between historical lessons and contemporary challenges.

The response of leaders to volatile historical contexts reflects a fusion of historical wisdom and contemporary action. history held lessons for navigating uncertainty, modern leaders employed their understanding of historical contexts to guide their decisions. The leadership responses, informed by the echoes of the past, underscore the enduring influence of history on the art and science of effective leadership—a timeless lesson for leaders striving to navigate the complexities of a rapidly changing world.

Civil Rights Movement and Transformational Leadership

The civil rights movement, a defining epoch of social change, heralded the emergence of transformational leadership. Leaders, inspired by the pursuit of justice and equality, galvanized communities with a vision for a better future. Leaders who ignited transformative shifts, these modern leaders utilized charisma, inspiration, and a sense of purpose to mobilize collective action and inspire change on a societal scale.

The Power of Charismatic Leadership

The civil rights movement illuminated the potency of charismatic leadership—leaders who possessed a magnetic allure that galvanized followers. This era showcased that leadership could transcend individual accomplishments, igniting movements that mirrored the history of unity and collective empowerment.

Charismatic leaders harnessed their influence to channel aspirations into action, reshaping societies and shaping the discourse of leadership.

The Dawn of Charismatic Leadership

In the annals of leadership history, few concepts shine as brightly as charismatic leadership—a force that galvanizes followers and propels movements forward. The civil rights movement emerged as a powerful testament to the transformative potential of charismatic leaders. This era showcased the profound influence that leaders with a magnetic allure could exert, echoing the essence of historical unity and collective empowerment.

Magnetic Allure and Follower Galvanization

Charismatic leaders possessed an innate magnetism that drew followers to their cause with an irresistible pull. Historical leaders commanded respect and allegiance, modern charismatic leaders captivated hearts and minds. In the civil rights movement, leaders like Sant Jarnail Singh exhibited a charisma that transcended individual accomplishments, channeling collective aspirations into a movement that aimed to reshape societal norms.

A Catalyst for Movement

Charismatic leaders catalyzed movements by harnessing their influence to inspire action. Historical leaders who ignited collective empowerment, these modern leaders transformed individual passion into a collective force. Their ability to articulate a compelling vision, coupled with their engaging presence, spurred individuals to rally together, transcending divisions and uniting under a common cause—like the historical unity observed in Punjab.

The Ripple Effect of Inspiration

The civil rights movement demonstrated that charismatic leaders had the power to create a ripple effect of inspiration. history witnessed the impact of collective action, the charisma of leaders like Martin Luther King, Rosa Parks and Malcolm X resonated far beyond their immediate spheres of influence. Their ability to kindle hope and determination fueled a wider movement for justice and equality, echoing the unity-driven aspirations seen throughout history.

Reshaping Societal Norms and Discourse

Charismatic leaders did more than inspire; they fundamentally reshaped societal norms and the discourse of leadership. leaders shaped cultural practices through their influence, charismatic leaders of the civil rights movement challenged the status quo and redefined the parameters of leadership. Their influence extended beyond their time, leaving an indelible mark on how leadership was perceived and enacted.

Influence of Punjab's Unity and Collective Empowerment

The civil rights movement's charismatic leadership drew parallel inspiration from Punjab's history of unity and collective empowerment. Leaders championed the aspirations of a united community, and charismatic leaders harnessed their influence to fuel collective action, demonstrating that leadership's impact extended beyond individual achievements.

Legacy of Charismatic Leadership

The legacy of charismatic leadership endures as a testament to the potent influence of individual charisma on collective aspirations. History informed cultural practices and charismatic leaders shaped the modern understanding of leadership. The ability to ignite movements for change, transcending individual achievements to drive societal transformation, remains a hallmark of charismatic leadership—a timeless lesson for leaders aiming to inspire and reshape the world around them.

Charismatic leadership's power to ignite movements for change resonates with historical narrative of unity and collective empowerment. The civil rights movement showcased the influence of magnetic leaders who inspired followers to rally behind a common cause. leaders shaped the region's cultural evolution, charismatic leaders left an enduring legacy that illustrates the profound impact of a single individual's ability to galvanize and transform society through the art of leadership.

Shaping Leadership Responses to Social Change

The civil rights movement's impact extended beyond its temporal confines, echoing the transformative capacities of historical shifts. Modern leaders were tasked with responding to the ripple effects of social change, adopting leadership approaches that fostered inclusivity, diversity, and social justice. These responses demonstrated the enduring influence of historical moments in shaping leadership's adaptive trajectory.

The Echoes of Transformation

The civil rights movement, a chapter in history that reverberated beyond its time, illuminated the transformative power of social change. Historical shifts that forged new paths, this movement underscored the profound capacity of human endeavors to reshape societal norms. As the civil rights movement's impact extended its influence, modern leaders found themselves navigating a world marked by dynamic social transformations, prompting them to reconsider their approaches to leadership.

Ripple Effects of Social Change

Punjab's historical shifts signaled the dawn of new eras and paradigms, just as the civil rights movement ushered in a transformative era for civil rights and social justice. This movement's influence reverberated far beyond its temporal confines. The modern world was marked by similar ripples of change, prompting leaders to grapple with how to effectively respond to the evolving expectations and demands of their societies.

Leadership Approaches for a Diverse Reality

Modern leaders recognized that the legacy of historical unity was mirrored in the need for leadership approaches that fostered inclusivity, diversity, and social justice. In the face of evolving societal landscapes, leaders were compelled to craft strategies that went beyond traditional hierarchies and embraced the principles of equity and fairness. The civil rights movement's emphasis on equality found resonance in leaders who understood the importance of providing opportunities and representation for all.

Adapting to Social Dynamics

Historical shifts were navigated by leaders who understood the importance of adapting to evolving dynamics, modern leaders responded to changing social dynamics by adopting innovative leadership approaches. The civil rights movement's call for justice was paralleled by leaders who recognized the need to engage with and empower marginalized communities, embracing change and fostering environments of collaboration and mutual understanding.

Resonance of Historical Moments

The enduring influence of historical moments, such as transformative shifts, echoed in the adaptive responses of modern leaders to social change. These leaders understood that the lessons of history could guide their actions in creating equitable and just societies. Historical transitions shaped cultural evolution, modern leaders engaged with historical moments to influence their leadership approaches, ensuring they aligned with the values and aspirations of their times.

Leadership's Adaptive Trajectory

The responses of modern leaders to social change underscored leadership's adaptive trajectory—an evolution that drew from the lessons of the past while embracing the demands of the present. Historical transitions exemplified the need for adaptable leadership in changing times. Modern leaders recognize that effective leadership requires continuous growth, a willingness to learn, and a commitment to embracing the challenges and opportunities presented by societal change.

The transformative impact of the civil rights movement and historical shifts underscored the malleability of societal norms and expectations. Modern leaders, confronted with dynamic social changes, embraced this lesson, responding with inclusive and diverse leadership approaches. The resonance between historical moments and modern leadership illuminated the timeless truth that effective leadership is a journey of adaptation—one that draws from the wisdom of the past to navigate the ever-changing landscapes of the present and future.

Postmodern Era and Distributed Leadership

As the postmodern era dawned, the leadership landscape shifted towards decentralization and networking. Diverse communities were connected by shared values, distributed leadership recognized that expertise and influence were not confined to hierarchical structures. This era illuminated the power of collaboration and the strength in recognizing that leadership was a collective endeavor.

Influence of Decentralization and Networking

The postmodern era drew lessons from historical power structures, recognizing that leadership's influence could extend beyond traditional hierarchies. historical leaders engaged in collaborative governance, modern leaders leveraged decentralized approaches to tap into the wisdom and strengths of a diverse array of contributors.

Embracing the Postmodern Shift

The postmodern era ushered in a transformative shift in the understanding of leadership—one that resonated with the principles of decentralization and networking. historical leaders recognized the power of collaborative governance, the postmodern era highlighted the potency of distributed leadership models that harnessed the collective potential of diverse individuals. This era marked a departure from traditional hierarchical structures, emphasizing the importance of shared authority and collaborative decision-making.

Influence of Decentralization and Networking

Drawing from the insights of historical practices, the postmodern era embraced the principles of decentralization and networking in leadership. leaders understood that strength lay in unity and collective action, modern leaders recognized that leadership's influence could be amplified through decentralized decision-making processes. This decentralized approach allowed for greater inclusivity, diversity of perspectives, and a more comprehensive understanding of complex issues.

Distributed Leadership

Distributed leadership models mirrored Punjab's historical emphasis on collaborative governance. In the postmodern era, leadership was no longer confined to a single individual or hierarchical position. Instead, it became an ecosystem where various individuals, each with unique expertise, contributed to the decision-making process. This approach recognized that leadership could emerge from any corner of the organization or community, fostering a culture of shared responsibility and innovation.

Unleashing Collective Potential

The influence of decentralization and networking in the postmodern era unlocked the latent potential of diverse voices. Historical leaders valued the contributions of various communities, modern leaders recognized that diversity enriched leadership's impact. By tapping into the collective wisdom and strengths of a diverse array of contributors, leaders were able to devise more robust solutions, respond more effectively to challenges, and drive innovation across sectors.

Adapting to Complex Environments

The postmodern era's embrace of decentralization and networking was particularly suited to the complexities of the modern world. historical leaders navigated diverse communities and challenges, modern leaders faced intricate global dynamics that demanded flexible and adaptable leadership approaches. Distributed leadership allowed organizations and communities to respond to these complexities with agility and resilience, leveraging the strengths of interconnected networks.

A Shift in Leadership Paradigms

The legacy of the postmodern era's focus on decentralization and networking continues to shape modern leadership paradigms. Historical leaders recognized the significance of collaborative governance, modern leaders understand that effective leadership involves cultivating an environment where leadership can emerge from any corner of the organization or community. This shift marks a departure from top-down models and emphasizes shared accountability, innovation, and the power of interconnected networks.

The postmodern era's adoption of distributed leadership models reflects the enduring influence of historical practices that recognized the strength of unity and collaboration. Historical leaders valued collective action, modern leaders leverage decentralization and networking to unleash the collective potential of diverse individuals. The postmodern era's legacy underscores the timeless wisdom that leadership is not confined to a single individual but is a collaborative endeavor that draws strength from the collective contributions of many.

Lessons from Historical Power Structures

In the intricate tapestry of history, the power structures that shaped civilizations offer a reservoir of lessons for contemporary leadership. Echoing the collaborative governance of historical leaders, these lessons transcend time, resonating with the postmodern era's emphasis on decentralized leadership and networking. As the world evolves, the enduring principles of collaboration, inclusivity, adaptability, and decentralization emerge as beacons guiding modern leaders on their journey to navigate complexities and build impactful, forward-thinking leadership approaches. Just as historical leaders harnessed the wisdom of their times, today's leaders can draw inspiration from history's pages to shape a more inclusive, innovative, and resilient leadership landscape.

Anchoring in Historical Wisdom

The annals of history hold invaluable insights for modern leadership, offering lessons drawn from the dynamics of historical power structures. historical leaders engaged in collaborative governance, modern leaders can glean wisdom from the past to shape their approaches. These lessons resonate with the postmodern era's emphasis on decentralized leadership and networking, underscoring the timeless principles that inform effective leadership.

Recognizing the Value of Collaboration

Lessons from historical power structures highlight the significance of collaboration. leaders recognized the strength of united communities, modern leaders understand that effective leadership involves harnessing the collective wisdom of diverse voices. Collaborative decision-making encourages a broader range of perspectives, resulting in more comprehensive solutions and fostering a sense of shared ownership and responsibility.

Embracing Decentralization

The lessons from historical power structures underscore the importance of decentralization. leaders understood the value of involving local expertise, modern leaders recognize that leadership influence extends beyond top-down structures. Decentralized leadership empowers individuals at all levels to contribute their insights, ensuring that decisions are informed by a holistic understanding of the complexities at hand.

Fostering Inclusive Decision-Making

Historical power structures echo the significance of inclusive decision-making. Similar to leaders valuing contributions from diverse communities, modern leaders prioritize diversity of thought and experience. By incorporating a variety of perspectives, leaders ensure that their decisions resonate with a broader range of stakeholders, leading to more well-rounded and effective outcomes.

Adapting to Changing Contexts

Lessons from historical power structures emphasize adaptability. leaders navigated changing historical landscapes, and modern leaders understand that flexibility is essential in a rapidly evolving world. The ability to adapt leadership approaches based on historical context enables leaders to respond effectively to shifting dynamics and challenges.

Guiding Leadership for the Future

The lessons from historical power structures provide a compass for modern leaders, guiding their approach to leadership in the postmodern era. The principles of collaboration, decentralization, inclusivity, and adaptability resonate across time, underscoring the enduring importance of these tenets in effective leadership. By drawing from the wisdom of history, modern leaders can shape a more inclusive, innovative, and responsive leadership landscape.

The lessons derived from historical power structures offer valuable guidance to modern leaders. Leaders recognized the strengths of collaborative governance and decentralized decision-making, and contemporary leaders can tap into these insights to navigate the complexities of the postmodern era. The echoes of history illuminate a path that leads to impactful, inclusive, and adaptable leadership, bridging the past with the present and forging a brighter future.

Synthesis and Reflection

In the intricate dance of time, history's footprints echo through the corridors of leadership, offering a reservoir of knowledge that informs and shapes the tapestry of modern leadership theories. historical leaders steered their communities through shifting landscapes, the lessons drawn from historical power structures weave a thread of continuity, connecting the past with the present. As we delve into this synthesis of historical influences and contemporary leadership theories, we embark on a reflective journey that uncovers the profound interplay between historical events and the development of leadership philosophies.

Connection Between Historical Influences and Contemporary Leadership Theories

Unraveling the tapestry of leadership theories reveals the threads woven by historical events. As history witnessed the ebb and flow of challenges and triumphs, so did the evolution of leadership theories capture the nuances of historical contexts. Modern leaders recognize that the struggles, innovations, and adaptations of the past have left indelible marks on leadership philosophies. By analyzing these historical shapers of theories, leaders gain insights into the transformative power of historical events on shaping leadership paradigms that resonate across time.

The enduring relevance of certain leadership concepts demonstrates the universality of effective leadership principles. Historical leaders held steadfast to enduring values, modern leaders unearth concepts that withstand the test of time. Lessons learned from historical power structures echo through contemporary leadership theories, highlighting the unwavering significance of collaboration, adaptability, and ethical decision-making. These concepts serve as guiding beacons, reminding leaders that the pulse of leadership beats to the rhythm of human nature and enduring values.

The exploration of historical influences in contemporary leadership theories is a journey of continuity—an acknowledgment that the echoes of history ripple through the fabric of leadership thought. Leaders crafted strategies rooted in their historical context, modern leaders draw from the wellspring of history to inform their strategies for the present and future. The connection between historical influences and contemporary theories bridges generations, reminding leaders that their decisions are not isolated acts but threads woven into the greater narrative of leadership's evolution.

The connection between historical influences and contemporary leadership theories is a bridge across time, uniting past experiences with present challenges. History shaped its cultural identity, and historical events have left an indelible mark on leadership philosophies. Modern leaders, recognizing this continuum of wisdom, embrace the insights of history to navigate complexities and create a leadership landscape that honors the lessons learned from eras long past.

How Historical Events Shaped the Development of Theories

The evolution of leadership theories is a tapestry intricately woven with the threads of historical events. History is imprinted with the imprints of cultural shifts and transitions, the development of modern leadership theories bears the marks of historical contexts that have shaped the course of leadership thought. By delving into this analysis, leaders gain insights into how the ebb and flow of history have influenced the very foundations of leadership theories, molding them to address the challenges and aspirations of their times.

Drawing Wisdom from Historical Milestones

The lens of historical analysis reveals that leadership theories are not static constructs, but dynamic responses to the changing landscapes of the past. Like historical leaders who responded to the currents of their age, contemporary leaders recognize that theories emerge from the cauldron of historical milestones. Through this analysis, leaders decipher how events like social movements, conflicts, and technological advancements have catalyzed shifts in leadership paradigms, adapting them to new societal and cultural currents.

Learning from the Evolution of Thought

Analyzing the interplay between historical events and leadership theories provides a roadmap of thought evolution. History witnessed the birth and transformation of ideas, modern leaders explore how historical events have led to shifts in leadership paradigms. This examination underscores the malleability of leadership theories, revealing how they adapt to address the complexities and challenges that societies face, thereby serving as mirrors reflecting the shifting tides of human progress.

Adapting Leadership to Historical Contexts

The analysis of historical influences unveils how leadership theories have been molded to suit the contours of specific historical contexts. Leaders adapted their strategies to the historical phases they traversed, modern leaders recognize the importance of contextual sensitivity in leadership theories. This analysis provides a nuanced understanding of how leadership principles shift in response to the unique challenges and opportunities posed by different historical periods.

Incorporating Historical Insights

By analyzing how historical events shaped the development of leadership theories, leaders arm themselves with a rich tapestry of insights. Leaders embraced wisdom from their history, modern leaders recognize that historical events have been instrumental in the development of theories that guide their decisions. Incorporating historical insights fosters a deeper understanding of leadership's adaptive nature and equips leaders to craft strategies that honor the lessons of the past while addressing the demands of the present and the future.

The analysis of how historical events shaped the development of theories enriches the tapestry of leadership thought. history imprints its influence on its cultural fabric, historical events have etched their mark on the evolution of leadership theories. By engaging in this analysis, leaders gain an appreciation for the fluidity and resilience of leadership thought, recognizing that theories are the result of dynamic interactions between history's tapestry and the aspirations of leadership.

Recognizing the Enduring Relevance of Leadership Concepts

Amid the currents of change that flow through history, certain leadership concepts stand as steadfast pillars of wisdom. History preserves the essence of cultural values, the leadership landscape too retains concepts that have proven their mettle across time. By acknowledging the enduring relevance of these principles, leaders find themselves grounded in a foundation of wisdom that transcends eras, guiding them through the intricacies of modern leadership challenges.

Lessons Carved in the Sands of Time

The recognition of enduring leadership concepts draws from the tapestry of history's lessons. leaders inherited legacies of wisdom, modern leaders uncover principles that have weathered the tests of time. These concepts, nurtured by historical power structures, serve as beacons that illuminate the path to effective leadership. By studying historical leaders who embraced these principles, contemporary leaders gain insights into the universal truths that continue to shape leadership excellence.

Collaboration

One such enduring concept is collaboration—an ageless virtue that echoes through both history and contemporary leadership thought. Just as historical leaders recognized the strength of united efforts, modern leaders embrace collaboration as a cornerstone of effective leadership. The resonance between historical collaborative practices and modern approaches underscores that collaboration transcends time, offering leaders the power to amplify their impact through collective synergy.

Ethical Decision-Making

Ethical decision-making is another timeless principle woven into both historical and contemporary leadership fabrics. Just as leaders upheld ethical values, modern leaders recognize the enduring importance of integrity, honesty, and accountability in their decisions. Lessons from history underscore that ethics are not confined to any particular era—they serve as guiding stars that illuminate the path to responsible leadership, even amidst the complexities of the modern world.

Inclusivity

The principle of inclusivity, the practice of embracing diversity, is a thread that unites historical power structures with the present. Just as historical leaders sought to incorporate diverse voices, modern leaders understand that inclusivity enriches decision-making and fosters a sense of belonging. By recognizing this enduring relevance, leaders shape environments where every voice is valued and diverse perspectives contribute to innovative solutions.

A Source of Strength and Guidance

Recognizing the enduring relevance of certain leadership concepts empowers leaders with a source of strength and guidance. Just as history imparts cultural wisdom, historical power structures offer leaders universal principles that transcend time. Incorporating these principles into contemporary leadership approaches not only honors the legacies of the past but also equips leaders to address the challenges of the present with the insights of generations gone by.

The recognition of enduring leadership concepts is a bridge that connects historical wisdom with modern leadership challenges. Just as cultural heritage informs its identity, historical power structures inform enduring principles that guide leadership excellence.

Key Takeaways

As we conclude our exploration of the foundations of leadership theories, a tapestry of insights emerges from the historical roots that have shaped the course of leadership thought. Just as history informs its cultural evolution, the historical power structures and philosophies discussed in this chapter offer key takeaways that bridge the past with the present. From the sagas of ancient civilizations to the enduring relevance of leadership concepts, our journey through history has illuminated the threads of wisdom that guide modern leadership. These insights, woven together, provide a foundation for understanding how leadership has evolved over time and how the echoes of the past continue to reverberate in the complexities of contemporary leadership challenges.

Understanding the Lineage of Leadership Theories from History

Delving into the lineage of leadership theories unveils a remarkable tapestry of continuity that stretches across the annals of time. Just as historical leaders drew inspiration from their predecessors, modern leadership theories are rooted in the evolution of thought that spans centuries. Our exploration of history's legacy has illuminated how ancient civilizations, military contexts, philosophical musings, and historical power structures have contributed to the rich lineage of leadership theories that guide modern leaders today. By understanding this lineage, leaders gain insights into the evolutionary process that has shaped leadership paradigms, fostering a deeper appreciation for the timeless principles that have stood the test of time.

Interplay between Historical Context and Theory Development

The interplay between historical context and theory development is a dynamic dance that shapes the evolution of leadership theories. Just as historical leaders were molded by the contexts they navigated, modern leadership theories are deeply intertwined with the historical landscapes that birthed them. By recognizing this intricate interplay, we gain insight into how historical events, societal norms, and cultural shifts have influenced the formulation and evolution of leadership theories, resulting in a tapestry of thought that reflects the complexities of the past and the aspirations of the present.

The Value of Historical Awareness in Leadership Practice

The value of historical awareness in leadership practice is akin to a compass that guides leaders through the intricate landscapes of modern challenges. historical leaders drew wisdom from their past, modern leaders who embrace historical awareness find themselves equipped with insights that illuminate the complexities of their roles. By recognizing the lessons, patterns, and context-specific strategies embedded in history, leaders gain a navigational tool that helps them navigate the ever-changing tides of leadership with a deeper understanding and more effective impact.

*****

CHAPTER THREE
Innate Leadership Theories

Leadership is a complex and dynamic concept that has intrigued scholars, practitioners, and researchers for centuries. In our quest to understand the theories of innate leadership, we delve into the realm of comprehending leadership not just as a skill that can be acquired through training, but as an inherent quality that some individuals possess naturally. This exploration seeks to reveal the mystery behind what makes a leader truly exceptional and how certain qualities set them apart from the rest. This chapter aims to help us understand innate leadership theories, the importance of comprehending inherent leadership qualities, and provide a preview of the theories we will be exploring, namely, The Great Man Theory and Trait Theory.

Understanding Innate Leadership Theories

Throughout the annals of history, the concept of leadership has remained a captivating enigma, characterized by its multidimensionality and often-elusive nature. As societies have evolved and cultures have shifted, leaders have risen to prominence, guiding their followers through challenges, shaping the course of events, and leaving an indelible mark on the world. Yet, within this tapestry of leadership, a central question continues to captivate our curiosity: What distinguishes a leader of exceptional caliber from the ordinary? This question has prompted the exploration of innate leadership theories – paradigms that propose the existence of innate qualities and attributes that imbue certain individuals with an inherent predisposition for effective leadership.

Historical Context and Ambiguity

The historical context of leadership is a kaleidoscope of leaders who have emerged across various eras and cultures, each possessing a unique blend of qualities and characteristics that have enabled them to exert influence over others. From the ancient rulers who commanded vast empires to the visionary artists and thinkers who led cultural revolutions, these leaders have cast their shadows on the canvas of history. However, as we examine their lives, the characteristics that propelled them to greatness often defy a standardized definition.

Inherent Qualities and Extraordinary Leadership

The notion of innate leadership theories arises from a recognition that there seems to be something exceptional – something beyond the grasp of conventional training and experience – that sets apart certain individuals in their leadership roles. These individuals are often able to inspire, motivate, and mobilize others with an innate charisma and confidence that defies easy explanation. This charisma might manifest as an aura of authority, an ability to communicate effectively, or an unwavering dedication to their cause.

While modern leadership research acknowledges the pivotal role of learned skills and adaptive behaviors in leadership development, innate leadership theories assert that a deeper, foundational element exists within some individuals. This foundational element, often thought of as a unique combination of personality traits, cognitive attributes, and emotional intelligence, seems to act as a catalyst for their leadership prowess. In essence, these theories suggest that some individuals are "wired" to be leaders from the outset, possessing an inherent disposition that aligns seamlessly with the demands of leadership.

Challenging Conventional Wisdom

The concept of innate leadership qualities challenges the conventional wisdom that leadership is solely the product of education, experience, and training. While these factors undoubtedly play a critical role in shaping leaders, innate leadership theories propose that there is an intangible factor – an "X-factor" – that transcends these elements. This idea challenges the prevailing notion that anyone can become a leader with the right set of skills and experiences.

The exploration of innate leadership theories offers a more nuanced understanding of leadership by acknowledging the uniqueness of individuals and the qualities that set them apart. It posits that leadership is not a uniform skill to be acquired but a complex interplay of nature and nurture. This perspective invites us to appreciate the diversity of leadership styles and approaches, recognizing that leaders are not simply products of their environments but also of their inherent attributes.

Exploring innate leadership theories allows us to peer beneath the surface of leadership, delving into the mysterious realm of qualities that seem to be present in exceptional leaders from the beginning. By navigating the landscape of leadership theories, we recognize that while education and experience play pivotal roles, there is an elusive element – an innate charisma, vision, or courage – that breathes life into leadership, setting apart those who merely lead from those who truly inspire and transform.

Significance of Understanding Inherent Qualities

The exploration of innate leadership theories extends far beyond theoretical curiosity; it holds profound implications across various dimensions of leadership development, education, and organizational success. By unraveling the mysteries of inherent qualities that shape extraordinary leaders, we gain invaluable insights that transcend traditional paradigms. This understanding offers a wealth of benefits across different domains, each contributing to the enhancement of leadership effectiveness and the realization of human potential.

Nuanced Perspective on Leadership

The significance of comprehending inherent qualities in leadership lies in its capacity to offer a more refined and multifaceted perspective on leadership itself. Traditionally, leadership has often been approached with a "one-size-fits-all" mentality, assuming that a predetermined set of skills and attributes universally define effective leadership. However, innate leadership theories challenge this notion by highlighting the diversity of qualities that contribute to exceptional leadership. By recognizing the unique interplay of traits, behaviors, and personal characteristics, this perspective liberates leadership from rigid molds, fostering a deeper appreciation for the myriad styles and approaches that can lead to success. This shift encourages leaders to embrace their individuality and leverage their innate strengths to make a lasting impact.

Identifying and Nurturing Leadership Potential

Understanding inherent qualities in leadership can act as a compass for identifying and nurturing leadership potential from an early stage. By acknowledging that certain individuals possess innate traits that predispose them to leadership roles, educators, mentors, and organizations can design tailored development programs that amplify these natural strengths. This proactive approach ensures that potential leaders receive the necessary guidance and support to harness their inherent attributes, facilitating their growth into impactful leaders. Moreover, this recognition can lead to a more inclusive approach to leadership development, as it acknowledges that leadership potential can manifest in various ways, transcending traditional molds.

Guiding Selection and Placement

One of the most pragmatic benefits of understanding inherent qualities in leadership lies in its ability to inform the selection and placement of leaders within diverse contexts. Recognizing the presence of specific innate traits can empower organizations to make more informed decisions about leadership assignments and team compositions. This insight enhances the likelihood of creating well-balanced and harmonious teams where leaders' inherent strengths align with the demands of their roles. As a result, team dynamics are optimized, collaboration is elevated, and performance outcomes are improved. This understanding also aids in mitigating potential mismatches between leaders and their roles, reducing the risk of leadership failures.

Enhancing Organizational Performance

The culmination of these benefits translates into improved organizational performance. When leadership is approached with a nuanced understanding of inherent qualities, organizations are better equipped to cultivate a leadership pipeline that aligns with their unique goals and values. This not only bolsters leadership effectiveness but also contributes to a more engaged and motivated workforce. The authenticity and resonance that emerge from leaders leveraging their innate qualities foster a sense of trust and connection, driving employees to perform at their best. Ultimately, this synergy between leadership styles and organizational objectives creates a more cohesive and high-performing environment.

The exploration of inherent qualities in leadership transcends theoretical speculation, offering practical and far-reaching implications across leadership development, education, and organizational success. By embracing the diversity of leadership attributes and recognizing the role of innate qualities, we usher in a new era of leadership enlightenment, where leaders are empowered to harness their uniqueness, educators tailor programs to individual strengths, and organizations optimize their human capital for unparalleled achievements.

Theories to be Explored

In our exploration of innate leadership theories, we embark on a journey through time and theory to uncover the foundational concepts that have shaped our understanding of leadership as an inherent quality. Our focus will be on two influential theories that have been instrumental in laying the groundwork for this fascinating line of research: The Great Man Theory and the Trait Theory. These theories provide insight into the notion that leadership is not solely a product of learning and experience but that certain inherent attributes play a pivotal role in shaping exceptional leaders.

The Great Man Theory

Dating back to the 19th century, the Great Man Theory stands as a pillar in the landscape of leadership theories. This theory, also known as the "Trait Theory of Leadership," proposes that remarkable leaders are not created through training or circumstances but are born with an innate predisposition for leadership. According to this theory, history is shaped by individuals who possess exceptional qualities that set them apart from the masses. These qualities, often characterized by attributes such as courage, vision, and charisma, align perfectly with the demands of leadership.

The essence of the Great Man Theory lies in the idea that certain individuals are destined to rise to leadership positions during pivotal moments in history, especially during times of crisis or transformation. These individuals are often seen as having a magnetic pull that draws followers to them and empowers them to lead with conviction. While this theory has been criticized for oversimplifying the complexities of leadership and failing to account for the influence of context and circumstances, its historical significance and exploration of innate qualities cannot be denied.

Trait Theory

Building upon the foundations of the Great Man Theory, Trait Theory takes a more systematic approach to understanding the inherent qualities that contribute to effective leadership. This theory seeks to identify a set of specific traits that are commonly found in successful leaders. These traits include intelligence, confidence, determination, decisiveness, and charisma, among others. Trait Theory operates on the premise that individuals who possess a certain combination of these traits are more likely to excel in leadership roles.

Unlike the Great Man Theory, Trait Theory aims to provide a structured framework for understanding leadership qualities. By isolating and categorizing specific attributes, this theory seeks to predict leadership effectiveness and success. While Trait Theory acknowledges that leadership development can occur through experience and education, it emphasizes that these inherent traits provide a foundation upon which leadership capabilities are built.

Exploring the Theories

Exploring these theories will critically examine their strengths, limitations, and implications for contemporary leadership understanding. By dissecting the key concepts and assumptions of the Great Man Theory and Trait Theory, we aim to gain a deeper appreciation for the complex interplay between inherent qualities and acquired skills in the development of exceptional leaders.

The Great Man Theory

The Great Man Theory stands as a captivating narrative that weaves together the essence of exceptional leadership with the fabric of history. This theory, rooted in the 19th century, introduces a perspective that leaders are not merely forged through experience and education but are born with inherent qualities that set them apart as destined figures of influence. At its core, the Great Man Theory posits that these exceptional individuals possess a distinctive amalgamation of traits and attributes that naturally elevate them to the forefront during pivotal moments in time. As we delve into the heart of this theory, we shall explore the concept of inherent leadership qualities within a historical context, revealing how the notion of "born leaders" and their intrinsic abilities has contributed to the shaping of history's most remarkable chapters.

In the rich tapestry of leadership theories, the Great Man Theory stands as a historically significant framework that seeks to unravel the mysteries of exceptional leadership. This theory, often regarded as a foundational concept in the realm of leadership studies, posits that individuals of extraordinary leadership prowess, often dubbed "great men," are not shaped solely by their experiences and learned skills. Instead, they are born with inherent qualities that naturally predispose them to assume leadership roles and leave an indelible mark on history.

At its core, the Great Man Theory suggests that exceptional leaders possess an intricate blend of traits, characteristics, and attributes that set them apart from the general population. The innate qualities are believed to equip them with an innate capacity to inspire, influence, and guide others in ways that ordinary individuals cannot replicate. This theory asserts that during critical junctures in history when societies and nations are at crossroads, these great men emerge as visionary figures who possess the exact qualities needed to lead and shape the course of events.

Inherent Qualities in Historical Context

The Great Man Theory was particularly influential during the 19th century, a time when society was captivated by the deeds of larger-than-life figures who seemed to single-handedly steer the course of events. These figures, such as military commanders, political leaders, and monarchs, were often viewed as possessing innate qualities that made them natural leaders. This theory found resonance in a historical context where the actions and decisions of a few could profoundly impact the lives of many.

The concept of inherent leadership qualities within the Great Man Theory is deeply intertwined with the idea that history is molded by individuals who embody qualities of courage, vision, charisma, and decisiveness. These qualities, it is believed, are not solely developed through education and experience but are present from birth, driving these leaders to step forward and command the attention of their contemporaries. This perspective paints a vivid picture of leaders who seem to possess an inner calling and destiny, guiding them toward roles of leadership even before circumstances beckon.

Concept of Inherent Leadership Qualities

The emergence of the Great Man Theory during the 19th century was deeply intertwined with the socio-political landscape of the time. This theory gained prominence in an era when societies were undergoing profound transformations, and leadership was often characterized by individuals who exhibited exceptional influence and authority across various domains. This historical backdrop sheds light on how the concept of inherent leadership qualities took root and flourished, shaping perceptions of leadership during this era.

Societal Structures and Exceptional Leadership

The 19th century was a period marked by rapid industrialization, political upheaval, and cultural shifts. As societies transitioned from agrarian economies to industrial powerhouses, traditional norms, and hierarchies were disrupted. Amid this upheaval, leaders emerged as guiding lights who could navigate the complexities of change and provide a sense of stability. Notable figures in military, political, and even artistic realms wielded immense influence over nations and populations, effectively shaping the course of events.

Noteworthy Figures and Larger-than-Life Personalities

The Great Man Theory found fertile ground in a historical context where certain individuals captured the collective imagination as larger-than-life personalities. Military commanders such as Sardar Sham Singh Attariwala and Napoleon Bonaparte, and political leaders like Veer Singh Dhillon in the court of Maharaja Ranjit Singh and Abraham Lincoln were celebrated for their exceptional leadership during times of crisis and transformation. These figures stood out for their achievements and the aura of authority and charisma they projected.

Inherent Qualities Beyond the Ordinary

Central to the Great Man Theory is the belief that these remarkable leaders possessed inherent qualities that extended beyond the ordinary. These qualities were often perceived as intrinsic to their very nature – an essence that set them apart from their contemporaries. This concept romanticized the notion of leadership, imbuing it with an air of mystique and heroism. These leaders were seen as possessing almost mythical attributes that endowed them with an innate ability to guide, inspire, and shape history.

Leadership Beyond Circumstances

One of the core tenets of the Great Man Theory is the idea that leaders do not simply rise to prominence due to favorable circumstances or opportunities. Rather, they ascend to positions of influence because of their unique inherent qualities. This perspective challenges the deterministic view that leadership is solely a product of external factors. Instead, it emphasizes the role of an individual's innate attributes as catalysts for leadership emergence.

Pivotal Events and Transformations

The theory suggests that these leaders were not products of their times; rather, their times were shaped by them. They appeared at pivotal junctures in history when their specific qualities were needed most. These qualities enabled them to navigate challenges, inspire followers, and propel societies forward. The inherent leadership qualities of these individuals were believed to align perfectly with the demands of the moment, making them natural leaders during times of crisis, innovation, or upheaval.

Belief in Born Leaders and Their Natural Abilities

At the core of the Great Man Theory resides a compelling belief that leaders possess an innate disposition, one that transcends the realm of education or training. This belief suggests that leaders are not molded through the acquisition of skills or knowledge, but are born with an inherent ability to inspire, guide, and influence others. These inherent qualities, often marked by traits such as courage, vision, charisma, and decisiveness, are thought to be woven into the very fabric of an individual's identity, shaping their actions, decisions, and the profound impact they have on society.

Intrinsic Traits and Identity

According to the Great Man Theory, the qualities that define a leader are not superficial or acquired; they are an integral part of who the individual is. These traits are believed to be so deeply embedded in the leader's essence that they naturally manifest in their behavior and interactions. Courage, for instance, might drive a leader to take bold risks in the face of adversity, while charisma enables them to galvanize followers with an effortless magnetism. These qualities are not adopted or put on display; they emanate naturally, underscoring the authenticity of the leader's influence.

Historical Parallels of Legendary Leaders

The annals of history abound with stories of leaders who, in the eyes of many, personified the ideals upheld by the Great Man Theory. Figures like Maharaja Ranjit Singh, Alexander the Great, Julius Caesar, and Napoleon Bonaparte are often viewed through the lens of this theory. These legendary leaders, who commanded vast empires and left indelible imprints on civilizations, exhibited qualities that seemingly surpassed the ordinary. Their exceptional leadership during times of upheaval and transformation resonates with the theory's premise that certain individuals possess inherent qualities that align perfectly with the needs of their era.

Complexities and Criticisms

While the Great Man Theory offers a captivating perspective on leadership, it has not escaped criticism. Detractors argue that this theory oversimplifies the intricate interplay of leadership and situational context. By attributing leadership solely to inherent qualities, the theory neglects the role of external circumstances, the influence of culture, and the power of learning in shaping leaders. It's important to note that leadership is a multidimensional phenomenon, influenced by both intrinsic attributes and external factors.

An Essential Historical Pillar

Despite its limitations, the Great Man Theory remains an essential historical pillar in the evolution of leadership thought. It challenges the prevailing notion that leadership can be attained solely through education and experience, ushering in a conversation about the role of innate qualities in driving exceptional leadership. By placing a spotlight on these qualities, the theory has ignited discussions that continue to shape our understanding of leadership attributes, their origins, and their impact on history.

Historical Figures and Their Impact

In the tapestry of human history, there are individuals whose presence and actions shape the course of nations and cultures, leaving an indelible mark that transcends time. These leaders, often regarded as embodiments of the "Great Man" Theory, are believed to possess inherent qualities that propel them to positions of extraordinary influence. Rooted in the notion that certain individuals are born with innate attributes that predispose them to leadership roles, this theory sheds light on the unique impact of these exceptional figures. In this exploration, we delve into the lives of three historical luminaries – Maharaja Ranjit Singh, Alexander the Great, and Abraham Lincoln – each frequently invoked as exemplars of the Great Man Theory. By scrutinizing their innate leadership qualities, we will uncover the traits that defined their leadership styles and the profound reverberations they initiated in their respective contexts. However, to traverse their legacies, it's essential to acknowledge the criticisms and controversies that surround the Great Man Theory, a theory that both magnifies and simplifies the intricate nature of leadership.

Prominent Historical Leaders

Within the annals of history, there stand figures whose leadership qualities are so remarkable that they have become emblematic of the "Great Man" Theory. This theory posits that exceptional leaders are endowed with innate attributes that elevate them beyond the ordinary and naturally position them as influencers of their time. Two such towering historical personalities, Alexander the Great, Abraham Lincoln, and Maharaja Ranjit Singh, are frequently invoked as exemplars of this theory, embodying leadership that transcends the norm.

Maharaja Ranjit Singh

In the Punjab subcontinent, Maharaja Ranjit Singh emerged as a charismatic and visionary leader during a time of turmoil. Rising to power in the early 19th century, Ranjit Singh's leadership was characterized by his strategic brilliance, administrative acumen, and ability to unite diverse communities under a single banner. His innate qualities enabled him to establish the Sikh Empire in Punjab, countering the fragmentation and disarray that plagued the region. Maharaja Ranjit Singh's reign not only marked a period of stability but also showcased his knack for fostering religious tolerance and cultural amalgamation.

Alexander the Great

In the ancient world, Alexander the Great stands as an archetype of charismatic and visionary leadership. His military prowess and conquests reshaped the geopolitical landscape of his era. Born in 356 BCE, Alexander's innate leadership qualities, such as unparalleled strategic acumen, unwavering determination, and the ability to inspire unyielding loyalty among his troops, cemented his status as a "Great Man." His ambition knew no bounds, as he undertook the audacious endeavor to forge an empire stretching from Greece to the far reaches of Asia. Alexander's innate qualities not only enabled his conquests but also fostered cultural exchange and the spread of Hellenistic civilization, leaving an enduring legacy.

Abraham Lincoln

In a different context and centuries later, Abraham Lincoln emerged as a leader whose moral courage and steadfast resolve made an indelible mark on American history. As the 16th President of the United States during its most tumultuous period, Lincoln's leadership qualities were defined by his deep empathy, unshakeable dedication to justice, and unparalleled oratory skills. Born in humble circumstances, Lincoln's journey from a log cabin to the White House exemplified the transformative power of leadership grounded in innate attributes. His unwavering commitment to preserving the Union during the American Civil War and his role in abolishing slavery showcased his embodiment of the Great Man Theory.

These historical leaders share a common thread: They possessed innate qualities that propelled them beyond the ordinary, enabling them to shape their respective contexts in profound ways. Their charisma, strategic insight, and transformative impact reflect the essence of the Great Man Theory, asserting that certain individuals are born with attributes that naturally align with the demands of leadership.

Analyzing Leadership Traits and the Impact

The historical figures of Maharaja Ranjit Singh, Alexander the Great, and Abraham Lincoln are not only emblematic of the "Great Man" Theory but also serve as captivating case studies to explore the innate leadership qualities that propelled them to reshape the course of history. Analyzing their distinct leadership traits provides insight into how these qualities contributed to their profound impact on their respective contexts.

Maharaja Ranjit Singh

Maharaja Ranjit Singh's leadership was characterized by a blend of strategic acumen, administrative prowess, and a unifying spirit. His innate qualities of decisiveness and the ability to bridge diverse communities played a pivotal role in consolidating the Sikh Empire in a region marked by fragmentation. His leadership traits enabled him to create a stable and multicultural kingdom, marked by religious tolerance and cultural vibrancy. Under his rule, the Punjab region experienced an era of stability and development, leaving a lasting imprint on the socio-political landscape.

Alexander the Great

Alexander's leadership was marked by a unique blend of strategic brilliance, unwavering determination, and an unparalleled ability to inspire his troops. His military campaigns were characterized by daring maneuvers, innovative tactics, and a relentless pursuit of victory. His innate qualities of charisma and vision enabled him to unite his troops under a common purpose, fostering an unbreakable bond that facilitated his conquests. The impact of his leadership extended beyond military triumphs; his cultural exchange initiatives ushered in the Hellenistic era, influencing art, philosophy, and politics for centuries to come.

Abraham Lincoln

Lincoln's leadership was grounded in moral integrity, empathy, and the power of his words. His innate qualities of humility and authenticity resonated deeply with the American populace during a time of unprecedented turmoil. As a masterful communicator, he harnessed the potency of oratory to convey his vision of a united nation and the abolition of slavery. His leadership traits enabled him to navigate the complexities of the Civil War, preserving the Union and setting the stage for a more just society. His Emancipation Proclamation marked a watershed moment, forever changing the course of American history.

Impact on Respective Contexts

These leaders' innate attributes had far-reaching impacts on their societies and beyond. Maharaja Ranjit Singh's unifying leadership not only brought stability to a region marked by strife but also fostered a multicultural society that embraced diversity. Alexander's conquests reshaped geopolitical boundaries and facilitated cultural exchange between the East and West. Lincoln's moral leadership and abolitionist stance transformed the United States, ending the scourge of slavery and paving the way for civil rights movements.

Their innate leadership traits allowed them to navigate tumultuous circumstances and drive change that extended beyond their lifetimes. Their legacy is a testament to the enduring influence of leaders who possess qualities that align naturally with the needs of their eras. These figures continue to inspire discussions about the interplay between innate attributes and the impact they have on shaping history.

Challenges and Controversies

While these leaders' impact is undeniable, the "Great Man" Theory has faced criticism for oversimplifying leadership dynamics. The theory's focus on individual attributes often neglects the role of broader societal, cultural, and situational factors in shaping leadership outcomes. While their qualities were undoubtedly remarkable, the context in which they operated cannot be ignored when analyzing their leadership legacies.

Evaluation and Relevance

As we traverse the landscapes of leadership theories, the Great Man Theory emerges as a captivating historical pillar that has shaped our understanding of leadership's origins and dynamics. Yet, with the passage of time and the evolution of society, it becomes imperative to critically examine the strengths and weaknesses of this theory. The Great Man Theory's assertion that exceptional leaders are born with inherent qualities that naturally predispose them to influence and guide challenges us to ponder its applicability in the complex leadership terrains of today. This exploration delves into the theory's merits and limitations, pondering its relevance in contemporary contexts. Moreover, it delves into the profound implications of this theory for the cultivation of leaders – the very individuals who carry the torch of progress, innovation, and change.

Critically Evaluating the Strengths and Weaknesses of The Great Man Theory

The Great Man Theory, a seminal concept in the realm of leadership theories, has sparked both admiration and skepticism. While it offers valuable insights into the role of innate qualities in leadership, a critical evaluation reveals a spectrum of strengths and weaknesses that shape its relevance in our understanding of leadership dynamics.

Strengths:

1. **Recognition of Inherent Leadership Qualities:** One of the theory's strengths lies in its acknowledgment of the impact of inherent qualities on leadership. It underscores that leaders possess certain attributes that distinguish them from the general population. This recognition aligns with historical accounts of influential figures whose exceptional qualities indeed contributed to their prominence and impact.

2. **Emphasis on Exceptional Influence:** The theory's focus on extraordinary leaders aligns with historical narratives of figures who have wielded exceptional influence during pivotal moments. By highlighting these exceptional individuals, the theory offers insights into how their inherent qualities played a role in guiding societies through times of change and uncertainty.

3. **Inspiration and Aspiration:** The notion of "Great Men" who possess innate qualities can serve as a source of inspiration for aspiring leaders. The idea that exceptional qualities can propel individuals to leadership roles can motivate individuals to develop and cultivate their own leadership attributes.

Weaknesses:

1. **Oversimplification of Leadership:** Critics argue that the theory oversimplifies the complexities of leadership.

Leadership is influenced by a myriad of factors, including situational context, cultural norms, and social dynamics. The theory's exclusive focus on inherent qualities neglects the interactive nature of leadership development.

2. **Exclusion of Other Factors:** The Great Man Theory downplays the significance of external circumstances and the role of education, experience, and learning in leadership development. Leadership is often a product of a combination of nature and nurture, and the theory's emphasis on nature alone disregards the importance of nurturing potential.

3. **Lack of Inclusivity:** The theory's language of "Great Men" implies a gendered perspective that excludes women and non-binary individuals. This limitation underscores the need for more inclusive theories that encompass a broader spectrum of leadership qualities and identities.

4. **Limited Application in Contemporary Contexts:** The theory's applicability in modern leadership landscapes is debated. In today's dynamic and interconnected world, leadership often requires adaptive skills, collaboration, and an understanding of complex systems. The theory's focus on inherent qualities might not fully capture the multifaceted nature of contemporary leadership challenges.

The strengths and weaknesses of the Great Man Theory underscore the complexity of leadership and the need for a nuanced understanding. While the theory offers valuable insights into the impact of innate qualities on leadership, it falls short in accounting for the intricate interplay of external factors and the evolving demands of leadership in the modern world. A comprehensive understanding of leadership requires the integration of multiple theories that collectively capture the rich tapestry of leadership dynamics.

Whether the Theory Holds True in Contemporary Leadership Landscapes

In a rapidly evolving world marked by technological advancements, global interconnectivity, and shifting societal norms, the question of whether the Great Man Theory holds true in contemporary leadership landscapes becomes both intriguing and complex. While the theory's emphasis on inherent leadership qualities has historical resonance, its applicability in the modern context requires careful examination.

Evolution of Leadership Dynamics

Contemporary leadership landscapes are characterized by fluidity, ambiguity, and the need for adaptive responses to dynamic challenges. Leadership is no longer confined to a select few who possess predetermined traits. Instead, effective leadership often necessitates the ability to collaborate, learn, and navigate complex systems. In this context, the theory's focus on fixed inherent qualities may not fully capture the versatility demanded of today's leaders.

Inclusive Leadership and Diversity

Modern leadership is increasingly characterized by diversity and inclusion. Recognizing the value of diverse perspectives and leadership styles challenges the notion of a singular prototype of a "Great Man." Leadership now spans a spectrum of identities, backgrounds, and approaches, highlighting that leadership qualities are not confined to specific gender, culture, or personality traits.

Learning and Adaptation

Contemporary leadership thrives on continuous learning and adaptation. The Great Man Theory's assertion that leaders are born with qualities that remain constant overlooks the importance of ongoing development. Leaders today need to continually refine their skills, embrace new knowledge, and adjust their strategies based on changing circumstances.

Collaboration and Interdependence

The interconnected nature of the modern world underscores the importance of collaboration and teamwork. Effective leadership often involves mobilizing a diverse group of individuals toward a common goal. The theory's individual-centric approach might not fully account for the collaborative and interdependent nature of many leadership endeavors.

Relevance in Limited Contexts

While the theory's applicability might be questioned in broad contemporary leadership contexts, it could hold some relevance in specific situations. In crisis scenarios, for instance, individuals with innate qualities such as resilience, decisiveness, and clarity of vision might emerge as pivotal leaders. However, even in such cases, the interplay between inherent qualities and situational dynamics remains crucial.

In contemplating whether the Great Man Theory holds true in contemporary leadership landscapes, it becomes evident that the theory's rigid focus on inherent qualities faces challenges in the face of the multifaceted demands of modern leadership. While there might be instances where certain inherent traits are advantageous, leadership in today's world requires flexibility, inclusivity, adaptability, and a commitment to ongoing growth. As leadership theories continue to evolve, the Great Man Theory's insights should be considered alongside other perspectives that better capture the complexities of leadership in our ever-changing global landscape.

Implications of the Theory for Leadership Development

The Great Man Theory's assertion that leaders are born with inherent qualities that naturally predispose them to influence and guide has profound implications for leadership development. While the theory has faced criticisms, it has also spurred discussions about the role of innate attributes in shaping exceptional leaders. Exploring these implications provides insights into how leadership development strategies can be enhanced in light of this theory.

Identification and Nurturing of Potential

The theory suggests that identifying individuals with innate leadership qualities is crucial. Leadership development programs can be tailored to identify and nurture these potential leaders from an early stage. By recognizing and amplifying these qualities, organizations can help individuals refine their inherent attributes and channel them toward effective leadership.

Fostering Self-Awareness

Understanding the implications of the theory can foster self-awareness among aspiring leaders. By reflecting on their own innate qualities, individuals can identify areas of strength and areas for growth. This awareness empowers individuals to leverage their strengths and work on developing additional skills that align with contemporary leadership demands.

Balancing Inherent Qualities and Skill Acquisition

While the theory emphasizes the role of inherent qualities, contemporary leadership development recognizes the importance of skill acquisition and learning. Effective leaders need a blend of adaptive skills, emotional intelligence, and domain expertise. Balancing inherent qualities with skill development ensures a comprehensive and well-rounded approach to leadership.

Creating Diverse Leadership Pipelines

Acknowledging the theory's limitations in accounting for diversity, leadership development initiatives should prioritize creating diverse pipelines of leaders. Recognizing that exceptional qualities can manifest in various ways across different individuals and cultures promotes inclusivity and ensures that leadership is not limited to a specific archetype.

Fostering a Growth Mindset

The theory's implications emphasize that while individuals might possess certain inherent attributes, leadership is a journey of continuous growth. Leadership development programs should encourage a growth mindset that embraces learning, adaptation, and evolution. This mindset empowers individuals to embrace change and seize opportunities for development.

Personalized Development Plans

By incorporating the theory's insights, leadership development can be tailored to individual needs. Personalized development plans can help aspiring leaders harness their inherent qualities while addressing areas that might require improvement. This approach aligns with the contemporary understanding that leadership is a combination of nature and nurture.

Trait Theory

Within the realm of leadership theories, Trait Theory emerges as a structured approach to unraveling the enigma of leadership qualities. This theory stands in contrast to the Great Man Theory, shifting the spotlight from inherent "greatness" to specific traits that underpin effective leadership. Trait Theory embarks on a journey to dissect the mosaic of characteristics that differentiate leaders from followers, offering a systematic lens to comprehend how certain attributes predispose individuals to leadership roles.

Foundations of Trait Theory

Trait Theory stands as a pillar of inquiry, offering a distinctive lens through which to examine the foundations of effective leadership. Unlike theories that attribute leadership to historical circumstances, situational dynamics, or learned behaviors,

Trait Theory shifts its focus to the intrinsic qualities that leaders possess. It proposes that certain inherent traits and attributes predispose individuals to excel in leadership roles.

The Essence of Trait Theory

At its core, Trait Theory represents a departure from the notion that leadership is a universally attainable skill acquired through experience and training. Instead, it suggests that leadership effectiveness is influenced by the innate qualities and characteristics individuals bring to the table. These traits form the foundational blueprint upon which leaders build their leadership styles, strategies, and approaches.

The Unique Configuration of Traits

Trait Theory proposes that some individuals possess a unique configuration of traits that naturally align with the demands of leadership, making them more likely to emerge as effective leaders in various contexts. The theory acknowledges that while leadership skills can be developed, certain traits create a predisposition for leadership success. These traits serve as the bedrock upon which leaders can develop their abilities and navigate complex challenges.

Classification of Traits: Cardinal, Central, and Secondary

Classification categorization enables us to understand the hierarchy and relative importance of different attributes in shaping leadership capabilities. Each category of traits contributes to the multifaceted nature of leadership, highlighting the diverse qualities that effective leaders possess.

Trait Theory as an Approach to Understanding Innate Leadership Qualities

Trait Theory emerges as a structured framework that delves into the core attributes that shape effective leaders. This theory offers a unique perspective by focusing on the inherent qualities that individuals bring to leadership roles. Unlike theories that emphasize situational factors or acquired skills, Trait Theory asserts that certain traits predispose individuals to become successful leaders.

The Lens of Innate Qualities

Trait Theory introduces us to a lens through which we can explore the innate qualities that are essential for effective leadership. Instead of attributing leadership solely to external circumstances or learned behaviors, the theory suggests that certain traits are integral to an individual's leadership potential. These traits serve as the building blocks upon which leadership skills and strategies are developed.

Beyond Situational Factors

This approach offers a departure from theories that attribute leadership solely to situational factors or the demands of a particular context. Trait Theory implies that while the context may influence how leadership is expressed, the core qualities that make a leader effective are rooted in their inherent traits. These traits provide leaders with the tools to navigate a wide range of situations and challenges.

Understanding Leadership Predisposition

Trait Theory highlights the idea of predisposition to leadership. It suggests that some individuals are naturally inclined to take on leadership roles due to their unique combination of traits. These traits encompass a spectrum of characteristics, from communication skills and decisiveness to empathy and resilience. Trait Theory enables us to identify these traits and understand how they contribute to leadership effectiveness.

A Holistic Approach to Leadership

By introducing Trait Theory as an approach to understanding innate leadership qualities, we recognize the significance of a holistic perspective on leadership development. While skills and experience undoubtedly play a role, innate traits serve as the underlying foundation that shapes an individual's leadership journey. This approach acknowledges that effective leadership encompasses a blend of nature and nurture.

Specific Traits that Contribute to Effective Leadership

Within the context of Trait Theory, a central tenet is the meticulous exploration of specific traits that underpin effective leadership. Unlike some theories that emphasize the circumstantial or learned aspects of leadership, Trait Theory directs its gaze toward the distinct attributes that leaders possess inherently. This approach recognizes that leadership effectiveness is not solely shaped by circumstances but is rooted in a collection of discernible traits that drive successful leadership.

The Essence of Trait Identification

Trait Theory's focus on identifying specific traits is a quest to unravel the essence of what distinguishes leaders from non-leaders. This exploration seeks to identify a set of characteristics that, when present in an individual, enhance their capacity to guide, motivate, and inspire others. By pinpointing these traits, we gain insight into the psychological and behavioral elements that contribute to effective leadership.

Diverse Range of Traits

Trait Theory acknowledges that effective leadership is a multidimensional construct, encompassing a wide array of traits. These traits span from cognitive abilities and emotional intelligence to social skills and personality attributes. The theory recognizes that there is no one-size-fits-all formula for effective leadership; rather, it's the synergy of these traits that shapes an individual's unique leadership style.

Mapping Traits to Leadership Effectiveness

Trait Theory strives to establish connections between specific traits and leadership effectiveness. For instance, traits such as emotional intelligence, assertiveness, and resilience are often linked to leaders who can manage their own emotions while effectively understanding and influencing the emotions of others. The focus on mapping traits to leadership outcomes enhances our understanding of how these attributes interact to foster successful leadership.

Advantages of Trait Identification

The identification of specific traits that contribute to effective leadership offers practical benefits for leadership development and selection. It allows organizations to create targeted training programs that enhance these specific attributes. Moreover, during the selection process, understanding the traits that align with leadership effectiveness enables organizations to identify and nurture individuals with leadership potential.

Complexity and Controversies

While Trait Theory's focus on specific traits is valuable, it's important to acknowledge the complexity and potential controversies. Leadership is influenced by a myriad of factors, and the interaction between traits and situational context cannot be overlooked. Moreover, the exclusion of certain traits in the assessment of leadership effectiveness challenges the completeness of this approach.

Cardinal Traits

Within the framework of Trait Theory, the concept of "cardinal traits" emerges as a pivotal component that sheds light on the core attributes that define effective leaders. Cardinal traits represent the dominant threads of an individual's personality that exert a pervasive influence on their behavior, choices, and leadership style. These traits are not only central to an individual's identity but also play a paramount role in shaping their leadership approach.

Cardinal traits can be envisioned as the defining pillars of an individual's personality, akin to the guiding principles that underpin their actions and interactions. These traits are not common to all individuals; rather, they are specific attributes that are distinctive to a particular leader. Cardinal traits encapsulate a unique configuration of characteristics that consistently manifest in various aspects of a leader's life.

Significance of Cardinal Traits

Cardinal traits are not mere surface-level attributes; they represent the deeply ingrained threads that weave through an individual's personality, shaping their behavior, decisions, and leadership style. Cardinal traits offer a unique perspective to grasp the core attributes that set leaders apart and significantly influence their impact. Cardinal traits can be thought of as the bedrock upon which a leader's identity is constructed. These traits encompass a distinct amalgamation of qualities that are intricately woven into an individual's character. Unlike secondary or fleeting traits, cardinal traits remain steady and unwavering, influencing how leaders navigate their responsibilities and interactions.

Linking Traits to Leadership Identity

Within the sphere of leadership, cardinal traits play a pivotal role in shaping a leader's identity and approach. Picture a leader with a cardinal trait of integrity – this characteristic infuses their decisions with ethical considerations, building trust and admiration from their team. Similarly, a leader endowed with a cardinal trait of resilience may showcase an unwavering determination to surmount challenges, motivating their team to persevere in challenging times.

Impact on Leadership Styles

Cardinal traits exert a profound impact on leadership styles, determining whether a leader inclines towards a transformational, collaborative, or authoritative approach. For instance, a leader embodying a cardinal trait of visionary thinking may be naturally inclined to inspire their team with a captivating vision of the future. These traits guide a leader's actions, establishing a cohesive link between their inherent attributes and their outward conduct.

The Authenticity Factor

Leaders who embody their cardinal traits often radiate authenticity – a quality that resonates deeply with their followers. When leaders wholeheartedly embrace and embody these traits, they communicate a sincere dedication to their principles and values. This authenticity not only elevates their credibility but also establishes a robust groundwork for fostering trust and commitment among their team members.

Navigating Complexity and Uniqueness

While cardinal traits provide insights into the core attributes that mold leaders, it's vital to acknowledge that each leader possesses a unique amalgamation of traits. The interplay between these traits contributes to the rich diversity of leadership styles and methodologies. Furthermore, how cardinal traits manifest can be influenced by situational contexts and the ever-evolving demands of leadership.

Examples of cardinal traits

The concept of "cardinal traits" within Trait Theory finds embodiment in historical leaders who have left an indelible mark on societies and cultures. These leaders' stories serve as a testament to the power of specific attributes that define their success. Examining historical figures through the lens of cardinal traits illuminates the essential qualities that have propelled them to leadership greatness and shaped their enduring legacies.

Resilience as a Cardinal Trait: Winston Churchill

Winston Churchill's leadership during World War II exemplified the cardinal trait of resilience. Faced with the daunting challenge of guiding Britain through one of its darkest hours, Churchill displayed unwavering determination and courage. His ability to rally the nation, deliver stirring speeches, and maintain resolve in the face of adversity demonstrated the power of resilience as a cardinal trait. Churchill's unyielding spirit not only inspired his country but also left an enduring legacy as a symbol of leadership in trying times.

Empathy as a Cardinal Trait: Bhai Kanhaiya Ji

Bhai Kanhaiya Ji, a historical figure in Sikh history, embodied the cardinal trait of empathy. His unwavering dedication to serving wounded soldiers, regardless of their affiliations, showcased an exceptional ability to connect with the suffering of others. His selflessness and compassion transcended societal divisions, setting a profound example of humanitarianism. Bhai Kanhaiya Ji's empathetic approach demonstrated how this trait can bridge differences and inspire acts of kindness and inclusivity.

Vision as a Cardinal Trait: Martin Luther King Jr.

Martin Luther King Jr. embodied the cardinal trait of vision, propelling the civil rights movement forward. His ability to articulate a powerful vision of equality and justice captured the hearts and minds of people across the United States. King's vision of a harmonious and just society was a rallying point that united diverse groups toward a common goal. His leadership showcased how a clear and compelling vision, when embraced as a cardinal trait, can galvanize movements and ignite transformative change.

Complexity and Individuality of Cardinal Traits

While these examples highlight cardinal traits that have historically defined successful leaders, it's important to acknowledge that leadership is multifaceted. Leaders often possess a combination of these and other traits, each contributing uniquely to their leadership style. The interplay of cardinal traits within different contexts and challenges showcases the dynamic nature of effective leadership.

Central Traits

In the intricate mosaic of leadership attributes, "central traits" emerge as the weaving threads that underpin a leader's behavior, decisions, and interactions. Central traits come to the forefront as essential components that contribute to a leader's unique identity and approach. These traits hold the power to influence how leaders navigate challenges, inspire their teams, and guide organizations toward success. Examining central traits provides a window into the pivotal qualities that form the nucleus of effective leadership, shedding light on their interplay with cardinal traits to create a multifaceted and comprehensive leadership profile.

Central Traits' Role in Shaping Leadership Behavior

Central traits, as elucidated within Trait Theory, encompass a spectrum of qualities that serve as the bedrock of an individual's personality and, consequently, their leadership behavior. These traits are not fleeting or situational; instead, they form the consistent threads that shape how leaders perceive, interact, and respond to their surroundings.

The Essence of Central Traits

Central traits are the pivotal characteristics that define an individual's overall demeanor and are prominent in various aspects of their life. When it comes to leadership, central traits are the compass that guides a leader's actions, decisions, and interactions with others. These traits may include qualities such as honesty, assertiveness, flexibility, and sociability. Their influence on leadership behavior is pervasive, impacting how leaders communicate, delegate, motivate, and manage conflicts.

Influencing Leadership Styles

Central traits profoundly influence the choice of leadership styles that individuals adopt. A leader with a central trait of assertiveness might gravitate towards a more directive and authoritative approach, while a leader with a central trait of adaptability may adopt a more collaborative and flexible style. These traits play a fundamental role in shaping the methods leaders employ to influence their teams and attain organizational objectives.

Guiding Decision-Making and Problem-Solving

Central traits are instrumental in guiding leaders' decision-making processes. For instance, a leader with a central trait of empathy might prioritize considering the well-being of team members when making choices. Similarly, a leader with a central trait of analytical thinking may meticulously analyze data and implications before arriving at conclusions. These traits contribute to a leader's capacity to make informed and effective decisions that align with their core attributes.

Interplay with Situational Context

While central traits are foundational, they also interact with situational factors to mold leadership behavior. A leader's central traits might manifest differently based on the demands of a given circumstance. For example, a leader with a central trait of assertiveness might exhibit more assertive behavior during times of crisis, showcasing adaptability in response to the situation. This interplay demonstrates the dynamic nature of leadership behavior.

Central Traits as the Bridge to Cardinal Traits

Central traits function as the bridge that connects cardinal traits to tangible leadership behavior. While cardinal traits set the broad principles that guide a leader's path, central traits serve as the channels through which these principles flow into practical actions. Imagine a leader with a cardinal trait of vision, coupled with a central trait of effective communication – their capability to convey visionary concepts hinges on their adeptness in communication, a central trait in their repertoire.

Crafting a Unified Leadership Profile

The fusion of central and cardinal traits yields a unified leadership profile that captures the intricate dimensions of effective leadership. This profile doesn't merely highlight strengths but also acknowledges potential challenges arising from the interplay between traits. Armed with this awareness, leaders can harness their strengths while proactively addressing potential limitations.

Secondary Traits

The exploration of "secondary traits" reveals the subtler threads that play a significant role in shaping leadership effectiveness. While central and cardinal traits often take the spotlight, secondary traits quietly orchestrate their own impact on a leader's capabilities. In the realm of Trait Theory, the study of secondary traits emerges as a crucial endeavor, shedding light on the traits that, although not as central, contribute indispensably to a leader's holistic prowess. These traits, while often operating behind the scenes, add depth and dimension to a leader's overall profile, further enriching their ability to navigate challenges, inspire others, and drive positive change.

Role of Secondary Traits

Secondary traits, often residing in the shadows of central and cardinal traits, play a pivotal role in influencing leadership effectiveness. While central and cardinal traits form the core of a leader's identity and behavior, secondary traits quietly contribute to the intricacies of leadership dynamics. These traits may not take center stage, but their presence weaves a tapestry of attributes that collectively define a leader's comprehensive capabilities.

The Subtle Forces of Secondary Traits

Secondary traits encompass a diverse range of characteristics that may not be as pronounced as central traits, yet they exert a significant influence on leadership behavior. These traits could include qualities like patience, adaptability, diplomacy, and attention to detail. Though they might not capture immediate attention, secondary traits subtly shape how leaders navigate challenges, manage relationships, and approach their responsibilities.

Fine-Tuning Leadership Styles

While central traits guide the broad outlines of leadership styles, secondary traits play a crucial role in fine-tuning these styles to suit specific contexts. For instance, a leader with a central trait of assertiveness might balance their approach with a secondary trait of diplomacy, allowing them to assert themselves while maintaining harmonious relationships. This balancing act showcases the synergy between different traits in creating an effective leadership demeanor.

Enhancing Communication and Collaboration

Secondary traits often amplify a leader's ability to communicate effectively and collaborate with others. Traits like active listening, empathy, and approachability facilitate open lines of communication and foster a sense of camaraderie among team members. Leaders who possess these traits can create a conducive environment for idea-sharing, problem-solving, and building strong interpersonal connections.

Navigating Complexity with Finesse

Secondary traits shine in complex situations where a leader's agility and adaptability are tested. Traits such as resilience and resourcefulness empower leaders to navigate ambiguity and uncertainty with finesse. These traits ensure that a leader can maintain composure, find innovative solutions, and lead their team through challenges, all while exemplifying their unique leadership attributes.

Contributing to Holistic Leadership

The inclusion of secondary traits in the leadership equation results in a more holistic and well-rounded profile. Leaders who leverage these traits, even if not central, demonstrate a level of versatility that enables them to adjust to various circumstances. This adaptability, rooted in secondary traits, equips leaders to tackle diverse challenges and maximize their impact across different scenarios.

Cultivating Versatility and Adaptability

Secondary traits enrich a leader's versatility by allowing them to adapt their approach to various circumstances. A leader with a secondary trait of adaptability can seamlessly transition between different roles and responsibilities, showing resilience in the face of change and demonstrating a capacity to lead effectively across diverse scenarios.

The Unsung Heroes of Leadership Attributes

Secondary traits, though less dominant than central and cardinal traits, play a crucial role in shaping a leader's behavior and interactions. These traits include qualities such as adaptability, patience, resilience, and empathy. While they might not always command attention, their presence underpins a leader's ability to navigate diverse situations and establish meaningful connections.

Building Trust and Connection

Traits like empathy, active listening, and approachability enable leaders to connect with their teams on a deeper level. These secondary traits create an environment of trust and openness, empowering leaders to understand their team members' perspectives, address concerns, and foster collaborative relationships.

Deconstructing Traits that Shape Effective Leadership

The objective is to dissect the essential components contributing to effective leadership. It delves into the intricate layers of leadership attributes to reveal the foundational elements defining successful leadership. From exploring the interplay between nature and nurture in shaping innate leadership traits to identifying key traits consistently associated with leadership effectiveness, the aim is to provide a comprehensive understanding of the attributes underpinning impactful leadership. Additionally, strategies to nurture and cultivate these traits are examined, offering a path for individuals to develop into proficient and inspiring leaders across various contexts. Through this process of deconstruction, the multifaceted nature of leadership attributes becomes clear, allowing individuals to tap into their inherent potential and lead with excellence.

Nature vs. Nurture

The nature vs. nurture debate is a longstanding and complex discourse that underscores the origins of human attributes, including those that contribute to effective leadership. This debate delves into the fundamental question of whether innate leadership traits are primarily influenced by one's genetic predisposition (nature) or by external environmental factors (nurture). This multifaceted debate raises intriguing questions about the genetic foundation of leadership qualities, the impact of upbringing and experiences, and the complex interplay between these factors in shaping the capabilities of leaders.

Nature

The "nature" perspective posits that individuals are born with a genetic blueprint that determines a range of traits, including those relevant to leadership. According to this view, some individuals possess inherent qualities such as charisma, empathy, confidence, and assertiveness due to their genetic makeup. Advocates of the nature perspective argue that these genetic predispositions create a foundation upon which effective leadership attributes are built.

Nurture

The "nurture" viewpoint emphasizes the role of environmental factors in shaping leadership attributes. This perspective suggests that experiences, upbringing, education, and cultural surroundings have a significant impact on the development of leadership traits. Proponents of this perspective argue that individuals acquire and refine leadership skills through exposure to diverse experiences, learning, and the influence of mentors and role models.

The Complexity of Interaction

It's important to recognize that the nature vs. nurture debate is not a strict dichotomy but rather a nuanced interplay between genetics and the environment. Genetic predispositions might provide a potential foundation for certain traits, but their actual expression and refinement often occur through environmental interactions. For instance, a genetically predisposed trait like adaptability might be honed through exposure to diverse challenges and experiences that nurture this quality.

A Balanced Perspective

The debate about whether leadership is nature or nurture highlights the complexity of developing leadership skills. Recognizing that both genetics and environment play a role in shaping effective leaders is crucial. This perspective stresses the importance of nurturing inherent qualities while also seeking opportunities for growth and learning to refine one's leadership abilities.

Genetic Predispositions and Environmental Factors

The intricacies of leadership development are shaped by the interplay between genetic predispositions and environmental factors. This interaction contributes to the formation of innate leadership traits and offers insights into how individuals cultivate and refine these attributes. Examining this intersection provides a deeper understanding of how leaders emerge with their unique qualities, skills, and capabilities.

Genetic Predispositions

Genetic predispositions lay the foundation for innate leadership traits. These predispositions refer to the genetic makeup that influences an individual's potential to exhibit certain qualities, such as emotional intelligence, adaptability, and assertiveness. For instance, a person might be genetically inclined to process emotions effectively, which can contribute to their ability to empathize and connect with others. These predispositions provide a baseline upon which environmental factors build.

Environmental Factors

Environmental factors encompass the experiences, upbringing, education, and cultural surroundings that individuals encounter throughout their lives. These factors play a crucial role in nurturing and shaping genetic predispositions into fully developed leadership traits. For instance, a person with a genetic predisposition for assertiveness might refine this trait through experiences that require taking charge and making decisions. A supportive environment, exposure to diverse perspectives, and mentorship can all contribute to the growth of leadership attributes.

Interaction and Adaptation

The dynamic interaction between genetic predispositions and environmental factors results in a process of adaptation.

Individuals with certain genetic traits are more likely to thrive in environments that align with those traits. However, the environment can also challenge individuals to adapt and refine their attributes. For instance, a genetically empathetic individual might further develop their emotional intelligence through exposure to diverse emotional contexts.

The Role of Self-Awareness

Understanding one's genetic predispositions and how they interact with the environment is a cornerstone of effective leadership development. Self-awareness allows individuals to leverage their strengths while actively working to address potential limitations. This awareness enables leaders to proactively seek experiences that align with their traits and to engage in targeted development efforts to enhance their capabilities.

The Power of Intentional Development

While genetic predispositions set a potential framework, intentional development efforts are what truly shape effective leaders. Deliberate learning, seeking out challenges, and practicing skills can refine and amplify innate traits. For example, a genetically adaptable individual can enhance their adaptability further by intentionally exposing themselves to unfamiliar situations and continuously learning from them.

A Holistic Approach

The interplay between genetic predispositions and environmental factors presents a holistic perspective on leadership development. It underscores the potential for both nature and nurture to contribute to effective leadership. Recognizing the intersection of these factors encourages leaders to embrace their inherent qualities while actively engaging in personal and professional growth to cultivate a robust repertoire of leadership attributes. This intersection provides a framework for understanding the complex journey of leadership development, offering insights into the emergence of impactful leaders across various contexts.

Effective Leadership Traits

This segment delves into the essence of effective leadership by unveiling the research-backed traits that consistently align with impactful leadership. These attributes serve as the bedrock upon which successful leaders stand, offering insights into the qualities that enable them to inspire, guide, and drive positive change. Furthermore, the exploration delves into the dynamic nature of certain traits, highlighting their potential for growth and development.

Traits that Consistently Correlate with Effective Leadership

The pursuit of effective leadership has spurred extensive research aimed at uncovering the attributes that consistently align with leadership excellence. Through systematic studies and empirical observations, researchers have identified a set of traits that not only differentiate successful leaders but also contribute significantly to their ability to guide and inspire others. These research-backed traits serve as guiding beacons, offering valuable insights into the qualities that underpin impactful leadership across various domains.

1. **Emotional Intelligence (EI):** One of the most well-established traits associated with effective leadership is emotional intelligence. Leaders with high EI are adept at recognizing, understanding, and managing their own emotions as well as those of others. This enables them to navigate complex interpersonal dynamics, foster positive relationships, and create a supportive and collaborative environment within their teams.

2. **Integrity and Authenticity:** Leaders who embody integrity and authenticity consistently earn the trust and respect of their teams. This trait involves aligning one's actions with ethical principles, being honest, and remaining true to oneself. Leaders who exhibit integrity and authenticity not only set a moral standard but also establish an environment of transparency and open communication.
3. **Vision and Strategic Thinking:** Effective leaders possess a clear vision for the future and the ability to translate that vision into actionable strategies. This trait enables leaders to set direction, make informed decisions, and lead their teams toward shared goals. Strategic thinking empowers leaders to anticipate challenges, identify opportunities, and adapt to changing circumstances.
4. **Adaptability and Flexibility:** In today's rapidly evolving landscape, adaptability is a trait of paramount importance. Effective leaders embrace change, remain flexible in the face of uncertainty, and encourage their teams to do the same. This quality allows leaders to navigate disruptions, pivot when necessary, and guide their organizations through transformative periods.
5. **Communication Skills:** Communication serves as the linchpin of effective leadership. Leaders who excel in communication can articulate their vision, provide clear instructions, actively listen to their team members, and foster a culture of open dialogue. Strong communication skills create a cohesive and informed workforce that is aligned with the leader's goals.
6. **Resilience:** Resilience is the trait that empowers leaders to bounce back from setbacks, learn from failures, and maintain a positive attitude in the face of challenges. Resilient leaders set an example for their teams, demonstrating the importance of perseverance, adaptability, and a growth mindset.

The malleability of Certain Traits and Their Potential

Within the landscape of leadership traits, an intriguing facet emerges the malleability of certain attributes and their potential for development. While some traits may appear inherent, research and experience illuminate the capacity for leaders to actively cultivate, refine, and amplify these qualities.

1. **Cultivating Emotional Intelligence (EI):** Emotional intelligence, often touted as a cornerstone of leadership, is a trait that can be nurtured and expanded. While some individuals may naturally possess a higher level of EI, others can engage in deliberate efforts to enhance their emotional self-awareness, empathy, and relationship management. Through self-reflection, active listening, and seeking feedback, leaders can hone their ability to connect with others on a deeper level.
2. **Expanding Communication Proficiency:** Communication skills are not solely the purview of those born with the gift of eloquence. Effective communication is a skill that can be developed through practice, observation, and refinement. Leaders can engage in workshops, seek mentorship, and dedicate time to improving their clarity, active listening, and persuasive abilities. As communication is at the heart of leadership, honing this skill is an investment with far-reaching impact.
3. **Fostering Adaptability and Resilience:** Adaptability and resilience, traits crucial in today's dynamic world, are qualities that can be cultivated through intentional efforts. Leaders can deliberately seek out challenges that take them out of their comfort zones, exposing them to new experiences and perspectives. Embracing failure as a learning opportunity and maintaining a growth mindset contribute to resilience, allowing leaders to bounce back from setbacks with renewed determination.

4. **Strengthening Vision and Strategic Thinking:** Leaders can actively develop their vision and strategic thinking by broadening their exposure to diverse information, industry trends, and innovative practices. Engaging in scenario planning, seeking input from cross-functional teams, and analyzing complex situations can sharpen a leader's ability to foresee potential opportunities and challenges, thereby enhancing their strategic decision-making.
5. **Nurturing Integrity and Authenticity:** Integrity and authenticity can be nurtured through continuous self-reflection and alignment with personal values. Leaders can engage in ethical dilemmas, making choices that reinforce their commitment to honesty and transparency. By consistently embodying these qualities, leaders create an organizational culture grounded in trust and ethical behavior.
6. **Embracing Continuous Learning:** Leadership development is an ongoing journey, and traits can be refined through a commitment to continuous learning. Leaders who acknowledge their areas for growth and engage in deliberate skill development, whether through formal education, mentorship, or self-guided learning, position themselves for constant improvement.

Cultivating Leadership Traits

Cultivating leadership traits is a transformative process that involves deliberate efforts to nurture and develop one's inherent qualities. This journey begins with self-awareness, where individuals reflect on their strengths and areas for growth. Through continuous learning, seeking mentorship, and engaging in purposeful experiences, aspiring leaders can refine their traits, amplifying their impact. By embracing challenges, learning from failures, and actively seeking opportunities for growth, individuals can cultivate a robust repertoire of leadership attributes. This ongoing cultivation equips leaders to navigate complexities, inspire teams, and leave a lasting legacy of impactful leadership.

Strategies for Individuals to Enhance Leadership Traits

Enhancing leadership traits is a dynamic and intentional endeavor that empowers individuals to elevate their leadership capabilities.

1. **Self-Awareness and Assessment:** A foundational step in enhancing leadership traits is developing self-awareness. This involves introspection to identify strengths, weaknesses, and areas for growth. Self-assessment tools, feedback from peers and mentors, and reflective practices can provide valuable insights into which traits to prioritize for development.
2. **Goal Setting:** Setting clear goals for leadership development provides direction and purpose. These goals can target specific traits, such as improving communication skills or cultivating adaptability. By articulating what they aim to achieve, individuals create a roadmap for their growth journey.
3. **Continuous Learning:** Leadership development is an ongoing process that benefits from continuous learning. Engaging in workshops, seminars, online courses, and reading materials related to leadership can expand knowledge and offer practical techniques for enhancing various traits.
4. **Seeking Mentorship and Feedback:** Mentorship from experienced leaders offers a unique opportunity for growth. Mentors can provide guidance, share insights, and offer constructive feedback that accelerates leadership development. Actively seeking feedback from colleagues, supervisors, and team members also provides valuable perspectives for improvement.
5. **Role Modeling and Observation:** Observing effective leaders in action can be a powerful way to learn. Studying leaders who exemplify desired traits allows individuals to

gain practical insights into how to apply those traits in real-world scenarios.
6. **Embracing Challenges:** Challenges and setbacks provide fertile ground for growth. Embracing challenging situations, taking calculated risks, and stepping out of comfort zones foster adaptability, resilience, and decision-making skills.
7. **Practicing Empathy and Active Listening:** Traits like empathy and active listening can be honed through intentional practice. Leaders can engage in active listening exercises, seek to understand diverse perspectives and cultivate empathy by putting themselves in others' shoes.
8. **Reflective Practice:** Regularly reflecting on experiences and interactions can deepen self-awareness and reinforce the development of leadership traits. Journaling, debriefing after significant events, and contemplating successes and failures provide insights for ongoing improvement.
9. **Applying Learned Techniques:** Putting learned techniques into practice is essential for real growth. Experimenting with new communication approaches, decision-making methods, and conflict-resolution strategies allows leaders to refine their skills in real-world contexts.
10. **Feedback Loop and Adaptation:** Leadership development is iterative. Regularly revisiting goals, seeking feedback, and adjusting strategies based on outcomes create a feedback loop that enables constant adaptation and refinement of leadership traits.

The journey of enhancing leadership traits is a purposeful and ongoing endeavor. By embracing self-awareness, learning, mentorship, practice, and adaptability, individuals can cultivate their inherent qualities, evolving into leaders who inspire, guide, and drive positive change. These strategies offer a roadmap for leaders to continually refine their traits and unlock their full potential as effective and influential leaders.

*****

CHAPTER FOUR
Leadership Styles and Approaches

Leadership serves as the compass guiding organizations through the uncharted territories of change and innovation. As we explore the multifaceted realm of leadership, we unveil a tapestry woven with diverse styles and approaches that both shape and are shaped by the dynamic landscapes they navigate. In this chapter, our journey embarks on a quest to understand the very essence of leadership by dissecting three distinct paradigms: Laissez-faire, Charismatic, and Autocratic. These styles, each with their own unique brushstrokes, contribute to the intricate mosaic of organizational culture, performance, and outcomes.

Importance of leadership styles

The fabric of an organization's success is intricately woven with the threads of leadership styles, casting a profound influence on the tapestry of its culture and outcomes. The significance of leadership styles transcends mere theoretical constructs, as they mold the very essence of how teams collaborate, innovate, and strive towards shared goals. Every leadership style, whether laissez-faire, charismatic, or autocratic, acts as a lens through which organizational dynamics are perceived, decisions are made, and actions are taken. The choice of leadership style is not a trivial matter; it reverberates throughout the organizational framework, shaping the work environment, employee engagement, and overall performance.

Influencing the organizational culture, leadership styles lay the groundwork for the attitudes and behaviors that permeate the workplace. A laissez-faire approach, characterized by its trust in employees' autonomy, can breed a culture of innovation and self-reliance, where individuals take ownership of their roles and collaborate on a foundation of independence. On the other hand, a charismatic leader's ability to infuse passion and inspiration into the fabric of the organization can create a culture that is not only goal-oriented but also deeply connected to a shared vision. Meanwhile, autocratic leadership can sculpt a culture of precision and efficiency, where decisive actions are taken swiftly, and directives are followed with rigor.

Crucially, leadership styles also serve as the architects of outcomes, steering the organization toward success or potential pitfalls. The chosen style shapes the pace and direction of decision-making, which in turn cascades into project timelines, resource allocation, and overall achievement. A laissez-faire approach, if applied judiciously, can stimulate creativity and adaptability, leading to innovative breakthroughs. Conversely, an autocratic style may prove effective in crises or situations requiring swift, centralized decision-making, ensuring that the organization can navigate challenges with agility.

1. **Laissez-faire Leadership:** This style embodies a hands-off approach, where leaders delegate decision-making authority and offer autonomy to their team members. The laissez-faire leader assumes a role of guidance rather than control, fostering an environment that nurtures individual creativity and innovation. However, the challenge lies in maintaining direction and accountability in the absence of direct supervision.
2. **Charismatic Leadership:** Charismatic leaders wield their personal magnetism to inspire and motivate their teams. Their visionary approach captivates and energizes followers, forging a shared sense of purpose and commitment. While charismatic leadership can spark enthusiasm and cohesion, it also presents the risk of creating dependency on the

leader's charisma, potentially overshadowing the importance of effective systems and structures.
3. **Autocratic Leadership:** Autocratic leadership is characterized by centralized decision-making and clear hierarchies. Leaders under this style assert authority and direct the course of action, leading to efficient execution and rapid responses in critical situations. Yet, the potential drawbacks include stifling creativity, limiting employee engagement, and creating an environment of dependency on the leader's directives.

Laissez-faire Leadership

In the realm of leadership, the laissez-faire style emerges as a distinct approach that hinges on the art of delegation and autonomy. Laissez-faire leadership entails providing individuals with the space to operate independently within predefined parameters. This style is a tribute to trust, recognizing that skilled professionals can flourish when granted the freedom to make decisions aligned with their expertise.

Laissez-faire leadership stands in stark contrast to more authoritative leadership approaches. Leaders adopting this style distance themselves from micromanagement, granting their team members a higher degree of autonomy in their decision-making processes.

1. **Facilitators of Innovation:** At its core, laissez-faire leaders act as facilitators. They offer guidance and resources, while simultaneously allowing team members the space to think creatively and implement solutions based on their unique perspectives. This approach fosters an environment where diverse ideas can flourish.
2. **Fostering a Culture of Self-Reliance:** An essential aspect of laissez-faire leadership is the promotion of self-reliance within the team. By entrusting team members with decision-

making power, leaders empower individuals to take ownership of their work and outcomes. This nurtures a culture of accountability and independence.
3. **Acknowledging Domain Expertise:** Laissez-faire leadership hinges on recognizing and respecting domain expertise. Leaders acknowledge that team members possess specialized knowledge, enabling them to make informed decisions in their areas of proficiency. This delegation of authority ensures that decisions are well-informed and aligned with organizational goals.
4. **Historical Roots and Philosophical Alignment:** The origins of laissez-faire leadership can be traced back to economic and political philosophies. Just as minimal government intervention is believed to spur economic growth, this leadership style applies a similar concept to organizational dynamics. It underscores the value of minimal interference, allowing capable individuals to excel within established parameters.
5. **Balancing Autonomy and Guidance:** While providing autonomy, finding the right balance is essential. Laissez-faire leadership requires clear boundaries and expectations to prevent ambiguity. Effective leaders in this style offer guidance when needed, ensuring that autonomy doesn't lead to chaos or misalignment.
6. **Nurturing Autonomy for Organizational Growth:** Laissez-faire leadership champions autonomy as a driver of growth and innovation. By cultivating an environment where creativity thrives and individuals take initiative, organizations can tap into the full potential of their teams. The strategic interplay between granting autonomy and providing occasional guidance enables leaders to harness the power of laissez-faire leadership to foster a culture of self-sufficiency and achievement.

Origins and Historical Context

The roots of the laissez-faire leadership style delve deep into historical, economic, and philosophical landscapes, tracing a path that intertwines notions of freedom, autonomy, and limited intervention. Understanding the origins and historical context of this leadership approach provides valuable insights into its evolution, relevance, and impact on modern organizational dynamics.

Historical Precursors

The term "laissez-faire" originates from French economic and political thought, signifying "let them do." It gained prominence during the 18th-century Enlightenment era when philosophers like Adam Smith advocated for minimal government intervention in economic affairs. This notion emerged as a response to the mercantilist policies of the time, which involved heavy government regulation and control over trade and commerce.

Adam Smith and the Invisible Hand

The Scottish economist Adam Smith, often considered the father of modern economics, championed the concept of the "invisible hand" in his seminal work "The Wealth of Nations" (1776). Smith argued that individuals pursuing their self-interest in a free market system inadvertently contribute to the overall welfare of society. This idea resonated with the laissez-faire philosophy, asserting that economies function most efficiently when left to their own devices, without excessive government intervention.

Evolution of Laissez-faire in Leadership

The principles of laissez-faire that were gaining traction in economics during the Enlightenment era began to influence other domains, including leadership and management. The idea of allowing individuals to operate autonomously within well-defined frameworks found resonance in leadership philosophy.

Leaders began to recognize the value of granting autonomy to employees, trusting them to make decisions aligned with their expertise.

Industrial Revolution and Its Impact

The Industrial Revolution, which commenced in the late 18th century, accelerated the evolution of the laissez-faire philosophy in organizational contexts. As industries transformed and economies shifted toward mechanization, hierarchical and autocratic leadership structures began to emerge. However, the laissez-faire approach still found its proponents who believed that giving employees more independence could enhance innovation and productivity.

20th Century Relevance and Critiques

The laissez-faire leadership style continued to be a subject of interest in the 20th century. Proponents argued that it empowered employees, encouraged creativity, and promoted a sense of ownership. However, critiques emerged, highlighting potential challenges such as lack of accountability, communication gaps, and the need for sufficient guidance.

Contemporary Applications and Adaptations

In the modern era, the principles of laissez-faire leadership remain relevant, but they have evolved to address the complexities of contemporary organizations. Organizations have recognized that a complete hands-off approach may not always be suitable, and thus, adaptations that strike a balance between autonomy and guidance have emerged. Contemporary leaders often adopt a more flexible approach, providing autonomy while still offering support and clear expectations.

A Historical Legacy

The origins and historical context of the laissez-faire leadership style offer a rich tapestry of ideas that have shaped its evolution. Stemming from economic and philosophical philosophies of the past, this approach continues to influence how leaders interact with their teams today. While its historical foundations underscore the importance of autonomy and trust, its contemporary applications reflect a nuanced understanding of the need for adaptability and balance.

Advantages and Disadvantages of Laissez-faire Leadership

The laissez-faire leadership style embodies a duality that presents both compelling advantages and noteworthy disadvantages.

Advantages

At the heart of the laissez-faire leadership style lies a profound emphasis on cultivating an environment that encourages creativity and independence among team members. This distinctive approach engenders a multitude of advantages that contribute to the growth and innovation of individuals and the organization as a whole.

1. **Unleashing Creative Potential:** One of the primary benefits of the laissez-faire leadership style is its potential to unleash the creative potential inherent within each team member. By offering autonomy and allowing individuals the freedom to make decisions related to their tasks, leaders empower employees to explore innovative solutions. This autonomy unshackles employees from the constraints of rigid directives, enabling them to think outside the box, experiment with new ideas, and generate novel approaches to challenges.
2. **Nurturing Intrinsic Motivation:** Laissez-faire leadership resonates deeply with intrinsic motivation—a key driver of individual performance and satisfaction. When team

members are trusted to take ownership of their tasks and decisions, they experience a heightened sense of responsibility and accomplishment. This, in turn, nurtures a genuine passion for their work, leading to increased engagement, commitment, and a desire to excel.

3. **Fostering Ownership and Accountability:** Empowering team members with autonomy fosters a sense of ownership over their responsibilities. As individuals take the reins of their tasks, they become more invested in their outcomes. This heightened sense of ownership naturally translates into increased accountability. Team members are motivated to see their initiatives succeed, taking proactive steps to ensure their efforts align with organizational goals.

4. **Encouraging Personal Growth and Skill Development:** The latitude granted by laissez-faire leadership encourages continuous personal growth and skill development. Team members have the opportunity to stretch their capabilities, experiment with new approaches, and refine their skills in a real-world context. This freedom to explore diverse roles and responsibilities enhances their skill set, making them more versatile and adaptable professionals.

5. **Fostering Collaboration and Diversity of Ideas:** In an environment where autonomy flourishes, collaboration takes on a new dimension. Team members, entrusted with decision-making authority, are more likely to collaborate and share ideas openly. This interaction leads to a rich exchange of perspectives, diverse viewpoints, and a collective brainstorming culture. As autonomy dissolves hierarchical barriers, team members become more receptive to integrating ideas from various sources, resulting in more holistic and innovative solutions.

6. **Empowering Emerging Leaders:** Laissez-faire leadership paves the way for the emergence of new leaders within the organization. As individuals are given the freedom to make decisions, those who demonstrate exceptional aptitude and initiative naturally rise to the occasion. This allows leaders

to identify and nurture potential leadership talent within the team, ensuring a robust succession pipeline.
7. **Enhancing Job Satisfaction and Retention:** The autonomy provided by the laissez-faire leadership style directly contributes to enhanced job satisfaction and higher rates of employee retention. Individuals who are trusted with decision-making authority feel valued and respected. This positive sentiment translates into a more positive work environment, where employees are more likely to stay committed to the organization over the long term.
8. **Empowerment as the Catalyst for Growth:** The advantages of the laissez-faire leadership style are far-reaching, touching every facet of organizational dynamics. By fostering creativity, independence, ownership, and collaboration, leaders create an ecosystem where employees thrive. The empowerment ingrained within this approach is a catalyst for individual growth, innovation, and organizational excellence.

However, while the benefits are undeniable, it is crucial to acknowledge the potential challenges that arise from striking a balance between autonomy and guidance. This balanced approach ensures that the advantages of the laissez-faire style are harnessed to their fullest potential, creating a harmonious synergy between individual autonomy and organizational success.

Disadvantages

While the laissez-faire leadership style offers numerous advantages, it is not without its notable disadvantages. One of the significant challenges associated with this approach is the potential for a lack of direction and accountability, which can have implications for team cohesion, performance, and the achievement of organizational objectives.

1. **Absence of Clear Direction:** A primary concern arising from the laissez-faire leadership style is the potential absence of clear direction. With leaders taking a hands-off approach, team members might lack explicit guidance on tasks, objectives, and priorities. This ambiguity can lead to confusion, inefficiencies, and instances where efforts are misaligned. Without a well-defined roadmap, individuals may struggle to understand their role within the larger context of the organization's goals.
2. **Erosion of Cohesion:** Laissez-faire leadership's emphasis on autonomy may inadvertently result in a fragmented team dynamic. Without a centralized authority overseeing coordination, communication, and decision-making, teams might function in isolated silos. This can impede collaboration, limit the exchange of critical information, and hinder the seamless flow of ideas across the organization. The erosion of team cohesion can undermine a sense of unity and shared purpose, potentially compromising the overall effectiveness of the team.
3. **Accountability Challenges:** While autonomy encourages ownership, it can also pose challenges related to accountability. With less direct oversight, individuals might feel less accountable for their actions and decisions. This can lead to instances where performance standards are not met, errors are not promptly rectified, and individuals avoid taking responsibility for outcomes. In the absence of clear lines of accountability, the overall effectiveness of teams and projects can suffer.
4. **Risk of Misalignment:** A lack of clear direction and accountability can create a risk of misalignment within the organization. Different teams or individuals might interpret goals and priorities differently, leading to conflicting efforts and priorities. This misalignment can slow down progress, hinder decision-making, and create an environment of uncertainty. In complex projects or rapidly changing

environments, this lack of cohesion can hinder the organization's ability to respond effectively to challenges.
5. **Reduced Support and Mentorship:** Laissez-faire leadership, by design, encourages autonomy and independence. However, this can inadvertently lead to reduced support and mentorship, particularly for individuals who may benefit from more guidance and supervision. Without regular feedback and mentorship, team members might struggle to develop their skills, make informed decisions, and navigate complex situations effectively.
6. **Addressing the Disadvantages:** While the disadvantages of laissez-faire leadership are significant, they are not insurmountable. Leaders can mitigate these challenges by striking a balance between autonomy and guidance. This can involve setting clear expectations, establishing regular check-ins, and creating open channels of communication. By providing a framework that offers the benefits of autonomy while addressing potential pitfalls, leaders can harness the strengths of this approach while minimizing its weaknesses.
7. **Navigating the Balance:** The potential lack of direction and accountability presents a compelling counterpoint to the advantages of laissez-faire leadership. While fostering autonomy and creativity, leaders must remain vigilant in ensuring that teams have the necessary guidance, alignment, and accountability structures in place. Navigating this delicate balance is key to reaping the benefits of laissez-faire leadership while mitigating the risks associated with potential directionless and unaccountable pursuits.

When Laissez-faire Leadership Works

Laissez-faire leadership finds its most conducive ground in contexts marked by experienced, self-motivated teams and a well-established foundation of trust. When team members possess a high degree of expertise and a proven track record of independent decision-making, the laissez-faire approach can flourish. This style thrives in environments where individuals are driven by intrinsic motivation, actively seeking opportunities to innovate and contribute. Additionally, industries characterized by rapidly evolving landscapes, where flexibility and adaptability are paramount, often provide fertile ground for laissez-faire leadership. In such scenarios, the hands-off approach empowers team members to respond swiftly to changing circumstances and seize emergent opportunities. By aligning laissez-faire leadership with these contexts, organizations can harness the potential of their teams, channeling autonomy into impactful outcomes that drive both personal growth and collective success.

Laissez-faire leadership, with its emphasis on autonomy and minimal intervention, thrives in specific situations where it can effectively harness the capabilities of experienced and self-motivated teams.

Experienced Teams and Specialized Expertise

Laissez-faire leadership shines brightest when applied to experienced teams comprising individuals who possess a wealth of specialized expertise. These professionals have demonstrated their ability to make informed decisions and navigate complex challenges within their respective domains. In such scenarios, the role of the leader transforms from a traditional directive figure to that of a facilitator and mentor. With a deep pool of expertise at their disposal, team members can effectively drive projects forward, contributing insights and innovative solutions that draw from their collective knowledge.

Intrinsic Motivation and Autonomy

Laissez-faire leadership finds a natural ally in teams fueled by intrinsic motivation. When team members are driven by a genuine passion for their work, the autonomy provided by this leadership style resonates profoundly. Autonomy aligns with their desire to take ownership of their tasks, make meaningful contributions, and explore avenues for innovation. Instead of relying on external directives, these individuals are motivated to excel on their own terms, leveraging their expertise to deliver results that are not only impactful but also personally fulfilling.

Cultivating Creativity and Problem-Solving

Experienced and self-motivated teams often excel in creative problem-solving. Laissez-faire leadership provides the ideal backdrop for channeling this propensity for innovation. By allowing individuals to take the lead, leaders enable the emergence of diverse perspectives and solutions. The inherent trust within this approach encourages team members to venture into uncharted territories, experiment with novel strategies, and collaborate on inventive approaches that might not be explored under more directive leadership styles.

Empowerment through Ownership

Laissez-faire leadership aligns seamlessly with the desire for ownership that characterizes experienced professionals. These individuals are not content with merely executing tasks; they yearn to shape the outcomes and drive projects to success. The autonomy provided by the laissez-faire style allows them to steer initiatives according to their vision, fostering a sense of pride, accomplishment, and accountability for the final results.

A Synergy of Expertise and Autonomy

The effectiveness of the laissez-faire leadership style is magnified when it aligns with the attributes of experienced and self-motivated teams. By granting autonomy to professionals with specialized expertise, leaders tap into a wellspring of creativity, intrinsic motivation, and problem-solving capabilities. In this symbiotic relationship, the leader acts as a guide, offering support and resources while allowing team members to harness their skills to the fullest. This harmony between expertise and autonomy not only fosters individual growth but also generates outcomes that drive the organization's success to new heights.

Decentralized Success

The efficacy of a decentralized leadership approach, synonymous with laissez-faire leadership, becomes most pronounced in specific industries and projects that thrive on innovation, adaptability, and the synergy of self-motivated teams.

Technology and Software Development

The technology and software development sector is a prime example of an industry where a decentralized leadership approach thrives. In this rapidly evolving landscape, innovation is paramount. Teams of experienced programmers and engineers thrive when given the autonomy to explore cutting-edge technologies, experiment with novel coding practices, and devise creative solutions to intricate problems. Laissez-faire leadership empowers them to embrace their natural curiosity, fostering an environment where independent decision-making drives the development of groundbreaking software products.

Design and Art

Industries centered around creativity and artistic expression, such as design, art, and creative content creation, benefit immensely from decentralized leadership. In these domains, professionals are often driven by their unique perspectives and creative instincts. A hands-off approach allows designers, artists, and creators to explore their creative impulses freely, resulting in diverse and original outcomes. Laissez-faire leadership nurtures an environment where innovation is nurtured, enabling these individuals to push boundaries, challenge conventions, and produce work that captivates and inspires.

Research and Development

In research and development (R&D) projects, the decentralized approach thrives. Laissez-faire leadership empowers research teams to delve into uncharted territories, explore new hypotheses, and experiment with varying methodologies. With autonomy to shape the course of their projects, scientists and researchers can pursue intellectual curiosity without the constraints of micromanagement. This style not only accelerates the discovery of new knowledge but also cultivates a culture of innovation, as researchers are motivated to uncover insights that can reshape entire fields.

Entrepreneurship and Startups

The world of entrepreneurship and startups is characterized by agility, risk-taking, and the pursuit of disruptive ideas. Laissez-faire leadership aligns naturally with the ethos of entrepreneurship, providing founders and their teams the autonomy to iterate quickly, pivot when necessary, and capitalize on emerging opportunities. By embracing a hands-off approach, leaders in startups foster a sense of ownership among team members, who are not only encouraged to think creatively but are also empowered to shape the trajectory of the company's growth.

Case Study

A case study is an in-depth examination and analysis of a specific instance, event, organization, individual, or phenomenon. It involves thorough research and investigation to gain a comprehensive understanding of the subject under scrutiny. Case studies are often used in various fields, including business, education, psychology, and social sciences, to provide insights into real-world situations, highlight successes or challenges, and extract valuable lessons or recommendations. A well-constructed case study typically includes a description of the context, a detailed account of the events or actions taken, an analysis of the outcomes, and an exploration of the factors that contributed to those outcomes. Case studies serve as powerful tools for learning, decision-making, and enhancing understanding by showcasing practical applications of theories and concepts.

Journeying into the historical tapestry of Punjab, we encounter a real-world case study that vividly demonstrates the application of laissez-faire leadership principles during the Misl period. This case study focuses on the leadership of Sardar Jassa Singh Ahluwalia, a prominent figure during the 18th century when the Sikh Misls emerged as significant political entities in the region.

Sardar Jassa Singh Ahluwalia's Leadership

Amidst the Misl period, Punjab was marked by political upheavals and power struggles. Sardar Jassa Singh Ahluwalia emerged as a charismatic leader who effectively employed laissez-faire leadership principles to unite and lead his followers. His leadership was pivotal during a time of flux and paved the way for the rise of the Sikh Misls as powerful players in the region.

The Implementation

Sardar Jassa Singh Ahluwalia's approach to leadership embraced the concept of decentralized governance. He understood the value of empowering local leaders within his Misl, allowing them to make decisions that aligned with their respective strengths and contexts. Instead of exerting authoritarian control, Jassa Singh Ahluwalia fostered an environment where individuals had the freedom to lead and contribute based on their expertise.

The Results

Under Jassa Singh Ahluwalia's laissez-faire leadership, the Sikh Misls experienced a period of unity and coordinated resistance against external powers. His decentralized approach enabled each Misl leader to adapt strategies to their specific circumstances, contributing to a collective effort while maintaining their autonomy.

This leadership style not only galvanized the Sikh community but also challenged the authority of external forces.

Factors Contributing to Success

Several pivotal factors contributed to the success of Jassa Singh Ahluwalia's laissez-faire leadership during the Misl period:

1. **Localized Expertise:** Decentralization allowed Misl leaders to leverage their knowledge of local conditions and tactics.

2. **Flexibility:** The approach facilitated swift adaptations to changing circumstances, which is essential during times of conflict.

3. **Unified Purpose:** The collective commitment to resisting external forces provided a common purpose that transcended individual leadership.

4. **Empowerment:** Local leaders felt a sense of ownership, which motivated them to contribute actively to the Misl's goals.

Analysis of Factors

The triumph of a laissez-faire leadership approach within the case study of Sardar Jassa Singh Ahluwalia's leadership during the Misl period can be attributed to a multitude of interwoven factors. This analysis delves into these factors, shedding light on how their synergy paved the path for success and influence within the complex historical landscape of Punjab.

1. **Decentralization and Local Empowerment:** At the core of the success lay the strategic decentralization of power. Sardar Jassa Singh Ahluwalia recognized that a top-down leadership style would neither harness the localized expertise nor inspire unity within the disparate Misls. By empowering local leaders with decision-

making authority, he leveraged their intricate knowledge of terrain, tactics, and conditions. This approach fostered a sense of ownership and accountability among the leaders, as they took charge of their Misl's affairs, driving the collective vision forward.

2. **Adaptability and Flexibility:** In an era of shifting alliances, external threats, and dynamic landscapes, adaptability was paramount. Laissez-faire leadership, which permitted each Misl to adapt strategies based on their unique context, facilitated swift responses to changing circumstances. Sardar Jassa Singh Ahluwalia's approach embraced this fluidity, ensuring that each Misl's actions aligned with its strengths and circumstances. This adaptability fortified the collective resistance and evoked the nimbleness required for effective leadership during tumultuous times.

3. **Unified Purpose and Collective Ownership:** The laissez-faire approach inherently encouraged ownership and unity. Each Misl leader, empowered to steer their respective forces, shared a common purpose: safeguarding Sikh interests and resisting external control. This collective sense of purpose transcended individual ambitions, fostering a unified movement that rallied under the banner of Sikh resistance. The leaders' ownership of their actions engendered a shared responsibility for the outcome, reinforcing their commitment to the cause.

4. **Cultural Synergy and Leadership Legacy:** Sardar Jassa Singh Ahluwalia's leadership aligned seamlessly with the cultural ethos of Sikhism and Punjab. Sikhs value self-reliance, community collaboration, and decentralized decision-making – values that mirrored the essence of laissez-faire leadership. This synergy between leadership approach and cultural beliefs forged a deep resonance among the leaders and their followers. Moreover, the legacy of Jassa Singh Ahluwalia's

leadership set a precedent for subsequent Sikh leaders, perpetuating the culture of empowerment and collaboration.

5. **Trust and Mentorship:** Sardar Jassa Singh Ahluwalia's role as a mentor within his leadership approach was pivotal. While advocating autonomy, he offered guidance, mentorship, and a framework for decision-making. This trust in his leaders and their abilities created an environment of mutual respect and collaboration. Leaders felt empowered, knowing they had a mentor to turn to when needed, while Jassa Singh Ahluwalia's trust fostered their confidence in decision-making.

The success of Sardar Jassa Singh Ahluwalia's laissez-faire leadership approach was a product of interconnected factors, each enhancing the efficacy of the other. Decentralization empowered local leaders, adaptability responded to the ever-changing context, unified purpose forged solidarity, cultural alignment resonated deeply, and trust cemented mentorship. This analysis underscores the intricate interplay of these factors, painting a vivid picture of how the synergies between them cultivated an environment of empowerment, unity, and strategic triumph within the complex fabric of the Misl period in Punjab's history.

Impact on Employee Morale and Engagement

Impact on Employee Morale and Engagement refers to the effects that a leadership style characterized by minimal intervention, where team members are given greater autonomy and independence, can have on the overall morale, motivation, and level of involvement exhibited by employees within an organization. This aspect of analysis involves assessing how the degree of hands-off leadership influences employees' sense of ownership, satisfaction, and commitment to their tasks and the organization as a whole. levels of employee morale and engagement, which are crucial drivers of productivity and success.

Minimal Intervention

Minimal intervention leadership, characterized by providing employees with autonomy and independence, can significantly influence their sense of ownership and commitment to their work and the organization. This impact is multifaceted, touching upon various aspects that shape the employees' perception, engagement, and dedication.

1. **Enhanced Ownership:** When employees are entrusted with the freedom to make decisions and contribute their ideas, they often develop a stronger sense of ownership over their work. They feel that their contributions matter and that their decisions have a direct impact on outcomes. This sense of ownership can drive a deeper connection to the work they do, as they feel responsible for its success and outcomes.
2. **Increased Accountability:** Autonomy often goes hand in hand with increased accountability. Employees who have the freedom to make decisions are more likely to take ownership of the results, whether positive or negative. Knowing that they have the power to shape outcomes can lead to a greater sense of responsibility for the quality and success of their work.
3. **Higher Engagement:** When employees feel that their opinions and contributions are valued and that they have the autonomy to make meaningful decisions, their level of engagement tends to increase. They become more invested in their tasks, motivated to excel, and eager to see projects through to completion. This heightened

engagement stems from the satisfaction of being in control of their work.
4. **Personal Investment:** Minimal intervention leadership encourages employees to take a more personal interest in their tasks and projects. They are more likely to invest additional effort, time, and creativity when they know that their individuality and decision-making abilities are recognized and encouraged. This personal investment can lead to higher-quality outcomes and a stronger commitment to achieving success.
5. **Pride in Contribution:** As employees exercise their autonomy and see the positive impact of their decisions, they develop a sense of pride in their contributions. This emotional attachment to their work fosters a deeper commitment to the organization's goals and values. The connection between autonomy and pride reinforces the employees' commitment to achieving the best possible outcomes.
6. **Development of Skills:** Autonomy provides employees with opportunities to develop and refine their skills. When they have the freedom to take on new challenges, experiment with different approaches, and learn from their experiences, employees become more capable and confident. This skill development further enhances their commitment as they see their growth aligning with the organization's success.
7. **Alignment with Organizational Goals:** Minimal intervention leadership allows employees to align their work more closely with the broader goals and vision of the organization. When they have the freedom to make decisions that align with their understanding of the organization's objectives, their commitment deepens as they perceive their contributions as integral to the organization's success.

Strategies to Maintaining Motivation without Direct Oversight

In a leadership approach characterized by minimal intervention, where employees are granted autonomy and independence, maintaining motivation becomes a critical consideration. While direct oversight might be limited, there are various strategies and practices that leaders can employ to ensure that employees remain motivated and engaged in their work.

1. **Clear Expectations and Goals:** Even in a hands-off leadership approach, it's crucial to establish clear expectations and goals. When employees understand what is expected of them and have a clear vision of the desired outcomes, they are more likely to stay motivated. Clear goals provide a sense of purpose and direction, guiding their efforts toward meaningful achievements.
2. **Regular Communication:** While minimal intervention allows autonomy, consistent communication is essential. Regular check-ins, updates, and feedback sessions help employees feel connected and informed about the organization's progress and their role within it. This communication demonstrates that their contributions are valued, sustaining their motivation.
3. **Recognition and Appreciation:** Acknowledging and appreciating employees' efforts is a powerful motivator. Even in an autonomous environment, recognizing their achievements, whether through public praise, rewards, or simple expressions of gratitude, reinforces the value of their work and encourages continued dedication.
4. **Professional Development Opportunities:** Offering avenues for skill enhancement and personal growth can keep employees motivated. Providing access to training, workshops, and opportunities to expand their expertise demonstrates the organization's investment in their development, motivating them to excel.

5. **Flexibility and Work-Life Balance:** Autonomy often extends to allowing flexibility in work arrangements. Empowering employees to manage their work hours and locations can enhance motivation by promoting a healthier work-life balance, which in turn contributes to overall job satisfaction.
6. **Challenging Projects and Responsibilities:** Offering challenging projects and responsibilities taps into employees' intrinsic motivation. Autonomy allows them to take on tasks that align with their interests and strengths, providing a sense of fulfillment as they push their boundaries and achieve meaningful goals.
7. **Encouraging Collaboration:** While autonomy is key, fostering a collaborative environment can be motivational. Encouraging cross-functional collaboration and sharing of ideas provides a sense of community and purpose beyond individual tasks.
8. **Providing Autonomy within Boundaries:** While minimal intervention involves autonomy, setting certain boundaries ensures that employees' actions are aligned with the organization's values and objectives. This framework gives them the freedom to make decisions while maintaining a sense of accountability.
9. **Emphasizing Impact:** Highlighting the impact of employees' work on the organization, its clients, or society can be a powerful motivator. When they see the positive outcomes of their contributions, their sense of purpose and motivation are reinforced.
10. **Cultivating a Positive Work Culture:** Creating a positive work environment that fosters trust, respect, and open communication contributes to sustained motivation. Employees are more likely to remain motivated when they feel that their well-being and growth are prioritized.

Challenges of Decision-making and Accountability in Minimal Intervention Leadership

Embracing a leadership approach characterized by minimal intervention and autonomy brings forth a unique set of challenges related to decision-making and accountability. While this style empowers employees, it also requires careful consideration of how decisions are made and how accountability is upheld.

1. **Lack of Clarity in Decision Authority**
   In an environment where autonomy is paramount, there might be instances where the lines of decision-making authority become blurred. Employees might be uncertain about who has the final say in certain matters, leading to confusion and potentially conflicting decisions.
   Strategy: Clearly define decision-making roles and responsibilities. Establish guidelines that outline the types of decisions that require centralized approval and those that can be made autonomously. This clarity ensures that decisions are aligned with the organization's objectives and values.

2. **Potential for Inconsistent Decisions**
   Without a structured oversight, there's a possibility that different individuals or teams might make decisions that are inconsistent with each other. This lack of coordination can hinder the organization's coherence and overall effectiveness.
   Strategy: Implement regular communication mechanisms where teams can share decisions, approaches, and outcomes. Encourage cross-functional collaboration to ensure decisions are aligned and contribute to the organization's larger goals.

3. **Accountability Ambiguity**
   In a hands-off leadership environment, holding individuals accountable for their decisions and actions can be challenging. It's possible for mistakes or oversights to occur

without a clear mechanism for identifying responsible parties.

Strategy: Define accountability parameters. While granting autonomy, emphasize the importance of ownership over decisions and their consequences. Encourage individuals to take responsibility for their actions and their impact on the organization's progress.

4. **Balancing Autonomy and Organizational**

   Maintaining a balance between individual autonomy and the organization's overarching vision can be intricate. Autonomous decisions might inadvertently deviate from the organization's strategic direction.

   Strategy: Foster a shared understanding of the organization's vision and values. Provide employees with context and guidance that help them align their autonomous decisions with the larger purpose, ensuring that individual actions contribute to the collective goals.

5. **Risk of Missed Opportunities:**

   Autonomous decision-making can sometimes result in missed opportunities due to limited perspectives. When decisions are made in isolation, innovative ideas might not be fully explored, hindering potential growth.

   Strategy: Encourage a culture of open idea-sharing. While granting autonomy, provide platforms for brainstorming and cross-pollination of ideas. This approach widens the scope of decision-making, allowing for a broader range of perspectives and possibilities.

6. **Potential Accountability**

   In an environment where minimal intervention is practiced, some employees might perceive the opportunity to evade accountability for unfavorable outcomes or mistakes, attributing them solely to their autonomy.

   Strategy: Promote a culture of learning from failures. Emphasize that accountability is integral to personal and professional growth. Frame mistakes as opportunities for improvement rather than as failures, encouraging individuals to take ownership of their actions.

Examination of Challenges within a Laissez-faire Environment

Adopting a laissez-faire leadership approach, which emphasizes minimal intervention and empowers employees with autonomy, brings with it a distinctive set of challenges in the realms of decision-making and accountability. While this leadership style encourages self-reliance and creativity, it is not without potential pitfalls.

1. **Decision Quality Variability:** In a laissez-faire setting, decision-making authority is distributed among team members. However, this can lead to inconsistent decision quality due to varying levels of expertise, perspectives, and information. Some decisions might lack thorough analysis, potentially impacting outcomes.
2. **Lack of Coordination:** The absence of centralized oversight can result in decisions that are not aligned with broader organizational goals or strategies. Teams might make decisions in isolation, leading to siloed efforts and misalignment with the bigger picture.
3. **Accountability Diffusion:** While autonomy is encouraged, the diffuse nature of decision-making authority can make it challenging to pinpoint accountability for outcomes, especially in situations where multiple individuals or teams are involved in a decision's execution.
4. **Potential for Inefficiency:** In an environment where each individual or team makes decisions independently, there might be a lack of standardization. This can lead to inefficiencies, redundant efforts, and even conflicts as different parties operate without cohesive coordination.
5. **Decision Paralysis:** Some team members might hesitate to make decisions without clear guidance or authorization,

fearing negative consequences. This hesitancy can slow down the decision-making process and impede progress.
6. **Risk of Missed Opportunities:** When decisions are distributed, innovative ideas might not gain traction due to limited visibility or a lack of collective evaluation. This can result in missing out on potentially valuable opportunities for growth.
7. **Accountability Evasion:** Without a well-defined accountability structure, individuals might avoid taking responsibility for unfavorable outcomes, attributing them solely to their autonomy rather than acknowledging their role in the decision.
8. **Alignment with Organizational Goals:** The pursuit of autonomy might lead to decisions that are not fully aligned with the organization's overarching goals and vision. This can result in divergent efforts that do not contribute to the organization's strategic direction.
9. **Communication Gaps:** Autonomous decision-making might sometimes omit crucial information from other team members who should be aware of the decisions being made. This can create communication gaps and hinder effective collaboration.
10. **Strain on Leadership Support:** Leaders might find themselves in a reactive position, being called upon to address the repercussions of autonomous decisions that may not align with organizational objectives.

Examination of potential challenges in decision-making and accountability within a laissez-faire environment highlights the need for a delicate balance. While autonomy can foster creativity and engagement, these challenges underscore the importance of setting clear guidelines, promoting effective communication, and creating a culture of accountability. Leaders must proactively address these challenges to harness the benefits of autonomy while ensuring that decisions align with organizational objectives and contribute to collective success.

Charismatic Leadership

At the heart of charismatic leadership lies a potent fusion of magnetic charisma and a compelling vision that captivates and inspires followers. Charismatic leaders possess a unique aura that draws people in, evoking admiration and trust. Their ability to articulate a vivid and inspiring vision ignites passion and commitment among their teams, compelling them to strive towards shared goals. This leadership style transcends traditional authority, relying instead on the force of the leader's personality and the allure of their vision to drive transformational change. Through the synergy of personal magnetism and an inspiring narrative, charismatic leadership becomes a dynamic force that propels organizations and individuals toward ambitious aspirations.

Charismatic leadership represents a dynamic and captivating style where a leader's magnetic charm and compelling vision become the driving forces behind their influence. At its core, charismatic leadership is not merely about authority but rather about the innate ability to inspire and guide through personal appeal. Charismatic leaders possess a rare aura that draws followers, engendering trust, respect, and a strong emotional connection. Their influence is not rooted in positional power alone but in the profound impact of their words, actions, and the vision they articulate. This leadership approach hinges on the power of persuasion and the art of shaping an aspirational narrative that ignites enthusiasm and commitment among those they lead.

The Charismatic Aura

Charismatic leadership hinges on the leader's exceptional ability to attract and engage followers through a magnetic personality. Their charm, confidence, and authenticity create an aura that captivates individuals, fostering trust and admiration. This personal allure transcends formal authority, allowing charismatic leaders to exert influence beyond traditional hierarchies.

The Power of Vision

At the heart of charismatic leadership is the art of crafting and communicating a compelling vision. Charismatic leaders possess an innate skill for formulating a clear and inspiring narrative about the future. This vision resonates deeply with followers' values and aspirations, serving as a rallying point that unites individuals around shared goals. The leader's ability to passionately articulate this vision ignites enthusiasm and commitment among the team.

Authenticity and Empathy

Charismatic leaders foster trust and loyalty by establishing genuine connections with their followers. Their emotional intelligence allows them to empathize with others, creating a sense of belonging and understanding. By valuing individual perspectives and demonstrating sincere care, they build strong relationships that enhance their influence. This emotional connection enhances the leader's credibility and strengthens their ability to guide and inspire.

Transformative Influence

Charismatic leadership goes beyond traditional forms of influence, driving followers to achieve extraordinary outcomes. The leader's magnetic presence and visionary guidance motivate individuals to go beyond their comfort zones and embrace challenges. Charismatic leaders empower their teams to exceed expectations, leveraging their influence to spark innovation, perseverance, and a collective drive for excellence.

Charismatic leadership's emphasis on the leader's personality and influence is a dynamic force that transcends conventional leadership approaches. By harnessing personal magnetism, articulating inspiring visions, nurturing authentic connections, and sparking transformative efforts, charismatic leaders have the unique ability to guide organizations and individuals toward remarkable achievements.

Qualities of a Charismatic Leader

Charismatic leadership is characterized by a distinct set of qualities that distinguish these leaders and enable them to exert a powerful and lasting influence on their followers. These qualities combine to create a magnetic aura that draws people in and inspires them to follow with passion and commitment. The primary essential qualities that define a charismatic leader are:

1. **Visionary Thinking:** Charismatic leaders possess a forward-looking mindset that enables them to envision bold and inspiring futures. Their ability to craft a compelling vision that resonates with their followers' aspirations sets them apart. This visionary thinking serves as a roadmap, guiding both the leader and their team toward meaningful goals.
2. **Confidence and Conviction:** Confidence radiates from charismatic leaders, instilling trust and belief in their capabilities. Their unwavering conviction in their vision and decisions empowers followers, assuring them that they are on a path worth pursuing. This confidence is contagious, boosting team morale and enthusiasm.
3. **Effective Communication:** A charismatic leader is a masterful communicator, adept at conveying their vision with clarity, passion, and conviction. They tailor their message to resonate with diverse audiences, ensuring that their ideas are understood and embraced by individuals at all levels of the organization.
4. **Empathy and Emotional Intelligence:** Charismatic leaders possess a deep understanding of human emotions

and motivations. Their capacity for empathy allows them to connect on a personal level, making individuals feel valued and heard. This emotional intelligence fosters trust and strengthens relationships.

5. **Adaptability and Resilience:** In the face of challenges and setbacks, charismatic leaders exhibit resilience and adaptability. Their ability to navigate uncertainties with grace and determination inspires confidence in their followers and demonstrates the importance of maintaining a steadfast commitment to their vision.

6. **Charisma and Presence:** Central to charismatic leadership is the magnetic charm exuded by these leaders. Their charisma captivates and engages others, creating an atmosphere of respect and admiration. Charismatic leaders have a presence that commands attention and evokes a sense of awe.

7. **Courageous Risk-Taking:** Charismatic leaders are unafraid to take calculated risks in pursuit of their vision. Their willingness to step outside their comfort zone encourages others to embrace innovation and embrace change as a means of achieving growth and progress.

8. **Inspirational Authenticity:** Authenticity is a hallmark of charismatic leaders. They stay true to their values and principles, which resonates with followers who appreciate their genuine nature. This authenticity fosters trust and encourages others to align with the leader's vision.

9. **Empowering Others:** Charismatic leaders empower their followers by instilling a sense of ownership and responsibility. They delegate tasks, trust their team's capabilities, and provide opportunities for growth, fostering a culture of self-confidence and initiative.

10. **Influence Through Action:** Actions speak louder than words for charismatic leaders. They lead by example, demonstrating commitment, dedication, and hard work.

This willingness to roll up their sleeves and engage in the work alongside their team earns respect and loyalty.

The Role of Vision and Inspiration in Charismatic Leadership

At the heart of charismatic leadership lies the potent interplay between an inspiring vision and the leader's magnetic influence. These two elements work in tandem to create a powerful force that captivates followers and propels organizations toward transformative change.

Charismatic leaders possess a unique ability to inspire and motivate their followers by articulating a compelling vision that resonates deeply with their aspirations and values. This vision serves as a powerful catalyst for change, igniting enthusiasm and commitment among individuals and driving them to exceed their potential. Here's an exploration of how charismatic leaders leverage a compelling vision to inspire and motivate:

1. **Evoking Emotion and Aspiration:** Charismatic leaders understand that a compelling vision must evoke emotions and tap into the aspirations of their followers. They craft a narrative that stirs excitement, hope, and a sense of purpose. By aligning the vision with the dreams and desires of their team members, charismatic leaders create a magnetic pull that draws individuals toward a shared goal.
2. **Painting a Vivid Picture:** Charismatic leaders are skilled storytellers who vividly illustrate the future they envision. They paint a clear and captivating picture of what success looks like, highlighting the positive impact that the vision will have on the organization, its members, and even the larger community. This imagery makes the vision tangible and relatable, fueling the motivation to work towards its realization.

3. **Linking to Core Values:** A charismatic leader's vision resonates with the core values and beliefs of their followers. They emphasize how the vision aligns with these values, reinforcing the idea that pursuing the vision is not just about achieving a goal but also staying true to one's principles. This alignment fosters a deep sense of connection and commitment.
4. **Fostering a Sense of Ownership:** Charismatic leaders involve their followers in shaping and refining the vision. This participatory approach fosters a sense of ownership and investment in the vision's success. When individuals feel their input is valued and integrated into the larger vision, they become more personally invested in its achievement.
5. **Highlighting Significance and Impact:** A compelling vision goes beyond day-to-day tasks; it showcases the larger significance and impact of the work being done. Charismatic leaders emphasize how the vision contributes to a larger purpose, emphasizing the positive change it will bring about. This perspective elevates the sense of importance attached to the vision, motivating individuals to contribute their best efforts.
6. **Instilling Confidence and Belief:** Charismatic leaders exude confidence in the attainability of the vision. Their unwavering belief in the vision's realization becomes infectious, spreading a sense of optimism and self-assuredness among their followers. This confidence boosts morale and encourages individuals to overcome challenges.
7. **Creating a Roadmap for Success:** Charismatic leaders break down the journey toward the vision into actionable steps. They provide a roadmap that outlines the path forward, making the vision seem achievable and guiding individuals on how to contribute effectively. This clarity eliminates ambiguity and empowers individuals to take concrete actions.

8. **Celebrating Milestones and Progress:** Charismatic leaders celebrate both small and significant milestones on the journey toward the vision. These celebrations reinforce the progress made, acknowledge the contributions of individuals, and keep the momentum alive. This recognition reinforces the importance of the vision and encourages continued dedication.

Example of Charismatic Leaders and the Impact of Their Visions

Maharaja Sher Singh, the son of Maharaja Ranjit Singh, serves as a historical example of a charismatic leader whose compelling vision had a profound impact on his followers and the course of history. Maharaja Sher Singh's leadership during a critical period in the Sikh Empire showcased the power of charismatic leadership and its ability to shape the destiny of nations.

Charismatic Aura and Leadership Style

Maharaja Sher Singh possessed a magnetic charisma that commanded the respect and loyalty of his followers. His confident demeanor, combined with his personal charm and regal presence, made him a compelling leader who could sway hearts and minds.

Vision of Unity and Sovereignty

Sher Singh's vision was rooted in preserving the unity and sovereignty of the Sikh Empire. After the demise of his father, Maharaja Ranjit Singh, Sher Singh faced internal strife and external threats. He envisioned a united Sikh state that upheld the legacy of his father's achievements and safeguarded Sikh values.

Inspiring Loyalty and Courage

Sher Singh's vision resonated deeply with his followers, inspiring them to rally behind his leadership. His commitment to Sikh principles and his determination to maintain the empire's integrity motivated his soldiers to exhibit unwavering loyalty and courage on the battlefield.

Uniting a Diverse Empire

Sher Singh's ability to unite a diverse empire with various ethnic and religious groups demonstrated his leadership prowess. His vision transcended cultural differences, fostering a sense of shared identity and purpose among his followers.

Transformative Change and Resilience

During his reign, Sher Singh faced challenges, including attempts to undermine his authority. However, his charismatic leadership and compelling vision enabled him to overcome these obstacles. His resilience and determination to realize his vision fueled his efforts to strengthen the empire.

Legacy of Unity and Inspiration

Although Maharaja Sher Singh's reign was relatively short, his legacy endures as a testament to the impact of charismatic leadership. His vision of unity and sovereignty continues to inspire discussions about the Sikh Empire's history and the role of charismatic leaders in shaping the fate of nations.

Maharaja Sher Singh's example illustrates how charismatic leadership, coupled with a compelling vision, can galvanize followers, inspire unity, and leave a lasting legacy. His ability to lead with charisma and articulate a vision that resonated with his followers showcases the transformative power of leadership guided by conviction and a shared sense of purpose.

Strategies for Cultivating Charisma as a Leader

Charisma, while often seen as an inherent trait, can be developed and enhanced through deliberate practices and mindful efforts. Leaders can take proactive steps to cultivate their personal magnetism, allowing them to inspire and influence others more effectively. Here are strategies to develop and enhance charisma as a leader:

1. **Authentic Self-Expression:** Embrace your authentic self. Cultivate self-awareness to understand your strengths, values, and passions. When you are genuine and transparent, people are drawn to your authenticity.
2. **Active Listening and Empathy:** Practice active listening to understand the perspectives and feelings of others. Show genuine empathy by putting yourself in their shoes. Empathetic leaders forge deeper connections and build trust.
3. **Positive Presence and Energy:** Cultivate a positive demeanor and exude enthusiasm. Your energy is contagious and can uplift the mood of those around you. A positive presence fosters engagement and creates a welcoming atmosphere.
4. **Strong Communication Skills:** Hone your communication skills to effectively convey your thoughts and ideas. Use clear and compelling language, maintain eye contact, and employ nonverbal cues that reinforce your message.
5. **Charismatic Body Language:** Mastering body language is crucial. Stand tall, maintain an open posture, and use gestures that are confident and purposeful. A commanding presence can enhance your overall charisma.
6. **Storytelling Ability:** Develop the skill of storytelling. Narratives capture attention, make ideas relatable, and

evoke emotions. Sharing anecdotes and personal experiences can make your message memorable.

7. **Building Rapport:** Work on building rapport with others. Find common ground and engage in meaningful conversations. Creating a sense of connection enhances your likability and influence.
8. **Demonstrating Confidence:** Confidence is magnetic. Believe in your abilities and decisions. When you project self-assuredness, others are more likely to trust your leadership.
9. **Continuous Learning and Growth:** Charismatic leaders are lifelong learners. Stay curious and open to new ideas. Your enthusiasm for learning is inspiring and showcases your dedication to personal growth.
10. **Charitable Behavior:** Demonstrate kindness and willingness to help others. Charitable behavior fosters a positive image and showcases your consideration for the well-being of those around you.
11. **Gratitude and Appreciation:** Express gratitude for the contributions of others. Acknowledge their efforts and accomplishments, reinforcing a culture of recognition and appreciation.
12. **Approachability and Availability:** Be approachable and accessible to your team. Encourage open communication and create an environment where individuals feel comfortable sharing their thoughts and concerns.
13. **Leading by Example:** Model the behavior you expect from others. When you demonstrate commitment, dedication, and integrity, you inspire your team to follow suit.
14. **Humility and Vulnerability:** Display humility by acknowledging your imperfections. Embrace vulnerability and admit when you don't have all the answers. This genuine approach enhances your relatability.

15. **Positive Impact and Purpose:** Connect your leadership to a larger purpose. When your actions align with a meaningful cause, you create a sense of purpose that resonates with others.

Steps for Communicating a Compelling and Achievable Vision

Crafting a compelling and achievable vision is a pivotal aspect of charismatic leadership. A well-crafted vision captures the imagination of your team, guiding their efforts toward a shared goal. Effectively communicating this vision ensures that it resonates with your audience, inspiring commitment and action. Here are the steps to create and communicate a vision that captivates and motivates:

1. **Clarify Your Purpose:** Understand the purpose of your vision. What transformative change do you want to bring about? Define the overarching goal and the impact you aim to achieve.
2. **Align with Core Values:** Ensure that your vision aligns with your personal values, the values of your team, and the organization's values. A vision rooted in shared principles garners greater buy-in.
3. **Envision the Future:** Imagine the future you aspire to create. Picture the ideal state and articulate the positive outcomes that will result from realizing this vision.
4. **Make it Specific and Concrete:** Craft a vision that is specific and tangible. Avoid vague or abstract language. Clearly outline what success looks like, providing concrete details that paint a vivid picture.
5. **Set Achievable Goals:** Break down your vision into smaller, achievable goals. These milestones create a roadmap that demonstrates progress and maintains motivation.

6. **Address Challenges:** Acknowledge potential challenges or obstacles that might arise. Show how your vision overcomes these hurdles, demonstrating your strategic thinking and commitment.
7. **Develop a Compelling Narrative:** Create a narrative that tells a story of transformation. Highlight the journey from the present to the future, emphasizing the positive impact on individuals and the organization.
8. **Engage Stakeholders:** Involve key stakeholders in shaping the vision. Seek their input and feedback to ensure a sense of ownership and commitment to its success.
9. **Use Inspiring Language:** Choose language that evokes emotion and enthusiasm. Use words that convey the significance and urgency of the vision.
10. **Visual Representation:** Create visual aids that illustrate your vision. Visual representations, such as diagrams or infographics, enhance understanding and retention.
11. **Tailor to the Audience:** Adapt your communication to resonate with your audience. Consider their values, aspirations, and concerns, and frame the vision accordingly.
12. **Share Real-World Examples:** Highlight real-world examples that demonstrate the vision's feasibility and impact. Stories of success inspire confidence in the attainability of the vision.
13. **Foster Two-Way Communication:** Encourage open dialogue. Invite questions, suggestions, and feedback to create a sense of collaboration and mutual understanding.
14. **Consistent Messaging:** Consistently reinforce the vision in your communications. Repetition helps embed the vision in the minds of your team.
15. **Lead by Example:** Exemplify the behaviors and actions that align with the vision. Your commitment serves as a model for others to follow.

16. **Measure Progress:** Establish metrics to measure progress toward the vision. Regularly assess milestones achieved and adjust strategies as needed.
17. **Celebrate Achievements:** Recognize and celebrate successes along the way. Acknowledging progress reinforces the significance of the vision and boosts morale.

Charisma's Role in Influencing Others

Charisma plays a pivotal role in influencing others, wielding a profound impact on people's perceptions and actions. Charismatic individuals possess an innate magnetism that immediately captures attention and fosters a positive first impression. Their confidence and authenticity build trust and credibility, making them more persuasive and trustworthy. What sets charisma apart is its ability to create emotional connections, as charismatic leaders often convey empathy and understanding, leaving individuals feeling valued and heard. Charismatic leaders inspire confidence in their vision and decisions, motivating others to follow their lead and invest more effort and dedication in shared goals. They excel in influencing attitudes and beliefs, adeptly changing minds and persuading others to adopt new perspectives. Moreover, charisma enhances conflict resolution skills, eases resistance to change, and fosters strong relationships, making charismatic individuals effective in leadership, communication, and networking roles. In essence, charisma's multifaceted role encompasses trust, credibility, emotional connection, motivation, persuasion, and the ability to inspire confidence and action, rendering charismatic individuals influential leaders and communicators across diverse contexts.

Psychology of Charisma

The psychology of charisma delves into the underlying factors that make charismatic individuals captivating and influential. At its core, charisma is anchored in a profound sense of confidence and self-assuredness. Charismatic leaders exude belief in their abilities, which in turn instills trust and confidence in their followers. Authenticity is another pivotal aspect of charisma. Charismatic individuals are authentic and true to themselves, a quality that resonates deeply with others, drawing them in. Charisma also involves a high degree of emotional intelligence, enabling charismatic leaders to empathize with others, understand their emotions, and respond with genuine care and consideration. Active listening skills play a vital role, as charismatic individuals make people feel heard and valued, fostering rapport and trust.

Nonverbal communication, including confident body language, eye contact, and purposeful gestures, plays a significant role in conveying charisma. Charismatic individuals are often skilled storytellers, able to craft compelling narratives that engage and inspire. Psychologically, charismatic leadership theories, such as transformational leadership theory, highlight how charismatic leaders create shared visions and emphasize values to inspire commitment and engagement. Additionally, the halo effect, where positive traits are attributed to charismatic individuals, and the phenomenon of emotional contagion, where their emotions influence others, contribute to their persuasive power. Ultimately, charisma draws on a deep understanding of human psychology, leveraging confidence, authenticity, empathy, and emotional connections to inspire trust, loyalty, and action in others.

Ethics and Potential Pitfalls of Charismatic Leadership

Charismatic leadership, while possessing numerous strengths and appeal, is not without its ethical considerations and potential pitfalls. At the core of ethical concerns lies the risk of charisma being used for self-serving purposes rather than the greater good. Charismatic leaders must navigate these challenges conscientiously to ensure that their influence remains positive and aligned with ethical principles.

One notable ethical concern is the potential for charismatic leaders to manipulate or exploit their followers' trust and admiration. Charisma can be a double-edged sword, as it can obscure the line between genuine inspiration and manipulation. Leaders who prioritize personal gain or power over the well-being of their followers can lead them down morally questionable paths.

Moreover, charismatic leaders may inadvertently foster a cult of personality, where their followers become overly reliant on their guidance and decisions. This can stifle independent thought and discourage constructive dissent, undermining the principles of open dialogue and diverse perspectives.

Another ethical consideration is the risk of charismatic leaders prioritizing short-term gains over long-term sustainability. Their persuasive abilities may lead to decisions that prioritize immediate gratification, potentially neglecting the long-term consequences or sustainability of those choices.

Furthermore, charismatic leaders may struggle with accountability and transparency. Their captivating personalities can make it challenging for followers to question their actions or hold them accountable for mistakes. This lack of accountability can lead to unchecked power and ethical lapses.

Examination of the Ethical Implications

Relying solely on charisma for leadership influence raises profound ethical questions and potential pitfalls that demand thorough examination. While charisma can be a compelling asset for leaders, its exclusive use can lead to several ethical concerns:

1. **Authenticity and Transparency:** Charismatic leaders who rely solely on their personal charm may be perceived as lacking authenticity and transparency. Their public persona may not align with their true character

and intentions, leading to doubts about their trustworthiness and ethical integrity.
2. **Meritocracy and Competence:** Charisma-driven leadership can overshadow meritocracy and competence. Leaders chosen primarily for their charismatic appeal may lack the necessary skills, experience, or qualifications to make informed and ethical decisions. This can lead to situations where leadership effectiveness is compromised, jeopardizing the welfare of their followers and organizations.
3. **Ethical Behavior and Manipulation:** Charismatic leaders, due to their persuasive abilities, may be tempted to manipulate or engage in unethical behavior while maintaining a positive image. The charisma that draws people to them can be used to conceal unethical actions, creating ethical dilemmas related to honesty and integrity.
4. **Cult of Personality and Followership:** Over-reliance on charisma can foster a cult of personality, where followers become unquestionably loyal to the leader, potentially sacrificing their critical thinking and ethical judgment. This unquestioning allegiance can hinder ethical decision-making and accountability.
5. **Abuse of Power and Lack of Checks:** Charismatic leaders who consolidate power without effective checks and balances can be prone to abusing their authority. The absence of ethical oversight can lead to ethical transgressions, as power becomes unchecked and potentially exploitative.

Charisma should not be the sole basis for leadership influence. Ethical leadership requires a holistic approach that encompasses transparency, competence, ethical behavior, accountability, and the well-being of followers and organizations. While charisma can enhance a leader's appeal, ethical leadership necessitates a commitment to values, integrity, and responsible decision-making to ensure that charisma serves as a force for good rather than an ethical liability. Balancing charisma with ethical responsibility is essential for effective and principled leadership.

Identification of Potential Downsides of Charismatic Leadership

While charismatic leadership can be highly effective, it is essential to identify and acknowledge potential downsides that may arise from over-reliance on personality and the susceptibility to manipulation. These downsides can impact both leaders and their followers, affecting the overall effectiveness and ethical integrity of leadership. Here are key areas of concern:

1. **Over-Reliance on Personality:** Charismatic leaders are often celebrated for their compelling personalities, which can overshadow other critical leadership attributes. Over-reliance on charisma alone may lead to neglecting essential leadership skills, such as strategic thinking, decision-making, and operational competence. When leadership depends primarily on personality, it can be less resilient in the face of challenges that require a broader skill set.
2. **Short-Term Orientation:** Charismatic leaders may prioritize short-term gains and immediate gratification, as their persuasive abilities can lead to swift results. This short-term focus may compromise long-term sustainability and strategic planning, potentially harming the organization's stability and growth.
3. **Unchecked Authority:** Charismatic leaders can accumulate significant authority and influence, which, if unchecked, may lead to an imbalance of power. An overreliance on the leader's personality can create an environment where dissenting voices are silenced, and critical thinking is discouraged, potentially resulting in poor decision-making and ethical lapses.

4. **Susceptibility to Manipulation:** Charismatic leaders themselves can be susceptible to manipulation, particularly if they surround themselves with a circle of loyal followers who reinforce their views without question. This insularity can lead to leaders making decisions based on inaccurate or biased information, increasing the risk of poor judgment and ethical transgressions.
5. **Ethical Dilemmas:** Charismatic leadership can pose ethical dilemmas if leaders prioritize their personal charisma over the ethical well-being of their followers and organizations. This may manifest as leaders making decisions that benefit their image or personal interests at the expense of ethical principles.
6. **Succession and Dependency Issues:** Organizations led by charismatic leaders may face challenges in identifying suitable successors. When leadership is synonymous with the leader's personality, transitioning to a new leader can be daunting, potentially destabilizing the organization.
7. **Vulnerability to Manipulative Leaders:** Followers of charismatic leaders may become vulnerable to manipulation by leaders who exploit their trust and loyalty. This susceptibility can lead to followers making decisions against their best interests due to their emotional attachment to the leader.

Recognizing these potential downsides is crucial for both leaders and organizations. Effective leadership involves a balance between charisma and a diverse skill set that encompasses ethical decision-making, strategic thinking, competence, and a focus on long-term sustainability. Leaders who are aware of these pitfalls can take proactive measures to mitigate their impact and ensure that their charismatic influence remains ethical and effective.

Autocratic Leadership

Autocratic leadership is characterized by a centralized decision-making approach, where the leader holds significant authority and control over the direction and decisions of the group or organization. In this style, the leader exercises strict command and control, often making decisions unilaterally and without substantial input from subordinates. This leadership dynamic is rooted in the leader's power and the expectation of unquestioning obedience from followers. Autocratic leaders tend to provide clear directives and closely supervise the work of their team, aiming for efficiency and consistency. While this style can be effective in certain situations, it may also stifle creativity, autonomy, and employee engagement due to its top-down and authoritative nature.

Autocratic leadership is a style where the leader holds most of the decision-making power and exercises control over the team or organization. Leaders in this style typically make decisions without seeking input from subordinates and expect strict adherence to their directives. Autocratic leaders are often seen as authoritative figures who prioritize efficiency and adherence to rules and procedures. This style is most effective in situations requiring quick decisions and clear direction, such as during emergencies or in highly regulated industries. However, it can also lead to decreased employee engagement and creativity when used excessively.

Key characteristics of autocratic leadership

1. **Centralized Decision-Making:** Autocratic leaders are the primary decision-makers in the organization or team. They have the final say on matters ranging from strategic planning to day-to-day operations. This centralized decision-making authority means that the leader's choices often shape the direction and actions of the group.

2. **Limited Input from Subordinates:** Autocratic leaders tend to make decisions independently, with little to no input from their team members. They may view their role as one of providing guidance and direction rather than seeking input or consensus from others.

3. **Strict Control:** Autocratic leaders exercise a high degree of control over various aspects of the organization or team. They closely monitor work processes, enforce rules and procedures rigorously, and may be inclined to micromanage to ensure that tasks are carried out according to their standards.

4. **Hierarchical Structure:** Autocratic leadership often aligns with a hierarchical organizational structure. The leader's authority is clearly delineated, and there is a strong emphasis on following the leader's directives.

While autocratic leadership has its merits in certain situations, such as when quick and decisive actions are needed, it can also have significant drawbacks. These drawbacks include:

1. **Limited Creativity:** The strict control and limited input in autocratic leadership can stifle creativity and innovation. Team members may feel hesitant to propose new ideas or solutions, fearing that their suggestions will not be welcomed or considered.

2. **Reduced Employee Engagement:** The lack of involvement in decision-making can lead to decreased employee engagement and motivation. Team members may feel disconnected from their work or undervalued, as their contributions and insights are not actively sought.

3. **Dependency on the Leader:** Autocratic leadership can create a culture of dependency on the leader. Team members may become reliant on the leader for direction and decision-

making, which can hinder their ability to make independent choices or take initiative.

4. **Potential for Resistance:** Over time, autocratic leadership may lead to resistance and frustration among team members who feel that their voices are not heard or respected. This can result in lower morale and productivity.

5. **Limited Adaptability:** Autocratic leaders may struggle to adapt to changing circumstances or evolving challenges since they are accustomed to a rigid decision-making process.

Historical Context and Examples of Autocratic Leaders

Autocratic leadership has historical roots that can be traced back to various periods and regions. Understanding the historical context of autocratic leadership provides insights into its evolution and impact. Here, we explore the historical context and provide examples of autocratic leaders from different eras and parts of the world:

1. Ancient Empires:
- **King Hammurabi (c. 1810–1750 BC):** The sixth king of the First Babylonian Dynasty, Hammurabi, is known for his code of laws, one of the earliest known legal codes in history. His rule in ancient Mesopotamia exemplifies autocratic leadership, where his decrees held supreme authority.

2. Roman Empire:
- **Julius Caesar (100–44 BC):** Julius Caesar, a military general and statesman, effectively ended the Roman Republic's era and established himself as a de facto autocrat. His assassination in 44 BC marked a turning point in Roman history.

3. **Medieval Europe:**

   - **King Louis XIV of France (1638–1715):** Known as the "Sun King," Louis XIV's reign epitomized autocratic rule in Europe. He centralized power, expanded the palace at Versailles, and ruled with absolute authority.

4. **Imperial China:**

   - **Emperor Qin Shi Huang (259–210 BC):** The first emperor of the Qin Dynasty, Qin Shi Huang, unified China and implemented centralized control, including the construction of the Great Wall. His autocratic style shaped Chinese governance for centuries.

5. **Sikh Khalsa Empire:**

   - **Maharaja Ranjit Singh (1780–1839):** Maharaja Ranjit Singh, the founder and leader of the Sikh Khalsa Empire in the early 19th century, is an example of an autocratic leader. He consolidated power, uniting various Sikh factions, and ruled with authority over a significant part of the Asia subcontinent. His rule is noted for its centralized governance and military prowess.

6. **Soviet Union:**

   - **Joseph Stalin (1878–1953):** As the leader of the Soviet Union from the mid-1920s until his death, Stalin exemplified autocratic leadership. His rule was characterized by centralized control, purges, and a cult of personality.

7. **Modern Autocratic Regimes:**

   - **Kim Jong-un (North Korea):** As the supreme leader of North Korea, Kim Jong-un exercises autocratic control over the country, continuing a dynastic regime characterized by centralized authority.

8. **Contemporary Autocratic Leaders:**

- **Vladimir Putin (Russia):** Vladimir Putin's leadership in Russia is often described as autocratic, marked by centralized power, restrictions on political opposition, and control over the media.

9. **Corporate World:**

- **Steve Jobs (Apple Inc.):** While not a political leader, Steve Jobs, as the co-founder and former CEO of Apple Inc., was known for his autocratic leadership style within the tech industry. His hands-on approach and insistence on design perfection are illustrative of this style.

These examples demonstrate that autocratic leadership has manifested in various forms and contexts throughout history. While some autocratic leaders have been associated with significant achievements, they have also faced criticism for their concentration of power and lack of inclusivity. Autocratic leadership remains a topic of study and debate in both historical and contemporary leadership analysis.

Efficiency and Rapid Decision-Making in Autocracy

In the realm of leadership, one style that stands out for its exceptional efficiency and rapid decision-making capabilities is autocracy. This style, marked by its centralized authority, empowers leaders to make swift choices without the encumbrance of lengthy discussions or consensus-seeking processes.

1. **Swift Decision-Making:** Autocratic leadership's hallmark is its ability to make decisions swiftly. This capacity is particularly advantageous in scenarios where time is of the essence, such as during crises or in time-sensitive projects.
2. **Clear Direction and Efficiency:** A key advantage of autocratic leadership is its provision of clear and efficient guidance to the team. This lucidity minimizes confusion and enhances efficiency in task execution.

3. **Agility in Response:** Autocratic leaders exhibit a remarkable agility in responding to evolving circumstances. This adaptability proves invaluable when addressing urgent issues or seizing fleeting opportunities.
4. **Streamlined Execution:** The unambiguous directives of autocratic leadership facilitate the efficient execution of tasks and projects. Team members are well-aware of their roles and responsibilities, which aids in meeting deadlines.
5. **Time-Critical Scenarios:** Autocratic leadership is especially well-suited for situations where time plays a pivotal role. The rapid decision-making it affords is instrumental in navigating crises and emergencies.
6. **Reduction of Ambiguity:** The clear and unequivocal direction provided by autocratic leaders significantly reduces ambiguity. This, in turn, augments team performance and ensures efficient task completion.
7. **Clarity in Roles:** Within an autocratic framework, team members possess a lucid understanding of their roles and responsibilities. This clarity promotes efficient task execution and streamlined project management.
8. **Decisiveness:** Autocratic leaders are distinguished by their decisiveness, a characteristic that proves invaluable in scenarios necessitating swift and effective choices. Such decisiveness contributes to overall efficiency in decision-making.
9. **Minimized Delays:** One of the paramount advantages of autocracy is its ability to minimize delays associated with protracted decision-making processes. This capacity proves advantageous in achieving organizational goals without unnecessary hindrances.
10. **Crisis Management:** Autocratic leadership often excels in crisis management due to its capacity for rapid decision-making and immediate action-taking. The swift response it enables is pivotal in effectively managing crises.
11. **Task Completion:** The efficient decision-making and task execution facilitated by autocratic leadership play a pivotal

role in ensuring timely task completion. Meeting objectives within established timeframes is a hallmark of this leadership style.

12. **Response to Opportunities:** Autocratic leaders are adept at swiftly seizing opportunities, allowing organizations to capitalize on favorable situations. Responsiveness to opportunities is a distinctive strength of autocratic leadership.

Exploring Disadvantages in Depth

While autocratic leadership has its merits, including efficiency and quick decision-making, it comes with significant disadvantages that warrant closer examination. There are two critical drawbacks associated with autocratic leadership: stifled creativity and employee dissatisfaction.

Stifled Creativity

Autocratic leadership, characterized by the centralization of decision-making in the hands of the leader, often restricts the flow of creative ideas within an organization. Here's a more comprehensive look at how stifled creativity manifests:

1. **Limited Input:** In autocratic settings, team members typically have limited opportunities to contribute their ideas or perspectives to decision-making processes. The leader's decisive approach may leave little room for divergent opinions or innovative solutions.

2. **Fear of Repercussions:** Team members may become hesitant to voice their creative ideas or challenge the status quo. They might fear that their input will be dismissed or discouraged, leading to a culture of conformity rather than innovation.

3. **Missed Opportunities:** Creativity thrives in environments that encourage diverse thinking and collaboration. When autocracy suppresses these qualities, the organization can miss out on valuable insights, novel approaches, and innovative solutions to complex problems.

4. **Adaptability Challenges:** In rapidly changing industries and markets, adaptability is a key asset. Autocratic leadership, by its nature, may hinder the organization's ability to adapt to evolving circumstances and capitalize on emerging opportunities.

5. **Innovation Drought:** Over time, the stifling of creativity can result in an innovation drought, where the organization fails to generate fresh ideas or keep pace with competitors who foster creative thinking.

Employee Dissatisfaction

Autocratic leadership can also lead to widespread employee dissatisfaction, which can have detrimental effects on organizational morale and productivity. Here's an in-depth exploration of this aspect:

1. **Limited Participation:** Autocratic leaders often make decisions independently, leaving team members feeling excluded from the decision-making process. This can create a sense of disempowerment and disconnect.

2. **Reduced Motivation:** When employees perceive themselves as mere executors of directives rather than active contributors to the organization's direction, their motivation can wane. They may lack a sense of ownership over their work, leading to decreased enthusiasm and commitment.

3. **Higher Turnover Rates:** Dissatisfied employees are more likely to seek opportunities elsewhere. High turnover rates can be costly for organizations, resulting in recruitment and training expenses and potential disruptions in workflow.

4. **Impact on Organizational Culture:** Autocratic leadership can shape the organization's culture in ways that discourage open communication, collaboration, and employee engagement. This can hinder the development of a positive and innovative workplace culture.

5. **Productivity Decline:** Low morale and job dissatisfaction often correlate with reduced productivity. Employees who are disengaged or unhappy with their work are less likely to perform at their best.

Situations Demanding Autocratic Leadership

Autocratic leadership, with its characteristic centralized decision-making and strict control, may not be the preferred leadership style in all scenarios. However, there are specific situations where this approach proves not only suitable but even essential.

Crisis Situations

Autocratic leadership shines in crisis management. When an organization faces a sudden and severe crisis, such as a natural disaster, a public relations nightmare, or a financial meltdown, decisive and rapid action is critical. Here's a closer look at why autocracy is valuable in crisis situations:

1. **Swift Decision-Making:** In crises, every moment counts. Autocratic leaders can make decisions promptly, ensuring that necessary actions are taken without delay. This speed is vital for mitigating the impact of the crisis and safeguarding the organization's reputation and resources.

2. **Unified Response:** Autocratic leadership provides a clear chain of command, helping to unify the organization's response to the crisis. With a single decision-maker, there's

less risk of confusion or conflicting directives during high-pressure situations.

3. **Resource Allocation:** In crises, resource allocation can be a make-or-break factor. Autocratic leaders can swiftly allocate resources where they are most needed, optimizing the organization's ability to respond effectively.

Highly Regulated Industries

Certain industries, such as healthcare, finance, and nuclear energy, are subject to stringent regulations and compliance requirements. Autocratic leadership may be particularly suitable in these contexts. Here's why:

1. **Compliance Assurance:** Highly regulated industries demand strict adherence to established protocols and guidelines. Autocratic leaders can enforce compliance more effectively by ensuring that procedures are followed rigorously.

2. **Risk Mitigation:** In industries where non-compliance can result in significant legal, financial, or safety risks, autocratic leadership can provide the necessary oversight to minimize these risks.

3. **Streamlined Decision-Making:** In highly regulated sectors, decisions often have legal and ethical implications. Autocratic leaders can make decisions that align with regulations and industry standards quickly and decisively.

It's important to note that while autocratic leadership can excel in these situations, it may still benefit from occasional input or feedback from subject-matter experts and stakeholders to ensure that decisions align with the organization's broader goals and values. Additionally, as the crisis subsides or regulatory environments evolve, a shift toward more collaborative leadership styles may be advisable to maintain long-term organizational health and adaptability.

Effective Use of Autocratic Leadership

Effective utilization of autocratic leadership involves leveraging the concentrated decision-making authority of a leader to achieve specific goals or navigate challenging situations. Autocracy shines in crisis management, where swift and decisive action is imperative, ensuring timely responses and resource allocation. It finds a niche in highly regulated industries, ensuring strict compliance with established protocols. A well-executed autocratic approach maintains a balance between efficiency and adherence to standards. To illustrate the practicality of autocracy, we examine a real-world case study, offering insights into its application and the factors contributing to its success. While autocratic leadership can be a valuable tool, it's essential to recognize when and how to transition to more collaborative styles as circumstances evolve, fostering long-term organizational adaptability.

Leader: Maharaja Ranjit Singh (1780-1839)

Effective Use of Autocratic Leadership in the Khalsa Empire

Maharaja Ranjit Singh, the founder and leader of the Sikh Empire in the early 19th century, stands as an exemplary figure in the effective application of autocratic leadership within the context of the Khalsa Empire. Ranjit Singh's autocratic rule was characterized by centralized authority and swift decision-making, which played a pivotal role in consolidating and expanding the Sikh Empire.

Key Accomplishments

1. **Territorial Expansion:** Under Ranjit Singh's autocratic leadership, the Sikh Empire expanded significantly, encompassing regions across Punjab, Kashmir, and parts of modern-day Pakistan and India.

2. **Military Strategy:** Ranjit Singh's decisiveness and control were instrumental in organizing and leading a formidable military force. His leadership style allowed for quick responses to threats and opportunities on the battlefield.

3. **Infrastructure Development:** Autocratic decision-making enabled Ranjit Singh to undertake ambitious infrastructure projects, including the construction of forts, roads, and the beautification of Lahore, the empire's capital.

4. **Cultural and Religious Tolerance:** Despite the autocratic nature of his rule, Ranjit Singh was known for his religious tolerance and respect for the diverse cultural and religious backgrounds of his subjects, earning him widespread support.

5. **Administration:** Ranjit Singh's centralized control ensured efficient administration, resource allocation, and governance throughout the empire.

While Maharaja Ranjit Singh's autocratic leadership played a significant role in the Sikh Empire's consolidation and expansion, it is essential to acknowledge that his leadership style also had its challenges, including maintaining unity among diverse groups and ensuring a smooth transition of power after his death. Maharaja Ranjit Singh's example illustrates that autocratic leadership, when used judiciously and with a clear sense of purpose, can be effective in achieving specific objectives, such as territorial expansion and centralized governance, within the framework of a historical empire like the Khalsa Empire.

Analysis of Factors Contributing to Maharaja Ranjit Singh's Successful Autocratic Leadership

Maharaja Ranjit Singh's effective use of autocratic leadership within the Khalsa Empire can be attributed to a combination of strategic factors and personal qualities that contributed to positive outcomes. Here is an analysis of these key factors:

1. **Visionary Leadership:** Maharaja Ranjit Singh possessed a clear vision for the expansion and consolidation of the Sikh Empire. His autocratic leadership allowed him to translate this vision into actionable strategies. He foresaw the potential for a united Sikh state and pursued this goal with determination.
2. **Decisive Decision-Making:** One of the hallmarks of autocratic leadership is swift decision-making. Maharaja Ranjit Singh's ability to make crucial decisions rapidly was instrumental in both military campaigns and administrative matters. This decisiveness allowed for quick responses to changing situations on the battlefield and efficient governance.
3. **Military Prowess:** Maharaja Ranjit Singh's autocratic control extended to the military, where he was a shrewd strategist and commander. Under his leadership, the Sikh army became a formidable force, securing territorial gains and deterring potential adversaries. His military acumen contributed significantly to the empire's expansion.
4. **Cultural and Religious Tolerance:** Despite his autocratic rule, Maharaja Ranjit Singh demonstrated an unusual degree of cultural and religious tolerance for his time. He embraced diversity and ensured that subjects of various backgrounds enjoyed religious freedom and cultural acceptance. This inclusive approach garnered support from diverse communities within the empire.
5. **Administrative Efficiency:** Autocratic leadership facilitated efficient administration. Maharaja Ranjit Singh's centralized control allowed for consistent governance, resource allocation, and infrastructure development. His ability to manage the empire's affairs effectively contributed to its stability and growth.

6. **Charismatic Authority:** While autocratic, Maharaja Ranjit Singh's leadership style also incorporated elements of charisma. He was a respected and revered figure who inspired loyalty among his followers. His personal charisma helped maintain unity within the empire and bolstered his authority.
7. **Pragmatic Diplomacy:** Maharaja Ranjit Singh was known for his pragmatic approach to diplomacy. He forged strategic alliances when necessary and navigated the complex geopolitics of the time with skill. His diplomatic efforts helped secure the Sikh Empire's borders and interests.
8. **Legacy of Unified Punjab:** Perhaps one of the most enduring legacies of Maharaja Ranjit Singh's autocratic rule was the unification of Punjab. His leadership laid the foundation for a region that remained relatively stable and cohesive even after his death.

Impacts of Directive Leadership

Understanding the impacts of directive leadership involves examining the consequences and effects of a leadership style characterized by clear, specific instructions, and a focus on task-oriented goals. This analysis delves into how directive leadership influences various aspects, including employee morale, decision-making processes, and the overall dynamics within an organization. By comprehending these impacts, leaders can make informed decisions about when and how to employ directive leadership in different contexts.

Balancing Control and Innovation in Directive Leadership

Balancing control and fostering innovation is a complex endeavor within directive leadership. Effective leaders in this style find ways to maintain structure while encouraging creative thinking. Here's how to strike that balance:

1. **Clearly Define Boundaries:** Establish and communicate clear boundaries within which employees can operate autonomously. These boundaries should provide a framework for innovation while ensuring alignment with organizational goals.
2. **Encourage Idea Generation:** Create dedicated channels for employees to share their innovative ideas. These channels can include suggestion platforms, brainstorming sessions, or innovation competitions. Recognize and reward innovative contributions to motivate creativity.
3. **Foster Collaborative Problem-Solving:** Involve teams in problem-solving and decision-making processes whenever possible. Collaborative approaches harness collective creativity and expertise.
4. **Provide Necessary Resources:** Allocate the required resources and tools for implementing innovative ideas. A lack of resources can impede creative efforts, so ensure teams have what they need to innovate effectively.
5. **Support Calculated Risk-Taking:** Encourage a culture of calculated risk-taking. Employees should feel empowered to experiment with new approaches, provided they assess potential risks and benefits.
6. **Offer Constructive Feedback:** Provide feedback on innovative ideas, even if they're not immediately feasible. Constructive input helps employees refine their thinking and fosters a culture of improvement.
7. **Lead by Example:** As a directive leader, demonstrate innovative thinking in your own approach. When employees see leaders embracing innovation, they're more likely to follow suit.
8. **Celebrate Successes:** Acknowledge and celebrate successful innovations and their impact on the organization.

Public recognition motivates employees to continue exploring creative solutions.
9. **Promote Continuous Learning:** Encourage ongoing learning and development among employees. A culture of learning often goes hand-in-hand with creativity and innovation.
10. **Embrace Adaptability:** Recognize that different situations may demand varying degrees of control and innovation. Be adaptable in your leadership style to align with the specific context.
11. **Monitor Progress:** Keep a close eye on the progress of innovative projects. Regular monitoring ensures that ideas are implemented effectively and can help identify areas for improvement.

Balancing control and innovation in directive leadership involves creating a structured environment that supports creative thinking and problem-solving. These strategies enable leaders to nurture innovation without compromising the essential structure and guidance provided by this leadership style.

Adapting Leadership Styles

Adapting leadership styles refers to the dynamic and flexible approach that leaders employ to tailor their leadership behaviors and strategies to the specific needs of a situation, team, or individual. It acknowledges that one leadership style does not fit all circumstances and that effective leaders are capable of adjusting their methods to achieve the best outcomes. Adapting leadership styles is a hallmark of effective leadership, allowing leaders to navigate diverse challenges and personalities while maximizing their team's potential and achieving organizational goals. The qualities of Leaders who excel at adapting leadership styles are:

1. **Assess the Situation:** They carefully evaluate the current context, including factors like the team's maturity, the nature of the task, and external pressures.

2. **Understand Team Dynamics:** They have a deep understanding of their team members' strengths, weaknesses, and preferences, enabling them to make informed leadership choices.

3. **Choose the Right Style:** Based on their assessments, they select the most appropriate leadership style from a range of options, including autocratic, democratic, laissez-faire, transformational, and more.

4. **Communicate Effectively:** They are skilled communicators who can articulate their vision, expectations, and goals while fostering open dialogue with their team.

5. **Adapt Over Time:** They recognize that situations evolve, and what worked yesterday may not work tomorrow. Hence, they remain adaptable and adjust their leadership style as needed.

The Significance of Flexibility in Leadership Style

Flexibility in leadership style is a crucial attribute that enables leaders to effectively respond to the evolving needs of the organization and its members. Flexibility in leadership style is not about being inconsistent but rather about being responsive and adaptable to the ever-changing landscape of the organization and the diverse needs of its members. It is a leadership quality that is increasingly valuable in today's fast-paced and complex business environment. Here's a discussion of why this flexibility is so important:

1. **Adapting to Changing Situations:** Organizations operate in dynamic environments where circumstances, challenges,

and opportunities can change rapidly. A flexible leader can adjust their approach to address these shifting conditions effectively. For example, during times of crisis, an autocratic style might be necessary for quick decision-making, while in periods of growth, a more participative style can encourage innovation and collaboration.
2. **Tailoring to Team Dynamics:** Different teams have unique compositions, strengths, and dynamics. Flexibility allows a leader to recognize these variations and adapt their leadership style accordingly. A team of experienced professionals might thrive with a laissez-faire approach, while a newer team may require more guidance and structure.
3. **Meeting Individual Needs:** Effective leadership involves understanding and catering to the individual needs and preferences of team members. Some employees may thrive when given a high degree of autonomy, while others may require more direction and support. Flexibility enables leaders to provide the right level of guidance and autonomy on a case-by-case basis.
4. **Fostering Employee Growth:** Flexibility in leadership style supports the professional development and growth of team members. Leaders who can adapt to individuals' changing skill sets and aspirations can provide opportunities for learning and advancement, ultimately benefiting both the employees and the organization.
5. **Building Resilience:** In a rapidly changing world, organizations must be adaptable and resilient. Flexible leaders set an example for their teams by demonstrating adaptability. This encourages a culture of resilience where employees are more willing to embrace change and innovate.
6. **Enhancing Employee Engagement:** Flexibility in leadership style can enhance employee engagement. When employees feel their leaders are responsive to their needs and

open to new ideas, they are more likely to be motivated, committed, and productive.
7. **Promoting Inclusivity:** Flexibility in leadership is essential for promoting inclusivity and diversity. Leaders who can adapt their styles to accommodate different backgrounds and perspectives create a more inclusive and equitable work environment.
8. **Navigating Organizational Transitions:** During times of change, such as mergers, acquisitions, or reorganizations, leaders must be flexible to navigate the transition smoothly. A one-size-fits-all approach is rarely effective in these situations.
9. **Achieving Organizational Goals:** Ultimately, the flexibility to tailor leadership styles based on evolving needs is instrumental in achieving organizational goals. Leaders who can pivot and adapt are better equipped to lead their teams to success, whether that means meeting financial targets, fostering innovation, or promoting a culture of excellence.

*****

CHAPTER FIVE
Behavioral and interactional theories

Behavioral and Interactional theories are psychological theories that focus on explaining and understanding human behavior, particularly in the context of how individuals interact with their environment and with other people. These theories have been influential in the fields of psychology, sociology, and communication studies. Here's a brief overview of both:

Behavioral Theories

Behavioral theories, also known as behaviorism, emphasize the role of observable behaviors in understanding human psychology. They propose that behavior is a result of conditioning and learning from the environment.

1. **Classical Conditioning:** This concept, developed by Ivan Pavlov, suggests that behavior is learned through associations. For example, a dog salivating at the sound of a bell after it has been paired with food.
2. **Operant Conditioning:** Proposed by B.F. Skinner, operant conditioning focuses on how behaviors are strengthened or weakened by consequences. Positive reinforcement, negative reinforcement, and punishment are key concepts in this theory.

Application

Behavioral theories have been applied in various fields, such as education, therapy, and parenting, to modify and shape behavior by using reinforcement and punishment techniques.

Interactional Theories

Interactional theories, also known as social interactionism, emphasize the significance of social interactions and communication in shaping human behavior and development.

1. **Symbolic Interactionism:** Developed by George Herbert Mead and Charles Horton Cooley, this theory suggests that individuals develop a sense of self and meaning through interactions with others. It focuses on symbols, gestures, and language as crucial elements of human interaction.
2. **Social Learning Theory:** Albert Bandura's social learning theory builds upon behaviorism but includes the idea that individuals can learn through observation and modeling. It also emphasizes the role of self-efficacy in motivating behavior.

Application

Interactional theories are often used in sociology and communication studies to analyze how individuals interpret symbols, engage in role-playing, and negotiate meanings in their social interactions. They are also relevant in understanding how individuals acquire social skills and adapt to different social contexts.

It is important to note that these theories are not mutually exclusive, and many psychologists and researchers integrate aspects of both behavioral and interactional theories in their work. They provide valuable insights into how individuals develop, learn, and adapt within their social and environmental contexts.

Significance of Behavioral and Interactional Theories

Behavioral and interactional theories have significant implications for leadership, as they offer insights into how leaders can influence and interact with their teams and organizations. Here's a breakdown of their significance in the context of leadership:

Behavioral Theories in Leadership

Behavioral theories of leadership focus on the actions and behaviors of leaders. They emphasize that leadership is not solely based on innate traits but can be developed through learned behaviors. This has several implications for leadership:

1. **Teaching Leadership Skills:** Behavioral theories suggest that leadership skills can be taught and learned. Leaders can undergo training and development programs to acquire and improve their leadership abilities.

2. **Focus on Observable Behaviors:** Leaders can be evaluated and assessed based on their observable behaviors and actions. This allows for more concrete feedback and development opportunities.

3. **Adaptive Leadership:** Leaders can adapt their leadership styles and behaviors to fit different situations and challenges. For example, they can be more autocratic in a crisis and more participative in routine decision-making.

4. **Use of Rewards and Punishments:** Leaders can apply principles of reinforcement to motivate and shape the behavior of their teams. Providing positive reinforcement for desired behaviors and addressing undesirable behaviors can be effective leadership strategies.

Interactional Theories in Leadership

Interactional theories, such as symbolic interactionism and social learning theory, highlight the importance of social interactions and communication in leadership. Here's how they are significant:

1. **Communication Skills:** Effective leaders need strong communication skills to convey their vision, build

relationships, and inspire their teams. Interactional theories emphasize the role of language and symbols in leadership communication.

2. **Understanding Followers:** Interactional theories underscore the importance of understanding the perspectives and needs of followers. Leaders who can empathize and adapt their communication and actions to different team members can build trust and rapport.

3. **Role Modeling:** Social learning theory suggests that leaders can influence their teams through modeling desired behaviors. When leaders demonstrate ethical behavior, commitment, and professionalism, they set an example for their followers.

4. **Contextual Leadership:** Interactional theories acknowledge that leadership effectiveness can vary depending on the context and culture. Leaders who are sensitive to cultural norms and adapt their communication styles accordingly are more likely to succeed in diverse environments.

Behavioral and interactional theories provide a comprehensive framework for understanding leadership. Behavioral theories emphasize the development of leadership skills and the importance of observable behaviors, while interactional theories focus on the role of communication, social interactions, and adaptability in leadership. Effective leaders often draw from both sets of theories to lead their teams and organizations successfully.

Behavioral Leadership

Behavioral leadership, in essence, is a leadership approach that places its primary emphasis on the observable actions, behaviors, and strategies employed by individuals in leadership roles. Instead of solely attributing effective leadership to inherent personality traits or characteristics, behavioral leadership theory contends that leadership can be better understood and cultivated by studying and refining specific actions and behaviors demonstrated by leaders in various situations. This approach contends that leadership is not an innate quality but a set of learned behaviors that can be assessed, developed, and applied in practical contexts. Behavioral leadership theory has practical implications for leadership development and training, as it allows leaders to receive feedback on their actions, encourages adaptability to different situations, and underscores the significance of ethical and interpersonal behaviors in influencing and guiding teams or organizations.

Behavioral leadership theory and its shift toward examining leadership behaviors

Behavioral leadership theory is a prominent approach in the field of leadership studies that focuses on the actions and behaviors of leaders as the primary determinant of their effectiveness. This theory represents a significant shift away from earlier trait-based theories of leadership that suggested leadership success was primarily a result of certain innate characteristics or traits possessed by leaders. Instead, the behavioral leadership theory argues that leadership is a set of behaviors and actions that can be observed, learned, and developed. Here's an explanation of the behavioral leadership theory and its shift toward examining leadership behaviors:

1. **Behavioral Focus:** Behavioral leadership theory places a central emphasis on what leaders do rather than who they are. It asserts that leadership is not solely dependent on inherent personality traits but is a set of behaviors that can be practiced, honed, and improved over time.

2. **Observable Actions:** In contrast to trait-based theories, which can be subjective and difficult to measure, behavioral

leadership theory is more objective and tangible. It highlights the significance of identifying specific leadership behaviors that can be observed, measured, and analyzed.

3. **Empirical Research:** The shift towards examining leadership behaviors has led to an increased emphasis on empirical research and data-driven analysis. Researchers and organizations can collect data on leader behaviors and their impact on followers and organizational outcomes, allowing for evidence-based leadership practices.

4. **Leadership Development:** Behavioral leadership theory has practical implications for leadership development and training. It enables leaders to receive feedback on their actions, behaviors, and communication styles, facilitating targeted improvements in their leadership skills.

5. **Leadership Styles:** This theory identifies different leadership styles, such as autocratic, democratic, and laissez-faire, based on observable behaviors. Leaders can adapt their styles to suit the needs and challenges of various situations and teams.

6. **Communication Skills:** Effective communication behaviors are considered a crucial component of behavioral leadership. Leaders who excel in communication can convey their vision, build relationships, and inspire their teams more effectively.

7. **Ethical Considerations:** Behavioral leadership theory also underscores the importance of ethical behavior and integrity. Leaders who demonstrate ethical behaviors and transparency are more likely to gain the trust and respect of their followers.

8. **Interpersonal Dynamics:** Examining leadership behaviors acknowledges the role of interpersonal dynamics in leadership effectiveness. Effective leaders understand and

respond to the needs, motivations, and perspectives of their team members.

The behavioral leadership theory represents a shift away from trait-based notions of leadership by emphasizing the critical role of observable behaviors and actions in effective leadership. This approach has practical implications for leadership development, encourages evidence-based leadership practices, and recognizes the importance of adaptability, communication, and ethical conduct in leadership effectiveness.

Historical Context and Emergence

The emergence of the behavioral leadership perspective can be understood within its historical context, which was influenced by several key factors and events in the 20th century. Here is an overview of the historical context and the emergence of the behavioral leadership perspective:

1. **Industrial Revolution and Shift to Large Organizations (Late 19th and Early 20th Century):** The late 19th and early 20th centuries witnessed the rapid growth of industrialization and the emergence of large, complex organizations. This shift from agrarian economies to industrial economies brought about a need for effective management and leadership within these organizations.

2. **Scientific Management (Early 20th Century):** Frederick W. Taylor and other proponents of scientific management focused on optimizing work processes and improving efficiency in organizations. This approach highlighted the importance of management practices and worker behavior in achieving organizational goals. It laid the groundwork for studying and understanding leadership behaviors in the workplace.

3. **World War I and World War II (Early to Mid-20th Century):** The two World Wars had a profound impact on leadership research and practice. The military's need for effective leadership in the face of complex challenges led to the study of leadership behaviors and the development of leadership training programs.

4. **Hawthorne Studies (1920s and 1930s):** The Hawthorne Studies, conducted at the Western Electric Hawthorne Works in Chicago, marked a significant turning point in leadership research. These studies, led by Elton Mayo and his colleagues, revealed the importance of social and psychological factors in the workplace. Researchers found that workers' attitudes and behaviors were influenced by interpersonal dynamics, group norms, and leadership styles, challenging the earlier emphasis on task efficiency.

5. **Behavioral Psychology (20th Century):** The rise of behavioral psychology, with figures like B.F. Skinner and Ivan Pavlov, contributed to the shift towards understanding behavior as a learned and observable phenomenon. This perspective influenced the idea that leadership could also be studied by observing and analyzing behaviors.

6. **Post-World War II Leadership Research:** After World War II, leadership studies continued to evolve. Researchers like Kurt Lewin and Douglas McGregor explored leadership behaviors and their impact on organizational dynamics. Lewin's work on leadership styles, including autocratic, democratic, and laissez-faire leadership, became influential.

7. **Ohio State Studies and Michigan Studies (1950s):** These research initiatives examined leadership behaviors and identified dimensions of leadership behavior, such as initiating structure (task-oriented) and consideration (relationship-oriented). These studies provided a framework for understanding leadership behaviors in organizations.

8. **Emergence of Contingency Theories (1960s and 1970s):** Contingency theories like Fiedler's Contingency Model and Hersey and Blanchard's Situational Leadership Model built upon the behavioral perspective by emphasizing that effective leadership behaviors depend on the context and the characteristics of followers.

The behavioral leadership perspective emerged in response to the changing industrial landscape, the need for effective leadership in large organizations, and the findings of influential studies like the Hawthorne Studies. It emphasized the study of observable behaviors and the impact of leadership actions on organizational outcomes, ultimately shaping the field of leadership research and practice in the 20th century and beyond.

Key Behavioral Traits of Effective Leadership

Effective leadership is characterized by a range of key behavioral traits that enable leaders to inspire, guide, and achieve success within their teams and organizations. Some of the key behavioral traits of effective leadership include clear communication, adaptability, empathy, decisiveness, and integrity. Clear communication allows leaders to articulate their vision, expectations, and goals while fostering open dialogue within their teams. Adaptability involves the ability to adjust leadership styles and strategies to suit various situations and challenges. Empathy enables leaders to understand and connect with their team members, fostering trust and cooperation. Decisiveness ensures that leaders can make timely and informed decisions, providing direction and clarity. Finally, integrity, demonstrated through ethical behavior and consistency, establishes leaders as role models and reinforces their credibility. These behavioral traits collectively contribute to effective leadership, facilitating team cohesion, motivation, and organizational success.

Specific behaviors that define effective leaders

Effective leaders exhibit a range of specific behaviors that set them apart and enable them to lead their teams and organizations successfully. Here is an exploration of some key behaviors that define effective leaders.

Effective Communication Skills

1. **Active Listening:** Effective leaders are skilled at active listening, which involves fully engaging with team members, understanding their perspectives, and validating their input. They give their full attention, ask clarifying questions, and provide feedback to demonstrate that they value and respect their team's ideas.
2. **Clear and Open Communication:** Effective leaders communicate clearly and openly. They convey their vision, goals, and expectations in a straightforward and transparent manner, ensuring that their team understands their direction and objectives.
3. **Adaptability in Communication:** Leaders adapt their communication style to suit the needs of different team members and situations. They can switch between being directive and participative, depending on the task and the individuals involved.

Decisiveness

1. **Timely Decision-Making:** Effective leaders make timely decisions. They gather relevant information, analyze options, and make choices when needed, preventing delays and uncertainty within the team.
2. **Accountability:** They take responsibility for their decisions, whether they result in success or failure. This accountability fosters trust within the team, as team members see that the leader stands behind their choices.

Conflict Resolution

1. **Conflict Management:** Effective leaders are skilled at managing conflicts within the team. They address disputes promptly and constructively, encouraging open communication and finding solutions that benefit the team as a whole.
2. **Mediation:** When necessary, leaders can serve as mediators to facilitate productive discussions and negotiations among team members. They maintain a neutral stance and guide the process toward resolution.
3. **Prevention:** Proactive leaders also work on preventing conflicts by creating a positive team culture, setting clear expectations, and encouraging open communication.

Empathy and Emotional Intelligence

1. **Understanding Team Members:** Effective leaders possess empathy and emotional intelligence, allowing them to understand the emotions, needs, and concerns of their team members. They connect on a personal level and build strong relationships.
2. **Support and Recognition:** They provide emotional support when needed and recognize the achievements and contributions of their team members. This boosts morale and motivation.
3. **Conflict Resolution:** Empathy helps leaders navigate conflicts with sensitivity, taking into account the feelings and perspectives of all involved parties.

Adaptability

1. **Flexibility:** Effective leaders are adaptable in response to changing circumstances or unexpected challenges. They adjust their strategies and plans as needed, demonstrating resilience and problem-solving skills.
2. **Learning Orientation:** They encourage a culture of continuous learning within the team, setting an example by

seeking feedback, embracing change, and demonstrating a growth mindset.

Integrity and Ethical Behavior:

1. **Consistency:** Effective leaders maintain consistency in their actions and decisions, which builds trust among team members.
2. **Ethical Decision-Making:** They adhere to ethical principles and values, making choices that align with the organization's ethical standards and societal expectations.

Effective leaders exhibit a combination of behavioral traits and skills that encompass clear communication, decisive decision-making, conflict resolution, empathy, adaptability, and integrity. These behaviors not only enable leaders to navigate challenges and achieve organizational goals but also create a positive and productive work environment that fosters teamwork and employee satisfaction.

Real-World Examples

Real-world examples can help illustrate the importance of the leadership behaviors mentioned earlier. Here are some examples that highlight the significance of effective communication, decision-making, conflict resolution, empathy, adaptability, and integrity in leadership:

1. **Effective Communication - Elon Musk (Tesla and SpaceX):** Elon Musk, CEO of Tesla and SpaceX, is known for his effective communication skills. He regularly communicates his vision for sustainable energy and space exploration to the public, investors, and employees. His clear and open communication has rallied support for ambitious projects like the Tesla electric car and the SpaceX Mars mission, attracting talent and investments.

2. **Decisiveness - Indra Nooyi (Former CEO of PepsiCo):** Indra Nooyi's tenure as CEO of PepsiCo is characterized by her decisive decision-making. She made bold choices, such as diversifying the company's product portfolio to include healthier snacks and beverages. These decisions not only boosted the company's market value but also addressed changing consumer preferences and health concerns.

3. **Conflict Resolution - Nelson Mandela (Former President of South Africa):** Nelson Mandela is a prominent example of a leader skilled in conflict resolution. He played a pivotal role in ending apartheid in South Africa by negotiating with the apartheid government and fostering reconciliation among different racial and ethnic groups. His approach to conflict resolution helped avoid a violent transition to democracy.

4. **Empathy and Emotional Intelligence - Satpreet Singh (CEO of Ardass):** Satpreet Singh, as the CEO of Ardass, exemplifies the significance of empathy and emotional intelligence in leadership. Ardass, a social enterprise, focuses on providing education and empowerment opportunities to underprivileged communities. Singh's leadership is marked by his deep understanding of the challenges faced by marginalized individuals and his commitment to addressing their needs. He actively engages with the communities Ardass serves, listens to their voices, and tailors programs to their specific requirements. His empathetic and emotionally intelligent approach has not only led to improved outcomes for the communities Ardass supports but has also garnered support and partnerships from stakeholders who share his vision of social impact through education and empowerment.

5. **Adaptability - Jeff Bezos (Former CEO of Amazon):** Jeff Bezos is known for his adaptability as a leader. He led Amazon from an online bookseller to a global e-commerce

and technology giant. Bezos constantly adapted to changes in the industry and consumer behavior, expanding Amazon's offerings and ventures, such as Amazon Web Services (AWS).

6. **Integrity and Ethical Behavior - Mary Barra (CEO of General Motors):** Mary Barra, as the CEO of General Motors, faced the ignition switch recall crisis in 2014. Her commitment to addressing the issue transparently and ethically, including taking responsibility and providing compensation to victims' families, demonstrated the importance of integrity and ethical behavior in leadership.

These real-world examples underscore how effective leadership behaviors can impact organizations, industries, and even nations. Leaders who exhibit these behaviors not only achieve success but also inspire and create lasting positive change.

Behavioral Leadership Models

Behavioral leadership models, also known as leadership style models, are theoretical frameworks that emphasize the observable behaviors and actions of leaders as the primary focus of leadership study and practice. These models move away from the traditional emphasis on innate traits or characteristics of leaders and instead concentrate on how leaders interact with their teams, make decisions, communicate, and manage various aspects of leadership. Behavioral leadership models typically categorize leadership styles based on specific patterns of behavior, such as autocratic, democratic, laissez-faire, or transformational. These models provide a valuable framework for understanding and analyzing leadership in practical terms, as they offer insights into the ways leaders influence their followers and achieve organizational goals through their actions and behaviors. By examining these observable behaviors, organizations can develop leadership development programs, provide targeted feedback, and cultivate effective leadership skills, contributing to improved leadership effectiveness and overall organizational success.

Notable Behavior Models

The Ohio State Studies and the University of Michigan Studies are two notable behavioral leadership models that emerged in the mid-20th century and contributed significantly to our understanding of leadership behaviors.

Ohio State Studies (1940s)

1. **Initiating Structure and Consideration:** The Ohio State Studies, conducted by researchers at Ohio State University in the late 1940s, were instrumental in categorizing leadership behaviors. They identified two primary dimensions of leadership behavior:

    - **Initiating Structure:** This dimension refers to the extent to which a leader defines and structures the roles of their team members. Leaders high in initiating structure provide clear expectations, set goals, and establish procedures to guide the work.

    - **Consideration:** Consideration pertains to the degree of warmth, support, and rapport-building a leader engages in with their team members. Leaders high in consideration show concern for the well-being and satisfaction of their team and maintain open communication.

2. **Leadership Grid:** The Ohio State Studies led to the creation of the Leadership Grid, a graphical representation of leadership styles based on the two dimensions. It identifies five leadership styles, ranging from impoverished management (low on both dimensions) to team management

(high on both dimensions), allowing for a nuanced understanding of leadership behaviors.

University of Michigan Studies (1950s)

1. **Employee-Centered and Job-Centered Leadership:** The University of Michigan Studies, conducted during the 1950s, aimed to identify effective leadership behaviors. Researchers at the University of Michigan categorized leadership styles into two primary dimensions:

   - **Employee-Centered Leadership:** This dimension reflects leaders who focus on building positive relationships with their team members, valuing their needs and opinions.

   - **Job-Centered Leadership:** Job-centered leaders prioritize task-oriented aspects of leadership, emphasizing efficiency and task completion.

2. **Leadership Styles:** These studies identified four leadership styles by combining the two dimensions:

   - **Group Leadership:** High on both employee-centered and job-centered dimensions. Leaders in this style are effective in both task accomplishment and maintaining good relationships.

   - **Human Relations Leadership:** High on employee-centered but low on job-centered dimension. These leaders prioritize building strong interpersonal relationships.

   - **Production-Centered Leadership:** High on job-centered but low on employee-centered dimension. These leaders focus on task efficiency.

   - **Laissez-Faire Leadership:** Low on both dimensions. Laissez-faire leaders are hands-off and provide minimal guidance or support.

Both the Ohio State and University of Michigan Studies contributed significantly to the understanding of leadership by highlighting the importance of specific behaviors and leadership styles. These models underscore that effective leadership is not limited to a single style but can be tailored to meet the needs of the situation and the team. They also laid the foundation for later leadership theories and models, further enriching our comprehension of leadership behaviors and their impact on organizational success.

Examination of how these models categorize leadership behaviors

The Ohio State Studies and the University of Michigan Studies categorize leadership behaviors by identifying specific dimensions and styles based on observable actions and interactions between leaders and their teams. Let's examine how these models categorize leadership behaviors in more detail:

Ohio State Studies (Initiating Structure and Consideration)

1. **Initiating Structure:** This dimension categorizes leadership behavior based on the extent to which leaders define roles, tasks, and responsibilities within the team. Leaders who score high on this dimension are considered to engage in task-oriented behaviors.

    - **High Initiating Structure:** Leaders who provide clear instructions, set goals, establish procedures, and structure work tasks in a precise manner. They ensure that the team members know what is expected of them, leading to efficient task accomplishment.

    - **Low Initiating Structure:** Leaders who are less directive in their approach, providing less structure and leaving room for team members to decide how to complete tasks. This approach can lead to greater autonomy but may require team members to self-organize.

2. **Consideration:** This dimension categorizes leadership behavior based on the degree of interpersonal support, warmth, and consideration leaders exhibit towards their team members.

    - **High Consideration:** Leaders who prioritize building strong relationships with their team members, showing empathy, active listening, and concern for their well-being. This fosters a positive work environment and team morale.

    - **Low Consideration:** Leaders who are less focused on interpersonal relationships and may appear less empathetic or warm. They are more task-oriented and less concerned with team members' feelings and needs.

University of Michigan Studies (Employee-Centered and Job-Centered Leadership)

1. **Employee-Centered Leadership:** This dimension categorizes leadership behavior based on the degree of attention leaders pay to the human aspects of leadership.

    - **High Employee-Centered Leadership:** Leaders who emphasize building positive relationships with their team members. They are supportive, considerate, and value the opinions and needs of their employees.

    - **Low Employee-Centered Leadership:** Leaders who prioritize task-oriented aspects of leadership, such as task efficiency and job completion. They may appear less concerned with team members' interpersonal relationships and emotions.

2. **Job-Centered Leadership:** This dimension categorizes leadership behavior based on the emphasis placed on task-oriented behaviors and goal achievement.

    - **High Job-Centered Leadership:** Leaders who focus on structuring tasks, maintaining discipline, and ensuring job completion. They may appear more directive and task-driven.

    - **Low Job-Centered Leadership:** Leaders who are less concerned with task efficiency and may provide more autonomy to their team members to decide how to accomplish tasks.

In both models, leadership behaviors are categorized based on these dimensions, resulting in different leadership styles:

- **Ohio State Studies:** The Leadership Grid categorizes leadership styles as combinations of high or low scores on initiating structure and consideration, resulting in five styles, including impoverished management, middle-of-the-road management, and team management.

- **University of Michigan Studies:** Leadership styles are classified into four categories based on the combinations of employee-centered and job-centered behaviors: group leadership, human relations leadership, production-centered leadership, and laissez-faire leadership.

These models emphasize that effective leadership behaviors can vary in their emphasis on task orientation and interpersonal relationships, highlighting the importance of adaptability and context in leadership. Leaders may exhibit different behaviors based on the situation and the needs of their team and organization.

Case Study

The application of behavioral leadership refers to the practical implementation of leadership theories and principles that emphasize observable behaviors, actions, and interactions of leaders within organizational contexts. This approach focuses on cultivating specific leadership behaviors and styles, such as effective communication, empathy, adaptability, and ethical conduct, to achieve desired outcomes and lead teams and organizations effectively. Applying behavioral leadership involves assessing and developing leadership skills, providing targeted feedback, and adapting leadership strategies to various situations and challenges. It recognizes that leadership is not solely dependent on inherent traits but can be learned, honed, and tailored to meet the needs of the team, organization, and its objectives. Ultimately, the application of behavioral leadership aims to enhance leadership effectiveness, foster a positive work culture, and drive organizational success by emphasizing practical, observable, and measurable leadership behaviors.

Starbucks Corporation

Starbucks Corporation, the global coffeehouse chain, has experienced remarkable growth and success under the leadership of Howard Schultz. Schultz's leadership approach aligns closely with behavioral leadership principles, particularly the concept of transformational leadership.

Leadership Behaviors Applied

1. **Transformational Leadership:** Howard Schultz is renowned for his transformational leadership style, which emphasizes inspiring and motivating employees to go above and beyond their roles. He applied the following key behavioral principles:

- **Visionary Communication:** Schultz articulated a compelling vision for Starbucks as a "third place" between work and home, where people could enjoy high-quality coffee and build community. His vision extended beyond profit and emphasized creating a positive social impact.

- **Empowerment and Development:** Schultz invested heavily in employee development programs, including health benefits, stock options, and tuition assistance. This approach demonstrated his commitment to employee well-being and personal growth.

- **Open Communication:** He encouraged open dialogue and feedback, creating a culture where employees felt heard and valued. This practice fostered a sense of inclusion and teamwork.

- **Adaptability:** Schultz demonstrated adaptability by overseeing significant changes during his tenure, such as introducing new products, expanding globally, and addressing issues like racial bias in stores. His ability to adapt to evolving circumstances and market trends was instrumental in Starbucks' success.

Outcomes

1. **Global Expansion:** Under Schultz's leadership, Starbucks expanded its presence from a few hundred stores to thousands worldwide. The brand became synonymous with quality coffee and a welcoming atmosphere.

2. **Financial Success:** Starbucks achieved impressive financial results, with consistent revenue growth and profitability. Schultz's focus on employee satisfaction translated into

satisfied customers, contributing to the company's financial performance.

3. **Social Responsibility:** Schultz's commitment to social responsibility led to initiatives like ethical sourcing of coffee beans, environmental sustainability efforts, and addressing social issues. These actions aligned with his vision of making Starbucks a force for positive change.

4. **Employee Engagement:** Starbucks consistently ranked as one of the best companies to work for, thanks to its employee-centric policies and practices. High employee morale contributed to customer satisfaction and loyalty.

5. **Brand Loyalty:** Schultz's leadership principles and vision cultivated a loyal customer base that identified with Starbucks' values and experiences, translating into brand loyalty and repeat business.

Key Takeaways

The Starbucks case study demonstrates how the application of behavioral leadership principles, particularly transformational leadership, can lead to exceptional organizational outcomes. Howard Schultz's visionary leadership, focus on employee well-being, open communication, and adaptability played pivotal roles in Starbucks' global success and its impact on the coffee industry. This case underscores the importance of leadership behaviors in shaping not only financial performance but also a company's social responsibility and reputation.

Analysis of specific behaviors

Analysis of specific behaviors involves a detailed examination and evaluation of the actions, conduct, and interactions of individuals within a particular context. This process seeks to understand the motivations, impacts, and outcomes associated with these behaviors. In the context of leadership and organizational success, analyzing specific behaviors entails dissecting the actions and practices of leaders and team members to determine their contribution to achievements or setbacks. It involves identifying patterns of behavior, assessing their effectiveness, and discerning their alignment with organizational goals and values. This analysis not only provides insights into what drives success but also offers opportunities for improvement and optimization. By scrutinizing behaviors within an organizational framework, leaders can make informed decisions, enhance performance, and foster a culture that cultivates behaviors conducive to positive outcomes and sustainable success.

Let's analyze the specific behaviors that contributed to the success of Starbucks under the leadership of Howard Schultz:

1. **Visionary Communication:** Schultz's ability to articulate a compelling vision for Starbucks as a "third place" between work and home, where people could gather, socialize, and enjoy high-quality coffee, was a key behavior that contributed to success. This vision went beyond mere profit and resonated with customers and employees alike, creating a sense of purpose and community.

2. **Empowerment and Development:** Schultz's emphasis on employee empowerment and development was another crucial behavior. By providing benefits like stock options, health coverage, and tuition assistance, he demonstrated a commitment to the well-being and personal growth of Starbucks employees. This behavior led to a motivated and dedicated workforce.

3. **Open Communication:** Schultz encouraged open communication and feedback within the organization, fostering a culture where employees felt valued and heard. This behavior created an environment of transparency and

trust, enabling Starbucks to address challenges effectively and make continuous improvements.

4. **Adaptability:** Schultz's ability to adapt to changing circumstances and market trends was instrumental in Starbucks' success. He oversaw significant changes, such as introducing new products, expanding globally, and addressing issues like racial bias in stores. This adaptability allowed Starbucks to remain relevant and resilient in a dynamic industry.

5. **Social Responsibility:** Schultz's commitment to social responsibility, including ethical sourcing of coffee beans and environmental sustainability efforts, was a significant behavior that contributed to success. This behavior aligned with his vision of making Starbucks a force for positive change and resonated with socially conscious consumers.

6. **Customer Engagement:** Schultz's hands-on involvement in enhancing the customer experience, such as creating welcoming store atmospheres and introducing innovative products like the Pumpkin Spice Latte, demonstrated his dedication to customer engagement. This behavior cultivated a loyal customer base and drove repeat business.

7. **Employee Engagement:** Schultz's focus on employee satisfaction and creating a positive work environment was a behavior that directly impacted the success of Starbucks. Satisfied employees contributed to a higher level of service quality and customer satisfaction, ultimately enhancing the brand's reputation.

Howard Schultz's leadership behaviors, including visionary communication, empowerment, open communication, adaptability, social responsibility, customer engagement, and employee engagement, played integral roles in Starbucks' success. These behaviors aligned with his transformational leadership style and created a culture that valued not only financial performance but also social responsibility, customer loyalty, and employee satisfaction. Schultz's leadership demonstrated the importance of specific behaviors in achieving organizational objectives and making a meaningful impact on the coffee industry.

Identifying Key Behaviors that Define Effective Leadership

Identifying key behaviors that define effective leadership involves pinpointing the specific actions, qualities, and conduct that contribute to a leader's ability to guide, inspire, and achieve success within an organization or team. It necessitates a comprehensive examination of a leader's behavior in various contexts, such as communication skills, decision-making processes, conflict resolution methods, and interpersonal interactions. Effective leadership behaviors often encompass qualities like active listening, clear and transparent communication, adaptability, empathy, decisiveness, ethical conduct, and the ability to motivate and inspire others. Identifying these behaviors is essential because it allows organizations to cultivate and reinforce leadership skills, provides a framework for assessing leadership effectiveness, and offers a basis for leadership development and training programs. Recognizing and fostering these key behaviors is instrumental in nurturing leadership talent and building a positive and productive work environment.

Communication as a Keystone Behavior

Communication as a keystone behavior refers to the central and foundational role that effective communication plays in leadership and interpersonal interactions. Just as a keystone in an arch holds the entire structure together, communication serves as the linchpin that binds leaders and teams, enabling collaboration, understanding, and alignment. It encompasses not only the spoken or written words but also active listening, non-verbal cues, and the ability to convey ideas, vision, and expectations clearly and persuasively. When communication is executed effectively, it fosters transparency, trust, and open dialogue within an organization. It allows leaders to convey their vision, provide guidance, resolve conflicts, and offer feedback. Recognizing communication as a keystone behavior emphasizes its pivotal role in leadership, as it underpins successful collaboration, decision-making, and the overall functioning of teams and organizations.

Role of communication in leadership

The critical role of communication in leadership cannot be overstated; it is a fundamental and multifaceted aspect that permeates every facet of leadership. Here is an in-depth exploration of its importance:

1. **Clarity of Vision and Direction:** Effective communication allows leaders to articulate their vision, mission, and objectives clearly. When leaders can convey their ideas and goals in a concise and understandable manner, team members are more likely to align with the vision and work toward shared objectives.

2. **Building Trust and Credibility:** Communication is at the heart of trust-building. Open, honest, and transparent communication fosters trust between leaders and team members. Leaders who consistently communicate with integrity and authenticity are more likely to earn the trust and respect of their teams.

3. **Conflict Resolution:** Conflict is an inevitable part of any organization. Strong communication skills enable leaders to address conflicts promptly and constructively. Effective communication can help de-escalate tensions, promote understanding, and facilitate resolution, thus maintaining a harmonious work environment.

4. **Motivation and Inspiration:** Leaders use communication to inspire and motivate their teams. By sharing stories, highlighting achievements, and providing positive feedback, leaders can boost team morale and engagement. Effective communication helps team members feel valued and appreciated, which can lead to increased productivity and commitment.

5. **Fostering Collaboration:** In a collaborative work environment, effective communication is essential. Leaders who promote open communication channels encourage team members to share ideas, collaborate on projects, and contribute their expertise. This collaborative spirit can lead to innovation and improved problem-solving.

6. **Adaptability and Flexibility:** Effective leaders are adaptable, and communication plays a crucial role in this aspect of leadership. Leaders must be able to communicate changes in direction, strategies, or priorities clearly and sensitively. Transparent communication helps team members understand the reasons behind changes and adapt more smoothly.

7. **Listening Skills:** Leadership is not just about speaking but also about active listening. Leaders who actively listen to their team members demonstrate empathy and respect. They gain insights, understand concerns, and can make more informed decisions.

8. **Influence and Persuasion:** Leadership often involves influencing others to support a particular idea, project, or direction. Effective communication allows leaders to persuade and convince others by presenting compelling arguments, evidence, and rationale.

9. **Crisis Management:** During challenging times, such as crises or emergencies, communication is critical. Leaders must provide timely and accurate information to reassure

and guide their teams. The absence of communication or misinformation can lead to confusion and panic.

10. **Feedback and Development:** Regular feedback is essential for personal and professional growth. Leaders who provide constructive feedback and communicate development opportunities help their team members improve their skills and reach their potential.

Communication is the lifeblood of effective leadership. It facilitates clarity of vision, trust-building, conflict resolution, motivation, collaboration, adaptability, active listening, influence, crisis management, and feedback. Leaders who prioritize and excel in communication are more likely to inspire, guide, and lead their teams to success while creating a positive and productive organizational culture.

Strategies for enhancing communication skills

Enhancing communication skills among leaders is a continuous process that involves self-awareness, practice, and feedback. Here are some effective strategies for leaders to improve their communication skills:

1. **Active Listening:** Leaders should practice active listening by giving their full attention when team members are speaking. This means refraining from interrupting, asking clarifying questions, and showing empathy and understanding.

2. **Receive and Act on Feedback:** Encourage open and honest feedback from team members and peers about your communication style. Use this feedback to identify areas for improvement and actively work on them.

3. **Invest in Communication Training:** Consider attending workshops or training programs focused on communication

skills. These sessions can provide practical tips and techniques for enhancing communication.

4. **Practice Empathy:** Understanding the perspectives and feelings of others is crucial for effective communication. Leaders should put themselves in others' shoes to empathize with their concerns and needs.

5. **Simplify Messages:** Avoid jargon and overly complex language. Keep messages clear, concise, and easily understandable. Use simple and relatable examples to illustrate your points.

6. **Non-Verbal Communication:** Be mindful of your body language, facial expressions, and tone of voice. These non-verbal cues can convey messages as effectively as words and should align with your intended message.

7. **Tailor Communication to the Audience:** Adapt your communication style to suit the needs and preferences of your audience. Some team members may prefer detailed explanations, while others may prefer a concise summary.

8. **Prepare and Organize:** Before important meetings or presentations, take the time to prepare and organize your thoughts. Having a clear structure and outline can help you convey your message more effectively.

9. **Use Visual Aids:** In presentations or discussions involving complex information, visual aids such as charts, graphs, or slides can help clarify key points and make the information more digestible.

10. **Seek Mentorship:** If possible, seek a mentor or coach who can provide guidance and feedback on your communication skills. Learning from an experienced communicator can be invaluable.

11. **Practice Public Speaking:** Public speaking skills can be beneficial for leaders in various contexts. Join a public speaking group, participate in speaking engagements, or practice delivering presentations regularly.

12. **Regular Check-Ins:** Conduct regular one-on-one or team check-ins to encourage open communication. Create a safe space for team members to share their thoughts, concerns, and ideas.

13. **Role-Play and Mock Scenarios:** Engage in role-playing exercises to practice challenging conversations or scenarios. This can help you become more comfortable and confident in handling difficult situations.

14. **Written Communication Skills:** Don't neglect written communication skills, as written messages, emails, and reports are integral in leadership roles. Pay attention to clarity, grammar, and tone in written communication.

15. **Self-Reflection:** Periodically reflect on your communication experiences and interactions. Consider what went well and what could have been improved. Use this self-awareness to refine your approach.

Enhancing communication skills is an ongoing journey that requires dedication and self-awareness. By implementing these strategies and actively working to improve their communication, leaders can foster better relationships with their teams, promote understanding, and ultimately become more effective in their roles.

Decision-making and problem-solving behaviors

Decision-making and problem-solving behaviors encompass the actions, processes, and approaches individuals or leaders employ when confronted with choices, challenges, or dilemmas. Decision-making involves the selection of a course of action from available alternatives, while problem-solving entails the identification and resolution of issues or obstacles. These behaviors may involve assessing information, weighing pros and cons, considering potential consequences, and making informed choices. Effective decision-making and problem-solving behaviors often include critical thinking, analytical skills, creativity, adaptability, and the ability to collaborate with others to reach optimal solutions. These behaviors are integral to leadership, as leaders are frequently tasked with making strategic decisions and addressing complex problems that impact their teams and organizations. Mastering these behaviors is crucial for leaders to navigate uncertainties, achieve goals, and drive success within their respective domains.

Effective decision-making and problem-solving behaviors

Effective decision-making and problem-solving behaviors are critical components of successful leadership. Here, we'll discuss these behaviors and their significance in leadership:

1. **Critical Thinking:** Leaders with strong critical thinking skills can objectively evaluate information, identify patterns, and consider multiple perspectives. This ability is invaluable for making well-informed decisions and effectively solving complex problems.

2. **Analytical Skills:** Analytical thinking allows leaders to break down complex issues into smaller, more manageable components. By dissecting problems and data, leaders can gain deeper insights and make data-driven decisions.

3. **Data-Driven Approach:** Effective leaders gather and analyze data to inform their decision-making and problem-solving processes. Data provides an objective foundation upon which decisions can be made, reducing the influence of bias.

4. **Creativity and Innovation:** Leaders who encourage creativity and innovation foster a culture where novel solutions to problems can emerge. Encouraging team members to think outside the box can lead to breakthroughs and competitive advantages.

5. **Adaptability:** The ability to adapt to changing circumstances and evolving challenges is crucial for leaders. Being open to new information and adjusting strategies when necessary allows leaders to navigate uncertainties effectively.

6. **Collaboration:** Effective leaders understand the value of teamwork in decision-making and problem-solving. They actively engage with team members, leveraging diverse perspectives and expertise to arrive at more comprehensive and robust solutions.

7. **Effective Communication:** Leaders must be adept at communicating their decisions and problem-solving approaches clearly to their teams. Transparent communication ensures that team members understand the rationale behind decisions and can align with the chosen path.

8. **Ethical Considerations:** Leaders should incorporate ethical considerations into their decision-making and problem-solving processes. Upholding ethical standards ensures that decisions are not only effective but also aligned with values and principles.

9. **Risk Management:** Effective leaders assess potential risks associated with decisions and problem-solving approaches. They weigh the potential rewards against the risks and develop strategies to mitigate adverse outcomes.

10. **Decisiveness:** While thoughtful consideration is important, leaders must also exhibit decisiveness. Procrastination or

indecision can lead to missed opportunities and stalled progress. Effective leaders strike a balance between deliberation and action.

11. **Feedback Incorporation:** Leaders actively seek feedback from team members and stakeholders, integrating diverse viewpoints into their decision-making and problem-solving processes. This fosters a culture of continuous improvement.

12. **Long-Term Perspective:** Effective leaders consider the long-term implications of their decisions and problem-solving approaches, aiming for sustainable solutions that align with organizational goals and values.

In leadership, the combination of these behaviors is crucial for addressing challenges, making strategic decisions, and driving the organization toward success. Leaders who possess these skills and behaviors can navigate complex environments, inspire confidence among their teams, and effectively steer their organizations through both routine and extraordinary circumstances.

Decision-making processes

Leaders can enhance their decision-making processes by implementing a range of strategies and approaches aimed at improving the quality, effectiveness, and efficiency of their decisions. Here are key ways in which leaders can enhance their decision-making:

1. **Develop Self-Awareness:** Leaders should start by gaining a deep understanding of their own decision-making biases and tendencies. Self-awareness allows them to recognize their strengths and weaknesses, enabling better decision-making.

2. **Gather Relevant Information:** Effective decision-making requires a solid foundation of information. Leaders should proactively seek out and gather all necessary data, facts, and

insights before making a decision. This may involve consulting experts, conducting research, or analyzing relevant metrics.

3. **Consider Alternatives:** Instead of rushing into a decision, leaders should explore multiple options and alternatives. Evaluating various courses of action helps ensure a more comprehensive and informed choice.

4. **Seek Diverse Perspectives:** Encourage input from team members and colleagues with diverse backgrounds and viewpoints. Different perspectives can uncover blind spots and lead to more creative solutions.

5. **Risk Assessment:** Leaders should assess the potential risks and rewards associated with each decision. A clear understanding of the risks allows for better risk mitigation strategies.

6. **Utilize Decision-Making Models:** Familiarize themselves with decision-making models and frameworks, such as SWOT analysis, cost-benefit analysis, or the Eisenhower Matrix, which can provide structured approaches to decision-making.

7. **Set Clear Criteria:** Define clear criteria and priorities that align with the goals and values of the organization. These criteria can serve as a guide for evaluating alternatives and making decisions that align with the organization's mission.

8. **Time Management:** Leaders should be mindful of time constraints and prioritize decisions accordingly. Some decisions require immediate attention, while others can be more thoroughly deliberated.

9. **Avoid Overthinking:** While thoughtful consideration is important, leaders should avoid overthinking or analysis paralysis. Sometimes, making a timely decision, even if it's not perfect, is better than prolonged indecision.

10. **Embrace Failure as a Learning Opportunity:** Leaders should recognize that not every decision will be perfect. When decisions do not yield the desired outcomes, view them as opportunities for learning and improvement.

11. **Communication:** Clearly communicate the rationale behind decisions to team members and stakeholders. Transparency helps build trust and understanding.

12. **Continuous Improvement:** Continuously seek to improve decision-making processes by soliciting feedback, conducting post-decision evaluations, and reflecting on past decisions.

13. **Mental and Emotional Well-being:** Ensure leaders are mentally and emotionally well-equipped to make decisions. Practices like mindfulness, stress management, and maintaining a healthy work-life balance can enhance decision-making.

14. **Ethical Considerations:** Leaders should always consider the ethical implications of their decisions and ensure they align with the organization's ethical standards and values.

15. **Delegate When Appropriate:** Leaders should recognize when it's suitable to delegate decision-making authority to team members who are closer to the situation or possess relevant expertise.

Improving decision-making is an ongoing process, and leaders should be committed to learning from their experiences and continuously refining their decision-making skills. By employing these strategies, leaders can make more effective, well-informed, and impactful decisions that benefit both their organizations and teams.

Conflict Resolution and Negotiation Behaviors

Conflict resolution and negotiation behaviors refer to the actions, strategies, and approaches individuals or leaders employ to address and resolve conflicts, disputes, or disagreements within a team, organization, or interpersonal relationships. Conflict resolution involves finding solutions to conflicts or tensions, while negotiation focuses on reaching agreements or compromises among parties with differing interests or positions. These behaviors often encompass skills such as active listening, empathy, effective communication, problem-solving, and the ability to de-escalate conflicts constructively. Conflict resolution and negotiation are essential leadership skills, as leaders frequently encounter conflicting interests, differing viewpoints, and interpersonal disputes. Mastery of these behaviors is crucial for maintaining harmonious relationships, fostering collaboration, and achieving mutually beneficial outcomes in both professional and personal contexts.

Analysis of conflict resolution and negotiation skills

Conflict resolution and negotiation skills are undeniably vital leadership behaviors with far-reaching implications for organizational success and team dynamics. Here's an analysis of their significance:

1. **Enhanced Collaboration:** Effective conflict resolution and negotiation skills promote collaboration and teamwork. Leaders who can navigate conflicts and disputes constructively foster an environment where diverse ideas are embraced, leading to innovation and improved problem-solving.

2. **Conflict Prevention:** Leaders skilled in conflict resolution can identify and address potential conflicts early, preventing them from escalating into more significant issues. This

proactive approach minimizes disruptions and maintains a harmonious work environment.

3. **Improved Decision-Making:** Conflict resolution and negotiation skills enable leaders to facilitate productive discussions and reach consensus. When team members feel heard and valued, they are more likely to support and implement decisions, enhancing decision-making processes.

4. **Stakeholder Management:** Effective negotiation skills are crucial when dealing with external stakeholders, such as clients, suppliers, or partners. Leaders who can negotiate mutually beneficial agreements build strong relationships and secure favorable deals.

5. **Conflict Transformation:** Skillful conflict resolution goes beyond surface-level solutions. It delves into the underlying issues, transforming conflicts into opportunities for growth and positive change within the organization.

6. **Conflict Diversity:** In diverse workplaces, leaders must navigate conflicts arising from differing cultural backgrounds, perspectives, and values. Proficiency in cross-cultural negotiation and conflict resolution is essential for fostering inclusivity and equity.

7. **Trust and Respect:** Successful conflict resolution builds trust and respect among team members. When conflicts are resolved fairly and respectfully, it strengthens the bonds between individuals and enhances overall team morale.

8. **Leadership Credibility:** Leaders who demonstrate proficiency in conflict resolution and negotiation earn credibility and respect from their teams. Team members are more likely to trust leaders who can navigate challenging situations effectively.

9. **Cost Savings:** Effective conflict resolution and negotiation can lead to cost savings for organizations. Resolving

disputes without resorting to litigation or protracted conflicts reduces legal expenses and other associated costs.

10. **Employee Retention:** A workplace marked by healthy conflict resolution and negotiation practices is more attractive to employees. High employee morale and satisfaction contribute to reduced turnover rates.

11. **Innovation and Creativity:** Conflict resolution encourages open dialogue and the sharing of diverse perspectives. This, in turn, fosters an environment where innovation and creativity thrive, as individuals feel safe expressing new ideas without fear of conflict.

12. **Conflict Resolution Models:** Leaders can adopt established conflict resolution models like win-win, compromise, or collaborate, depending on the situation. These models provide structured approaches to addressing conflicts effectively.

Conflict resolution and negotiation skills are indispensable leadership behaviors that promote collaboration, improve decision-making, build trust, and enhance organizational effectiveness. Leaders who prioritize these skills create a positive work culture where conflicts are seen as opportunities for growth and where individuals feel empowered to contribute their best efforts. Ultimately, these skills contribute significantly to the overall success and sustainability of both leaders and their organizations.

Techniques for Managing Conflicts and Negotiations

Managing conflicts and negotiations effectively requires a combination of strategies and techniques to facilitate constructive resolutions and mutually beneficial agreements. Here are some techniques that leaders can employ:

Conflict Management Techniques

1. **Active Listening:** Actively listen to all parties involved to understand their perspectives, concerns, and emotions. This demonstrates empathy and helps uncover the root causes of the conflict.

2. **Stay Calm and Neutral:** Maintain composure and avoid taking sides in the conflict. A neutral stance encourages open dialogue and minimizes defensiveness.

3. **Define the Problem:** Clearly identify and define the issues at the core of the conflict. Ensure all parties have a shared understanding of what needs to be addressed.

4. **Encourage Open Communication:** Create a safe space for open and honest communication. Set ground rules that promote respectful discourse and encourage everyone to share their views.

5. **Mediation:** Consider involving a neutral third party, such as a mediator or facilitator, to help navigate the conflict and guide discussions toward resolution.

6. **Brainstorm Solutions:** Collaboratively generate potential solutions to the conflict. Encourage creativity and exploration of various options.

7. **Conflict Resolution Models:** Employ established conflict resolution models, such as the Thomas-Kilmann Conflict Mode Instrument (TKI) or the Win-Win approach, to structure the resolution process effectively.

8. **Agree on Action Steps:** Once a resolution is reached, outline specific action steps and timelines for implementation. Ensure all parties commit to these steps.

9. **Follow-Up:** Periodically follow up to assess progress and ensure that the conflict resolution remains effective. Address any new issues that may arise promptly.

Negotiation Techniques

1. **Prepare Thoroughly:** Prior to negotiations, research and gather relevant information about the issues, parties involved, and potential solutions. Preparation is key to building a strong negotiation strategy.

2. **Set Clear Objectives:** Define your goals and desired outcomes clearly. Know what you are willing to concede and where you must stand firm.

3. **Best Alternative to a Negotiated Agreement (BATNA):** Identify your BATNA, which is your alternative plan if negotiations fail. Understanding your BATNA provides leverage and informs your negotiation strategy.

4. **Active Listening:** Just as in conflict resolution, active listening is critical in negotiations. Understand the other party's needs, concerns, and interests to find areas of compromise.

5. **Use Effective Communication:** Clearly and persuasively communicate your position and the benefits of your proposal. Be concise and avoid confrontational language.

6. **Seek Win-Win Solutions:** Aim for solutions that benefit all parties involved. This approach fosters goodwill and increases the likelihood of reaching an agreement.

7. **Trade-offs:** Be willing to make concessions, but do so strategically. In return for giving up something, request something of value in return.

8. **Maintain Flexibility:** Be adaptable and open to exploring alternative solutions. Negotiations often require compromise and adjustment to reach an agreement.

9. **Pause for Reflection:** If negotiations become heated or reach an impasse, consider taking a break to allow both parties to cool off and reflect on their positions.

10. **Put Agreements in Writing:** Once an agreement is reached, document the terms and expectations in a written contract or agreement to avoid misunderstandings later.

11. **Build Relationships:** Focus on building positive relationships throughout the negotiation process. Strong relationships can lead to more successful negotiations in the future.

Effective conflict management and negotiation require a combination of these techniques, adapted to the specific circumstances and parties involved. Leaders who can navigate conflicts and negotiations skillfully are better equipped to achieve positive outcomes and maintain productive relationships within their organizations.

Relationship Leadership

Surrounding Attractions and Interactions is a concept that underscores the pivotal role of relationships and interpersonal dynamics in effective leadership. It emphasizes that leaders are not isolated figures but are deeply intertwined with their teams, colleagues, and stakeholders. The phrase "Surrounding Attractions" suggests that leaders must create an environment that attracts and retains talented individuals, fostering a culture of trust, respect, and collaboration. This involves building strong connections, inspiring loyalty, and being a source of motivation. "Interactions" emphasize the day-to-day engagement and communication between leaders and their teams. Relationship leadership centers on the idea that leaders who prioritize building meaningful and positive relationships with those they lead can enhance team cohesion, productivity, and ultimately, organizational success. It acknowledges that leadership extends beyond mere authority, recognizing that effective leaders understand and leverage the power of human connections.

Understanding relationship leadership involves recognizing that effective leadership is not solely about positional authority but is deeply rooted in building and nurturing positive and meaningful relationships with individuals, teams, and stakeholders. It emphasizes that leadership goes beyond directing tasks and making decisions; it's about fostering trust, respect, and collaboration. Leaders who practice relationship leadership prioritize connecting with their team members on a personal level, understanding their needs, motivations, and aspirations. They actively engage in open and empathetic communication, actively listen to concerns, and provide support. This approach acknowledges that people are not merely resources but valued contributors to the organization, and strong relationships between leaders and their teams are essential for achieving common goals, promoting teamwork, and creating a positive work culture. Understanding relationship leadership is about recognizing that the success of a leader is often intertwined with the quality of their interpersonal interactions and their ability to inspire and motivate through authentic connections.

Relationship-based leadership is a multifaceted approach that recognizes the significance of building and maintaining positive and meaningful relationships within the context of leadership. It encompasses several key principles and characteristics:

1. **Trust and Respect:** Relationship-based leadership begins with trust and respect as foundational elements. Leaders earn the trust of their team members through consistency, honesty, and reliability. They also respect the unique perspectives, skills, and contributions of each individual.

2. **Open and Transparent Communication:** Effective communication is at the heart of relationship-based leadership. Leaders foster open dialogue, actively listen to team members, and encourage them to voice their ideas, concerns, and feedback. Transparent communication builds transparency and mutual understanding.

3. **Empathy and Understanding:** Leaders practice empathy by understanding and acknowledging the feelings, needs, and experiences of their team members. They consider the human aspect of leadership and show compassion when team members face challenges or setbacks.

4. **Building Connections:** Relationship-based leaders invest time and effort in building personal connections with their team members. They get to know individuals on a deeper level, learning about their aspirations, strengths, and areas of development.

5. **Individualized Leadership:** Recognizing that each team member is unique, relationship-based leaders tailor their leadership approaches to align with the preferences and needs of each individual. This personalized approach enhances engagement and motivation.

6. **Collaborative Decision-Making:** Leaders involve team members in decision-making processes whenever possible. They seek diverse input and perspectives to arrive at more informed and inclusive decisions.

7. **Conflict Resolution:** Conflict is addressed in a constructive manner, with a focus on maintaining and repairing relationships. Leaders help team members navigate conflicts and encourage open dialogue to find mutually agreeable solutions.

8. **Recognition and Appreciation:** Relationship-based leaders regularly acknowledge and appreciate the contributions of their team members. They provide positive feedback and recognition to reinforce desired behaviors and efforts.

9. **Mentorship and Development:** Leaders actively support the professional and personal development of their team members. They provide guidance, mentorship, and opportunities for growth.

10. **Crisis Management:** During challenging times or crises, relationship-based leaders are a source of stability and reassurance. They communicate openly, provide support, and help team members navigate uncertainties.

11. **Long-Term Perspective:** Relationship-based leadership takes a long-term view, recognizing that building strong relationships is an ongoing process. Leaders invest in nurturing connections that endure over time.

12. **Positive Organizational Culture:** By fostering positive relationships, leaders contribute to the creation of a healthy and inclusive organizational culture. This culture, in turn, attracts and retains talent, fosters innovation, and enhances overall organizational performance.

Relationship-based leadership prioritizes people and relationships as the driving forces behind effective leadership. It acknowledges that leadership is not solely about authority and control but also about the ability to connect, inspire, and collaborate with others. Leaders who embrace this approach tend to create a work environment where individuals feel valued, motivated, and empowered, ultimately leading to increased engagement, productivity, and organizational success.

Importance of Interpersonal Dynamics

The shift towards recognizing the importance of interpersonal dynamics in leadership reflects a fundamental change in how leadership is understood and practiced. Traditionally, leadership was often associated with a top-down approach focused on authority, decision-making, and task management. However, contemporary leadership theories and practices have evolved to emphasize the critical role of relationships, communication, and collaboration in effective leadership. Several key factors contribute to this shift:

1. **Team-Centric Work Environments:** In today's collaborative work environments, teams are central to achieving organizational goals. Effective leadership is increasingly seen as the ability to facilitate teamwork, promote synergy, and build trust among team members.

2. **Diversity and Inclusion:** Diverse workplaces with individuals from various backgrounds and perspectives require leaders who can navigate and leverage these differences. Understanding interpersonal dynamics is essential for fostering inclusivity and equity.

3. **Employee Engagement:** Research consistently shows that engaged employees are more productive and committed. Leaders who prioritize interpersonal relationships can create an environment where team members feel valued, heard, and motivated.

4. **Emotional Intelligence:** The concept of emotional intelligence, which includes self-awareness, empathy, and social skills, has gained prominence in leadership. Leaders with high emotional intelligence are better equipped to understand and manage interpersonal dynamics effectively.

5. **Collaborative Problem-Solving:** Complex challenges often require collaboration and the exchange of ideas. Leaders who can facilitate open communication and collaboration are more likely to find innovative solutions.

6. **Flat Hierarchies:** Many organizations are moving towards flatter hierarchies, where decision-making is distributed. In such structures, leaders rely on their ability to influence and connect with others rather than relying solely on positional power.

7. **Customer-Centric Focus:** In customer-focused industries, understanding customer needs and feedback is critical. Leaders who excel in interpersonal dynamics can gather

valuable customer insights and translate them into actionable strategies.

8. **Adaptive Leadership:** Leaders need to adapt to rapidly changing environments and uncertainties. Interpersonal skills enable leaders to lead in ambiguous situations by maintaining trust and providing stability.

9. **Crisis Management:** During crises, effective leaders must communicate clearly, provide reassurance, and manage stakeholder relationships effectively. Interpersonal dynamics play a crucial role in crisis leadership.

10. **Leadership Styles:** Transformational leadership, which emphasizes inspiration and motivation, is increasingly valued. This style relies heavily on leaders' ability to connect with and inspire their teams.

The shift towards recognizing the importance of interpersonal dynamics in leadership reflects the evolving nature of work, the value of diverse teams, and the recognition that leadership is not solely about authority but also about relationships, collaboration, and emotional intelligence. Leaders who embrace this shift are better equipped to navigate the complexities of today's organizations and to inspire and motivate their teams to achieve shared goals.

Interpersonal Skills and Relationship Building

Interpersonal skills and relationship building are crucial components of effective leadership and successful interactions in both professional and personal contexts. Interpersonal skills encompass a range of abilities and behaviors that enable individuals to communicate, connect, and collaborate with others effectively. These skills include active listening, empathy, effective communication, conflict resolution, and the ability to convey ideas and information clearly and persuasively.

Relationship building, on the other hand, extends beyond mere interactions and involves the intentional effort to establish and nurture positive and meaningful connections with others. It is about fostering trust, mutual respect, and rapport. Relationship building requires authenticity, patience, and the willingness to invest time and energy in getting to know individuals on a deeper level.

Interpersonal skills are the tools individuals use to engage with others, while relationship building is the ongoing process of cultivating and strengthening these connections. Together, these concepts emphasize the importance of genuine and empathetic communication, fostering collaboration, and building a network of trusted relationships, all of which are foundational for effective leadership and personal growth.

Key Interpersonal Skills

Effective leaders possess a range of key interpersonal skills that enable them to build strong relationships, communicate effectively, and navigate complex interpersonal dynamics. Here are some essential interpersonal skills that leaders should possess:

1. **Active Listening:** Active listening involves not only hearing what others are saying but also fully understanding their perspectives and emotions. Leaders who actively listen demonstrate empathy and create an environment where team members feel heard and valued.

2. **Empathy:** Empathy is the ability to understand and share the feelings of others. Leaders with empathy can connect on a deeper level with team members, demonstrating understanding and support in both challenging and positive situations.

3. **Effective Communication:** Clear and concise communication is a hallmark of effective leadership. Leaders should convey their ideas, expectations, and

feedback clearly and persuasively, both in written and spoken communication.

4. **Conflict Resolution:** Leaders should be skilled in addressing and resolving conflicts constructively. This includes the ability to remain neutral, listen to all parties, and facilitate discussions that lead to mutually beneficial solutions.

5. **Emotional Intelligence:** Emotional intelligence involves recognizing and managing one's own emotions and understanding and influencing the emotions of others. Leaders with high emotional intelligence can navigate interpersonal relationships more effectively.

6. **Adaptability:** In rapidly changing environments, leaders must be adaptable and open to new ideas and approaches. Being willing to adjust to different personalities and situations enhances leadership effectiveness.

7. **Negotiation Skills:** Negotiation skills are essential for reaching agreements and compromises in various situations. Leaders who can negotiate effectively can find solutions that satisfy all parties involved.

8. **Feedback and Coaching:** Providing constructive feedback and coaching is a critical skill for leadership development. Leaders should offer feedback that is specific, actionable, and focused on growth.

9. **Cultural Sensitivity:** In diverse workplaces, cultural sensitivity is vital. Leaders should be aware of and respectful of cultural differences, recognizing how they can impact interactions and communication.

10. **Influence and Persuasion:** Leaders often need to influence others to support their ideas or initiatives. The ability to persuade and convince others through logical reasoning and compelling arguments is invaluable.

11. **Team Building:** Leaders should know how to foster a sense of unity and collaboration within their teams. Team-building skills involve bringing diverse individuals together to work toward common goals.

12. **Networking:** Building a network of professional relationships both within and outside the organization can provide valuable support, insights, and opportunities for a leader's career and the organization's growth.

13. **Conflict Avoidance:** While conflict resolution is essential, leaders should also possess skills for conflict avoidance through effective communication, proactive problem-solving, and creating a positive work environment.

These interpersonal skills collectively empower leaders to connect with their teams, build trust, inspire motivation, and effectively navigate the complexities of leadership. Leaders who continually develop and refine these skills are better equipped to foster productive working relationships and drive organizational success.

Strategies for Building Strong Relationship

Building strong relationships within teams and organizations is a fundamental aspect of effective leadership. Here are some strategies to help leaders foster positive and enduring relationships:

1. **Lead by Example:** Demonstrate the behaviors and values you expect from your team members. When leaders exhibit professionalism, respect, and integrity, they set a standard for others to follow.

2. **Open and Honest Communication:** Encourage open, transparent, and frequent communication. Create an environment where team members feel safe sharing their

thoughts, concerns, and ideas. Listen actively and provide constructive feedback.

3. **Get to Know Your Team:** Take the time to understand each team member individually. Learn about their strengths, weaknesses, career aspirations, and personal interests. This knowledge allows you to tailor your interactions and support to each person.

4. **Regular Check-Ins:** Schedule regular one-on-one meetings with team members to discuss their goals, challenges, and progress. These check-ins demonstrate your commitment to their growth and well-being.

5. **Recognize and Appreciate:** Acknowledge and celebrate achievements, both big and small. Publicly recognize team members for their contributions and efforts. Feeling appreciated boosts morale and reinforces positive behavior.

6. **Empower and Delegate:** Empower team members by delegating responsibilities and decision-making authority. Trusting your team fosters a sense of ownership and responsibility, enhancing their commitment to the organization's goals.

7. **Resolve Conflicts Constructively:** When conflicts arise, address them promptly and constructively. Encourage open dialogue, listen to all perspectives, and work towards mutually agreeable solutions. Conflict resolution can strengthen relationships when handled well.

8. **Promote Inclusivity:** Create an inclusive work environment where diversity is valued and everyone feels welcome. Encourage diverse perspectives and foster a culture of respect and equality.

9. **Provide Development Opportunities:** Support your team's professional and personal growth. Offer training,

mentorship, and opportunities for skill development. Show that you are invested in their long-term success.

10. **Lead with Empathy:** Understand and consider the feelings and perspectives of your team members. Show empathy during challenging times and offer support when needed. Compassion strengthens bonds.

11. **Celebrate Milestones:** Recognize personal milestones and achievements outside of work, such as birthdays, anniversaries, or life events. This personal touch demonstrates that you care about your team members as individuals.

12. **Encourage Collaboration:** Foster a collaborative culture where team members are encouraged to work together, share knowledge, and learn from one another. Create opportunities for cross-functional projects and teamwork.

13. **Be Accessible:** Be approachable and accessible to your team. Maintain an open-door policy or provide other means for team members to reach out when they need guidance or support.

14. **Promote Work-Life Balance:** Encourage a healthy work-life balance and lead by example. Support flexible work arrangements when possible and respect personal time boundaries.

15. **Feedback and Growth:** Provide constructive feedback for improvement while highlighting strengths. Offer guidance on how team members can further develop their skills and advance their careers.

Building strong relationships within teams and organizations is an ongoing process that requires dedication and a genuine commitment to the well-being and success of your team members. By consistently applying these strategies, leaders can create a cohesive and motivated team that collaboratively works towards achieving common goals.

Influence and Persuasion in Leadership

Influence and persuasion in leadership are two closely related concepts that refer to a leader's ability to guide and inspire others to adopt certain viewpoints, make specific decisions, or take particular actions. Influence involves the capacity to affect the thoughts, behaviors, and beliefs of individuals or groups, often through personal credibility, expertise, or charisma. Persuasion, on the other hand, is the art of convincing or motivating others to willingly embrace a particular idea, plan, or course of action. Both influence and persuasion are integral to effective leadership as they enable leaders to rally support, gain buy-in, and navigate complex organizational dynamics. Successful leaders leverage these skills to build consensus, overcome resistance, and drive positive change within their teams and organizations, ultimately contributing to the achievement of shared objectives.

How Leaders Use Influence and Persuasion to Achieve Goals

Leaders use influence and persuasion as powerful tools to achieve their goals by effectively mobilizing their teams and stakeholders. Here's how these strategies are employed:

1. **Building Credibility:** Leaders establish credibility through their expertise, track record, and consistency. When team members and stakeholders trust a leader's judgment, they are more likely to be influenced by their ideas and vision.

2. **Clear and Compelling Communication:** Leaders use persuasive communication to articulate their goals and vision clearly and passionately. They employ storytelling,

data, and compelling narratives to make their message resonate with others.

3. **Stakeholder Alignment:** Leaders identify key stakeholders and work to align their interests with organizational goals. They engage in conversations that demonstrate how achieving these goals benefits all parties involved.

4. **Inclusive Decision-Making:** Leaders involve team members and stakeholders in the decision-making process, seeking their input and ideas. This not only fosters ownership but also increases the chances of achieving consensus.

5. **Social Proof:** Leaders leverage social proof by showcasing the support and endorsement of others. When team members see colleagues or respected individuals backing a leader's vision, they are more inclined to follow suit.

6. **Emotional Appeal:** Leaders understand the power of emotions in persuasion. They connect with others on an emotional level, empathizing with their concerns and demonstrating a genuine commitment to their well-being and success.

7. **Reciprocity:** Leaders initiate positive actions and gestures, creating a sense of reciprocity. When they go above and beyond to support their teams, team members are more likely to reciprocate by supporting the leader's vision and goals.

8. **Leveraging Authority:** Leaders who possess positional authority can use it judiciously to influence decisions and actions. However, they do so while respecting the autonomy and input of team members.

9. **Adaptability:** Effective leaders tailor their approach to their audience. They understand the unique preferences, motivations, and communication styles of individuals and adjust their persuasion strategies accordingly.

10. **Framing and Context:** Leaders frame their goals and messages in a way that resonates with the values and aspirations of their audience. They consider the cultural, organizational, and contextual factors that influence perceptions.

11. **Overcoming Resistance:** Leaders anticipate and address resistance by empathetically listening to concerns, providing evidence, and offering solutions to mitigate potential challenges.

12. **Consistency and Commitment:** Leaders demonstrate unwavering commitment to their goals, reinforcing their dedication through consistent actions and messaging over time.

13. **Measurable Outcomes:** Leaders provide concrete metrics and indicators that highlight progress toward achieving the goals. This data-driven approach reinforces the persuasiveness of their vision.

14. **Empowerment:** Leaders empower individuals by giving them the autonomy and resources to contribute to the achievement of goals. When people feel their contributions are valued, they become more invested in the leader's vision.

15. **Celebrating Success:** Leaders acknowledge and celebrate milestones and achievements along the way. Recognizing progress reinforces commitment and motivates continued effort.

Leaders use influence and persuasion as strategic tools to rally support, foster alignment, and drive actions that lead to goal attainment. Effective leadership involves a keen understanding of human behavior, effective communication, and the ability to build consensus and commitment among diverse groups of individuals.

Case Study: Successful Relationship Leadership

A successful relationship leadership case study exemplifies how effective leadership built on strong interpersonal connections and relationship-building can yield positive outcomes within an organization or team. In such a case, a leader has displayed exceptional skills in fostering trust, communication, and collaboration among team members. This leader likely values and invests time in getting to know team members individually, understanding their strengths and weaknesses, and aligning their goals with those of the organization. By actively listening, offering support, and demonstrating empathy, the leader has created an environment where team members feel valued, motivated, and empowered. As a result, the team experiences higher morale, improved communication, enhanced problem-solving abilities, and a shared commitment to achieving common objectives. Ultimately, the success of the team or organization in this case study can be attributed, at least in part, to the leader's ability to leverage strong relationships to drive productivity, innovation, and organizational excellence.

Baba Banda Singh Bahadur, a revered Sikh leader and military commander in the 18th century, provides a compelling example of relationship-based leadership. His approach was grounded in building strong interpersonal connections and fostering trust among his followers, which played a crucial role in his success:

1. **Inclusivity:** Baba Banda Singh Bahadur welcomed individuals from diverse backgrounds into his ranks, emphasizing the importance of unity and a shared mission over distinctions of caste or religion. This inclusive approach strengthened the bonds among his followers.

2. **Trust and Empowerment:** He built trust among his soldiers by treating them as equals and empowering them to actively participate in decision-making. This approach not only

boosted their confidence but also reinforced their commitment to the cause.

3. **Communication:** Effective communication was a hallmark of his leadership. He engaged in open dialogue with his followers, actively listening to their ideas and concerns. This transparent communication fostered a sense of belonging and trust.

4. **Shared Values:** Baba Banda Singh Bahadur instilled a strong sense of shared values, emphasizing principles of justice, equality, and religious freedom. These shared values united his diverse army and inspired their dedication to the cause.

5. **Conflict Resolution:** When conflicts arose within his ranks, he addressed them with empathy and fairness. His approach to conflict resolution reinforced the sense of belonging and unity among his followers.

6. **Recognition:** He provided support and recognition to his soldiers by acknowledging their bravery and sacrifices. This boosted morale and motivated them to continue fighting for their shared objectives.

7. **Leading by Example:** Baba Banda Singh Bahadur led by example, demonstrating courage, resilience, and selflessness in the face of adversity. His personal sacrifices inspired unwavering loyalty among his followers.

8. **Long-Term Vision:** His leadership was guided by a long-term vision of justice and religious freedom. He tirelessly worked toward achieving this vision, inspiring others to remain committed to the cause even in the most challenging circumstances.

Baba Banda Singh Bahadur's relationship-based leadership was instrumental in rallying a diverse group of individuals behind a shared mission of justice and freedom. His ability to build trust, communicate effectively, and foster unity among his followers demonstrates the profound impact of relationship-based leadership, not only in building strong teams but also in driving societal change and upholding shared values.

Analysis of the Interpersonal Dynamics that Contributed to Success

The success of Baba Banda Singh Bahadur as a leader can be attributed to several critical interpersonal dynamics that he cultivated among his followers. These dynamics were instrumental in achieving his goals and fostering a sense of unity and commitment within his diverse army:

1. **Inclusivity and Unity:** Baba Banda Singh Bahadur's emphasis on inclusivity, regardless of caste or religion, fostered a sense of unity among his followers. By transcending social divisions, he created a cohesive and diverse force that was united by a common cause—justice and religious freedom.

2. **Trust and Empowerment:** The leader's trust in his soldiers and empowerment of individuals within his ranks instilled confidence and a sense of responsibility among his followers. They felt valued and capable of contributing to the cause, which motivated them to perform at their best.

3. **Open and Transparent Communication:** Effective communication was a cornerstone of his leadership. By engaging in open and transparent dialogue, Baba Banda Singh Bahadur ensured that his followers' voices were heard. This communication helped to address concerns, build consensus, and strengthen bonds.

4. **Shared Values:** The leader instilled a strong sense of shared values among his followers. Principles of justice, equality, and religious freedom served as the foundation of their

collective mission. These shared values not only united diverse individuals but also inspired their unwavering dedication.

5. **Conflict Resolution:** Baba Banda Singh Bahadur's empathetic approach to conflict resolution reinforced the sense of belonging and unity within his ranks. By addressing conflicts with fairness and empathy, he prevented division and maintained a harmonious atmosphere.

6. **Recognition and Motivation:** Providing recognition and support to his soldiers for their bravery and sacrifices boosted morale and motivation. This acknowledgment reinforced their commitment to the cause and to their leader.

7. **Leading by Example:** The leader's personal sacrifices, courage, and unwavering commitment to justice set a powerful example for his followers. They respected and admired his dedication, which inspired them to emulate his selflessness.

8. **Long-Term Vision:** His leadership was guided by a long-term vision of justice and religious freedom. This vision provided a sense of purpose and direction, enabling his followers to persevere even in the face of formidable challenges.

The interpersonal dynamics cultivated by Baba Banda Singh Bahadur, including inclusivity, trust, effective communication, shared values, conflict resolution, recognition, leading by example, and a compelling long-term vision, collectively contributed to the success of his leadership. These dynamics created a sense of belonging and commitment among his followers, resulting in their unwavering dedication to the cause of justice and religious freedom.

Interpersonal Dynamics in Leadership

Exploring interpersonal dynamics in leadership involves a deep examination of the complex and multifaceted interactions that occur within a leadership context. It delves into the ways leaders and their team members communicate, collaborate, build relationships, and influence one another. Interpersonal dynamics encompass a wide range of elements, including trust, communication styles, conflict resolution, motivation, empathy, and the overall group dynamics that shape decision-making and team cohesion. Understanding these dynamics is crucial for effective leadership, as it allows leaders to navigate interpersonal relationships, build strong teams, and inspire individuals to work cohesively toward shared goals. By exploring interpersonal dynamics, leaders can enhance their self-awareness, adapt their leadership styles, and cultivate positive and productive working relationships, ultimately contributing to the success of their teams and organizations.

Team Dynamics and Group Leadership

Team dynamics and group leadership pertain to the intricate interactions and behaviors that occur when individuals come together to work as a collective unit, whether in a formal team or informal group setting. Team dynamics involve the complex interplay of factors such as team cohesion, roles and responsibilities, communication patterns, and conflict resolution within a group. Effective group leadership focuses on guiding, facilitating, and influencing these dynamics to achieve common objectives. Group leaders are responsible for fostering a positive team environment, aligning individual efforts with collective goals, promoting collaboration, and managing conflicts when they arise. Understanding team dynamics and group leadership is essential for orchestrating the collective potential of a group, ensuring that members work together harmoniously and efficiently, and ultimately achieving desired outcomes or results. It involves recognizing the unique strengths and weaknesses of team members, leveraging their diverse skills and perspectives, and providing the necessary guidance and support to maximize their collective performance.

How to navigate team dynamics and group leadership

Leaders navigate team dynamics and group leadership by employing a range of strategies and skills to foster collaboration, communication, and productivity within a team or group. Here's how leaders effectively manage these aspects:

1. **Building Trust:** Leaders understand that trust is foundational to team dynamics. They lead by example, act with integrity, and keep their commitments to build trust among team members. Trust fosters open communication and a sense of security within the group.

2. **Defining Roles and Goals:** Leaders establish clear roles, responsibilities, and objectives for each team member. By defining expectations and ensuring everyone understands their contributions, leaders minimize confusion and conflict.

3. **Effective Communication:** Leaders prioritize clear and open communication within the group. They encourage active listening and provide opportunities for team members to express their ideas, concerns, and feedback. Regular team meetings and updates help maintain transparency.

4. **Conflict Resolution:** Leaders are skilled in managing conflicts constructively. They address disagreements promptly, encouraging respectful dialogue and finding solutions that benefit the team and the organization as a whole.

5. **Motivation and Recognition:** Leaders motivate their teams by recognizing individual and collective achievements. They

provide positive reinforcement, celebrate milestones, and offer constructive feedback to keep team members engaged and motivated.

6. **Empowerment:** Leaders empower team members by giving them autonomy and decision-making authority within their areas of expertise. Empowered team members feel a greater sense of ownership and responsibility for their work.

7. **Adaptability:** Leaders are adaptable and responsive to changing circumstances or team dynamics. They adjust their leadership style to accommodate the needs and preferences of different team members, fostering inclusivity.

8. **Conflict Avoidance:** While addressing conflicts is essential, leaders also aim to create a positive work environment that minimizes unnecessary disputes. By fostering a culture of respect and open communication, leaders reduce the likelihood of conflicts arising.

9. **Team Building:** Leaders actively engage in team-building activities and initiatives to enhance cohesion and camaraderie among team members. These activities can include team-building exercises, retreats, or bonding experiences outside of work.

10. **Cultural Sensitivity:** In diverse teams, leaders demonstrate cultural sensitivity by recognizing and respecting differences in backgrounds, perspectives, and communication styles. They promote an inclusive culture that values diversity.

11. **Feedback and Coaching:** Leaders provide constructive feedback and coaching to help team members develop their skills and reach their potential. They focus on individual growth while emphasizing the importance of collective success.

12. **Decision-Making:** Leaders involve the team in decision-making processes whenever possible. They seek input,

weigh options, and make informed decisions that align with the team's goals and values.

13. **Monitoring Progress:** Leaders track team progress toward goals, ensuring that objectives are met. They offer support and resources when needed and make adjustments to plans as circumstances evolve.

14. **Celebrating Success:** Leaders celebrate team successes, both big and small. Recognizing achievements reinforces the team's sense of accomplishment and motivates continued effort.

Leaders must navigate team dynamics and group leadership with a keen awareness of their team's unique characteristics, challenges, and goals. By effectively managing these dynamics, leaders can create a productive and harmonious work environment where team members are motivated, engaged, and aligned with the organization's mission and objectives.

Strategies for promoting collaboration and synergy

Promoting collaboration and synergy within teams is crucial for achieving collective goals and fostering a positive work environment. Here are strategies that leaders can employ to encourage collaboration and synergy among team members:

1. **Clear Goals and Objectives:** Start with well-defined and shared goals. Ensure that every team member understands the team's purpose and the individual roles and responsibilities needed to achieve those goals.

2. **Effective Communication:** Foster open and transparent communication within the team. Encourage active listening, regular team meetings, and platforms for sharing ideas and feedback. Ensure that everyone has a chance to voice their opinions and concerns.

3. **Building Trust:** Trust is the foundation of collaboration. Leaders should lead by example, be honest, and demonstrate integrity. Encourage team members to trust one another by creating a safe and supportive atmosphere.

4. **Diverse Teams:** Embrace diversity within the team, as it brings different perspectives and ideas to the table. Encourage inclusivity and ensure that all voices are heard and valued.

5. **Roles and Responsibilities:** Clearly define roles and responsibilities for each team member to avoid confusion and duplication of efforts. Ensure that everyone knows their unique contributions to the team's success.

6. **Empowerment:** Empower team members by giving them autonomy and decision-making authority within their areas of expertise. When team members feel trusted and capable, they are more likely to collaborate effectively.

7. **Team-Building Activities:** Organize team-building exercises and activities to strengthen bonds and build camaraderie among team members. These activities can improve interpersonal relationships and communication.

8. **Conflict Resolution:** Equip team members with conflict resolution skills and encourage a healthy approach to resolving disputes. Address conflicts promptly and constructively to prevent them from escalating.

9. **Shared Tools and Resources:** Provide the necessary tools, resources, and technology that facilitate collaboration, such as collaboration software, project management tools, or shared workspaces.

10. **Regular Feedback:** Offer regular feedback to team members on their performance and contributions. Acknowledge and celebrate successes, and provide constructive feedback for improvement.

11. **Leadership Support:** As a leader, actively support and advocate for collaboration. Encourage cross-functional collaboration and be available to address any issues or concerns that may hinder teamwork.

12. **Recognition and Rewards:** Recognize and reward collaborative efforts and achievements. Highlight the value of teamwork and acknowledge individuals who go above and beyond to support their colleagues.

13. **Training and Development:** Invest in training and development programs that enhance collaboration skills, including communication, teamwork, and conflict resolution.

14. **Lead by Example:** Model collaborative behavior as a leader. Engage in teamwork, seek input from others, and demonstrate a willingness to collaborate with team members.

15. **Continuous Improvement:** Regularly assess the team's collaborative efforts and seek feedback from team members. Use this feedback to make necessary adjustments and improvements to collaboration processes.

16. **Celebrate Diversity:** Embrace and celebrate the unique strengths and perspectives that each team member brings to the table. Recognize that diversity is an asset that can lead to innovative solutions.

Promoting collaboration and synergy within teams requires ongoing effort and commitment from both leaders and team members. By implementing these strategies and fostering a culture of collaboration, teams can work cohesively, leverage their collective strengths, and achieve outstanding results.

Leadership Styles and Interpersonal Compatibility

Leadership styles and interpersonal compatibility are essential components of effective leadership within a team or organization. Leadership styles refer to the approaches and methods leaders use to guide and influence their teams. These styles can vary widely, from autocratic and directive to democratic and collaborative. Interpersonal compatibility, on the other hand, pertains to the alignment or congruence between a leader's style and the personalities, communication preferences, and work styles of their team members.

Effective leadership hinges on the ability of a leader to assess and adapt their leadership style to the unique needs and characteristics of their team. For instance, a transformational leader might be highly effective in an environment where team members are inspired by visionary leadership and open communication. However, the same leadership style might not yield the same results in a team that values structure and clear directives, where a more transactional leadership approach may be better suited.

Interpersonal compatibility involves understanding how team members interact with each other and with their leader. It's about recognizing the diverse personalities and communication styles within a team and adjusting leadership behaviors accordingly. Leaders who are attuned to the interpersonal dynamics within their teams can foster trust, effective communication, and collaboration.

Ultimately, successful leadership styles are those that align with the interpersonal compatibility of the team. Leaders who adapt their approach to accommodate the unique characteristics of their team members are more likely to build strong, cohesive teams that work together harmoniously to achieve common goals. In essence, leadership styles and interpersonal compatibility are intricately connected, and effective leaders are those who can navigate and balance both elements to create a productive and harmonious work environment.

How leadership styles impact interpersonal compatibility

Leadership styles have a profound impact on interpersonal compatibility within a team or organization. The way a leader chooses to lead directly influences how team members interact with each other and with the leader.

1. **Autocratic Leadership:** Autocratic leaders make decisions unilaterally and provide strict directives to team members. This style can lead to interpersonal challenges when team members desire more autonomy and involvement in decision-making. Incompatibility may arise if team members feel disempowered or unheard.

2. **Democratic Leadership:** Democratic leaders involve team members in decision-making and value their input. This style often promotes positive interpersonal compatibility as team members feel engaged and empowered. Collaboration and open communication are encouraged.

3. **Transformational Leadership:** Transformational leaders inspire and motivate their teams through a shared vision and enthusiasm. This style typically enhances interpersonal compatibility, as team members are inspired by the leader's charisma and vision. They often share a sense of purpose and commitment.

4. **Transactional Leadership:** Transactional leaders emphasize clear expectations, rewards for performance, and consequences for non-compliance. Interpersonal compatibility can be positive when team members appreciate structure and accountability. However, those who prefer more autonomy may find this style less compatible.

5. **Servant Leadership:** Servant leaders prioritize the needs of their team members above their own. This style often fosters strong interpersonal compatibility, as team members feel

valued, supported, and cared for. Trust and collaboration are common outcomes.

6. **Laissez-Faire Leadership:** Laissez-faire leaders provide autonomy and minimal guidance. Interpersonal compatibility can vary widely with this style, as it suits self-directed and highly skilled teams but may lead to confusion or frustration when more guidance is needed.

7. **Coaching Leadership:** Coaching leaders focus on developing the skills and potential of their team members. Interpersonal compatibility is typically positive, as team members appreciate the investment in their growth. Open communication and trust are common features.

8. **Charismatic Leadership:** Charismatic leaders rely on their charm and persuasion to influence others. Interpersonal compatibility can be strong when team members are inspired by the leader's charisma. However, if team members have contrasting personalities or values, compatibility may be less positive.

It is essential for leaders to recognize that no single leadership style is universally effective or compatible with all team members. Leaders who adapt their style to fit the needs, preferences, and personalities of their team can enhance interpersonal compatibility and create a more harmonious and productive work environment. Effective leaders also encourage open communication, actively seek feedback, and remain flexible in their approach to leadership, ensuring that interpersonal dynamics are conducive to team success.

How leaders can adapt their styles to foster better relationships

Leaders can adapt their leadership styles to foster better relationships by recognizing the unique needs, preferences, and characteristics of their team members. Here are ways in which leaders can make these adaptations:

1. **Assess Individual Preferences:** Leaders should take the time to understand the personalities, communication styles, and work preferences of their team members. This can be done through one-on-one conversations, personality assessments, or team-building exercises.

2. **Flexibility in Communication:** Adapt communication styles to match those of team members. Some individuals may prefer written communication, while others may thrive in face-to-face interactions. Tailoring communication to individual preferences enhances understanding and rapport.

3. **Provide Autonomy When Desired:** Recognize that some team members may prefer autonomy in their work, while others may seek more guidance. Leaders can adapt by giving more freedom to self-directed individuals and offering additional support to those who require it.

4. **Engage in Active Listening:** Actively listen to team members' concerns, ideas, and feedback. Demonstrate empathy and understanding by acknowledging their perspectives. This fosters trust and demonstrates that their voices are valued.

5. **Adjust Decision-Making Approaches:** Leaders can involve team members in decision-making processes when appropriate, especially for matters that directly affect them. This democratic approach can lead to more buy-in and better relationships.

6. **Offer Constructive Feedback:** Tailor feedback to individual needs and preferences. Some team members may prefer direct, concise feedback, while others may appreciate a more nurturing and coaching-oriented approach.

7. **Adapt to Cultural Differences:** In diverse teams, leaders should be sensitive to cultural differences and adapt their leadership styles accordingly. Respect for cultural norms and values can enhance relationships and teamwork.

8. **Provide Recognition and Rewards:** Recognize and reward team members in ways that align with their preferences. Some may prefer public acknowledgment, while others may appreciate private recognition. Personalizing recognition efforts strengthens relationships.

9. **Conflict Resolution Styles:** Understand how team members approach conflict and adapt conflict resolution approaches accordingly. Some may prefer direct confrontation, while others may prefer a more collaborative and consensus-based resolution.

10. **Lead by Example:** Demonstrate the behaviors and values you expect from your team members. Modeling effective communication, empathy, and respect fosters better relationships by setting a positive example.

11. **Invest in Team Development:** Facilitate team-building activities and opportunities for skill development that can improve relationships. These activities can promote trust, cooperation, and understanding among team members.

12. **Seek Feedback:** Continuously seek feedback from team members about your leadership style and its impact on their relationships and performance. Be open to making adjustments based on their input.

13. **Adapt to Changing Needs:** Recognize that team dynamics and individual needs can evolve over time. Leaders should be agile and adapt their leadership styles as circumstances change.

By being adaptable and responsive to the needs and preferences of team members, leaders can build better relationships, enhance trust, and create a collaborative and productive work environment. Effective leadership isn't about imposing a fixed style but rather about tailoring one's approach to best serve the team and its goals.

Emotional Intelligence in Leadership

Emotional intelligence (EI) in leadership refers to a leader's ability to recognize, understand, manage, and effectively utilize their own emotions and the emotions of others in the workplace. It encompasses a range of emotional competencies that contribute to effective leadership, such as empathy, self-awareness, self-regulation, social awareness, and interpersonal skills.

Leaders with high emotional intelligence can navigate complex interpersonal relationships, communicate effectively, and make informed decisions that consider the emotional well-being of their team members. They are attuned to the emotions and needs of both individuals and groups, enabling them to foster a positive work environment, resolve conflicts, and motivate their teams.

Emotional intelligence is not just about being in touch with one's own emotions; it also involves recognizing and responding to the emotions of others. Leaders who possess EI can inspire trust, build strong relationships, and lead with empathy and authenticity. They can adapt their leadership styles to different situations, demonstrating emotional flexibility and resilience.

Emotional intelligence in leadership goes beyond technical skills and knowledge; it encompasses the ability to connect with and influence people on an emotional level. Leaders who excel in EI can create a workplace culture that promotes collaboration, engagement, and overall well-being, ultimately contributing to the success and satisfaction of their teams and organizations.

Role of emotional intelligence in leadership

Emotional intelligence plays a pivotal role in effective leadership, influencing various aspects of how leaders interact with their teams and organizations. The significant role of emotional intelligence in leadership is:

1. **Self-Awareness:** Leaders with high EI possess self-awareness, which means they understand their own emotions, strengths, weaknesses, and triggers. This self-awareness allows them to regulate their emotions effectively and make sound decisions based on self-reflection rather than impulsivity.

2. **Self-Regulation:** EI enables leaders to self-regulate their emotions. They can manage stress, frustration, and anxiety, which are common in leadership roles. This emotional control prevents outbursts or rash decisions and maintains a composed and collected demeanor.

3. **Empathy:** Empathy, a core component of EI, enables leaders to understand and resonate with the emotions of their team members. This empathetic connection fosters trust, as team members feel understood and valued. Leaders can anticipate needs and concerns, making them more approachable.

4. **Social Awareness:** Leaders with high EI possess strong social awareness. They can read social cues, recognize non-verbal communication, and understand group dynamics. This awareness allows them to adapt their communication and leadership style to different situations and individuals.

5. **Effective Communication:** EI enhances communication skills. Leaders can convey their ideas clearly and persuasively, but more importantly, they actively listen to others. This open, empathetic listening fosters better relationships and a more inclusive work environment.

6. **Conflict Resolution:** Conflict is inevitable in any organization, but leaders with high EI excel at resolving conflicts constructively. They can navigate emotionally charged situations, de-escalate tensions, and facilitate productive dialogue to find mutually beneficial solutions.

7. **Motivation:** EI drives intrinsic motivation. Leaders with high EI set a positive tone, inspire their teams, and encourage a shared sense of purpose. They recognize the emotional rewards of achieving collective goals, driving higher levels of engagement and commitment.

8. **Adaptability:** EI promotes adaptability. Leaders can flexibly adjust their leadership styles to meet the needs of changing situations or individual team members. This adaptability is particularly valuable in dynamic work environments.

9. **Decision-Making:** Leaders with EI make more emotionally intelligent decisions. They consider the emotional impact of choices on their team members, stakeholders, and the organization as a whole, resulting in decisions that are not only rational but also sensitive to people's feelings.

10. **Team Building:** EI contributes to effective team building. Leaders can assemble diverse teams, foster collaboration, and leverage the strengths of each team member. The emotional resonance they establish within the team promotes cohesiveness and mutual support.

11. **Organizational Culture:** Leaders with high EI shape the organizational culture. They model emotional intelligence, which influences how employees interact with each other and with customers or clients. A culture of emotional intelligence promotes trust, innovation, and overall well-being.

Emotional intelligence is a cornerstone of effective leadership. It enhances a leader's ability to understand themselves and others, manage emotions, communicate effectively, and create a positive work environment. Leaders who prioritize and develop their emotional intelligence not only lead with authenticity but also foster stronger, more resilient, and more motivated teams that contribute to organizational success.

Strategies for developing emotional intelligence skills

Developing emotional intelligence skills is essential for leaders who want to enhance their effectiveness in leading teams and organizations. Here are strategies to help leaders develop their emotional intelligence:

1. **Self-Awareness:**
   - Practice self-reflection: Regularly assess your emotions, triggers, and reactions to various situations.
   - Keep a journal: Document your emotional responses and reflect on them to gain insights into your patterns of behavior.
   - Seek feedback: Ask for honest feedback from colleagues, mentors, or coaches to gain an external perspective on your emotional strengths and areas for improvement.
2. **Self-Regulation:**
   - Practice stress management techniques: Incorporate stress-reduction practices like mindfulness, meditation, or deep breathing exercises into your daily routine.

- Delay responses: When faced with a challenging situation, take a moment to pause and consider your response rather than reacting impulsively.
- Set clear boundaries: Define personal and professional boundaries to prevent emotional spillover from one area of life to another.

3. **Empathy:**
   - Active listening: Listen attentively to others without interrupting or judgment. Focus on understanding their perspective.
   - Put yourself in others' shoes: Try to imagine how others might feel in a given situation to enhance your ability to empathize.
   - Practice perspective-taking: Deliberately seek different viewpoints and engage in conversations with people from diverse backgrounds to broaden your empathy.

4. **Social Awareness:**
   - Observe non-verbal cues: Pay attention to body language, facial expressions, and tone of voice to better understand people's emotions.
   - Attend training and workshops: Participate in courses or workshops on emotional intelligence and social awareness to build these skills.
   - Engage in active social listening: Actively engage in conversations and discussions to gain insights into the needs and concerns of others.

5. **Effective Communication:**
    - Practice assertiveness: Express your thoughts and feelings honestly and respectfully, while also actively listening to others.
    - Use "I" statements: Frame your communication by expressing your own emotions and needs rather than making assumptions about others' feelings.
    - Solicit feedback: Encourage open and honest feedback from team members to improve your communication style.

6. **Conflict Resolution:**
    - Develop conflict resolution skills: Learn and practice conflict resolution techniques, such as negotiation, mediation, and compromise.
    - Role-play scenarios: Engage in role-playing exercises to simulate conflict situations and practice effective resolution strategies.
    - Seek guidance: Consider seeking advice or mentoring from experienced leaders who excel in conflict resolution.

7. **Motivation:**
    - Set meaningful goals: Identify and pursue goals that align with your values and passions to maintain motivation.
    - Celebrate successes: Acknowledge your achievements and those of your team members to stay motivated and inspire others.
    - Stay resilient: Embrace setbacks as learning opportunities and maintain a positive outlook, even in the face of challenges.

8. **Team Building:**
    - Foster a supportive team culture: Create an environment where team members feel comfortable expressing their emotions and concerns.
    - Facilitate team-building activities: Organize activities that promote trust, collaboration, and emotional bonds among team members.

9. **Continuous Learning:**
    - Read books and articles: Explore literature on emotional intelligence, leadership, and psychology to deepen your understanding.
    - Attend workshops and seminars: Participate in professional development events focused on emotional intelligence and leadership.

10. **Coaching and Mentoring:**
    - Engage a coach or mentor: Seek guidance from experienced individuals who can provide personalized feedback and support your EI development.

*****

CHAPTER SIX
Situational and Contextual Theories

Situational and contextual theories are frameworks in psychology and social sciences that emphasize the significance of the environment and specific circumstances in understanding human behavior and decision-making. These theories acknowledge that individuals' actions and choices are not solely determined by their inherent traits or characteristics but are heavily influenced by the situation in which they find themselves and the broader context in which they operate.

Situational theories, also known as contingency theories, propose that there is no one-size-fits-all approach to understanding or predicting behavior. Instead, they assert that people's actions and responses can vary depending on the specific situation they are in. In other words, the same individual may exhibit different behaviors or make different choices when faced with varying circumstances. A classic example of a situational theory is Fiedler's Contingency Model, which suggests that leadership effectiveness depends on the match between a leader's style and the situation.

Contextual theories broaden the perspective to consider not only immediate situations but also the broader social, cultural, and historical context that surrounds individuals. These theories argue that understanding behavior requires analyzing the larger context within which it occurs. For instance, cultural relativism in anthropology recognizes that norms and values vary across cultures and that what is considered acceptable behavior in one culture may be different from another. Similarly, in developmental psychology, Bronfenbrenner's Ecological Systems Theory underscores the importance of the multiple layers of context, from the immediate family environment to the larger societal and cultural influences, in shaping human development.

Situational theories highlight the importance of specific, immediate circumstances in influencing behavior, while contextual theories emphasize the broader social, cultural, and historical factors that shape human actions and choices. Both approaches contribute to a more comprehensive understanding of human behavior by recognizing that it is not solely determined by individual traits but is profoundly influenced by the situations and contexts in which people find themselves.

Importance of Situational and Contextual Theories

Situational and contextual theories are highly significant in the realm of leadership because they provide a more nuanced and adaptable approach to understanding and practicing effective leadership. Here's an understanding of their importance in leadership:

1. **Adaptability:** Situational leadership theories, such as the Hersey-Blanchard Situational Leadership Model, emphasize the need for leaders to adapt their leadership style to the specific needs and readiness levels of their followers. In different situations, followers may require different types of leadership – from a directive approach to a more supportive or delegative one. Leaders who can flexibly adjust their leadership behaviors are more likely to be successful in guiding their teams.

2. **Effective Decision-Making:** Contextual theories of leadership, like the Contingency Theory, recognize that the effectiveness of leadership styles depends on various external factors. Leaders who consider the broader context, such as the organization's culture, industry trends, and market conditions, can make more informed decisions about

how to lead their teams. For example, in a rapidly changing industry, a leader might need to adopt a more adaptive and transformational leadership style.

3. **Cultural Sensitivity:** Cultural context plays a crucial role in leadership. Leadership behaviors that are effective in one culture may not be as successful in another. Cross-cultural leadership theories, like the GLOBE Study, emphasize the importance of understanding cultural dimensions and adapting leadership practices accordingly. Leaders who are culturally sensitive and can adjust their leadership behaviors to align with the values and expectations of diverse teams can foster better relationships and cooperation.

4. **Long-Term Success:** Contextual theories also consider the long-term impact of leadership decisions. Leaders who focus on the broader context are more likely to make sustainable decisions that benefit the organization in the long run. This can include decisions related to ethical leadership, corporate social responsibility, and environmental sustainability, which are increasingly important in today's business landscape.

5. **Conflict Resolution:** Situational leadership theories can be valuable in resolving conflicts within teams. Leaders who understand the situational factors contributing to conflicts can employ the appropriate conflict resolution strategies. For instance, they may use a more assertive approach when addressing a performance-related conflict and a more collaborative approach when dealing with interpersonal disputes.

6. **Employee Engagement:** Both situational and contextual approaches can enhance employee engagement. Leaders who tailor their leadership styles to individual and situational needs can create a more positive work environment, leading

to higher job satisfaction and motivation among team members.

Situational and contextual theories of leadership underscore the importance of flexibility, adaptability, and a deep understanding of the specific circumstances and broader context in which leadership occurs. Leaders who embrace these theories are better equipped to navigate the complexities of modern organizations and effectively lead diverse teams toward success.

Dynamic Nature of Leadership and the Need to Adapt to Various Contexts

Emphasizing the dynamic nature of leadership and the need to adapt to various contexts is crucial in contemporary leadership theory and practice.

1. **Changing Environments:** Today's business and social environments are characterized by rapid change and uncertainty. Technological advancements, shifting market dynamics, and global interconnectedness mean that leaders must continuously adapt to new challenges and opportunities. A leader who fails to adapt to changing circumstances may find their leadership ineffective or obsolete.

2. **Situational Awareness:** Effective leaders possess situational awareness, which means they are attuned to the specific conditions, challenges, and opportunities at hand. They don't rely on a one-size-fits-all approach but instead analyze the current situation to determine the most appropriate leadership style and actions. This adaptability is crucial for making informed decisions and leading with precision.

3. **Leadership Styles:** Adaptable leaders are proficient in employing various leadership styles, such as

transformational, transactional, servant, or laissez-faire, depending on the context. They understand that what works in one situation may not work in another. For example, during a crisis, a more directive and authoritative leadership style might be necessary, while in times of stability, a collaborative and empowering approach may be more suitable.

4. **Cultural Sensitivity:** In a globalized world, leaders often work with diverse teams and stakeholders from different cultural backgrounds. Adapting leadership behaviors to accommodate cultural differences is essential for building trust, fostering collaboration, and avoiding misunderstandings. Leaders who appreciate and respect cultural nuances can bridge gaps and lead effectively in multicultural environments.

5. **Flexibility in Decision-Making:** Leaders must be adaptable in their decision-making processes. They may need to switch between centralized and decentralized decision-making based on the urgency and complexity of the situation. Being open to feedback and considering various viewpoints can lead to better decisions and greater buy-in from team members.

6. **Change Management:** In organizational leadership, change is a constant. Leaders need to guide their teams through transitions, whether it's implementing new technologies, restructuring, or adapting to market shifts. Effective change leaders understand that the approach to change management must be tailored to the specific circumstances and the readiness of their teams.

7. **Continuous Learning:** Adaptable leaders are committed to lifelong learning. They seek out new knowledge and skills, staying updated on industry trends and leadership best

practices. This continuous learning enables them to stay relevant and effective in ever-changing contexts.

8. **Resilience:** Adaptability also involves resilience in the face of setbacks and challenges. Leaders who can bounce back from failures, learn from them, and adjust their strategies are more likely to succeed in the long run.

Leadership is not a static concept but a dynamic one that requires constant adaptation to various contexts. Leaders who embrace this dynamism and cultivate the ability to adapt their styles, strategies, and behaviors to suit different situations are better positioned to navigate the complexities of the modern world and inspire their teams to achieve success.

Contingency Theory

Contingency Theory, in the field of management and organizational studies, posits that there is no one universally effective way to manage or lead organizations. Instead, it asserts that the most effective approach to management or leadership depends on the specific circumstances or contingencies faced by an organization. In other words, there is a direct relationship between the effectiveness of a management or leadership style and the context in which it is applied. Contingency Theory suggests that various factors, such as an organization's size, its environment, the complexity of tasks, and the personalities of individuals within the organization, all play a role in determining the optimal management or leadership approach. Therefore, leaders and managers should analyze and assess the unique situation of their organization before choosing a particular strategy or style. For instance, in a rapidly changing and turbulent industry, a more flexible and adaptive leadership style might be necessary, whereas in a stable and well-established organization, a more bureaucratic or structured approach might work best. Overall, Contingency Theory highlights the need for leaders and managers to be adaptable and context-sensitive, as there is no one-size-fits-all solution to effective leadership or management. By carefully considering the contingencies they face, they can make more informed decisions and increase the likelihood of achieving success within their specific organizational context.

Fundamental Principle of Contingency Theory

The contingency theory of leadership is based on the fundamental premise that leadership effectiveness is contingent on specific situations or contexts. This theory asserts that there is no one-size-fits-all approach to leadership, and the most effective leadership style or behavior depends on the unique circumstances in which a leader operates.

Key points regarding the contingency theory and its premise are as follows:

1. **Situational Dependency:** Contingency theory suggests that different situations require different leadership approaches. What works in one situation may not work in another. For example, a crisis may demand a more directive and autocratic leadership style, whereas a creative brainstorming session may benefit from a participative and democratic approach.

2. **Various Contingency Factors:** Contingency theory identifies several contingency factors that influence leadership effectiveness. These factors can include the organization's size, structure, culture, the complexity of tasks, the level of employee experience and expertise, and the external environment, among others. Each of these factors can interact to determine the most appropriate leadership style.

3. **Leader Adaptability:** Effective leaders must be adaptable and capable of adjusting their leadership behaviors to fit the specific situation. This adaptability involves recognizing the

cues and demands of a given context and responding accordingly. It also implies that a leader may need to switch between different leadership styles or behaviors as circumstances change.

4. **No Universal Best Style:** Contingency theory challenges the notion of a universally "best" leadership style. Instead, it suggests that leadership effectiveness is relative and context-dependent. The most effective leader in one organization or situation may not be effective in another due to differences in contingencies.

5. **Continuous Assessment:** Leaders following contingency theory principles must continuously assess the situational factors at play and make adjustments accordingly. This means that leadership is an ongoing, dynamic process that requires vigilant monitoring and adaptation.

The contingency theory of leadership underscores the idea that there is no single blueprint for effective leadership. Instead, leadership effectiveness is contingent on specific situations, and leaders must adapt their styles and behaviors to align with the unique circumstances they face. This theory promotes a flexible and context-sensitive approach to leadership, recognizing that what works in one context may not be suitable in another.

Historical Context and Key Proponents

The contingency theory of leadership emerged during the mid-20th century as a response to earlier leadership theories that had failed to fully explain the complexities of leadership effectiveness. This theory takes into account the historical context of organizational and leadership studies during that time and has had several key proponents who have contributed to its development.

Historical Context

The contingency theory of leadership gained prominence in the 1960s and 1970s, coinciding with a period of significant change and evolution in both organizational studies and leadership research. Several factors contributed to the emergence of this theory:

1. **Post-World War II Era:** After World War II, organizations were growing in size and complexity. This led to a greater need for more sophisticated theories of leadership that could address the diverse and evolving challenges facing organizations.

2. **Industrial and Technological Advances:** Rapid industrialization and technological advancements were transforming the business landscape. Organizations needed adaptable leadership strategies to navigate these changes.

3. **Challenges to Earlier Theories:** Prior leadership theories, such as trait theory and behavioral theory, failed to provide a comprehensive understanding of leadership effectiveness. Researchers sought a more nuanced approach that considered the contextual factors influencing leadership outcomes.

Key Proponents

Several scholars and researchers have played significant roles in developing and popularizing the contingency theory of leadership. Some of the key proponents include:

1. **Fred Fiedler:** Fiedler is often considered one of the founding figures of contingency theory. His Contingency Model of Leadership, introduced in the 1960s, posits that the effectiveness of a leader depends on the match between their leadership style (relationship-oriented or task-oriented) and the situation's favorableness, as determined by the leader-

member relations, task structure, and position power. Fiedler's work laid the foundation for understanding the interaction between leadership style and situational variables.

2. **Paul Hersey and Kenneth Blanchard:** Hersey and Blanchard developed the Situational Leadership Theory (SLT) in the late 1960s and early 1970s. SLT focuses on the readiness or maturity of followers and suggests that effective leadership requires adjusting one's leadership style to the readiness level of the followers. This theory emphasizes that leadership is not a fixed trait but rather a dynamic relationship.

3. **Joan V. Gallos:** Gallos is known for her contributions to the field of leadership and her work in contextualizing leadership theories. She has written extensively on leadership in educational contexts and has emphasized the importance of considering the specific environment and context when studying leadership effectiveness.

4. **Victor H. Vroom:** Vroom developed the Vroom-Yetton-Jago Decision Model in the 1970s. While not exclusively a contingency theory of leadership, it incorporates situational factors in decision-making processes. The model helps leaders determine the appropriate level of participation and decision-making style based on the characteristics of the situation.

These key proponents, among others, have contributed to the development and refinement of contingency theory, each offering unique perspectives and models for understanding how leadership effectiveness is contingent on specific situations and contexts. Their work has had a lasting impact on leadership research and practice, emphasizing the need for leaders to be adaptable and context-sensitive in their approach.

Contingency Factors in Leadership

Contingency factors in leadership refer to the specific situational variables or circumstances that can significantly influence the effectiveness of a leader's approach or style. These factors are the core elements of the contingency theory of leadership, which posits that leadership effectiveness is contingent upon the interplay between a leader's behaviors or traits and the particular context in which they lead. Contingency factors encompass a range of variables, including the organization's structure, the nature of tasks or goals, the quality of leader-follower relationships, the level of authority and power held by the leader, and the external environment in which the organization operates. Understanding these contingent elements is essential for leaders as it helps them determine the most appropriate leadership strategies and behaviors that will yield the best results in a given situation. In essence, contingency factors remind us that leadership is not a one-size-fits-all concept but requires adaptability and contextual awareness for effective decision-making and leadership outcomes.

Examination of the various contingency factors

Examining the various contingency factors that impact leadership effectiveness is crucial in understanding how leadership operates within different contexts. These factors are integral to the contingency theory of leadership, emphasizing the need for leaders to adapt their approaches to suit specific situations. Three important key contingency factors are: task structure, team dynamics, and organizational culture.

1. **Task Structure:** The structure of tasks or goals within an organization is a critical contingency factor. It can be classified as either high or low in terms of clarity, complexity, and the presence of established procedures. In situations with well-structured tasks, where objectives are clear, and there are established guidelines, leaders may adopt

a more directive or task-oriented leadership style. Conversely, in situations with loosely structured or complex tasks, leaders might need to be more participative, involving team members in decision-making processes to leverage their expertise and insights. Task structure thus directly influences the most effective leadership approach.

2. **Team Dynamics:** Team dynamics encompass factors related to the composition, cohesion, and collaboration within a group or team. Effective leaders recognize that team dynamics can vary widely, depending on the personalities, skills, and experiences of team members. In cohesive and high-performing teams, leaders may adopt a more hands-off or delegative approach, allowing members to leverage their skills and collaborate autonomously. Conversely, in teams with conflicts or low cohesion, leaders may need to be more interventionist, using conflict resolution skills and fostering a sense of unity. Team dynamics strongly influence the need for supportive or directive leadership behaviors.

3. **Organizational Culture:** Organizational culture represents the shared values, beliefs, and norms that guide behavior within an organization. It plays a significant role in shaping leadership effectiveness. In organizations with a strong culture that values innovation and employee autonomy, leaders who encourage creativity and give employees a degree of freedom tend to be more effective. Conversely, in organizations with a highly structured or hierarchical culture, leaders may need to align with these cultural norms by being more directive and adhering to established procedures. Leaders who understand and align with the prevailing organizational culture can build trust and foster greater acceptance of their leadership.

These three contingency factors are not exhaustive, and there are other variables, such as leader-member relations, external environmental factors, and the power or authority of the leader, which also play a role in determining leadership effectiveness. The key takeaway is that leadership is not a fixed concept but must adapt to the specific context. Effective leaders assess these contingency factors to make informed decisions about their leadership styles and behaviors, ultimately increasing their ability to achieve organizational goals and motivate their teams.

Examples

1. **Task Structure:** Imagine a software development project with a well-defined scope, clear requirements, and established coding standards. In this scenario, the task structure is high. A leader who adopts a directive leadership style, providing specific instructions and closely monitoring progress, may be more effective. This ensures that the project stays on track, adheres to established guidelines, and meets the defined objectives.

    On the other hand, consider a research project in a highly specialized scientific field where the goals are less clear, and the approach requires frequent adaptation. Here, the task structure is low. A leader who takes a more participative approach, involving team members in decision-making and encouraging them to explore various research avenues, is likely to be more effective. This approach leverages the team's expertise and adaptability in navigating complex and evolving tasks.

2. **Team Dynamics:** In a sports team context, think about a highly cohesive and motivated basketball team. The players have a deep sense of trust and camaraderie, which positively influences team dynamics. The coach, in this case, can adopt a more supportive leadership style, empowering players to make decisions on the court, trusting their judgment, and focusing on motivation and encouragement rather than micromanagement. This approach capitalizes on the team's strong cohesion and collaborative spirit.

In contrast, consider a team with conflicting personalities and a lack of cohesion, perhaps in a corporate setting. Here, the leader may need to take a more hands-on approach, facilitating conflict resolution, setting clear expectations, and closely monitoring progress. This interventionist leadership style helps address team dynamics challenges and ensures that the team can work together effectively despite internal conflicts.

4. **Organizational Culture:** Suppose you are leading a team within a startup known for its innovative culture. In this environment, the organizational culture encourages experimentation and autonomy. As a leader, you would be effective by adopting a transformational leadership style, inspiring team members, providing them with autonomy to explore new ideas, and encouraging a culture of creativity and risk-taking.

Conversely, imagine leading a team in a government agency with a highly bureaucratic and rule-bound culture. Here, adherence to established procedures and hierarchy is paramount. In this context, a more bureaucratic and transactional leadership style that ensures compliance with regulations and established processes would be more effective in aligning with the prevailing organizational culture.

These illustrative examples showcase how task structure, team dynamics, and organizational culture can significantly influence the most effective leadership approach. Effective leaders recognize the importance of adapting their leadership styles and behaviors to align with these contingency factors, ultimately enhancing their ability to lead and motivate their teams in diverse contexts.

Matching Leadership Styles to Contingencies

Matching leadership styles to contingencies is a fundamental concept in contingency theory, emphasizing the importance of aligning a leader's approach with the specific situational factors or contingencies at play. It recognizes that leadership effectiveness is not a one-size-fits-all proposition, and the most suitable leadership style or behavior varies depending on the circumstances. This approach involves a leader's ability to assess and adapt to factors such as task complexity, team dynamics, organizational culture, and external influences. For instance, in situations where tasks are highly structured and team members are experienced and cohesive, a more hands-off or participative leadership style may be appropriate. Conversely, in complex and uncertain environments, leaders may need to be more directive or transformational to provide clear guidance and motivation. Matching leadership styles to contingencies is a dynamic and context-sensitive approach that recognizes the need for leaders to be flexible and responsive, ultimately optimizing their effectiveness in diverse situations.

Concept of "fit" in contingency theory

The concept of "fit" in contingency theory refers to the alignment or compatibility between a leader's chosen leadership style or behavior and the specific demands or contingencies of a given situation. It underscores the idea that effective leadership hinges on finding the right match between a leader's approach and the context in which they operate. Here, we will delve into the significance of "fit" in contingency theory and how it plays a pivotal role in leadership effectiveness.

1. **Adaptability and Context Sensitivity:** The concept of "fit" acknowledges that there is no one-size-fits-all leadership style. Rather, leaders must be adaptable and context-sensitive. It emphasizes that leaders should assess the unique characteristics of a situation, such as task complexity, team

dynamics, and organizational culture, and then select a leadership style that aligns with those characteristics. This adaptability is a hallmark of effective leadership.

2. **Maximizing Leadership Effectiveness:** "Fit" is essential for maximizing leadership effectiveness. When a leader's style aligns with the contingencies of the situation, it enhances the leader's ability to influence, motivate, and guide their team or organization effectively. For example, in a highly structured environment, a leader who adopts a directive style that provides clear instructions and guidance is more likely to achieve the desired outcomes.

3. **Achieving Organizational Goals:** Leadership "fit" is closely tied to achieving organizational goals. By choosing the right leadership approach that fits the specific demands of a situation, leaders can steer their teams toward success. For instance, in a crisis situation, a leader who employs a decisive and authoritative style can help the organization navigate through challenges and maintain stability.

4. **Improved Team Morale and Satisfaction:** When leaders match their leadership style to the situation, it often results in improved team morale and satisfaction. This is because team members feel that their leader understands and responds to their needs and the unique challenges they face. In turn, this fosters a positive work environment and can lead to higher levels of employee engagement and commitment.

5. **Flexibility and Continuous Learning:** Embracing the concept of "fit" encourages leaders to be flexible and continuously learn. Leaders must stay attuned to changes in their environment and adapt their leadership styles accordingly. This requires ongoing self-assessment and a willingness to develop new skills and approaches as the situation dictates.

6. **Risk Mitigation:** By matching leadership styles to contingencies, leaders can mitigate risks associated with ineffective leadership. Inconsistent or misaligned leadership styles can lead to conflicts, misunderstandings, and decreased productivity. A "fit" leadership approach helps prevent these issues and promotes smoother operations.

The concept of "fit" in contingency theory highlights the importance of leaders' ability to select and adapt their leadership styles to suit the unique demands of each situation. Effective leadership requires an ongoing assessment of the contingencies at play and a commitment to aligning one's leadership behaviors with those contingencies. By achieving this alignment, leaders enhance their effectiveness, increase their chances of achieving organizational goals, and foster a more positive and productive work environment.

Strategies for Leaders to Assess Situation

Leaders can employ several strategies to assess situations effectively and adapt their leadership approaches accordingly, in alignment with the principles of contingency theory. These strategies help leaders make informed decisions about the most suitable leadership style or behavior for a given context:

1. **Gather Information:** Leaders should actively seek information about the current situation. This includes understanding the goals and objectives, the level of task complexity, team dynamics, and any external factors that may be influencing the situation. Gathering data through observation, feedback, and open communication with team members is essential.

2. **Assess Task Structure:** Determine the structure of the tasks or goals at hand. Is the task well-defined and straightforward, or is it complex and uncertain? Assessing

task structure provides insights into whether a more directive or participative leadership style is appropriate.

3. **Evaluate Team Dynamics:** Analyze the composition of the team, their levels of experience, cohesion, and any conflicts or challenges within the group. Understanding team dynamics helps leaders gauge the need for support, guidance, or intervention.

4. **Consider Organizational Culture:** Recognize the prevailing culture within the organization. Is it hierarchical and rule-bound, or is it characterized by innovation and autonomy? Leaders should align their behaviors with the organizational culture to build trust and credibility.

5. **Assess External Factors:** Take into account external factors that may impact the organization or team, such as market conditions, competition, regulatory changes, or economic trends. These external factors can influence the urgency and complexity of the situation.

6. **Reflect on Past Experiences:** Leaders can draw on their past experiences and lessons learned from similar situations. Reflecting on what worked and what didn't in the past can guide decision-making in the current context.

7. **Consult with Others:** Seek input and perspective from trusted colleagues, mentors, or advisors. These external viewpoints can provide valuable insights and help leaders avoid biases or blind spots in their assessments.

8. **Use Decision-Making Models:** Consider decision-making models, such as the Vroom-Yetton-Jago Decision Model, to systematically determine the most appropriate level of involvement and decision-making style based on the situation's characteristics.

9. **Stay Flexible and Open-Minded:** Maintain a flexible mindset and be open to adjusting leadership approaches as

the situation evolves. Leaders should be willing to adapt and make necessary course corrections based on ongoing assessments.

10. **Continuous Learning:** Invest in ongoing learning and leadership development. Staying current with leadership theories and best practices can provide leaders with a broader toolkit to draw from when assessing and adapting to situations.

11. **Feedback Mechanisms:** Establish feedback mechanisms within the team or organization to regularly gather input from team members about their needs, concerns, and perceptions of leadership effectiveness. This feedback can inform leadership adjustments.

12. **Regular Reviews:** Periodically review and reassess the alignment between leadership approaches and situational contingencies. Situations can change over time, and leaders should ensure that their strategies remain relevant.

By implementing these strategies, leaders can enhance their ability to assess situations effectively and make informed decisions about how to adapt their leadership approaches in a way that aligns with the unique demands of each context. This adaptability is central to the success of leaders operating within the framework of contingency theory.

Case Study: Successful Application of Contingency Theory

A case study illustrating the successful application of contingency theory in leadership showcases how this approach can lead to favorable outcomes in real-world situations. In such a case, leadership effectiveness is demonstrated by aligning leadership styles and behaviors with the specific contingencies or challenges faced by an organization or team. For instance, consider a technology startup navigating a rapidly changing industry landscape. The CEO of this startup recognizes the dynamic nature of their environment as a high-contingency factor. To succeed, the CEO adopts a flexible and adaptive leadership style that encourages innovation, empowers employees to make decisions, and fosters a culture of continuous learning. This approach proves effective in keeping the organization agile, responsive to market shifts, and able to seize emerging opportunities. The CEO's ability to tailor their leadership behaviors to the ever-changing context demonstrates the successful application of contingency theory, resulting in the startup's growth and resilience in a highly competitive market. This case study underscores how leaders who understand and adapt to situational contingencies can achieve success and drive organizational effectiveness.

Hari Singh Nalwa

Hari Singh Nalwa, a historical figure from the early 19th century, provides a compelling real-life case study that demonstrates the effective application of contingency theory in leadership. Nalwa was a prominent military general in the army of Maharaja Ranjit Singh, who ruled the Sikh Empire in the Indian subcontinent during a period of political turmoil and change.

Context (Contingencies)

1. **Highly Turbulent Period:** Nalwa's era was marked by frequent wars, political instability, and territorial disputes among various regional powers.
2. **Diverse and Multicultural Army:** Nalwa commanded a diverse army comprising Sikhs, Muslims, Hindus, and soldiers from various backgrounds, each with different languages, customs, and loyalties.
3. **Volatile Borders:** The Sikh Empire shared borders with several rival states and faced constant threats from external forces, including the British East India Company.

Effective Application of Contingency Theory

1. **Adaptation of Leadership Style:** Nalwa demonstrated a remarkable ability to adapt his leadership style to fit the contingencies of the situation. During times of war and military campaigns, he exhibited a decisive and directive leadership style. He was known for leading from the front, making quick decisions on the battlefield, and providing clear instructions to his troops.

2. **Cultural Sensitivity:** Given the diversity within his army, Nalwa recognized the importance of cultural sensitivity. He ensured that the soldiers of different backgrounds felt respected and valued. This inclusive approach fostered loyalty and unity among his troops, crucial for success in a multicultural environment.

3. **Strategic Flexibility:** Nalwa displayed strategic flexibility, shifting his tactics and strategies based on the evolving geopolitical landscape. He understood that the external threats and alliances were constantly changing, requiring him to adapt his military plans accordingly.

4. **Collaborative Leadership:** In addition to his directive approach during battles, Nalwa also employed a more participative and consultative leadership style during peacetime and in administrative matters. This approach encouraged open communication, collaboration, and the exchange of ideas among his officers.

Outcomes

Hari Singh Nalwa's effective application of contingency theory in leadership yielded several notable outcomes:

1. The Sikh Empire, under his leadership, expanded its territories and consolidated power during a tumultuous era.

2. Nalwa's ability to adapt to the diverse and ever-changing environment helped maintain the loyalty of his troops, enabling him to face external threats effectively.
3. His leadership was instrumental in securing and defending the empire's borders against numerous adversaries.

Hari Singh Nalwa's historical legacy exemplifies how a leader who comprehends the specific contingencies of their time and adapts their leadership style accordingly can achieve remarkable success in the face of complex challenges. His leadership demonstrates the enduring relevance of contingency theory in understanding and effectively addressing the demands of real-world situations.

Analysis of Style with Specific Context

Hari Singh Nalwa, a prominent military general in the Sikh Empire during the early 19th century, demonstrated a remarkable ability to match his leadership style to the specific context in which he operated. His success can be attributed to his keen understanding of the contingencies of his time and his adaptability in response to these factors:

1. **Adaptive Leadership Style:** Nalwa displayed an adaptive leadership style that varied based on the situational demands. In times of warfare and military campaigns, he adopted a directive and authoritative leadership style. This approach was well-suited to the high-stakes, structured, and often volatile nature of military operations. Nalwa's decisiveness and clear instructions during battles instilled confidence in his troops and contributed to their success.

2. **Cultural Sensitivity:** Recognizing the diverse composition of his army, which included Sikhs, Muslims, Hindus, and individuals from various backgrounds, Nalwa was culturally sensitive in his leadership. He promoted an inclusive and

respectful environment that acknowledged and respected the different customs, languages, and beliefs of his soldiers. This cultural sensitivity fostered loyalty and unity among his troops, a critical element for success in a multicultural and diverse army.

3. **Strategic Flexibility:** Nalwa's strategic flexibility was instrumental in his achievements. He understood that the external geopolitical landscape was constantly changing. Whether facing rival powers or shifting alliances, he adapted his military plans accordingly. His ability to pivot strategically and adjust his leadership approach ensured that the Sikh Empire could respond effectively to evolving contingencies.

4. **Collaborative Leadership:** Beyond his directive approach during battles, Nalwa also employed a more participative and consultative leadership style during peacetime and in administrative matters. This approach encouraged open communication, collaboration, and the exchange of ideas among his officers. Nalwa recognized that different situations called for different leadership behaviors.

5. **Continuous Learning:** Nalwa's success was also influenced by his commitment to continuous learning and self-improvement. He learned from his experiences and applied those lessons to future endeavors, adapting his leadership style based on these lessons. This commitment to growth and development contributed to his effectiveness in diverse situations.

Hari Singh Nalwa's success as a leader can be attributed to his exceptional ability to match his leadership style to the specific context or contingencies he encountered. His adaptive leadership, cultural sensitivity, strategic flexibility, collaborative approach, and commitment to learning all played vital roles in his achievements. Nalwa's leadership exemplifies the principles of contingency theory, emphasizing the importance of aligning leadership behaviors with the unique demands of each situation for effective leadership outcomes.

Adapting Leadership Styles to Situational Demands

Adapting leadership styles to situational demands is a fundamental concept that underscores the importance of tailoring one's leadership approach to the specific circumstances and challenges of a given situation. It recognizes that there is no one-size-fits-all leadership style, and effective leaders must be flexible and context-sensitive. This approach involves a leader's ability to assess the unique aspects of a situation, including its complexity, the characteristics of team members, the organization's culture, and external factors. Based on this assessment, leaders can adjust their leadership behaviors and strategies to align with the demands of the situation. For example, in a crisis, leaders may need to adopt a more directive and authoritative style to provide clear guidance and maintain stability, while in a creative brainstorming session, a more participative and democratic approach may be suitable to encourage idea generation. Adapting leadership styles to situational demands ensures that leaders are responsive and effective in addressing the unique challenges and opportunities presented by each context.

Understand the Flexibility of Leadership Styles

Understanding the flexibility of leadership styles refers to recognizing and appreciating that effective leadership is not confined to a single, rigid approach. Instead, it acknowledges that leadership is adaptable and should be responsive to the varying needs, contingencies, and contexts that leaders encounter. Flexibility in leadership styles entails the capacity to shift, modify, or blend different leadership behaviors and strategies as situations dictate. Leaders who comprehend this flexibility are better equipped to tailor their approaches to specific challenges, team dynamics, and organizational cultures, maximizing their effectiveness. This understanding acknowledges that leadership is not a fixed or one-dimensional concept but a dynamic and context-sensitive practice that demands versatility and the ability to adjust to the ever-changing demands of the environment.

Why Leadership Flexibility is Essential

In today's fast-paced and ever-changing world, the need for leadership flexibility in dynamic environments has become increasingly evident. Leaders are confronted with complex challenges, evolving technologies, diverse workforces, and shifting market landscapes. To navigate these turbulent waters successfully, leaders must possess the ability to adapt and demonstrate flexibility in their leadership styles and approaches. Here's why leadership flexibility is essential in dynamic environments:

1. **Rapid Change and Uncertainty:** Dynamic environments are characterized by rapid and often unpredictable changes. Whether it's disruptive technologies, global economic shifts, or unforeseen crises, leaders must be prepared to respond swiftly and effectively. Rigid leadership styles that worked in stable contexts may prove ineffective in the face of such unpredictability.

2. **Diverse Workforces:** Organizations today consist of diverse teams with varied backgrounds, perspectives, and expectations. Leadership flexibility is crucial in managing and motivating this diverse workforce. Different team members may respond better to different leadership approaches, making adaptability a key factor in achieving cohesion and productivity.

3. **Complex Problem-Solving:** Dynamic environments often present complex and multifaceted problems that demand

creative solutions. Leaders who can adapt their leadership styles to encourage innovation, collaboration, and critical thinking are better positioned to tackle these challenges successfully.

4. **Globalization:** In an interconnected global economy, leaders frequently deal with cross-cultural teams, international markets, and diverse stakeholders. Leadership flexibility includes cultural sensitivity and the ability to navigate cultural nuances, as well as adapting to different business practices and regulations across borders.

5. **Employee Engagement:** Flexibility in leadership styles contributes to higher levels of employee engagement and job satisfaction. Leaders who can tailor their approaches to meet the unique needs and aspirations of their team members foster a positive work environment, which, in turn, enhances productivity and retention.

6. **Resilience and Adaptability:** Leaders who embody flexibility serve as role models for adaptability and resilience. In dynamic environments, setbacks and challenges are commonplace. Leaders who demonstrate adaptability inspire their teams to bounce back from adversity and embrace change as an opportunity for growth.

7. **Strategic Agility:** Flexibility in leadership is closely tied to strategic agility. Leaders who can pivot quickly in response to emerging trends and opportunities are more likely to lead their organizations to sustainable growth and success.

8. **Competitive Advantage:** Organizations that cultivate flexible leadership have a competitive advantage. They can respond rapidly to market shifts, innovate more effectively, and attract top talent who appreciate an adaptable and forward-thinking leadership culture.

Leadership flexibility in dynamic environments is a critical asset for achieving organizational success and resilience. Leaders who can adjust their leadership styles, strategies, and behaviors to meet the evolving demands of their environments are better positioned to thrive amidst uncertainty and lead their teams to sustainable growth and achievement.

Drawback of Rigid Leadership

Rigid leadership styles, characterized by an inflexible and unchanging approach to leading others, can have several significant drawbacks. While there may be situations where a more directive or authoritarian style is appropriate, relying exclusively on rigid leadership styles can lead to various negative consequences:

1. **Low Adaptability:** Rigid leaders are often resistant to change and may struggle to adapt to evolving circumstances. This lack of adaptability can hinder an organization's ability to respond effectively to external challenges or opportunities.

2. **Low Employee Morale:** Rigid leaders may create an environment where employees feel stifled, undervalued, or unheard. This can lead to low morale, decreased job satisfaction, and, ultimately, high turnover rates.

3. **Innovation Stifling:** Creativity and innovation thrive in environments where employees feel empowered to share their ideas and take calculated risks. Rigid leaders who discourage input or experimentation can stifle innovation and hinder an organization's ability to stay competitive.

4. **Resistance to Feedback:** Leaders with rigid styles may be resistant to receiving feedback, which is essential for personal and organizational growth. This resistance can create a culture of silence, where employees are afraid to voice concerns or suggestions.

5. **Limited Perspective:** Rigid leaders often have a limited perspective and may not consider alternative viewpoints or approaches. This can result in suboptimal decision-making and missed opportunities for improvement.

6. **Decreased Team Engagement:** Team members may disengage or become disinterested in their work when they feel their contributions are not valued or that their leader is unresponsive to their needs. This can lead to decreased productivity and collaboration.

7. **Poor Communication:** Rigid leaders may struggle with effective communication. They may be unable to convey their expectations clearly or may fail to provide necessary information to their teams, leading to misunderstandings and confusion.

8. **Micromanagement:** Some rigid leaders resort to micromanagement, closely monitoring and controlling every aspect of their team's work. This not only erodes trust but also hampers individual autonomy and creativity.

9. **Resistance to Change:** In rapidly evolving industries or markets, rigid leaders who resist change can lead their organizations into obsolescence. Adaptation to new technologies or market trends may be delayed, resulting in a loss of competitiveness.

10. **Team Disunity:** Rigid leadership styles can create a sense of division within teams, as employees may become polarized or divided into factions based on their support or opposition to the leader's approach. This can lead to internal conflicts and reduced cohesion.

While rigid leadership styles may have their place in certain contexts, relying on them exclusively can result in various drawbacks that affect both leaders and their organizations. To foster a more adaptive and effective leadership approach, it's crucial for leaders to recognize the limitations of rigid styles and be open to exploring more flexible and context-appropriate leadership behaviors.

Assessing Situational Demands

Assessing situational demands in a leadership context involves the systematic evaluation of the unique characteristics, challenges, and requirements of a specific situation or context. It requires leaders to thoroughly understand the conditions they are operating in, including factors such as the complexity of tasks, the composition and dynamics of their team, the organization's culture, external influences, and any potential risks or opportunities. The goal of assessing situational demands is to gather the necessary information to make informed decisions about the most suitable leadership approach or style. This process allows leaders to tailor their behaviors and strategies to align with the specific needs and contingencies of the situation, ultimately increasing their effectiveness in achieving desired outcomes. Assessing situational demands is a foundational step in applying contingency theory and emphasizes the importance of context-aware leadership.

Strategies and Tools for Leaders to Assess the Demands of Different Situations

Assessing the demands of different situations is a crucial skill for leaders to make informed decisions about their leadership approach. Important strategies and tools that leaders can use to assess the demands of various situations are:

1. **Active Listening:** Leaders can practice active listening, which involves fully concentrating, understanding, and responding to what others are saying. This helps in gathering valuable insights about team dynamics, challenges, and concerns within the group.

2. **Feedback Mechanisms:** Establishing formal and informal feedback channels within the organization or team allows leaders to receive insights from team members about their experiences, needs, and perceptions of the situation. Tools such as surveys, suggestion boxes, or regular one-on-one meetings can be employed.

3. **SWOT Analysis:** Conducting a SWOT (Strengths, Weaknesses, Opportunities, Threats) analysis provides leaders with a structured framework to assess the internal and external factors affecting a situation. It helps identify key issues and potential areas of focus.

4. **PESTEL Analysis:** PESTEL (Political, Economic, Social, Technological, Environmental, Legal) analysis helps leaders evaluate external macro-environmental factors that might influence a situation, such as economic trends, regulatory changes, or societal shifts.

5. **Task Analysis:** Breaking down the tasks or goals associated with a situation can provide clarity about the level of complexity, resources needed, and potential challenges. Tools like task lists, project management software, or Gantt charts can aid in task analysis.

6. **Competitor Analysis:** For leaders in competitive industries, analyzing competitors' strategies, strengths, and weaknesses can provide insights into the external landscape. Tools like competitive intelligence reports and market research can aid in this assessment.

7. **Benchmarking:** Benchmarking involves comparing the performance or practices of your organization or team against industry best practices or peer organizations. This helps leaders identify areas where improvements or changes are needed.

8. **Scenario Planning:** Leaders can engage in scenario planning, which involves developing multiple future scenarios based on different assumptions. This helps in assessing potential risks and opportunities in uncertain situations.

9. **Cultural Assessments:** Understanding the organizational culture is crucial. Leaders can employ tools like culture surveys, interviews, or cultural assessments to gauge the prevailing norms, values, and beliefs within the organization.

10. **Consultation and Expertise:** Seeking advice from subject matter experts, mentors, or advisors can provide valuable perspectives and insights when assessing complex situations. External consultants can also offer specialized expertise.

11. **Data Analytics:** In data-rich environments, leaders can utilize data analytics tools to gather quantitative insights. This can include performance metrics, customer data, or market trends, which can inform decision-making.

12. **Risk Assessment:** Conducting a risk assessment helps leaders identify potential threats and vulnerabilities associated with a situation. Risk matrices or probability-impact analyses can be employed.

13. **Stakeholder Analysis:** Identifying key stakeholders and their interests, influence, and needs related to a situation is vital. Stakeholder mapping tools can assist in this assessment.

14. **Scenario-Based Role-Playing:** Leaders can engage in scenario-based role-playing exercises to simulate potential situations and evaluate how they and their teams would respond.

15. **Market Research:** In business contexts, market research tools and methodologies, such as surveys, focus groups, or trend analysis, can provide insights into customer preferences and market dynamics.

16. **Environmental Scanning:** Leaders can regularly scan their external environment for relevant news, trends, and events that may impact the situation. This can include news alerts, industry publications, and economic indicators.

17. **Cross-Functional Teams:** In complex situations, assembling cross-functional teams with diverse expertise can facilitate a comprehensive assessment of the demands and challenges.

18. **Psychological Safety:** Creating an environment of psychological safety within the team encourages open and honest communication, enabling team members to share their concerns and perspectives freely.

19. **Regular Self-Assessment:** Leaders should engage in regular self-assessment, reflecting on their leadership behaviors and effectiveness in various situations. Tools like leadership assessments or 360-degree feedback can aid in this process.

20. **Continuous Learning:** Leaders should invest in continuous learning to stay updated on industry trends, leadership theories, and best practices. This enhances their ability to assess and respond to changing demands.

By employing these strategies and tools, leaders can systematically assess the demands of different situations, gather relevant information, and make informed decisions about their leadership approaches. This adaptability and context-awareness are essential for effective leadership in today's dynamic and evolving environments.

Recognizing the Signs

Recognizing the signs that a situational shift may be necessary is a crucial skill for leaders who want to adapt their approaches effectively. Here are some key indicators that can signal the need for a change in leadership style or strategy:

1. **Declining Team Performance:** A noticeable decrease in team performance, such as missed deadlines, increased errors, or decreased productivity, may indicate that the current leadership style is not motivating or guiding the team effectively.

2. **Increased Conflict:** Rising tensions, conflicts among team members, or a hostile work environment could suggest that the current leadership approach is not promoting collaboration or addressing underlying issues.

3. **Low Employee Morale:** A noticeable drop in employee morale, evidenced by disengagement, absenteeism, or negative attitudes, may be a sign that the leadership style is not meeting the emotional and motivational needs of team members.

4. **Unresponsive to Feedback:** If team members consistently provide feedback about the leadership style or approach and the leader fails to acknowledge or address it, this can indicate a lack of responsiveness to the evolving needs of the situation.

5. **Resistance to Change:** An unwillingness or resistance among team members to adapt to changes in processes, strategies, or goals may suggest that the current leadership style is not effectively communicating the rationale for change or providing necessary guidance.

6. **Stagnation or Decline in Results:** A plateau or decline in key performance indicators, despite efforts to maintain or

improve them, may signal that the leadership approach is no longer effective in driving results.

7. **Lack of Innovation:** If the organization or team struggles to generate new ideas, embrace innovation, or adapt to evolving industry trends, the leadership style may not be fostering a culture of creativity and adaptation.

8. **High Turnover Rates:** Elevated turnover rates, particularly among high-performing employees, can indicate dissatisfaction with the current leadership style or a failure to retain top talent.

9. **Mismatched Team Dynamics:** Changes in the composition or dynamics of the team, such as the addition of new members, shifts in roles, or increased diversity, may necessitate adjustments to the leadership style to ensure cohesion and effectiveness.

10. **External Changes:** Shifts in the external environment, such as new regulations, market trends, or competitive pressures, may require a change in leadership strategies to adapt to the changing landscape.

11. **Feedback from Peers or Superiors:** If peers, superiors, or external stakeholders provide feedback or express concerns about the leadership style or approach, it should be taken seriously as an indicator of potential issues.

12. **Ineffective Communication:** Difficulty in communicating expectations, goals, or changes may suggest that the current leadership approach is not facilitating effective information flow within the organization.

13. **Lack of Trust or Respect:** A noticeable erosion of trust and respect between the leader and team members can indicate that the current leadership style is not fostering positive relationships or ethical behavior.

14. **Emotional Intelligence:** A leader's ability to recognize the emotional states of team members can be a valuable sign. If team members exhibit signs of stress, frustration, or burnout, the leader should consider adjusting their approach to support their emotional well-being.

15. **Situational Complexity:** Changes in the complexity or urgency of tasks, projects, or goals may require a different leadership style to address the specific demands of the situation effectively.

Leaders who remain vigilant and responsive to these signs are better equipped to make timely adjustments in their leadership styles or strategies, ensuring that they continue to meet the evolving needs of their teams and organizations.

Communication and Feedback

Communication and feedback play pivotal roles in the process of adapting leadership styles based on situational demands. These elements are essential for leaders to understand the needs of their teams, align their leadership approaches with specific situations, and continually refine their strategies. Here's how communication and feedback contribute to this process:

1. **Assessing Situational Demands:** Effective communication channels enable leaders to gather information about the current situation, including its challenges, opportunities, and complexities. Through open dialogue with team members and stakeholders, leaders can gain insights that inform their assessment of the situation's demands.

2. **Understanding Team Members:** Regular communication with team members fosters an understanding of their individual preferences, strengths, weaknesses, and motivations. This knowledge allows leaders to tailor their

leadership styles to match the unique characteristics of team members and the situation.

3. **Setting Clear Expectations:** Communication is crucial for setting clear expectations regarding roles, responsibilities, and objectives in any given situation. When everyone understands their roles and the desired outcomes, it becomes easier for leaders to adapt their leadership approach to align with these expectations.

4. **Empowering Decision-Making:** Open lines of communication promote a culture of inclusivity and empowerment. Leaders who actively seek input and encourage team members to participate in decision-making processes are better equipped to adapt their styles to situations that require collaborative problem-solving.

5. **Offering Timely Feedback:** Providing regular feedback ensures that team members are aware of their performance and progress. Leaders can adapt their feedback styles to match individual needs, offering support and guidance when required and acknowledgment and praise when merited.

6. **Flexibility in Conflict Resolution:** Effective communication is essential when addressing conflicts. Leaders should maintain open lines of dialogue to resolve disputes and adapt their conflict resolution strategies to the nature and severity of the conflict.

7. **Cultural Sensitivity:** In diverse teams or international contexts, cross-cultural communication and feedback are vital. Leaders must adapt their communication styles to accommodate cultural differences and foster understanding.

8. **Regular Reflection and Feedback Seekings:** Leaders can actively seek feedback from team members regarding their leadership styles and the impact on team dynamics and performance. Constructive feedback allows leaders to adjust

their approaches for better alignment with situational demands.

9. **Continuous Learning:** Communication channels, such as participation in training, workshops, or professional networks, facilitate leaders' ongoing learning and development. This exposure to new ideas and practices enriches their leadership toolkit and enhances adaptability.

10. **Transparency and Trust Building:** Transparent communication fosters trust within the team. Leaders who communicate openly about their intentions, decisions, and plans create an environment where team members are more receptive to changes in leadership style.

11. **Monitoring and Evaluation:** Feedback mechanisms are essential for monitoring the effectiveness of leadership adaptations. Leaders can use feedback to evaluate whether their adjusted approach is producing the desired results or if further modifications are necessary.

12. **Adaptive Leadership Response:** Effective communication allows leaders to respond to emerging needs and contingencies swiftly. When leaders are aware of changing circumstances, they can adapt their styles proactively to address evolving challenges.

Communication and feedback are the lifeblood of leadership style adaptation. They provide leaders with the information, insights, and insights they need to make informed decisions about how to lead effectively in different situations. By fostering open and honest communication and actively seeking feedback, leaders can refine their approaches, enhance their adaptability, and promote organizational success.

Situational Leadership

Situational leadership, also known as adaptive leadership, is a leadership approach that emphasizes the need to adapt one's leadership style to suit the varied demands of different situations. The core concept is that there is no single, universally effective leadership style; instead, leaders must be flexible and responsive to the unique characteristics and requirements of each situation they encounter. Situational leadership recognizes that the dynamics of a crisis, a creative project, a team development initiative, or routine day-to-day operations can vary significantly. Therefore, leaders must assess the specific demands of a given situation, such as the level of task complexity, the competence and commitment of their team members, and the external factors at play. Based on this assessment, leaders can adjust their leadership behaviors, ranging from being more directive and hands-on to being more empowering and supportive, to align with the situation's needs. In essence, situational leadership is about achieving the right balance and adapting one's leadership approach to optimize team performance and achieve desired outcomes in any context.

Situational Leadership Model

The Situational Leadership Model, developed by Paul Hersey and Ken Blanchard in the late 1960s, is a widely recognized leadership framework that provides a structured approach for leaders to adapt their leadership styles to the readiness level of their followers or team members. This model is based on the premise that effective leadership is not static but should vary depending on the specific situation and the development level of those being led. The Situational Leadership Model defines leadership along two key dimensions:

1. **Leadership Behavior:** It classifies leadership behavior into four distinct styles: Telling (S1), Selling (S2), Participating (S3), and Delegating (S4). Each style ranges from high

directive behavior (providing specific instructions and close supervision) to high supportive behavior (emphasizing collaboration and autonomy).

2. **Follower Readiness:** It assesses the readiness or development level of followers based on their competence and commitment. Followers are categorized into four readiness levels: R1 (Low Competence, Low Commitment), R2 (Some Competence, Low Commitment), R3 (Moderate to High Competence, Variable Commitment), and R4 (High Competence, High Commitment).

The Situational Leadership Model provides a valuable framework for leaders to assess the readiness of their team members and adjust their leadership styles accordingly. It underscores the importance of flexibility in leadership, recognizing that what works best in one situation may not be suitable for another. By aligning leadership behavior with follower readiness, the model aims to maximize the likelihood of achieving team goals and individual development effectively.

Situational Model's Four Leadership Styles

The Situational Leadership Model defines four distinct leadership styles, each with its specific characteristics and applicability to different situations. These styles are Telling, Selling, Participating, and Delegating.

Telling (S1 - Directing)

- **Characteristics:** This style is characterized by high directive behavior and low supportive behavior. Leaders who adopt the Telling style provide specific instructions, closely supervise tasks, and make decisions for their team members.

- **Applicability:** The Telling style is most appropriate when team members are at the lowest readiness level (R1 - Low Competence, Low Commitment). In situations where followers lack the necessary skills or knowledge and are also hesitant or resistant, a directive approach is essential. It helps establish clarity and build competence.

Selling (S2 - Coaching)

- **Characteristics:** The Selling style combines high directive behavior with a higher level of supportive behavior. Leaders who use this style not only provide clear direction but also engage in active communication to persuade and motivate team members.

- **Applicability:** The Selling style is suitable when team members exhibit low to moderate readiness (R2 - Some Competence, Low Commitment). In such situations, followers may have the required skills but lack confidence or commitment. Leaders must provide guidance, support, and encouragement to boost commitment while reinforcing competence.

Participating (S3 - Supporting)

- **Characteristics:** This style involves low directive behavior and high supportive behavior. Leaders adopting the Participating style encourage team members to participate in decision-making, problem-solving, and goal-setting. They offer guidance when needed but allow team members to take the lead.

- **Applicability:** The Participating style is suitable when team members demonstrate moderate to high readiness (R3 - Moderate to High Competence, Variable Commitment). In these situations, followers possess the necessary skills but may have varying levels of commitment. Leaders should involve them in decision-making to enhance commitment and maintain their competence.

Delegating (S4 - Empowering)

- **Characteristics:** Delegating involves low directive behavior and low supportive behavior. Leaders who use this style provide minimal guidance and allow team members to take control of their tasks and decisions independently.

- **Applicability:** The Delegating style is appropriate when team members are at the highest readiness level (R4 - High Competence, High Commitment). In this scenario, followers are both highly skilled and motivated. Leaders can step back, entrust responsibilities to team members, and focus on providing support when needed. This style encourages autonomy and fosters a sense of ownership.

It's important to note that the Situational Leadership Model emphasizes the need for leaders to assess the readiness level of their team members before selecting the most appropriate leadership style. Effective leaders should be flexible and capable of transitioning between these styles as the situation and the readiness of their followers evolve. By adapting their leadership behaviors to match the specific needs of each situation, leaders can enhance team performance, facilitate development, and achieve desired outcomes more effectively.

Real World Examples

Real-world examples can help illustrate how leaders effectively adapt their styles using the Situational Leadership Model. A few examples are:

1. **Steve Jobs at Apple:** Steve Jobs, the co-founder and former CEO of Apple Inc., is known for his adaptability in leadership. He could be highly directive when introducing new products or strategies (Telling) to ensure that the team understood his vision. However, he also demonstrated the Selling style by actively involving teams in product development, encouraging creative input. His adaptability contributed to Apple's success in delivering innovative products like the iPhone and iPad.
2. **Nelson Mandela's Leadership in South Africa:** Nelson Mandela's leadership during South Africa's transition from apartheid to democracy is a prime example of situational adaptability. While in prison, he used a Participating leadership style to maintain unity among diverse political groups. After his release, he transitioned to a Selling style, persuading various factions to work together for a peaceful transition. Once he became President, he adopted a Delegating style, empowering his government to lead the country's transformation.
3. **Elon Musk at Tesla:** Elon Musk, CEO of Tesla, demonstrates situational leadership by adjusting his style depending on the company's needs. In the early days, he used a Telling style to set the company's vision and direct product development. As Tesla matured, he shifted to a Participating style, collaborating with engineers and designers. Musk also delegates responsibilities to his teams, focusing on his strengths and overarching strategy (Delegating).
4. **Effective School Principals:** School principals often use the Situational Leadership Model to manage their staff effectively. For example, when introducing a new

curriculum, they may adopt a Telling style to provide specific guidelines. In mentoring new teachers, they might use a Selling style, offering guidance and support. As experienced teachers demonstrate readiness, principals may transition to a Delegating style, allowing them more autonomy in classroom decisions.

5. **Emergency Response Leaders:** Leaders in emergency response situations, such as firefighters or paramedics, exhibit situational adaptability. In high-stress scenarios, they often employ a Telling style to provide clear instructions. As the situation stabilizes, they may shift to a Selling style to coordinate efforts with other teams. In post-emergency phases, they adopt a Delegating style to oversee recovery operations.

These real-world examples highlight how leaders from various fields apply the Situational Leadership Model to adapt their styles according to the specific demands and readiness levels of their teams or followers. This adaptability allows them to navigate complex situations, motivate teams, and achieve their objectives effectively.

Challenges and Criticisms

The Situational Leadership Model, while widely respected and applied, is not without its challenges and criticisms. One major challenge lies in the complexity of consistently assessing the readiness level of team members accurately. Determining whether individuals possess the necessary competence and commitment can be subjective and may vary from one leader to another. Additionally, readiness levels may change rapidly, making it challenging to maintain a precise assessment.

Critics argue that the model oversimplifies the complexities of leadership by categorizing individuals into four discrete readiness levels, potentially neglecting the nuances of each person's unique development needs. Some assert that it lacks a deeper consideration of individual personality traits, values, and cultural factors that can influence leadership effectiveness.

Furthermore, the Situational Leadership Model can be criticized for emphasizing leadership adaptation without providing clear guidance on how to make these adaptations effectively. This might leave leaders unsure of how to transition between styles seamlessly and how to communicate these shifts transparently to their teams.

While the Situational Leadership Model offers valuable insights into leadership flexibility and adaptation, it faces challenges related to the accuracy of readiness assessments and criticism for potential oversimplification and lack of detailed guidance. Despite these concerns, many leaders continue to find it a useful framework for enhancing their leadership effectiveness in various situations.

1. **Complexity of Readiness Assessment:** One of the primary challenges lies in accurately assessing the readiness level of team members. Determining whether individuals have the necessary competence and commitment can be subjective and prone to errors. Additionally, readiness levels can change rapidly, making consistent assessment a challenging task.
2. **Oversimplification of Leadership:** Critics argue that the model oversimplifies the multifaceted nature of leadership by categorizing individuals into four discrete readiness levels (R1, R2, R3, R4). This oversimplification may neglect the nuances of individual personality traits, values, and cultural factors that can profoundly influence leadership effectiveness.
3. **Lack of Contextual Nuance:** The Situational Leadership Model does not always account for the unique contextual factors that may impact leadership effectiveness in specific situations. Leaders may find it challenging to adapt the

model to the idiosyncrasies of their organizations, industries, or cultural environments.
4. **Absence of Personality Considerations:** Critics argue that the model places greater emphasis on situational adaptation and readiness levels while downplaying the influence of a leader's personality traits and characteristics. In reality, a leader's personality can significantly impact their leadership style and effectiveness.
5. **Transitioning Between Styles:** The model may not provide clear guidance on how to transition between leadership styles effectively. Leaders may struggle with understanding when and how to shift from one style to another, leading to inconsistency in leadership approaches.
6. **Communication of Style Shifts:** Communicating style shifts to team members can be challenging. Abrupt changes in leadership style without proper explanation or transparency can lead to confusion and resistance among team members.
7. **Lack of Prescriptive Guidance:** The model does not offer prescriptive guidelines for leaders, which can be seen as both an advantage and a drawback. Some leaders may prefer more concrete instructions on how to adapt their styles effectively.
8. **Applicability in Complex Environments:** In highly complex and rapidly changing environments, the Situational Leadership Model may not provide sufficient guidance for leaders facing multifaceted challenges and uncertainty.
9. **Training and Implementation Challenges:** Effectively training leaders in the model's principles and ensuring consistent implementation across an organization can be challenging. Without proper training and support, leaders may struggle to apply the model effectively.

The Situational Leadership Model is a valuable framework for leadership adaptation, but it is not without its challenges and criticisms. Leaders should be mindful of these limitations and consider how to complement the model with additional leadership approaches and tools to address the complexities of their unique situations and teams.

Strategies for mitigating potential drawbacks

To mitigate potential drawbacks associated with the Situational Leadership Model, leaders can employ several strategies to enhance its effectiveness and address its limitations:

1. **Enhance Readiness Assessment:** Invest in improving the accuracy of readiness assessments. Provide training to leaders on how to evaluate competence and commitment more effectively, including the use of performance metrics and regular feedback.
2. **Combine with Other Leadership Theories:** Use the Situational Leadership Model in conjunction with other leadership theories and approaches. This allows leaders to draw from a broader toolkit and adapt their strategies more comprehensively.
3. **Consider Individual Differences:** Recognize that individuals have unique traits, values, and experiences. While applying the model, consider how these individual differences may influence leadership effectiveness and adapt your approach accordingly.
4. **Contextualize the Model:** Adapt the model to the specific context of your organization or industry. Consider the unique challenges, cultural factors, and organizational dynamics that may affect leadership effectiveness and tailor your approach accordingly.
5. **Include Personality Assessment:** Incorporate personality assessments or leadership style assessments alongside the Situational Leadership Model. This can help leaders better

understand their own leadership preferences and adapt more consciously.
6. **Provide Training and Guidance:** Offer training and guidance to leaders on how to transition between leadership styles effectively. Provide practical examples and case studies to illustrate successful style transitions in different situations.
7. **Transparent Communication:** Communicate style shifts transparently to team members. Explain the reasons for the change, the expected outcomes, and how it aligns with the team's goals. Encourage open dialogue and feedback.
8. **Customize Leadership Development:** Tailor leadership development programs to address the specific needs and challenges of your organization. Ensure that leaders receive ongoing support and training to master the Situational Leadership Model.
9. **Seek External Expertise:** Consider bringing in external experts or consultants to provide insights and guidance on implementing the model effectively. They can offer a fresh perspective and help identify areas for improvement.
10. **Flexibility and Adaptability:** Encourage leaders to embrace flexibility and adaptability in their leadership approaches. Empower them to make real-time adjustments based on evolving circumstances and team dynamics.
11. **Continuous Evaluation and Improvement:** Continuously evaluate the effectiveness of the model within your organization. Collect feedback from leaders and team members, and be willing to make refinements to your approach as needed.
12. **Foster a Learning Culture:** Promote a culture of learning and growth within your organization. Encourage leaders to experiment with different leadership styles and approaches, emphasizing the importance of ongoing development.

By implementing these strategies, organizations and leaders can better address the potential drawbacks of the Situational Leadership Model and maximize its benefits in fostering adaptable and effective leadership.

Broader Perspective

A Broader Perspective refers to an expanded understanding and application of adaptive leadership principles that extend beyond the traditional organizational context. While adaptive leadership initially emerged as a framework for addressing leadership challenges within organizations, it has evolved to encompass a broader perspective that recognizes its relevance in various domains, including community leadership, social change, and global issues.

In this context, adaptive leadership goes beyond managing internal organizational dynamics and focuses on addressing complex, adaptive problems that transcend traditional boundaries. These problems often involve multiple stakeholders, diverse perspectives, and systemic challenges that require innovative and collaborative approaches.

It signifies the evolution of adaptive leadership concepts to address complex and systemic challenges that extend beyond the boundaries of organizations. It emphasizes a holistic and inclusive approach that engages diverse stakeholders, fosters innovation, and seeks sustainable solutions to pressing issues in our interconnected and rapidly changing world.

Beyond Individual Behaviors

The concept of adaptive leadership extends beyond individual behavior to tackle complex challenges and systems by recognizing that leadership is not confined to personal attributes or behaviors but is inherently intertwined with the broader context in which it operates. Adaptive leadership, as introduced by Ronald Heifetz and Martin Linsky, reframes traditional notions of leadership and acknowledges that many problems organizations and societies face are not just complicated but genuinely complex and adaptive in nature. Here's a detailed exploration of this concept:

1. **Complex Challenges vs. Complicated Problems:** Adaptive leadership differentiates between complicated and complex problems. Complicated problems have known solutions that require expertise and technical know-how, while complex challenges lack clear solutions and involve numerous interconnected factors, diverse stakeholders, and often, unforeseeable consequences.
2. **Leadership Beyond Authority:** Adaptive leadership goes beyond the idea that leadership is solely the domain of designated leaders or authorities. Instead, it recognizes that anyone can exhibit leadership behaviors, regardless of their formal position, when addressing complex challenges.
3. **Technical vs. Adaptive Challenges:** In the context of leadership, adaptive challenges are those that require changes in people's beliefs, behaviors, or values. Technical challenges, on the other hand, can be addressed through existing expertise and established procedures.
4. **Disruptive Change and Resistance:** Adaptive leadership acknowledges that introducing disruptive changes, especially in deeply entrenched systems, often generates resistance and discomfort. Leaders must navigate this resistance and mobilize stakeholders for change effectively.
5. **Balancing Authority and Adaptation:** Adaptive leaders need to strike a delicate balance between exercising authority to maintain order and creating the necessary adaptive disturbance to stimulate change. They must recognize when to intervene and when to allow adaptive work to occur.

6. **Creating Adaptive Spaces:** Adaptive leadership involves creating safe spaces for open dialogue and experimentation. Leaders encourage diverse perspectives, challenge assumptions, and promote learning from failures as essential components of addressing complex challenges.
7. **Systemic View:** Leaders employing adaptive approaches view challenges systemically, considering how various interconnected elements contribute to the problem and how changes in one part of the system may affect others.
8. **Learning Orientation:** Adaptive leadership is fundamentally a learning-oriented approach. Leaders continuously learn from their experiences, adapt their strategies, and encourage adaptive learning among stakeholders.
9. **Empowering Stakeholders:** Adaptive leaders empower stakeholders, enabling them to play active roles in problem-solving and decision-making processes. This approach fosters ownership and commitment among those affected by the change.
10. **Long-Term Sustainability:** Adaptive leadership is often concerned with long-term sustainability. Leaders aim to address the root causes of complex challenges, rather than implementing quick fixes that may not endure.
11. **Ethical Considerations:** Ethical principles are integral to adaptive leadership. Leaders prioritize fairness, justice, and the well-being of all stakeholders in their efforts to address complex challenges.
12. **Global and Cross-Sector Engagement:** Adaptive leadership extends to global and cross-sector engagement, recognizing that many complex challenges, such as climate change and global health crises, require collaborative efforts across borders and industries.

Adaptive leadership introduces a paradigm shift in understanding leadership by emphasizing the importance of addressing complex challenges and systems that cannot be solved through technical expertise alone. It underscores the need for leaders to navigate uncertainty, foster learning, and mobilize stakeholders in the pursuit of sustainable solutions to pressing societal and organizational issues.

Application on Organizations

Applying adaptive leadership in organizations means adopting a leadership approach that acknowledges and addresses complex challenges within the organizational context. Unlike traditional leadership models, adaptive leadership recognizes that many issues faced by organizations are not straightforward but involve intricate, interconnected factors, requiring shifts in behaviors, beliefs, and values. Leaders who apply adaptive leadership principles focus on creating a supportive environment that encourages open dialogue, diversity of thought, and constructive conflict. They mobilize leadership across various levels of the organization, recognizing that effective solutions often emerge from collective efforts. Additionally, they prioritize long-term sustainability, ethical considerations, and continuous learning, fostering a culture of adaptability and resilience. By embracing adaptive leadership, organizations can better navigate the complexities of their internal and external environments, fostering innovation and facilitating positive change.

Tackle Organizational Challenges

Adaptive leadership can be effectively applied to address various organizational challenges, including change management and fostering innovation. Here's an exploration of how adaptive leadership principles can be applied in these contexts:

Change Management

1. **Diagnosing the Challenge:** Adaptive leaders begin by diagnosing the nature of the change required. They distinguish between technical changes (those with known solutions) and adaptive changes (those necessitating shifts in behaviors, beliefs, and values).

2. **Creating a Holding Environment:** To manage change effectively, adaptive leaders create a "holding environment" where employees feel safe to express concerns, uncertainties, and fears associated with the change. This environment encourages open dialogue and helps address resistance.

3. **Mobilizing Leadership at All Levels:** Adaptive leaders understand that successful change requires the engagement of individuals at all levels of the organization. They empower employees to play active roles in the change process, recognizing that leadership is not confined to top management.

4. **Managing Conflict Constructively:** Change often brings about conflict. Adaptive leaders facilitate constructive conflict resolution, allowing stakeholders to voice their opinions and concerns. They view conflict as an opportunity for learning and growth.

5. **Embracing Experimentation:** Adaptive leadership encourages experimentation as a means of finding innovative solutions and learning from failures. Leaders foster a culture where employees are encouraged to test new approaches and adapt as needed.

6. **Leveraging Diversity:** Diversity of thought and experience is valued in adaptive leadership. Leaders actively seek diverse perspectives when addressing change, recognizing that varied viewpoints can lead to more robust solutions.

Innovation

1. **Creating an Innovation-Supportive Environment:** Adaptive leaders establish an environment that encourages and rewards innovative thinking. They promote a culture where employees feel comfortable proposing new ideas, taking risks, and challenging the status quo.

2. **Mobilizing Leadership for Innovation:** Innovation is not limited to R&D departments. Adaptive leaders encourage employees from all departments and levels to contribute to innovation efforts. They recognize that innovation can come from unexpected sources.

3. **Managing Creative Conflict:** Adaptive leadership acknowledges that innovative processes may involve creative conflict. Leaders facilitate healthy debates and discussions to refine ideas and identify the best solutions.

4. **Experimentation and Learning:** Leaders foster a culture of experimentation, where employees are encouraged to prototype and test new concepts. Adaptive leaders support learning from both successes and failures, viewing setbacks as opportunities for growth.

5. **Long-Term Sustainability:** Adaptive leaders ensure that innovation efforts align with the organization's long-term goals and values. They focus on creating innovations that have lasting impacts and contribute to the organization's overall success.

6. **Global Collaboration for Innovation:** In today's interconnected world, innovation often benefits from global perspectives and partnerships. Adaptive leaders engage with diverse stakeholders, both within and outside the organization, to drive innovation efforts forward.

Adaptive leadership principles are highly applicable to tackling organizational challenges such as change management and innovation. By creating supportive environments, mobilizing leadership at all levels, managing conflict constructively, and fostering experimentation and learning, adaptive leaders can navigate these challenges effectively and drive positive organizational transformation and innovation.

Case Study 1: IBM's Transformation under Ginni Rometty

Background

IBM, a global technology and consulting company, faced significant challenges as it grappled with the rapid evolution of the tech industry. Ginni Rometty, who served as IBM's CEO from 2012 to 2020, demonstrated adaptive leadership throughout her tenure.

Application of Adaptive Leadership

1. **Diagnosing the Challenge:** Rometty recognized that IBM needed to shift its focus from hardware to software and services to remain competitive in the changing technology landscape. She diagnosed the challenge as a complex adaptive problem.

2. **Creating a Holding Environment:** Rometty created a "holding environment" by fostering a culture of open dialogue and experimentation. She encouraged employees to voice concerns, share innovative ideas, and challenge conventional thinking.

3. **Mobilizing Leadership at All Levels:** Rometty believed that innovation could come from anywhere within the organization. She empowered employees at all levels to lead change and contribute to IBM's transformation.

4. **Managing Conflict Constructively:** During IBM's transformation, conflicts naturally arose as the company

pivoted its business model. Rometty and her leadership team managed conflicts constructively by engaging stakeholders in productive discussions and addressing concerns transparently.

5. **Embracing Experimentation:** Rometty promoted experimentation and risk-taking by investing in emerging technologies like artificial intelligence and cloud computing. IBM's willingness to experiment led to the development of innovative solutions and services.

Results

Under Ginni Rometty's adaptive leadership, IBM successfully transformed itself into a leading cloud and cognitive solutions provider. The company embraced change, diversified its offerings, and maintained its position as a key player in the tech industry. Rometty's adaptive approach played a pivotal role in IBM's resurgence.

Case Study 2: The Apollo 13 Mission

Background

The Apollo 13 mission, launched by NASA in 1970, faced a life-threatening crisis when an oxygen tank in the spacecraft exploded, jeopardizing the lives of the astronauts onboard. Gene Kranz, the flight director, and his team demonstrated adaptive leadership in managing the crisis.

Application of Adaptive Leadership

1. **Diagnosing the Challenge:** The Apollo 13 mission faced a highly complex and life-threatening challenge. Kranz and his team quickly diagnosed the problem and understood it to be a complex, adaptive issue requiring innovative solutions.

2. **Creating a Holding Environment:** Kranz established a "holding environment" in the mission control center, where team members felt safe to voice concerns, brainstorm solutions, and challenge assumptions.

3. **Mobilizing Leadership at All Levels:** The crisis required leadership contributions from all team members. Engineers and astronauts collaborated closely, contributing their expertise to develop solutions for various aspects of the mission.

4. **Managing Conflict Constructively:** Conflicting opinions and concerns emerged during critical decision-making. Kranz facilitated constructive conflict resolution, ensuring that the team's discussions led to informed and effective decisions.

5. **Embracing Experimentation:** The team had to rapidly prototype solutions to address the mission's challenges, such as creating a makeshift carbon dioxide removal system. They embraced experimentation and learned from their attempts.

Results

Through adaptive leadership, Gene Kranz and his team successfully guided the Apollo 13 mission back to Earth safely, overcoming numerous technical and logistical challenges. Their ability to adapt, innovate, and collaborate under extreme pressure remains a remarkable example of adaptive leadership in a high-stakes environment.

These case studies illustrate how adaptive leadership principles can be applied to navigate complex challenges and drive successful outcomes, whether in the context of organizational transformation or life-threatening situations. Adaptive leaders diagnose challenges, create supportive environments, mobilize leadership at all levels, manage conflict constructively, and embrace experimentation to lead effectively in dynamic and uncertain circumstances.

The Role of Continuous Learning and Feedback

The role of learning and feedback in adaptive leadership is paramount. Learning is an ongoing process that enables leaders to gather insights, refine their strategies, and adapt to changing circumstances. Adaptive leaders embrace a continuous learning orientation, seeking opportunities to expand their knowledge and understanding of complex challenges. Feedback, both from stakeholders and the environment, serves as a critical source of information for leaders to assess the impact of their actions and make necessary adjustments. It provides valuable insights into what is working and what needs improvement, facilitating course corrections and informed decision-making. Learning and feedback in adaptive leadership contribute to resilience, innovation, and the ability to navigate complex issues successfully.

Importance of Continuous Learning

Continuous learning and feedback are of paramount importance in the practice of adaptive leadership. Here's why they are essential:

1. **Navigating Complexity:** In adaptive leadership, leaders often confront complex and ambiguous challenges. Continuous learning helps leaders develop a deeper understanding of these challenges, enabling them to make informed decisions and take appropriate actions.
2. **Resilience:** Adaptive leaders need to adapt to changing circumstances and setbacks. Continuous learning allows leaders to build resilience by acquiring new skills, insights, and perspectives, helping them bounce back from adversity.

3. **Innovation:** Learning fosters creativity and innovation. Adaptive leaders who continuously seek new knowledge and ideas can drive innovation within their organizations by challenging the status quo and exploring novel solutions to complex problems.

4. **Enhanced Decision-Making:** Feedback from stakeholders and the environment provides critical information for leaders to evaluate the effectiveness of their strategies. This feedback loop helps leaders make data-informed decisions and refine their approaches.

5. **Engagement and Trust:** Leaders who actively seek and value feedback from their teams and stakeholders demonstrate a commitment to collaboration and improvement. This builds trust and engagement among team members, as they see their voices are heard and their input is valued.

6. **Alignment with Changing Needs:** The external environment and organizational context are subject to change. Continuous learning allows leaders to stay attuned to these changes and adjust their strategies accordingly, ensuring alignment with evolving needs and expectations.

7. **Adaptive Culture:** Leaders who prioritize continuous learning and feedback help create a culture of adaptability within their organizations. This cultural shift encourages employees to embrace change and contribute to the organization's adaptive capacity.

8. **Personal Growth:** Adaptive leaders view their own development as an ongoing journey. Continuous learning enables personal growth, expanding leaders' skills and capabilities, which, in turn, benefit the organization.

9. **Conflict Resolution:** Feedback provides insights into conflicts and challenges within the organization. Adaptive

leaders can use feedback to address issues, mediate conflicts, and promote healthy working relationships.
10. **Sustainability:** Continuous learning helps leaders focus on long-term sustainability rather than short-term fixes. Leaders who adapt their strategies based on ongoing learning are more likely to achieve lasting solutions to complex challenges.

Continuous learning and feedback are integral to adaptive leadership, as they enable leaders to navigate complexity, build resilience, drive innovation, make informed decisions, foster engagement and trust, align with changing needs, cultivate an adaptive culture, promote personal growth, resolve conflicts, and pursue sustainability. These elements collectively contribute to the effectiveness of adaptive leaders in addressing complex and ever-evolving challenges.

Strategies for Creating a Culture of Learning

Creating a culture of learning and adaptation within organizations is vital for fostering innovation, resilience, and long-term success. Some strategies to establish such a culture are:

1. **Leadership Commitment:** Leadership plays a pivotal role in setting the tone for a learning culture. Leaders should exemplify a commitment to learning and adaptation through their actions, decisions, and behaviors.
2. **Clear Vision and Values:** Establish a clear vision that emphasizes the importance of learning and adaptation. Align organizational values with these principles, making it evident that they are integral to the organization's identity.
3. **Open Communication:** Encourage open and transparent communication channels. Create forums where employees can share ideas, concerns, and feedback without fear of reprisal.

4. **Empowerment and Autonomy:** Empower employees by granting them autonomy to make decisions related to their work. This autonomy fosters a sense of ownership and encourages innovative thinking.
5. **Continuous Feedback:** Implement regular feedback mechanisms, including performance evaluations, surveys, and suggestion boxes. Use feedback to drive improvements and inform decision-making.
6. **Learning Opportunities:** Provide ample learning opportunities, such as training programs, workshops, and access to educational resources. Support employees in acquiring new skills and knowledge.
7. **Experimentation and Risk-Taking:** Encourage a culture of experimentation and risk-taking. Celebrate both successes and failures as opportunities for learning and growth.
8. **Cross-Functional Collaboration:** Promote cross-functional collaboration by breaking down silos and encouraging teams from different departments to work together on projects. Diverse perspectives often lead to innovative solutions.
9. **Recognition and Rewards:** Recognize and reward employees who actively contribute to the culture of learning and adaptation. Acknowledging their efforts reinforces the desired behavior.
10. **Storytelling:** Share success stories and lessons learned within the organization. These narratives inspire others to embrace learning and adaptation.
11. **Leaders as Coaches:** Encourage leaders to take on coaching roles, guiding and mentoring employees in their development. This personal touch can significantly impact employees' growth.
12. **Data-Driven Decision-Making:** Promote the use of data and analytics to inform decision-making processes. Demonstrating how data can lead to better outcomes reinforces the value of learning and adaptation.

13. **Regular Assessments:** Periodically assess the organization's culture and the effectiveness of its learning and adaptation initiatives. Use the results to make improvements and adjustments.
14. **Celebrate Diversity:** Embrace diversity in all its forms, including diversity of thought and background. Recognize that diverse perspectives are essential for innovation and adaptation.
15. **Long-Term Focus:** Encourage a long-term perspective rather than seeking quick fixes. Learning and adaptation efforts should align with the organization's long-term goals.
16. **Lead by Example:** Leaders should actively participate in learning and adaptation initiatives. Their engagement sends a powerful message to the entire organization.

By implementing these strategies, organizations can cultivate a culture where learning and adaptation are not just encouraged but ingrained in the organization's DNA. Such a culture fosters agility, innovation, and the ability to thrive in an ever-changing business environment.

*****

CHAPTER SEVEN
Transformational and Modern Approaches

The terms "Transformational" and "Modern Approaches" are often used in various contexts, including business management, leadership, technology, and more. The specific meaning of these terms can vary depending on the context in which they are used.

Transformational Approaches

Transformational approaches typically refer to methods, strategies, or leadership styles that aim to bring about significant and positive change or transformation within an organization, group, or system. These approaches are characterized by a focus on inspiring and motivating individuals or teams to achieve higher levels of performance and reach new goals. Transformational leaders often lead by example, set clear visions, and encourage innovation and creativity. In the context of leadership, transformational leaders are known for their ability to inspire and empower their followers, fostering a sense of ownership and commitment among team members. They often emphasize values and a shared vision to drive change and improvement.

Modern Approaches

Modern approach is a broad term that refers to contemporary or up-to-date methods, practices, or techniques that have evolved with changing times and advancements in various fields. These approaches are characterized by their adaptability and relevance to current circumstances, often incorporating the latest technologies, knowledge, and best practices. In business, for instance, modern approaches may include adopting digital transformation strategies, agile project management methodologies, data-driven decision-making, and utilizing cutting-edge technologies like artificial intelligence and automation. In education, modern approaches may involve incorporating online learning platforms, personalized learning, and innovative teaching methods to enhance the educational experience.

Importance of Transformation and Modern Approaches

Understanding the significance of transformational and modern leadership approaches is crucial for leaders and organizations seeking to thrive in today's rapidly changing and competitive environments. Let's delve into the significance of each approach:

Significance of Transformational Leadership

1. **Inspires and Motivates:** Transformational leaders have the ability to inspire and motivate their teams to achieve extraordinary results. They create a shared vision that inspires a sense of purpose and commitment among team members.

2. **Fosters Innovation:** This leadership style encourages innovation and creativity. Team members are more likely to think outside the box and propose new ideas when they are motivated by a transformational leader.

3. **Builds Strong Teams:** Transformational leaders often build strong, cohesive teams where members are united by a common vision and trust in their leader. This can lead to improved teamwork and collaboration.

4. **Personal Growth:** Transformational leadership can lead to personal growth and development among team members. Leaders invest in their team's development, helping them reach their full potential.

5. **Adaptability:** Transformational leaders are often adaptable and open to change. This is essential in today's dynamic

business environment where flexibility and agility are key to success.

Significance of Modern Leadership Approaches

1. **Adaptation to Technology:** Modern leadership approaches incorporate the latest technologies and digital tools to improve efficiency and decision-making. This is vital in a world where technology is advancing rapidly.

2. **Data-Driven Decision-Making:** Modern leaders use data and analytics to inform their decisions. This approach ensures that decisions are based on objective information rather than gut feelings.

3. **Agility and Flexibility:** Modern leaders recognize the importance of being agile and adaptable. They can pivot quickly in response to changing market conditions and customer needs.

4. **Remote Work:** With the rise of remote work, modern leaders have had to adapt to leading virtual teams effectively. They understand how to manage remote teams, foster collaboration, and maintain productivity.

5. **Diversity and Inclusion:** Modern leaders place a strong emphasis on diversity and inclusion in the workplace. They recognize the value of diverse perspectives and work to create inclusive environments where everyone can thrive.

6. **Environmental and Social Responsibility:** Many modern leadership approaches incorporate a focus on environmental and social responsibility. Leaders consider the impact of their decisions on sustainability and social issues.

Transformational leadership inspires and motivates, while modern leadership approaches adapt to the evolving landscape of business and technology. The significance of these approaches lies in their ability to drive innovation, foster growth, and ensure relevance and competitiveness in today's ever-changing world. Effective leaders often combine elements of both approaches to meet the complex challenges of contemporary leadership.

Shift from the Traditional Leadership Models

The shift from traditional leadership models to more contemporary and values-driven paradigms reflects the evolving expectations and demands of today's organizations and society. This transition is significant for several reasons:

1. **Alignment with Modern Values:** Traditional leadership models often focused on hierarchical structures, command-and-control approaches, and profit-driven goals. Contemporary leadership paradigms align with modern values such as ethics, sustainability, diversity, and social responsibility. This shift resonates with the values of employees, customers, and stakeholders who increasingly prioritize these aspects.

2. **Employee Engagement and Well-Being:** Contemporary leadership models emphasize employee engagement, well-being, and work-life balance. Leaders who prioritize these factors tend to have more satisfied and motivated teams, leading to higher productivity and retention rates.

3. **Innovation and Adaptability:** Traditional leadership models can be rigid and resistant to change. Contemporary leadership emphasizes innovation and adaptability, recognizing the need to stay agile in rapidly evolving markets. Leaders who embrace this paradigm encourage a culture of experimentation and learning.

4. **Diversity and Inclusion:** Modern leadership models recognize the importance of diversity and inclusion. They promote a diverse workforce and ensure that all voices are

heard and valued. This not only fosters creativity but also aligns with principles of fairness and equality.

5. **Transparency and Trust:** Values-driven leadership often entails transparency and open communication. Leaders who are honest and trustworthy can build stronger relationships with their teams and stakeholders. Trust is crucial for collaboration and long-term success.

6. **Sustainability and Social Impact:** Many contemporary leadership paradigms incorporate sustainability and social impact into their strategies. Leaders are increasingly held accountable for their organizations' environmental and social practices, and values-driven leaders prioritize these aspects to make a positive difference in the world.

7. **Globalization and Digitalization:** In a globalized and digital world, leadership transcends borders and time zones. Modern leaders must navigate diverse cultural contexts and leverage technology effectively. Values-driven leadership promotes inclusivity and harnesses the power of technology for positive change.

8. **Long-Term Vision:** While traditional leadership models may prioritize short-term gains, contemporary paradigms often have a longer-term perspective. Leaders focus on building sustainable, enduring organizations that contribute positively to society over time.

9. **Resilience and Crisis Management:** Values-driven leaders tend to be more resilient in the face of crises. They prioritize ethical decision-making, crisis preparedness, and the well-being of their teams, which helps organizations weather storms more effectively.

10. **Competitive Advantage:** Organizations that embrace contemporary and values-driven leadership can gain a competitive edge. They attract top talent, resonate with

customers, and adapt more readily to changing market dynamics.

The shift from traditional leadership models to contemporary and values-driven paradigms is significant because it reflects the evolving needs and expectations of individuals, organizations, and society as a whole. This transition is not just about leadership style but also about the core values and principles that guide leaders in an ever-changing world.

Transformational Leadership

Transformational leadership is a leadership style that focuses on catalyzing change and inspiration within an organization or team. Leaders who adopt this approach inspire and motivate their followers by creating a compelling vision and fostering a sense of purpose. They encourage innovation, challenge the status quo, and promote personal growth among team members. Transformational leaders lead by example, demonstrating high levels of commitment and enthusiasm, which inspires their teams to achieve exceptional results. This leadership style is particularly effective in times of change and uncertainty, as it encourages adaptability, creativity, and a shared commitment to a common goal, ultimately driving positive transformation within the organization.

Paradigm Focused on Inspiring and Motivating Teams to Achieve Remarkable Goals

1. **Visionary Leadership:** Transformational leaders are known for their ability to articulate a compelling vision for the future. They paint a vivid picture of what success looks like and create a shared sense of purpose among team members. This vision serves as a guiding light, inspiring individuals to work toward remarkable goals.

2. **Motivation and Inspiration:** Transformational leaders go beyond simply assigning tasks and setting goals. They inspire and motivate their teams through charisma, enthusiasm, and a genuine passion for the vision they've outlined. By connecting on an emotional level and demonstrating their commitment, these leaders energize and engage their followers.
3. **Individualized Consideration:** Transformational leaders recognize the unique strengths and needs of each team member. They provide individualized support, coaching, and mentoring to help individuals develop their skills and reach their full potential. This personalized approach fosters a sense of trust and loyalty.
4. **Intellectual Stimulation:** Transformational leaders encourage creativity and innovation. They challenge their teams to think critically, question assumptions, and come up with new ideas. This intellectual stimulation leads to fresh approaches and solutions, which can help teams achieve remarkable goals.
5. **Idealized Influence:** Transformational leaders lead by example. They set high ethical and performance standards and model the behavior they expect from their teams. Their integrity and commitment inspire trust and admiration among team members.
6. **Continuous Learning and Growth:** Transformational leaders are committed to the personal and professional development of their team members. They provide opportunities for learning, skill-building, and advancement, which not only benefits the individual but also contributes to the team's ability to achieve remarkable goals.
7. **Extraordinary Performance:** Under the guidance of transformational leaders, teams often surpass ordinary expectations. The collective motivation, alignment with a meaningful vision, and encouragement of innovation result in outstanding performance and the achievement of goals that may have seemed unattainable.

8. **Adaptability:** Transformational leadership is particularly effective in dynamic and uncertain environments. Leaders who inspire and motivate their teams to adapt, embrace change, and stay resilient are better equipped to navigate challenges and seize opportunities.
9. **Long-Term Impact:** Transformational leaders aim for lasting change. By instilling a shared vision and a commitment to values, they leave a legacy of positive transformation within organizations and inspire a culture of continuous improvement.

Transformational leadership is a powerful paradigm that focuses on creating an environment where individuals are not just motivated but genuinely inspired to work together towards remarkable goals. This leadership style taps into the emotional and intellectual aspects of leadership, ultimately driving extraordinary achievements and fostering long-term organizational success.

Historical Context and Key Contributors

Transformational leadership has evolved over time and is deeply rooted in both historical context and the contributions of key thinkers and researchers in the field of leadership. The historical context and key contributors to this leadership approach are:

Historical Context

1. **Early Leadership Theories:** The study of leadership can be traced back to the early 20th century when researchers focused on identifying traits and qualities of effective leaders. This period gave rise to trait theory, which suggested that certain innate qualities were essential for leadership.
2. **Behavioral Theories:** Following trait theory, behavioral theories emerged in the mid-20th century. Researchers like Kurt Lewin and his colleagues conducted studies that explored the impact of leadership behaviors on group

dynamics. This shift emphasized that leadership could be learned and was not solely dependent on traits.

3. **Contingency Theories:** In the 1960s and 1970s, contingency theories, such as Fiedler's Contingency Model and Hersey and Blanchard's Situational Leadership Model, gained prominence. These theories recognized that effective leadership depended on the situation and the leader's ability to adapt.

4. **Social and Cultural Changes:** The latter half of the 20th century saw significant social and cultural changes, including the civil rights movement, the women's rights movement, and increased awareness of diversity and inclusion. These changes influenced leadership paradigms, emphasizing the importance of values, ethics, and social responsibility.

Key Contributors

1. **James MacGregor Burns (1978):** Burns is often credited with introducing the concept of transformational leadership. In his book "Leadership," he distinguished between transactional and transformational leadership styles. He emphasized that transformational leaders inspire and motivate their followers beyond self-interest and personal gain.

2. **Bernard M. Bass (1985):** Building on Burns's work, Bass further developed the theory of transformational leadership. He expanded the concept, emphasizing four components of transformational leadership: idealized influence, inspirational motivation, intellectual stimulation, and individualized consideration. Bass's research and writings helped solidify the theoretical foundation of transformational leadership.

3. **James Kouzes and Barry Posner (1987):** In their book "The Leadership Challenge," Kouzes and Posner popularized transformational leadership in the business world. They introduced the Five Practices of Exemplary Leadership: Model the Way, Inspire a Shared Vision, Challenge the Process, Enable Others to Act, and Encourage the Heart.

4. **Additional Scholars and Researchers:** Over the years, numerous scholars, including Avolio, Yammarino, and Bass, have contributed to the development and refinement of transformational leadership theory. Their research has explored various aspects of this leadership style, including its effects on organizational performance, employee motivation, and ethical leadership.

5. **Practical Application:** Transformational leadership has been applied in various settings, from business to education to healthcare. Organizations like General Electric, under the leadership of Jack Welch, embraced transformational leadership principles to drive change and innovation.

Transformational leadership has its roots in the evolution of leadership theories over the 20th century. It emerged as a response to changing social and cultural dynamics and has been further developed and refined by key contributors in the field. This approach emphasizes the importance of inspiring and motivating individuals to achieve remarkable goals by fostering a shared vision and a commitment to values and ethical leadership.

Four Components of Transformational Leadership

Transformational leadership is characterized by four distinct components that collectively contribute to its effectiveness. Firstly, Idealized Influence entails leaders becoming role models, exemplifying ethical behavior, and instilling trust and respect among their followers. They inspire admiration and set high standards for their teams to emulate. Secondly, Inspirational Motivation involves leaders creating a compelling vision of the future that ignites enthusiasm and commitment within their teams. Through effective communication, they motivate their followers to strive for excellence and take ownership of their work. Thirdly, Intellectual Stimulation encourages innovation and critical thinking. Transformational leaders challenge the status quo, foster an environment where new ideas are valued, and promote continuous learning and personal growth. Lastly, Individualized Consideration reflects a leader's genuine concern for the well-being and development of each team member. They offer personalized support and guidance, helping individuals realize their potential while fostering trust and loyalty within the team. These four components together form the bedrock of transformational leadership, inspiring individuals and teams to achieve extraordinary goals and drive positive change within organizations.

Idealized Influence

Idealized Influence is the first component of transformational leadership, also known as charisma or role modeling. It involves leaders becoming exemplary role models and earning the trust and respect of their followers. Here are key aspects of Idealized Influence:

1. **High Moral and Ethical Standards:** Transformational leaders uphold strong moral and ethical values, demonstrating honesty, integrity, and fairness in their actions and decisions. They are consistent in adhering to these principles.
2. **Inspiration and Trust:** Leaders inspire their teams by setting an example of dedication, commitment, and

unwavering belief in the shared vision. This behavior generates trust and admiration among followers.
3. **Shared Values:** They align their actions with the values of the organization and encourage others to do the same. This shared value system helps create a sense of unity and purpose within the team.
4. **Personal Sacrifice:** Transformational leaders are willing to make personal sacrifices for the benefit of the team or organization, further reinforcing their commitment to the cause.

Inspirational Motivation

Inspirational Motivation is the second component of transformational leadership. It involves leaders inspiring and motivating their teams to work towards a common vision or goal. Here are key aspects of Inspirational Motivation:

1. **Visionary Leadership:** Transformational leaders articulate a compelling vision of the future that excites and energizes their followers. They paint a vivid picture of what success looks like and communicate this vision effectively.
2. **Passion and Enthusiasm:** Leaders convey their passion and enthusiasm for the vision, creating a sense of urgency and commitment among team members. They use powerful and persuasive communication to inspire others.
3. **Setting High Expectations:** Transformational leaders challenge their teams to achieve high levels of performance and excellence. They foster a belief that these goals are attainable and worth pursuing.
4. **Empowerment:** Leaders empower their followers by involving them in the decision-making process and giving them autonomy to contribute to the vision. This sense of ownership enhances motivation and engagement.

Intellectual Stimulation

Intellectual Stimulation is the third component of transformational leadership. It involves leaders encouraging creativity, innovation, and critical thinking within their teams. Here are key aspects of Intellectual Stimulation:

1. **Challenging the Status Quo:** Transformational leaders challenge conventional thinking and encourage their teams to question assumptions and existing practices. They create an environment where creativity is valued.
2. **Problem-Solving:** Leaders promote problem-solving and decision-making at all levels of the organization. They encourage team members to explore new solutions and approaches to challenges.
3. **Open Communication:** Leaders foster open and free-flowing communication, where ideas and feedback are welcomed without fear of reprisal. They listen actively to diverse perspectives and encourage constructive dissent.
4. **Continuous Learning:** Transformational leaders promote a culture of continuous learning and personal development. They provide opportunities for skill-building and growth to enhance individual and team capabilities.

Individualized Consideration

Individualized Consideration is the fourth component of transformational leadership. It involves leaders showing genuine concern for the well-being and development of each team member as individuals. Here are key aspects of Individualized Consideration:

1. **Personalized Support:** Leaders take the time to understand the unique needs, strengths, and aspirations of each team member. They offer individualized guidance and support tailored to help individuals thrive.

2. **Mentorship and Coaching:** Transformational leaders serve as mentors and coaches, helping individuals set and achieve their goals. They provide constructive feedback and assist with career development.
3. **Recognition and Appreciation:** Leaders acknowledge and appreciate the contributions of each team member. They celebrate achievements and provide positive reinforcement to boost morale.
4. **Creating Trust:** By demonstrating care and concern, transformational leaders build trust and loyalty within their teams. This trust fosters a sense of psychological safety, where team members feel comfortable taking risks and expressing themselves.

The four core components of transformational leadership—Idealized Influence, Inspirational Motivation, Intellectual Stimulation, and Individualized Consideration—work together to inspire and motivate teams to achieve remarkable goals. These components form the foundation of a leadership style that values ethics, shared vision, innovation, and the personal growth and well-being of individuals within the organization.

Real World Example

Maharaja Ranjit Singh's leadership exemplified the core components of transformational leadership by embracing ethical values, inspiring a shared vision, encouraging intellectual stimulation and innovation, and demonstrating genuine concern for individual well-being. His leadership played a pivotal role in the historical development of the Sikh Empire and left a lasting legacy in the history of Punjab and the world.

1. **Idealized Influence:** Maharaja Ranjit Singh's leadership was built on a foundation of moral and ethical values. As a devout Sikh, he embraced the principles of equality, religious tolerance, and social justice that are central to

Sikhism. He not only practiced these values himself but also expected his administration to uphold them. His unwavering commitment to these principles earned him the respect and trust of people from diverse religious and cultural backgrounds within his empire. His ethical conduct set a powerful example for his followers and subjects.
2. **Inspirational Motivation:** Ranjit Singh possessed a clear and compelling vision for a unified Sikh Empire. He aimed to create a state where justice, prosperity, and religious freedom prevailed. His visionary leadership and ability to communicate this inspiring vision motivated thousands to rally behind his cause. Under his leadership, Sikhs, Hindus, Muslims, and people of other faiths were united in their pursuit of a brighter future. Ranjit Singh's inspirational motivation not only galvanized his troops but also won the hearts of his subjects.
3. **Intellectual Stimulation:** The Maharaja recognized the importance of intellectual stimulation and innovation. He actively supported and patronized scholars, artists, and thinkers from various backgrounds. Under his rule, the Punjabi language and culture thrived, and he encouraged the creation of literary and artistic works. Additionally, he welcomed advisers and experts from diverse religious and cultural backgrounds, fostering an environment where different perspectives were valued. This intellectual openness encouraged critical thinking and contributed to the growth and development of the Sikh Empire.
4. **Individualized Consideration:** Ranjit Singh's leadership was marked by his genuine concern for the well-being of his subjects. He was accessible to common people and listened to their grievances. He promoted social welfare initiatives and cared for the welfare of individuals regardless of their religious or social backgrounds. His leadership style created a sense of belonging and security among the people, reinforcing their loyalty to the empire. His approach to

individualized consideration was an important aspect of his popularity and success as a leader.

5. **Legacy of Transformation:** Maharaja Ranjit Singh's transformational leadership had a profound and lasting impact on the Sikh Empire. Under his rule, the empire expanded its territories, embraced modern administrative reforms, promoted trade and commerce, and provided a stable and inclusive environment for its subjects. His legacy extended beyond his lifetime, as his principles of justice, unity, and religious tolerance continued to influence the Sikh community and the broader region long after his death.

Impact of Transformational Leadership

The impact of transformational leadership is profound and far-reaching, influencing individuals, teams, organizations, and even entire societies. This leadership style fosters a range of positive outcomes, including increased motivation, enhanced performance, improved organizational culture, and long-term growth. Transformational leaders inspire and empower their followers to reach remarkable goals, driving meaningful change and innovation.

At the individual level, transformational leadership can lead to heightened job satisfaction, greater engagement, and personal growth. Employees feel a stronger sense of purpose and connection to the organization's mission, which often results in higher levels of productivity and commitment. Moreover, transformational leaders often serve as mentors, helping individuals develop their skills and advance their careers.

Within teams, this leadership style promotes collaboration and cohesion. Teams led by transformational leaders tend to be more innovative, as leaders encourage members to think creatively, challenge the status quo, and contribute their unique perspectives. This collective creativity can lead to the development of groundbreaking solutions and products.

On the organizational level, the impact of transformational leadership extends to improved performance and competitiveness. Leaders who inspire and motivate their teams to exceed expectations can drive increased productivity, efficiency, and profitability. Moreover, transformational leaders often create a positive work culture characterized by trust, open communication, and a shared commitment to the organization's goals.

Transformational leadership also contributes to long-term organizational growth and sustainability. Leaders who focus on values, ethics, and a compelling vision for the future can guide their organizations through periods of change and uncertainty. They foster adaptability and resilience, enabling the organization to thrive in evolving markets and industries.

In societies and communities, the impact of transformational leadership can be transformative. Leaders who prioritize social responsibility, diversity, and inclusion can inspire positive change beyond the workplace. They may advocate for social justice, environmental sustainability, and other important causes, influencing broader societal values and behaviors.

The impact of transformational leadership is multi-faceted, touching upon individual, team, organizational, and societal levels. It generates motivation, innovation, and growth, creating a ripple effect of positive change that can lead to improved well-being and progress in various spheres of life.

Transformational leadership has a profound impact on organizations, leading to improvements in various key areas, including employee engagement, innovation, and change management.

Employee Engagement

Transformational leaders excel in engaging and inspiring their teams. They achieve this through several means:

1. **Shared Vision:** Transformational leaders create and communicate a compelling vision for the organization's future. This vision provides a sense of purpose and direction, aligning employees with a common goal.
2. **Emotional Connection:** They establish an emotional connection with employees by demonstrating passion, enthusiasm, and a commitment to the shared vision. This fosters a sense of belonging and pride among team members.
3. **Individualized Consideration:** Transformational leaders show genuine concern for the well-being and development of each employee. This personalized approach makes employees feel valued and appreciated.
4. **Empowerment:** Leaders empower employees by granting them autonomy and decision-making authority. This sense of ownership over their work contributes to higher levels of engagement.

The impact of transformational leadership on employee engagement is evident in increased job satisfaction, greater enthusiasm for tasks, and higher levels of commitment to the organization.

Innovation

Transformational leaders cultivate a culture of innovation within organizations, driving creativity and groundbreaking ideas:

1. **Intellectual Stimulation:** They encourage employees to think critically, challenge assumptions, and explore new approaches. This intellectual stimulation leads to innovative problem-solving and solutions.
2. **Support for Risk-Taking:** Transformational leaders create an environment where calculated risks are welcomed, as they understand that innovation often involves experimentation and some degree of failure.

3. **Inspirational Motivation:** Through their inspiring communication, they motivate employees to reach their full creative potential, fostering a culture where innovation is celebrated and rewarded.

This impact of transformational leadership on innovation results in the development of new products, services, and processes, which can give organizations a competitive edge.

Change Management

Transformational leaders are well-equipped to manage change effectively:

1. **Visionary Leadership:** They articulate a clear vision of the desired future state, which helps employees understand the purpose and benefits of change.
2. **Emotional Resonance:** Their ability to inspire and connect with employees emotionally reduces resistance to change. Employees are more likely to embrace change when they believe in their leader's vision.
3. **Individualized Support:** Transformational leaders provide individualized consideration during periods of change. They offer support, address concerns, and facilitate the transition for each team member.

The impact of transformational leadership on change management is evident in smoother transitions, quicker adaptation to new circumstances, and a higher likelihood of achieving the desired outcomes of change initiatives.

Transformational leadership significantly impacts organizations by enhancing employee engagement, fostering innovation, and facilitating effective change management. Leaders who embrace this approach inspire and empower their teams to reach remarkable goals and navigate organizational challenges with confidence and enthusiasm.

Measurement and Assessment of Effectiveness

The measurement and assessment of transformational leadership effectiveness involve evaluating how well leaders are applying transformational leadership principles and the impact of their leadership on individuals, teams, and the organization as a whole. Several methods and tools can be employed to assess transformational leadership effectiveness:

Surveys and Questionnaires

- **Multifactor Leadership Questionnaire (MLQ):** Developed by Bernard M. Bass and Bruce J. Avolio, this widely used tool assesses transformational leadership behaviors. It consists of items that measure various leadership dimensions, including idealized influence, inspirational motivation, intellectual stimulation, and individualized consideration.

- **Employee Engagement Surveys:** These surveys gauge the level of employee engagement, which is often a result of effective transformational leadership. Questions may explore employees' perceptions of leadership inspiration, trust, and alignment with the organization's vision.

- **360-Degree Feedback:** Collecting feedback from peers, subordinates, supervisors, and self-assessment can provide a comprehensive view of a leader's effectiveness in practicing transformational leadership behaviors.

Performance Metrics

- **Organizational Performance Indicators:** Assessing key performance indicators (KPIs) related to productivity, profitability, and other organizational outcomes can help gauge the impact of transformational leadership. Improved performance can be an indicator of effective leadership.

- **Employee Performance Appraisals:** Evaluating the performance of individual team members can provide insights into how well a leader is motivating and supporting their team.

Qualitative Interviews and Focus Groups

Conducting interviews and focus groups with employees can offer qualitative insights into the perceived effectiveness of transformational leadership. Participants can share their experiences, describe the impact of their leader's behaviors, and provide suggestions for improvement.

Observations

Observations of leaders in action can provide valuable insights into their leadership behaviors. Trained observers can assess how frequently leaders exhibit transformational leadership behaviors, such as setting a vision or providing individualized support.

360-Degree Assessment

In addition to self-assessments, a 360-degree assessment involves gathering feedback from a leader's peers, subordinates, and supervisors. This comprehensive view can help identify strengths and areas for development in transformational leadership.

Case Studies

Analyzing case studies or success stories within the organization can illustrate the impact of transformational leadership. These narratives can highlight instances where leaders inspired change, fostered innovation, or created a positive organizational culture.

Employee Retention and Satisfaction

High levels of employee retention and job satisfaction often correlate with effective transformational leadership. Monitoring turnover rates and conducting employee satisfaction surveys can provide insights into leadership effectiveness.

Long-Term Organizational Outcomes

Assessing long-term organizational outcomes, such as growth, innovation, and adaptability, can help measure the sustained impact of transformational leadership over time.

It's important to note that assessing transformational leadership effectiveness should be an ongoing process, as leadership impact may evolve as circumstances change. Combining multiple assessment methods, both quantitative and qualitative, can provide a comprehensive understanding of how transformational leadership contributes to organizational success and individual well-being.

Transformational Leadership in Action

Transformational Leadership in Action refers to an in-depth examination and analysis of a specific real-world situation or scenario where transformational leadership principles are actively practiced and demonstrated. In such a case study, researchers or analysts scrutinize the actions, behaviors, and decisions of a leader who embodies transformational leadership qualities. They explore how this leader has inspired and motivated individuals or teams, encouraged innovation, fostered a positive organizational culture, and contributed to achieving remarkable goals or driving positive change within their organization. By dissecting such real-life examples, scholars and practitioners gain insights into the practical application of transformational leadership and its impact on individuals and organizations, providing valuable lessons and guidance for leadership development and organizational improvement.

Case Study

One real-life case study that exemplifies the successful implementation of transformational leadership is the story of Nelson Mandela, the former President of South Africa. Mandela's leadership during and after the apartheid era serves as a powerful example of transformational leadership in action.

Background

Nelson Mandela's journey to leadership began during South Africa's oppressive apartheid regime, which institutionalized racial segregation and discrimination. In 1962, he was arrested and later sentenced to life in prison for his involvement in anti-apartheid activities. He spent 27 years behind bars, emerging as a symbol of resistance and hope.

Transformational Leadership in Action

1. **Idealized Influence:** Mandela embodied high moral and ethical standards. He consistently advocated for non-violence, reconciliation, and forgiveness, even in the face of immense personal suffering. His unwavering commitment to these values earned him the respect and trust of not only the oppressed black majority but also international leaders and communities.
2. **Inspirational Motivation:** Throughout his imprisonment, Mandela's vision of a non-racial and democratic South Africa remained steadfast. He inspired hope in others through his resilience and unwavering belief in the possibility of a better future. His speeches and letters from prison served as a source of inspiration and motivation for the anti-apartheid movement.
3. **Intellectual Stimulation:** Mandela encouraged critical thinking and dialogue. He engaged in secret negotiations with apartheid leaders while in prison, demonstrating a willingness to explore new solutions. His willingness to

consider alternative paths to peace and reconciliation showed intellectual openness.
4. **Individualized Consideration:** Mandela was deeply concerned about the well-being of individuals and the nation as a whole. After his release from prison, he focused on reconciliation and healing, rather than retribution. He sought to address the needs and fears of all South Africans, regardless of their racial background.

Impact

Mandela's transformational leadership played a pivotal role in ending apartheid and transitioning South Africa into a democracy. His commitment to reconciliation and forgiveness prevented a potential civil war and paved the way for peaceful negotiations that led to the dismantling of apartheid. He served as South Africa's first black president from 1994 to 1999 and continued to promote unity and reconciliation during his tenure.

Legacy

Nelson Mandela's legacy extends far beyond his presidency. His leadership serves as an enduring symbol of transformation, resilience, and the power of forgiveness. He exemplifies how transformational leadership can bring about remarkable change, unite disparate groups, and inspire a nation to overcome the most challenging circumstances.

Nelson Mandela's life and leadership provide a powerful real-life case study of the successful implementation of transformational leadership principles. His unwavering commitment to values, his inspirational vision, and his focus on reconciliation transformed a deeply divided nation and left an indelible mark on the world.

Analysis of how four Components bring change and Inspiration

Nelson Mandela's leadership during South Africa's transition from apartheid to democracy exemplifies how he applied the four components of transformational leadership—Idealized Influence, Inspirational Motivation, Intellectual Stimulation, and Individualized Consideration—to bring about change and inspiration:

1. **Idealized Influence:** Mandela embodied high moral and ethical standards. He consistently advocated for non-violence, reconciliation, and forgiveness, even in the face of immense personal suffering. His unwavering commitment to these values earned him the respect and trust of not only the oppressed black majority but also international leaders and communities. Mandela became a symbol of hope and justice for those who believed in his vision for a united, non-racial South Africa.
2. **Inspirational Motivation:** Mandela's vision of a non-racial and democratic South Africa was inspiring and powerful. He communicated this vision effectively through his speeches and actions. Even during his long imprisonment, he continued to inspire hope and determination among his supporters. His resilience and belief in a better future motivated not only South Africans but also people worldwide to support the anti-apartheid movement.
3. **Intellectual Stimulation:** Mandela encouraged critical thinking and dialogue. While in prison, he engaged in secret negotiations with apartheid leaders, demonstrating a willingness to explore new solutions beyond violence. This approach showed his intellectual openness and adaptability. He recognized that achieving his vision required innovative, non-violent strategies, such as negotiations and reconciliation.
4. **Individualized Consideration:** Mandela demonstrated genuine concern for the well-being of individuals and the

nation as a whole. After his release from prison, he focused on reconciliation and healing, rather than retribution. He sought to address the needs and fears of all South Africans, regardless of their racial background. This individualized consideration was instrumental in easing tensions and fostering trust among the diverse communities in South Africa.

Nelson Mandela's leadership applied the four components of transformational leadership to remarkable effect. He led by example with unwavering moral integrity, inspired a nation with his visionary ideals, encouraged innovative approaches to conflict resolution, and showed genuine concern for the well-being of individuals and the entire nation. Through these actions, he brought about profound change and inspiration, leading South Africa through a peaceful transition from apartheid to democracy and leaving an enduring legacy of leadership.

Analyzing the Components of Transformational Leadership

Analyzing each component of Transformational Leadership involves a comprehensive assessment of the four core elements that constitute this leadership style. These components are Idealized Influence, Inspirational Motivation, Intellectual Stimulation, and Individualized Consideration. Idealized Influence pertains to leaders as role models, earning trust and respect through integrity; Inspirational Motivation involves creating a compelling vision and motivating teams; Intellectual Stimulation fosters creativity and critical thinking; Individualized Consideration focuses on personalized support and development for each team member. Evaluating these components allows for a deep understanding of a leader's ability to inspire, motivate, challenge, and support individuals and teams, ultimately shaping their effectiveness and the organization's success.

Idealized Influence

Idealized Influence, the first component of Transformational Leadership, refers to the leader's ability to serve as a role model and inspire trust and respect in their followers. Leaders who embody idealized influence are characterized by their strong moral and ethical values, demonstrating honesty, integrity, and fairness in their actions and decisions. They consistently adhere to these principles, setting an example that their team members want to emulate. By earning the admiration and trust of their followers, leaders who exhibit idealized influence foster a sense of unity and shared values within the team, which can have a profound impact on team cohesion and commitment. This component of transformational leadership is all about leading by example and inspiring others through the leader's own actions and values.

1. **Setting a Positive Example:** Idealized Influence involves leaders serving as role models for their followers. They exhibit a strong sense of ethics, integrity, and moral values in their words and actions. They consistently demonstrate honesty, fairness, and a commitment to doing what is right, even in challenging circumstances. This exemplary behavior inspires trust and admiration among team members, as they see their leader as someone they want to emulate.
2. **Earning Trust and Respect:** Leaders who practice idealized influence are adept at building trust and respect within their teams. They do this by consistently aligning their actions with their stated values and principles. When followers witness their leader's unwavering commitment to ethical conduct and fairness, it creates a sense of reliability and credibility. This trust is essential for effective leadership, as it fosters an environment where team members feel secure and confident in their leader's guidance.
3. **Fostering Shared Values:** Idealized influence goes beyond personal integrity; it extends to promoting shared values within the team or organization. Transformational leaders

actively work to create a culture where everyone upholds the same ethical standards and principles. This shared value system helps unify the team, as individuals feel a sense of belonging and alignment with the organization's mission and goals.
4. **Impact on Team Cohesion:** A leader who practices idealized influence can significantly impact team cohesion and morale. When team members have faith in their leader's character and values, they are more likely to work together harmoniously and commit to collective objectives. This sense of unity can lead to increased collaboration, reduced conflicts, and improved team performance.
5. **Long-Term Trustworthiness:** Idealized influence is not a one-time effort but an ongoing commitment to ethical leadership. Leaders must consistently uphold their values and act as role models to maintain the trust and respect of their followers over the long term. This sustained trustworthiness contributes to the stability and effectiveness of leadership within the organization.

Idealized Influence in transformational leadership involves leaders setting a positive example through their ethical conduct and values, earning the trust and respect of their followers. By fostering shared values and promoting a sense of unity, leaders who practice this component contribute to team cohesion, high morale, and long-term trustworthiness, ultimately leading to more effective leadership and organizational success.

Strategies for Leaders to Cultivate Idealized Influence

Leaders can cultivate and embody idealized influence by employing various strategies that promote ethical behavior, trust, and the alignment of values. Here are some key strategies:

1. **Lead by Example:** Leaders should consistently model the ethical behavior and values they expect from their team

members. This involves practicing honesty, integrity, fairness, and other positive qualities in their daily actions and decisions. Demonstrating these qualities consistently helps build trust and respect.

2. **Communicate Core Values:** Leaders should clearly communicate their core values and principles to their team. This includes sharing their personal values and the values that guide the organization. By openly discussing these values, leaders ensure that their expectations are transparent and understood by everyone.

3. **Be Transparent and Accountable:** Transparency is crucial for idealized influence. Leaders should be open and honest about their actions and decisions, especially in difficult or controversial situations. If mistakes are made, they should take responsibility and use them as opportunities for growth and learning.

4. **Act with Empathy and Compassion:** Leaders who genuinely care about their team members and demonstrate empathy and compassion create a sense of connection and belonging. Taking the time to understand the concerns and needs of individuals fosters trust and strengthens the leader's influence.

5. **Promote a Culture of Integrity:** Leaders can actively promote a culture of integrity within the organization by recognizing and rewarding ethical behavior, while addressing unethical behavior promptly and decisively. This sends a clear message that ethical conduct is a priority.

6. **Share Personal Stories and Experiences:** Sharing personal stories and experiences that illustrate how values have guided the leader's life and decisions can be inspiring. These stories help team members relate to their leader on a personal level and see the authenticity of their values.

7. **Encourage Ethical Decision-Making:** Leaders should encourage team members to make ethical decisions and provide guidance when dilemmas arise. By supporting

ethical decision-making at all levels, leaders empower their teams to act in alignment with the organization's values.
8. **Seek Feedback and Self-Reflection:** Leaders should actively seek feedback from team members about their leadership and ethical conduct. Self-reflection and a willingness to improve are essential for continuously embodying idealized influence.
9. **Invest in Personal Development:** Leaders can invest in personal development, including ethics training and leadership development programs, to enhance their ability to embody and cultivate idealized influence.
10. **Recognize and Celebrate Ethical Behavior:** Publicly recognizing and celebrating individuals or teams that exhibit ethical behavior reinforces the importance of ethical conduct within the organization.

By employing these strategies, leaders can not only embody idealized influence themselves but also create a culture that values ethical behavior and inspires trust and respect among team members, ultimately fostering a positive and productive work environment.

Inspirational Motivation

The second component of Transformational Leadership, Inspirational Motivation, is about leaders inspiring and motivating their teams to achieve remarkable goals. Leaders who excel in this aspect possess a unique ability to communicate a compelling vision for the future that captivates and energizes their followers. They paint a vivid picture of what success looks like, instilling a sense of purpose and enthusiasm within their team members. Inspirational leaders use their words, actions, and communication skills to convey a shared sense of destiny and a belief that collective efforts can overcome challenges and accomplish great feats. This component is essential for driving motivation, commitment, and a sense of unity among team members, propelling them toward the realization of the envisioned goals.

1. **Articulating a Compelling Vision:** Transformational leaders begin by crafting a clear and inspiring vision for the future. This vision serves as a beacon, outlining the organization's overarching goals, values, and direction. It is often ambitious and forward-looking, challenging the status quo and igniting enthusiasm among team members.
2. **Effective Communication:** Inspirational leaders are skilled communicators. They convey the vision with passion, clarity, and conviction. Through compelling speeches, storytelling, and vivid imagery, they paint a picture of what success looks like and why it matters. Their communication is inclusive, ensuring that every team member understands their role in achieving the vision.
3. **Instilling a Sense of Purpose:** Leaders who excel in inspirational motivation help team members connect their daily tasks to the larger mission. They show how individual contributions contribute to the realization of the shared vision, instilling a sense of purpose and meaning in each team member's work.
4. **Empowering and Encouraging:** Inspirational leaders empower their teams by giving them a sense of ownership over the vision. They encourage creativity and innovation, welcoming ideas and solutions from all levels of the organization. This approach fosters a culture where team members feel valued and motivated to contribute their best.
5. **Leading by Example:** Leaders who inspire motivation lead by example, embodying the passion and dedication they expect from their teams. They are visible, accessible, and actively involved in the pursuit of the vision, demonstrating their commitment to the cause.
6. **Resilience in the Face of Challenges:** Inspirational leaders acknowledge that the journey toward the vision may involve obstacles and setbacks. However, they maintain unwavering

faith in the attainability of the vision and inspire resilience in their teams. They view challenges as opportunities for growth and learning.
7. **Celebrating Achievements:** Recognizing and celebrating milestones and achievements along the way is a crucial part of inspirational motivation. Leaders acknowledge the progress made toward the vision, reinforcing the team's commitment and enthusiasm.
8. **Continuous Inspiration:** Inspirational motivation is not a one-time effort but an ongoing process. Leaders consistently remind their teams of the vision and its significance, ensuring that motivation remains high and that everyone remains aligned with the shared goal.
9. **Adapting and Evolving:** Effective inspirational leaders recognize that circumstances may change, and the vision may need to adapt. They are open to revisiting and refining the vision to ensure it remains relevant and inspiring.

Inspirational Motivation in transformational leadership involves articulating a compelling vision, communicating it effectively, and inspiring teams to work collectively toward its realization. Leaders who excel in this component create a sense of purpose, enthusiasm, and commitment among their teams, driving them to achieve remarkable goals and overcome challenges in pursuit of the shared vision.

Techniques for Crafting and Communication

Crafting and communicating a motivating vision is a fundamental aspect of transformational leadership. Here are techniques to help leaders effectively develop and convey a compelling vision:

1. **Clarity and Simplicity:** Craft a clear and concise vision statement that is easy to understand. Avoid jargon or overly

complex language. A straightforward and simple vision is more likely to resonate with team members.
2. **Paint a Vivid Picture:** Use descriptive language to create a mental image of what success looks like. Share stories and examples that illustrate how achieving the vision will positively impact the organization and its members.
3. **Relate to Core Values:** Align the vision with the organization's core values and principles. When the vision is rooted in shared values, it becomes more meaningful and motivating.
4. **Be Inspiring and Aspirational:** Make the vision aspirational and ambitious. It should inspire individuals to strive for excellence and to push their limits. Aim high and convey the idea that achieving the vision is a noble and worthwhile pursuit.
5. **Involve Stakeholders:** Engage team members and stakeholders in the vision-crafting process. Seek their input and feedback to ensure that the vision resonates with their aspirations and concerns. This involvement fosters a sense of ownership and commitment.
6. **Focus on Purpose:** Emphasize the purpose or "why" behind the vision. Explain why it matters and how it will contribute to a better future, whether for the organization, its customers, or society as a whole.
7. **Storytelling:** Share stories and anecdotes that illustrate the vision in action. Stories can be powerful tools for conveying the emotional and human aspects of the vision.
8. **Use Visual Aids:** Visual aids like charts, graphs, or images can help illustrate the vision in a compelling way. Visuals make the abstract concept of the vision more tangible and memorable.
9. **Repeat and Reinforce:** Continuously communicate the vision. Repetition is key to ensuring that the vision remains at the forefront of team members' minds. Use various communication channels, such as meetings, emails, and social media, to reinforce the message.

10. **Lead by Example:** As a leader, embody the values and behaviors associated with the vision. Be a role model by demonstrating your commitment to the vision through your actions and decisions.
11. **Encourage Questions and Dialogue:** Create an environment where team members feel comfortable asking questions and providing feedback about the vision. Encourage open dialogue to clarify any doubts and build a shared understanding.
12. **Adapt as Needed:** Be open to refining and adapting the vision as circumstances change. A vision should remain relevant and motivating, so it may require adjustments over time.

By using these techniques, leaders can craft and communicate a motivating vision that resonates with team members, inspiring them to work passionately toward the shared goal and fostering a sense of purpose and unity within the organization.

Intellectual Stimulation

The third component of Transformational Leadership, Intellectual Stimulation, involves leaders challenging the status quo and encouraging innovative thinking and problem-solving within their teams. Leaders who excel in this component foster an environment where team members are stimulated to think critically, explore new ideas, and question existing practices. They value diverse perspectives and actively seek out input from their team members, promoting a culture of continuous learning and growth. Intellectual stimulation ignites creativity, inspires innovative solutions to challenges, and empowers individuals to stretch their intellectual boundaries, contributing to a dynamic and forward-thinking organization.

1. **Fostering a Culture of Curiosity:** Leaders who practice intellectual stimulation cultivate a culture of curiosity within their teams. They encourage team members to question

assumptions, challenge the status quo, and seek new perspectives. This culture of inquiry drives a continuous quest for knowledge and improvement.
2. **Encouraging Critical Thinking:** Transformational leaders stimulate critical thinking by posing thought-provoking questions and presenting challenges that require innovative solutions. They encourage team members to analyze problems from various angles, consider unconventional approaches, and engage in in-depth analysis.
3. **Embracing Diverse Perspectives:** Intellectual stimulation involves valuing diverse viewpoints and backgrounds. Leaders actively seek input from team members with different experiences and expertise. By embracing this diversity, leaders tap into a broader range of ideas and insights.
4. **Promoting Risk-Taking:** Leaders who promote intellectual stimulation understand that innovation often involves risk. They create an environment where calculated risks are not only accepted but encouraged. Team members are empowered to experiment, learn from failures, and continuously improve.
5. **Providing Resources and Support:** Effective leaders ensure that team members have access to the resources, training, and support needed to pursue innovative ideas. This includes providing opportunities for skill development and fostering an atmosphere of psychological safety where team members feel comfortable expressing their ideas.
6. **Recognizing and Rewarding Creativity:** Leaders reinforce the importance of creative thinking and problem-solving by recognizing and rewarding innovative efforts and successes. This recognition can be both intrinsic (acknowledgment and praise) and extrinsic (bonuses, promotions, or special projects).
7. **Leading by Example:** Transformational leaders lead by example when it comes to intellectual stimulation. They demonstrate a commitment to continuous learning, critical

thinking, and openness to new ideas. Their own behavior serves as a model for their team members.
8. **Setting Challenging Goals:** Leaders set high standards and challenging goals that require innovative thinking to achieve. These goals provide a sense of purpose and motivation for the team, driving them to explore creative solutions.
9. **Nurturing a Learning Organization:** Intellectual stimulation contributes to the development of a learning organization—a place where learning and innovation are woven into the fabric of daily operations. Leaders encourage ongoing education, knowledge sharing, and a growth mindset.
10. **Monitoring Progress:** Leaders monitor the progress of innovative projects and initiatives, offering guidance and feedback as needed. They ensure that creativity is not just encouraged but effectively harnessed to achieve organizational objectives.

Intellectual Stimulation in transformational leadership fosters a culture of curiosity, critical thinking, and innovation. Leaders who excel in this component encourage team members to challenge norms, embrace diverse perspectives, and seek creative solutions to problems. By nurturing an environment that values intellectual exploration, leaders contribute to the organization's adaptability, competitiveness, and capacity for continuous improvement.

Methods for Stimulating Intellectual Growth

Stimulating intellectual growth within teams is essential for fostering innovation, problem-solving, and overall team development. Here are several methods and strategies leaders can use to promote intellectual growth among team members:

1. **Encourage Open Communication:** Create an open and inclusive communication environment where team members

feel comfortable expressing their ideas, asking questions, and sharing their viewpoints without fear of judgment.
2. **Promote Continuous Learning:** Support and encourage ongoing learning by providing access to training, workshops, webinars, and educational resources. Encourage team members to seek out opportunities for professional development and self-improvement.
3. **Facilitate Brainstorming Sessions:** Organize regular brainstorming sessions where team members can collaborate on generating creative solutions to challenges or exploring new ideas. Ensure that these sessions are inclusive and that everyone has a chance to participate.
4. **Foster Cross-Functional Collaboration:** Encourage team members from different departments or disciplines to collaborate on projects or initiatives. Cross-functional teams bring diverse perspectives and expertise to the table, promoting intellectual growth through knowledge exchange.
5. **Assign Challenging Projects:** Provide team members with assignments and projects that require them to stretch their intellectual boundaries and develop new skills. Assignments that push individuals out of their comfort zones foster growth.
6. **Encourage Feedback and Constructive Criticism:** Promote a culture of constructive feedback, where team members are encouraged to offer insights, suggestions, and constructive criticism. Feedback should be focused on growth and improvement.
7. **Create a Knowledge-Sharing Culture:** Establish a culture of knowledge sharing, where team members freely share their expertise, best practices, and lessons learned. Implement platforms or systems that facilitate knowledge sharing and collaboration.
8. **Recognize and Reward Intellectual Growth:** Acknowledge and reward team members for their intellectual growth and contributions. Recognition can be in

the form of promotions, bonuses, or simply public praise for their innovative ideas or accomplishments.
9. **Provide Autonomy and Ownership:** Give team members ownership over their work and projects, allowing them the autonomy to make decisions and take responsibility for outcomes. Autonomy fosters intellectual growth as individuals learn from their experiences and choices.
10. **Encourage Reading and Research:** Encourage team members to read books, articles, and research papers related to their field or industry. Share relevant materials and discuss insights collectively.
11. **Support Diverse Perspectives:** Create an inclusive and diverse team composition that brings together people with varying backgrounds, experiences, and viewpoints. Diverse teams are more likely to generate innovative ideas and stimulate intellectual growth.
12. **Lead by Example:** As a leader, model a commitment to intellectual growth by demonstrating your own willingness to learn, adapt, and seek knowledge. Share your experiences and insights with the team.
13. **Implement Regular Knowledge Sharing Meetings:** Hold regular team meetings or sessions dedicated to sharing knowledge, discussing industry trends, and exploring new ideas. Invite guest speakers or experts to contribute to these sessions.

By implementing these methods, leaders can create a stimulating environment that encourages intellectual growth within their teams, fostering creativity, innovation, and personal development among team members.

Individual Considerations

The fourth component of Transformational Leadership, Individualized Consideration, involves leaders recognizing and addressing the unique needs, strengths, and aspirations of each team member. Leaders who practice individualized consideration prioritize personalized support and development. They take time to understand the individual goals and challenges of team members, offering guidance, mentoring, and opportunities for growth tailored to each person. This component emphasizes the importance of treating team members as individuals rather than mere employees, fostering a sense of trust, loyalty, and well-being within the team by acknowledging and respecting their individuality.

1. **Fostering Trust and Rapport:** Recognizing and supporting individual team members builds trust and rapport. When leaders show a genuine interest in each person's well-being and growth, it creates a sense of psychological safety. Team members feel valued and understood, which enhances their commitment to the leader and the organization.
2. **Motivation and Engagement:** Tailoring support and development to individual needs motivates team members. It acknowledges their aspirations and helps align their personal goals with those of the organization. This motivation leads to increased engagement, higher job satisfaction, and a willingness to go the extra mile.
3. **Maximizing Potential:** Individualized consideration enables leaders to identify and leverage the unique strengths and talents of each team member. By providing opportunities that match individual capabilities, leaders can maximize the potential of the entire team, leading to higher performance and productivity.
4. **Personalized Development:** Leaders can offer personalized development plans that address specific skills or areas of improvement for each team member. This targeted approach ensures that individuals receive the support and resources needed to advance their careers and contribute effectively.
5. **Adaptive Leadership:** In a rapidly changing work environment, leaders who practice individualized consideration are better equipped to adapt their leadership

style to suit different team members' needs. This flexibility is crucial for navigating diverse challenges and fostering a culture of continuous learning.
6. **Employee Retention:** Recognizing and supporting individual team members enhances job satisfaction and loyalty. When employees feel that their growth and well-being are valued, they are more likely to stay with the organization, reducing turnover and associated recruitment costs.
7. **Enhancing Team Dynamics:** Individualized consideration contributes to healthier team dynamics. When team members perceive that their leader values and respects their individuality, it reduces conflicts and fosters a cooperative and collaborative atmosphere.
8. **Meeting Diverse Needs:** In diverse teams, individualized consideration is particularly important. It recognizes that different team members may have unique cultural, personal, or professional backgrounds, and leaders must adapt their approach to accommodate these differences.
9. **Empowerment and Autonomy:** Leaders who offer individualized consideration empower team members to take ownership of their roles and decisions. This autonomy fosters a sense of responsibility and self-efficacy, leading to greater job satisfaction and performance.

Individualized Consideration is a cornerstone of transformational leadership that emphasizes the significance of recognizing and supporting the individual needs and aspirations of team members. By doing so, leaders create an environment where trust, motivation, and engagement flourish, ultimately leading to higher performance, job satisfaction, and overall team success.

Practical Approaches to Provide Individualized Support and Mentorship

Providing individualized support and mentorship to team members is essential for effective leadership. Here are practical approaches that leaders can use to offer personalized guidance and development:

1. **Regular One-on-One Meetings:** Schedule regular one-on-one meetings with each team member. Use these sessions to discuss their career goals, challenges, and development needs. Offer guidance and feedback tailored to their unique circumstances.
2. **Personalized Development Plans:** Work with team members to create personalized development plans. Identify their strengths and areas for improvement and outline specific actions, training, or resources needed to achieve their goals.
3. **Mentorship Programs:** Establish mentorship programs within your organization. Pair team members with experienced mentors who can provide individualized guidance, share insights, and offer career advice.
4. **Tailored Training and Learning Opportunities:** Identify training and learning opportunities that align with each team member's career aspirations and skills development needs. Invest in courses, workshops, or certifications that are relevant to their individual goals.
5. **Recognition and Acknowledgment:** Publicly recognize and acknowledge the achievements and contributions of individual team members. Tailor your recognition efforts to their preferences, whether it's a simple acknowledgment during team meetings or a more formal recognition ceremony.
6. **Job Rotation and Stretch Assignments:** Offer opportunities for team members to take on challenging assignments or job rotations that align with their career

interests. This exposes them to new experiences and helps them acquire new skills.

7. **Listen Actively:** Practice active listening during conversations with team members. Pay attention to their concerns, aspirations, and feedback. Demonstrating that you value their input fosters trust and engagement.
8. **Provide Constructive Feedback:** Offer constructive and specific feedback that helps individuals grow and improve. Highlight their strengths and offer guidance on areas where they can enhance their performance.
9. **Encourage Networking and Professional Development:** Encourage team members to build their professional networks and seek opportunities for growth outside the organization. Offer guidance on attending industry conferences, joining associations, or participating in relevant events.
10. **Flexibility in Work Arrangements:** Be flexible in accommodating individual work arrangements that support work-life balance and personal needs. Recognize that each team member may have unique circumstances.
11. **Assess Individual Learning Styles:** Understand the individual learning styles of team members—whether they are visual, auditory, or kinesthetic learners. Adapt your mentoring and support strategies accordingly.
12. **Set Clear Expectations:** Clearly communicate performance expectations and objectives for each team member. Regularly review progress toward these objectives and provide guidance on how to meet or exceed them.
13. **Encourage Self-Reflection:** Encourage team members to engage in self-reflection and self-assessment. Help them identify their strengths, areas for growth, and career aspirations through exercises like journaling or self-assessment tools.
14. **Offer Emotional Support:** Be attuned to the emotional well-being of team members. Offer support and

understanding during challenging times, such as personal crises or work-related stress.
15. **Create a Supportive Team Culture:** Foster a team culture where team members support each other's growth and development. Encourage peer mentoring and the sharing of knowledge and experiences.

By applying these practical approaches, leaders can provide individualized support and mentorship that aligns with each team member's unique needs and aspirations, ultimately fostering their professional growth and success.

Authentic Leadership

Authentic Leadership is a leadership approach centered on leading with values and self-discipline. It emphasizes the importance of leaders being true to themselves, their principles, and their core values. Authentic leaders are transparent, genuine, and consistent in their actions and decisions, which builds trust and credibility among their team members. This style of leadership encourages leaders to be self-aware and understand their strengths and weaknesses, allowing them to make more informed choices. Self-discipline is a key component, as authentic leaders must consistently demonstrate their commitment to their values and principles, even when faced with challenges or difficult decisions. Authentic Leadership fosters a positive organizational culture built on honesty, integrity, and ethical behavior, ultimately promoting trust, engagement, and long-term success.

Understanding Authentic Leadership involves recognizing and appreciating a leadership style that prioritizes genuineness, honesty, and alignment with one's core values. Authentic leaders lead from a place of self-awareness, staying true to themselves while inspiring trust and confidence in their team members. This leadership approach emphasizes being transparent about one's beliefs, strengths, and weaknesses, which fosters open and honest communication within the organization. Authentic leaders are not only guided by their principles but also exhibit self-discipline in upholding them, even when faced with challenges. This leadership style creates a positive work environment where ethical behavior and authenticity are celebrated, ultimately contributing to stronger relationships, increased engagement, and the achievement of shared goals.

Key Principles and Characteristics

Authentic leadership is characterized by several key principles and characteristics that guide leaders in their approach to leadership. Here are the fundamental principles and characteristics of authentic leadership:

1. **Self-Awareness:** Authentic leaders possess a deep understanding of themselves, including their values, strengths, weaknesses, and emotions. This self-awareness enables them to make conscious and authentic choices in their leadership.
2. **Transparency:** Authentic leaders are open, honest, and transparent in their communications and actions. They do not hide their true selves or intentions, fostering trust among team members.
3. **Consistency:** Consistency is a hallmark of authentic leadership. Authentic leaders maintain their values and principles in all situations, avoiding hypocrisy or inconsistency in their behavior.
4. **Ethical Behavior:** Authentic leaders prioritize ethical conduct and integrity. They hold themselves to high ethical standards and expect the same from their team members.
5. **Relational Transparency:** They build genuine and meaningful relationships with their team members. They are approachable, empathetic, and actively listen to others' perspectives.

6. **Leading with Values:** Authentic leaders align their leadership with their personal values and the organization's values. Their actions and decisions reflect these values, promoting a sense of shared purpose.
7. **Self-Regulation and Self-Discipline:** They exercise self-regulation and self-discipline to control their emotions, impulses, and reactions. This self-control is essential for rational decision-making.
8. **Adaptability:** Authentic leaders are adaptable and open to change. They are willing to evolve and learn from their experiences and mistakes.
9. **Empowerment:** They empower their team members, giving them a sense of ownership and autonomy in their roles. They encourage individual growth and development.
10. **Positive Organizational Culture:** Authentic leadership contributes to a positive organizational culture characterized by trust, respect, and open communication.
11. **Resilience:** Authentic leaders exhibit resilience in the face of challenges and setbacks. They remain steadfast in their values and beliefs, inspiring their team members to do the same.
12. **Authenticity as a Model:** They serve as role models for authenticity and ethical behavior, setting a standard for integrity and sincerity that others aspire to emulate.
13. **Inclusivity:** They value diversity and inclusivity, recognizing that different perspectives enrich the organization and contribute to better decision-making.
14. **Listening and Empathy:** Authentic leaders actively listen to the concerns and needs of their team members and demonstrate empathy and understanding.
15. **Positive Influence:** They use their influence positively, inspiring and motivating their team members to achieve their best.
16. **Personal Growth:** Authentic leaders are committed to personal growth and self-improvement, continuously learning and evolving as leaders.

Authentic leadership is rooted in self-awareness, transparency, ethical behavior, and the ability to build meaningful relationships. Leaders who embody these principles and characteristics create an environment of trust and authenticity, leading to higher team morale, engagement, and organizational success.

Importance of Authenticity

The importance of authenticity in leadership cannot be overstated. Authentic leaders inspire trust and credibility among their team members because they are genuine, transparent, and true to their values. This trust fosters open communication and collaboration, which are essential for organizational success. Authentic leaders also create a positive work culture where individuals feel valued and respected, leading to higher job satisfaction and engagement. Moreover, authenticity sets a standard for ethical behavior and integrity within the organization, promoting a culture of honesty and accountability. In a world where transparency and trust are increasingly valued, authenticity is a cornerstone of effective leadership, contributing to both personal and organizational growth and success.

The significance of authenticity in leadership extends to several crucial aspects that are essential for personal and organizational success. Let's delve into the detailed significance of authenticity, focusing on building trust, fostering transparency, and making ethical decisions:

1. **Building Trust:** Authentic leaders inspire trust among their team members. When leaders are genuine and sincere in their actions, they create an environment where people feel safe and confident in their leadership. Team members are more likely to trust leaders who are consistent and transparent about their intentions, values, and expectations. Trust is the foundation of strong working relationships, and

it leads to improved collaboration, cooperation, and overall team cohesion.
2. **Fostering Transparency:** Authenticity and transparency go hand in hand. Authentic leaders are open and honest in their communication, willingly sharing information and insights. This transparency cultivates a culture of openness within the organization. When leaders are forthright about challenges, successes, and decision-making processes, it encourages team members to do the same. In a transparent environment, problems are identified and addressed more promptly, and solutions are developed collaboratively.
3. **Making Ethical Decisions:** Authentic leaders prioritize ethical behavior and integrity. Their actions are guided by a strong moral compass rooted in their personal values. This commitment to ethical conduct sets the tone for the entire organization, reinforcing the importance of honesty and fairness. Team members are more likely to follow ethical standards when they see their leaders consistently adhering to them. Authentic leaders make tough decisions with fairness and a sense of justice, which fosters a culture of trust and accountability.
4. **Enhancing Employee Engagement:** Authentic leadership significantly contributes to employee engagement. When leaders are sincere and genuine, employees are more likely to feel valued and respected. This sense of recognition and appreciation leads to higher job satisfaction and a greater sense of purpose in their work. Engaged employees are more committed to their roles, leading to increased productivity, innovation, and overall organizational success.
5. **Encouraging Personal Growth:** Authentic leaders not only focus on the growth and development of their team members but also emphasize personal growth for themselves. They are open to self-reflection and acknowledge their own areas for improvement. This willingness to learn and evolve sets a positive example and encourages others to do the same, promoting a culture of continuous improvement.

6. **Resolving Conflicts Effectively:** Authentic leaders are skilled at resolving conflicts because they approach conflicts with transparency and empathy. They actively listen to the concerns of all parties involved and seek to understand different perspectives. This empathetic approach helps in finding equitable solutions that address the root causes of conflicts, maintaining a harmonious work environment.
7. **Promoting Organizational Alignment:** Authentic leaders ensure that their personal values align with the organization's values and mission. This alignment fosters a sense of shared purpose and direction, making it easier to rally the team around common goals. When leaders and team members are on the same page regarding values and objectives, the organization can achieve greater cohesion and effectiveness.

Authenticity in leadership plays a pivotal role in building trust, fostering transparency, and making ethical decisions. It creates a culture where openness, honesty, and integrity are highly valued, ultimately leading to improved employee engagement, effective conflict resolution, and a stronger, more ethically grounded organization. Authentic leaders serve as beacons of trustworthiness and inspire their teams to reach higher levels of performance and success.

Embracing Authenticity as a Leader

Embracing authenticity as a leader is about being true to oneself and one's values while inspiring trust and confidence in others. It involves the willingness to show vulnerability and admit mistakes, creating an atmosphere of openness and honesty. Authentic leaders lead by example, consistently aligning their actions with their values, which fosters credibility and respect. Embracing authenticity also means valuing diversity and inclusivity, respecting different viewpoints, and listening actively to team members. Authentic leaders create a culture where people feel safe to express themselves, enabling better communication and collaboration. Overall, embracing authenticity as a leader not only strengthens personal and professional relationships but also contributes to a positive organizational culture and long-term success.

Strategy and Practice to Embrace

Embracing authenticity and self-discipline in leadership roles requires deliberate strategies and practices. Here are some key approaches for leaders to cultivate authenticity and self-discipline:

1. **Self-Reflection:** Regularly engage in self-reflection to understand your values, strengths, weaknesses, and areas for improvement. This self-awareness is the foundation of authentic leadership.
2. **Clarify Your Values:** Clearly define your core values and principles. Knowing what you stand for makes it easier to align your actions with your beliefs.
3. **Lead by Example:** Model the behavior you expect from others. Demonstrating authenticity and self-discipline sets the standard for your team to follow.
4. **Be Transparent:** Practice transparency by sharing your thoughts, intentions, and decisions openly. Authentic leaders are honest and forthright in their communication.
5. **Active Listening:** Develop active listening skills to understand the perspectives and concerns of your team members. Authenticity involves valuing others' input and experiences.
6. **Admit Mistakes:** Be willing to admit when you make a mistake and take responsibility for your actions. Authentic leaders acknowledge imperfections and learn from them.
7. **Develop Emotional Intelligence:** Enhance your emotional intelligence to understand and manage your emotions

effectively. This self-regulation is crucial for maintaining composure and making rational decisions.

8. **Set Ethical Standards:** Establish clear ethical standards and hold yourself accountable to them. Ethical behavior is a cornerstone of authenticity and self-discipline.
9. **Cultivate Resilience:** Develop resilience to handle setbacks and challenges with grace and determination. Resilient leaders remain true to their values during difficult times.
10. **Seek Feedback:** Solicit feedback from peers, mentors, and team members to gain insights into your leadership style and areas for improvement. Use this feedback to make necessary adjustments.
11. **Continuous Learning:** Commit to continuous learning and personal growth. Stay open to new ideas, perspectives, and experiences that can help you evolve as a leader.
12. **Practice Self-Discipline:** Build self-discipline by setting clear goals, prioritizing tasks, and managing your time effectively. Self-discipline enables you to stay focused on your values and objectives.
13. **Surround Yourself with Authenticity:** Encourage authenticity in your team by valuing diversity and inclusivity. Create an environment where team members feel safe to express themselves authentically.
14. **Reflect on Decisions:** Before making important decisions, take time to reflect on how they align with your values and principles. This reflective practice ensures that your choices are consistent with your authenticity.
15. **Lead with Purpose:** Connect your leadership to a higher purpose or vision. Leaders who lead with purpose are more likely to exhibit authenticity and self-discipline in their actions.
16. **Seek Role Models:** Identify authentic leaders you admire and seek inspiration from their practices. Learn from their experiences and apply relevant insights to your own leadership journey.

By implementing these strategies and practices, leaders can embrace authenticity and self-discipline, creating an environment that fosters trust, openness, and ethical behavior. Authentic leadership benefits not only the leader but also the entire team and organization, contributing to long-term success and positive organizational culture.

Self-Assessment Tolls for Developing Authenticity

Self-assessment tools can be valuable for leaders looking to develop authenticity in their leadership style. These tools help leaders gain insights into their strengths, weaknesses, values, and areas for improvement. Here are some self-assessment tools and resources that can aid in the development of authenticity:

1. **360-Degree Feedback Surveys:** These surveys collect feedback from peers, subordinates, and superiors to provide a comprehensive view of a leader's strengths and weaknesses. They can highlight areas where a leader's behavior aligns or diverges from their intended values and authenticity.

2. **Emotional Intelligence (EQ) Assessments:** EQ assessments, such as the Emotional Intelligence Appraisal by Travis Bradberry and Jean Greaves, help leaders understand and improve their emotional self-awareness, self-regulation, empathy, and social skills. Emotional intelligence is closely tied to authenticity.

3. **Values Assessment:** Tools like the Values in Action (VIA) Survey or the Barrett Values Centre Cultural Transformation Tools help individuals identify their core values and assess how well their actions align with these values.

4. **Strengths-Based Assessments:** Assessments like the CliftonStrengths (formerly StrengthsFinder) can identify a leader's natural talents and strengths. Building on one's

strengths can enhance authenticity by allowing leaders to leverage what comes naturally to them.

5. **Leadership Style Assessments:** Assessments such as the Myers-Briggs Type Indicator (MBTI) or DiSC Personality Assessment can provide insights into leadership styles and preferences. Understanding one's style can help leaders align their leadership with their authentic selves.

6. **Ethical Decision-Making Surveys:** Tools like the Ethical Leadership Self-Assessment from the Ethics and Compliance Initiative (ECI) can help leaders assess their ethical decision-making and adherence to ethical principles.

7. **Journaling:** Regularly keeping a journal where leaders reflect on their thoughts, actions, and decisions can be a valuable self-assessment tool. It allows leaders to track their progress in aligning their behavior with their values.

8. **Mentoring and Coaching:** Seek guidance from mentors or coaches who can provide feedback and help you assess your authenticity as a leader. Their insights and experience can be invaluable in your development journey.

9. **Online Courses and Workshops:** Many online platforms offer courses and workshops on leadership and authenticity. Platforms like Coursera, LinkedIn Learning, and edX offer a variety of resources.

10. **Books and Publications:** Reading books and articles on authentic leadership, emotional intelligence, and self-awareness can provide valuable insights and self-assessment opportunities. Authors like Brené Brown, Daniel Goleman, and Stephen Covey have written extensively on these topics.

When using self-assessment tools, it's important to approach them with an open and self-reflective mindset. The goal is not just to identify areas for improvement but also to develop a deeper understanding of oneself and how authenticity can be nurtured in leadership. Additionally, combining multiple assessment tools and seeking feedback from trusted sources can provide a more comprehensive view of one's authentic leadership journey.

Embracing Authenticity for Genuine Leadership

Embracing authenticity for genuine leadership is a powerful approach where leaders align their actions and decisions with their true selves and values. It involves being sincere, open, and honest in all interactions, fostering trust among team members. Genuine leaders prioritize ethical behavior and self-discipline, making choices that reflect their principles. This approach promotes transparency, encourages open communication, and inspires team members by setting a positive example. By embracing authenticity, leaders create a work environment where people feel valued, motivated, and empowered, ultimately leading to stronger relationships and more meaningful and successful leadership outcomes.

Leading the Value

Leading with values is a leadership approach centered on guiding and influencing others based on a set of core principles and beliefs. It involves consistently making decisions and taking actions that align with these values, even in the face of challenges or pressure. Leaders who lead with values prioritize ethical conduct, integrity, and a commitment to doing what is right over personal gain or expediency. This approach not only fosters trust and credibility but also sets a clear moral and cultural tone for the organization. Leading with values is about being an exemplar of the principles one holds dear and using them as a guiding compass to inspire and guide both individual and collective efforts within a team or organization.

Role of Value in Authentic Leadership

The role of values in authentic leadership is pivotal as it forms the foundation upon which leaders build trust, credibility, and a sense of purpose within their teams and organizations. Values guide decision-making, shape ethical behavior, and define the character of a leader. Here's a detailed explanation of the role of values in authentic leadership and how leaders can align their actions with their core values:

1. **Values as Guiding Principles:** Authentic leaders have a clear understanding of their core values. These values represent their deeply held beliefs about what is right, just, and important in both personal and professional life. Values serve as guiding principles that influence decision-making and actions.
2. **Shaping Ethical Behavior:** Values play a fundamental role in shaping ethical behavior. Authentic leaders prioritize ethical conduct and integrity, and their values act as a moral compass in making decisions. They consider not only the immediate impact of their choices but also the long-term ethical implications.
3. **Building Trust and Credibility:** Authentic leaders who consistently align their actions with their core values are seen as trustworthy and credible by their team members and stakeholders. When values are upheld consistently, it fosters a sense of reliability and predictability, which is essential for building trust.
4. **Defining Organizational Culture:** Leaders' values have a significant influence on organizational culture. When leaders lead by example and prioritize values, it sets the tone for the entire organization. Employees are more likely to embrace and embody these values, contributing to a positive and ethical workplace culture.
5. **Inspiring Commitment:** Authentic leaders inspire commitment and dedication among their team members.

When values are clearly articulated and consistently demonstrated, team members feel a sense of purpose and alignment with the organization's mission.

6. **Aligning with Personal and Organizational Values:** Leaders must ensure that their personal values align with the values of the organization they lead. This alignment creates a seamless integration of individual and organizational values, contributing to a stronger sense of shared purpose.
7. **Self-Awareness:** Leaders need self-awareness to identify and articulate their core values. Regular self-reflection and introspection help leaders gain clarity about what truly matters to them.
8. **Articulating Values:** Authentic leaders should clearly articulate their values to their team members. Open and transparent communication about these values helps team members understand the leader's guiding principles.
9. **Consistent Modeling:** Leaders must consistently model their values through their actions and decisions. Their behavior should serve as a tangible example of how these values are put into practice.
10. **Accountability:** Leaders should hold themselves accountable for aligning their actions with their values. They should acknowledge and rectify any lapses that might occur.
11. **Encouraging Dialogue:** Create an environment where team members feel comfortable discussing values and ethical dilemmas. Encourage open dialogue about how values can guide decision-making and problem-solving.
12. **Adaptability and Growth:** While values provide a stable foundation, leaders should also be open to growth and change. Values may evolve over time, and leaders should adapt while remaining true to their core principles.

Values are at the heart of authentic leadership. Leaders who consistently align their actions with their core values create a culture of trust, integrity, and ethical behavior. They inspire commitment, foster a sense of purpose, and drive positive change within their organizations, ultimately leading to greater success and a more meaningful leadership experience.

Example of Leaders led by Authenticity

Several leaders from various fields have successfully led with authenticity and values. These leaders have demonstrated their commitment to ethical behavior, transparency, and aligning their actions with their core principles. Here are some examples:

1. **Kartar Singh Sarabha:** Kartar Singh Sarabha was a Sikh revolutionary and freedom fighter who played a significant role in India's struggle for independence from British colonial rule. His authenticity and commitment to the values of justice, freedom, and self-determination were evident in his actions. At a young age, he joined the Ghadar Movement, an organization of Indian expatriates advocating for India's independence. Sarabha's unwavering dedication and sacrifices, including his involvement in planning an armed rebellion, showcased his alignment with his core values. Although he was arrested and executed at a young age, his legacy as an authentic leader who fearlessly fought for his beliefs continues to inspire generations of freedom fighters in Punjab and around the world.

2. **Oprah Winfrey:** Media mogul Oprah Winfrey is known for her authenticity and commitment to values like empathy, education, and empowerment. Her career has been marked by open and honest communication, particularly in her talk show and philanthropic endeavors, where she empowers individuals to live their best lives.

3. **Nelson Mandela:** Nelson Mandela, the former President of South Africa, exemplified authenticity and values by advocating for reconciliation, forgiveness, and equality. Despite enduring years of imprisonment, he remained

steadfast in his commitment to justice and democracy, uniting a divided nation.
4. **Abigail Disney:** Abigail Disney, a filmmaker, philanthropist, and activist, has used her platform to speak out against income inequality and unethical corporate practices. Her authenticity lies in her commitment to social justice and using her wealth to advocate for change.
5. **Howard Schultz (Starbucks):** Former Starbucks CEO Howard Schultz led with values by emphasizing employee well-being, ethical sourcing, and community engagement. He took a stand on issues like race and immigration, demonstrating a commitment to social responsibility in business.
6. **Ratan Tata (Tata Group):** Ratan Tata, the former Chairman of Tata Group, emphasized values such as integrity and social responsibility in the conglomerate's operations. He consistently demonstrated his commitment to these values by leading various philanthropic initiatives and promoting ethical business practices.
7. **Rosa Parks:** Civil rights activist Rosa Parks is an exemplar of authenticity and values. Her refusal to give up her bus seat to a white passenger in 1955 was a powerful act of civil disobedience rooted in her commitment to justice and equality.
8. **Paul Polman (Unilever):** Former Unilever CEO Paul Polman led with a strong focus on sustainability and social responsibility. He committed the company to the Sustainable Living Plan, aligning its business practices with environmental and social goals.
9. **Elon Musk (Tesla, SpaceX):** While known for his bold vision and innovation, Elon Musk has also been open about his commitment to values like environmental sustainability and human colonization of Mars. His companies, Tesla and SpaceX, reflect these values in their missions and actions.
10. **Melinda Gates:** Philanthropist Melinda Gates, co-chair of the Bill & Melinda Gates Foundation, demonstrates

authenticity through her commitment to global health, gender equality, and education. Her work is a reflection of her values and dedication to making the world a better place.

These leaders serve as role models for authentic leadership by consistently aligning their actions with their values, promoting ethical behavior, and striving to create positive change in their respective fields and the world at large.

Self-Reflection and Growth

Self-reflection and growth are essential components of personal and professional development. Self-reflection involves introspection and examining one's thoughts, actions, and experiences to gain a deeper understanding of oneself. It's a process of assessing one's values, goals, strengths, weaknesses, and areas for improvement. Growth, on the other hand, signifies the continuous process of evolving and improving oneself based on the insights gained through self-reflection. It involves setting goals, acquiring new knowledge and skills, and making intentional efforts to become a better version of oneself. Self-reflection and growth go hand in hand, as the awareness gained through self-reflection often leads to personal and professional development and the pursuit of meaningful goals. This ongoing cycle of self-awareness and improvement is crucial for individuals seeking to reach their full potential and lead authentically.

Importance of Self-Reflection and Personal Growth

Ongoing self-reflection and personal growth are paramount in maintaining authentic leadership. Here's why it is crucial:

1. **Enhanced Self-Awareness:** Self-reflection allows leaders to gain a deeper understanding of their values, beliefs,

strengths, and weaknesses. This self-awareness is foundational for authentic leadership, as leaders must first be in touch with their own principles before they can effectively lead with authenticity.
2. **Alignment with Values:** Authentic leaders consistently align their actions with their core values. Through self-reflection, they can assess whether their decisions and behaviors are in harmony with their principles. This alignment fosters credibility and trust among team members.
3. **Adaptability:** The business landscape is constantly evolving. Personal growth ensures that leaders remain adaptable and open to change. They acquire new knowledge and skills that enable them to navigate challenges and opportunities effectively while remaining true to their values.
4. **Resilience:** Personal growth contributes to leaders' resilience. When they continuously develop their emotional intelligence and coping mechanisms, they are better equipped to handle setbacks and adversity without compromising their authenticity.
5. **Inspiration:** Authentic leaders lead by example. When they actively pursue personal growth, they inspire their team members to do the same. This can create a culture of continuous improvement and learning within the organization.
6. **Problem-Solving:** Personal growth often involves enhancing problem-solving skills. Leaders who continually develop their critical thinking abilities are better equipped to make ethical decisions and address complex challenges while upholding their values.
7. **Enhanced Communication:** Leaders who engage in self-reflection and personal growth are typically more skilled communicators. They are better at active listening, empathizing with others, and conveying their thoughts and values effectively, which is essential for authentic leadership.

8. **Long-Term Sustainability:** Authentic leadership is not a one-time accomplishment; it's a continuous journey. Self-reflection and personal growth sustain authenticity over the long term, ensuring that leaders remain true to their values throughout their leadership tenure.
9. **Positive Organizational Culture:** Leaders who prioritize self-reflection and personal growth contribute to the development of a positive organizational culture. This culture values self-awareness, learning, and ethical behavior, fostering a more engaged and motivated workforce.

Ongoing self-reflection and personal growth are essential for authentic leadership. They enable leaders to maintain alignment with their values, adapt to changing circumstances, inspire others, and lead with integrity. Authentic leaders understand that growth is a continuous process, and by investing in their own development, they can effectively lead their teams and organizations towards success while staying true to their authentic selves.

Strategies and Resources for Continuous Improvement

Continuous self-improvement is a lifelong journey that authentic leaders actively pursue to enhance their personal and professional growth. Here are some strategies and resources for ongoing self-improvement:

Self-Reflection

- Regularly set aside time for introspection and self-assessment.
- Journal your thoughts, experiences, and insights.
- Ask reflective questions such as "What did I learn today?" and "How can I improve?"

Reading and Learning

- Read books, articles, and research papers related to your field and areas of interest.
- Utilize online courses and platforms like Coursera, edX, and LinkedIn Learning.
- Join professional organizations and attend conferences to stay updated in your industry.

Seeking Feedback

- Solicit feedback from mentors, peers, and team members.
- Actively listen to constructive criticism and use it as a tool for growth.
- Consider using 360-degree feedback assessments.

Goal Setting

- Set SMART (Specific, Measurable, Achievable, Relevant, Time-bound) goals for personal and professional development.
- Break larger goals into smaller, actionable steps.

Networking

- Build a diverse network of professionals and thought leaders.
- Engage in meaningful conversations and exchange insights with others in your field.

Skill Development

- Identify specific skills you want to develop and create a plan to acquire them.
- Practice deliberate practice, focusing on areas that challenge you the most.

Emotional Intelligence (EQ)

- Enhance your emotional intelligence by developing self-awareness, self-regulation, empathy, social skills, and motivation.
- Consider EQ assessments and training programs.

Time Management

- Improve time management skills to make the most of your day.
- Use techniques like the Pomodoro Technique or time blocking to increase productivity.

Mindfulness and Well-Being

- Practice mindfulness and meditation to reduce stress and enhance focus.
- Prioritize physical health through regular exercise, balanced nutrition, and sufficient sleep.

Leadership Development Programs

- Enroll in leadership development programs offered by universities, organizations, or professional coaching services.
- These programs often provide structured learning and development opportunities.

Personal Development Books

- Explore books on personal development, leadership, and self-improvement by renowned authors like Stephen Covey, Brené Brown, and Daniel Goleman.

Accountability Partners

- Partner with a friend, colleague, or mentor who can hold you accountable for your self-improvement goals.

- Regular check-ins can help maintain your commitment.

Online Communities

- Join online communities, forums, or social media groups related to your interests and goals.
- Engage in discussions, share experiences, and learn from others.

Talks and Podcasts

- Watch Talks and listen to podcasts that cover topics of personal and professional growth.
- These platforms offer insights from experts and thought leaders.

Workshops and Webinars

- Attend workshops and webinars on leadership, communication, and personal development.
- Many organizations and institutions offer these events.

Remember that continuous self-improvement is a personalized journey, and what works for one person may not work for another.

Create an Authentic Organizational Culture

Creating an authentic organizational culture is about fostering an environment where transparency, honesty, and ethical behavior are valued and practiced at all levels. It begins with leaders setting a clear example by consistently aligning their actions with the organization's core values. Authenticity should be embedded in the organization's mission and vision statements, guiding principles, and code of conduct. This culture encourages open communication, where employees feel safe to voice their opinions and concerns. Leaders actively seek and act on feedback, demonstrating a commitment to improvement and growth. When authenticity is ingrained in the organizational culture, it promotes trust among employees, leading to higher engagement, better decision-making, and a shared sense of purpose.

How Authentic Leadership Can Shape the Organizational Culture

Authentic leadership can profoundly shape the culture of an organization by influencing the behaviors, values, and norms that guide how individuals and teams operate within that environment. Here's a detailed explanation of how authentic leadership can shape an organizational culture:

1. **Setting a Clear Example:** Authentic leaders lead by example, consistently aligning their actions with their core values. When employees witness leaders demonstrating honesty, integrity, and ethical behavior, they are more likely to emulate these qualities in their own work.
2. **Fostering Trust and Transparency:** Authentic leaders prioritize transparency and open communication. They create an atmosphere where employees feel safe sharing their thoughts and concerns without fear of retribution. This fosters trust among team members and between employees and leadership.
3. **Encouraging Open Dialogue:** Authentic leaders actively seek feedback and diverse perspectives. They promote a culture of open dialogue and constructive criticism, allowing for the free exchange of ideas and fostering an environment where innovation and creativity can thrive.
4. **Values-Driven Decision-Making:** Authentic leaders base their decisions on their core values. This consistent adherence to principles guides the organization's decision-making processes, ensuring that choices are aligned with ethical and moral standards.
5. **Empowering Employees:** Authentic leaders empower their employees by valuing their contributions and providing

opportunities for growth and development. This empowerment leads to a more engaged and motivated workforce.
6. **Inclusivity and Diversity:** Authentic leaders value diversity and inclusivity, recognizing that different perspectives contribute to innovation and problem-solving. They actively promote these principles in the organization's hiring and promotion practices.
7. **Resilience in Adversity:** Authentic leaders demonstrate resilience in the face of challenges and setbacks. They maintain their commitment to their values and principles, serving as a source of inspiration and motivation for the entire organization during difficult times.
8. **Long-Term Orientation:** Authentic leaders focus on long-term sustainability rather than short-term gains. This perspective promotes a culture of stability and ethical decision-making, which can lead to sustained success.
9. **Promoting Learning and Growth:** Authentic leaders encourage continuous learning and personal growth among employees. They invest in training and development programs, reinforcing the value of self-improvement and skill enhancement.
10. **Cultivating a Shared Purpose:** Authentic leaders connect the organization's mission and vision to a higher purpose. This shared sense of purpose creates a cohesive culture where employees understand the significance of their work and its impact on the world.
11. **Accountability:** Authentic leaders hold themselves and others accountable for their actions. This reinforces the importance of taking responsibility for one's behavior and the consequences of decisions made within the organization.
12. **Employee Well-Being:** Authentic leaders prioritize the well-being of their employees, recognizing that a healthy work-life balance and a supportive environment contribute to overall satisfaction and productivity.

Authentic leadership shapes the culture of an organization by infusing it with values such as transparency, trust, ethical behavior, and a commitment to the greater good. When leaders consistently exhibit these qualities, they inspire their teams to do the same, ultimately creating a positive and values-driven organizational culture that fosters employee engagement, innovation, and long-term success.

Steps for Leaders

Fostering an environment where authenticity is valued and encouraged is essential for promoting authentic leadership and creating a positive organizational culture. Here are steps that leaders can take to achieve this:

1. **Lead by Example:** Demonstrate authenticity in your own actions and decision-making. Be transparent, honest, and true to your values. Your behavior sets the standard for the organization.
2. **Communicate Openly:** Encourage open and honest communication throughout the organization. Create channels for employees to voice their opinions, concerns, and ideas without fear of retribution.
3. **Articulate Core Values:** Clearly define and communicate the organization's core values and guiding principles. Ensure that these values are integrated into the company's mission and vision statements.
4. **Empower Employees:** Give employees autonomy and ownership over their work. Encourage them to take initiative and make decisions aligned with the organization's values.
5. **Seek Feedback:** Actively seek feedback from employees at all levels. Use surveys, one-on-one discussions, and anonymous feedback mechanisms to gather insights into the organizational culture.

6. **Promote Inclusivity:** Value diversity and inclusion in all aspects of the organization. Create a culture where different perspectives are welcomed and celebrated.
7. **Encourage Growth and Development:** Invest in training and development programs that promote personal and professional growth. Support employees in acquiring new skills and advancing in their careers.
8. **Recognize and Reward Authenticity:** Acknowledge and reward behaviors that exemplify authenticity and align with the organization's values. Celebrate employees who demonstrate ethical conduct and integrity.
9. **Provide Mentorship and Coaching:** Offer mentorship and coaching opportunities for employees to enhance their leadership skills and foster authenticity. Encourage leaders to serve as mentors.
10. **Establish Accountability:** Hold leaders and employees accountable for their actions and decisions. Consistently apply consequences for behavior that contradicts the organization's values.
11. **Promote Work-Life Balance:** Encourage a healthy work-life balance among employees. Support flexible work arrangements and initiatives that prioritize employee well-being.
12. **Celebrate Success and Learning from Failure:** Celebrate both successes and failures as opportunities for growth. Encourage a culture that values learning from mistakes and adapting for improvement.
13. **Create a Shared Purpose:** Help employees connect their work to a higher purpose. Emphasize the impact of their contributions on the organization's mission and societal well-being.
14. **Address Conflicts Constructively:** When conflicts arise, encourage a respectful and constructive approach to resolution. Provide conflict resolution training if necessary.

15. **Review and Adapt:** Regularly assess the organization's progress in fostering authenticity and adjust strategies as needed. Continuously seek ways to improve the culture.

By taking these steps, leaders can actively promote authenticity within their organizations, creating an environment where employees feel empowered, valued, and encouraged to bring their true selves to work. This, in turn, leads to enhanced employee engagement, a positive organizational culture, and ultimately, greater success and fulfillment for all involved.

*****

CHAPTER EIGHT
Decision-making and influence theories

Decision-Making and Influence Theories are fundamental concepts in the fields of psychology, sociology, and organizational behavior. These theories provide insights into how individuals and groups make choices and how they are influenced by various factors. Let's delve into their meanings and what they entail:

Decision-Making Theories

Decision-making theories explore the processes and factors that influence an individual's or a group's choices and actions. These theories help us understand why people make specific decisions and how they weigh different options. Some key decision-making theories include:

1. **Rational Decision-Making Theory**: This theory posits that individuals make choices based on a rational analysis of available information, aiming to maximize their utility or benefits while minimizing costs or risks. It assumes that people have complete information, make consistent choices, and have clear preferences.
2. **Bounded Rationality Theory**: Proposed by Herbert Simon, this theory acknowledges that human decision-makers often operate with limited information and cognitive resources. They make decisions that are "good enough" rather than perfectly rational, considering constraints such as time and cognitive abilities.
3. **Prospect Theory**: Developed by Daniel Kahneman and Amos Tversky, this theory suggests that people tend to evaluate potential gains and losses relative to a reference

point. They are more sensitive to perceived losses than equivalent gains, leading to risk-averse behavior in some situations and risk-seeking behavior in others.
4. **Behavioral Economics**: This interdisciplinary field combines elements of psychology and economics to study how cognitive biases and heuristics can affect decision-making. It explores how people deviate from purely rational choices due to emotional and psychological factors.

Influence Theories

Influence theories examine the ways in which individuals and groups are persuaded or guided by external factors, such as social norms, authority figures, and peer pressure. These theories shed light on how people are influenced to adopt certain behaviors or make specific decisions. Some prominent influence theories include:

1. **Social Influence Theory**: This theory explores how people are affected by the attitudes, beliefs, and behaviors of others in their social environment. It encompasses concepts like conformity, obedience, and social norms, illustrating how individuals adjust their behavior to fit in with a group or comply with authority figures.
2. **Informational and Normative Influence**: Informational influence occurs when individuals conform to the group's behavior because they believe the group possesses valuable knowledge. Normative influence, on the other hand, is driven by the desire to gain social approval or avoid rejection, even if one disagrees with the group's stance.
3. **Reciprocity and Persuasion**: These theories examine how the principle of reciprocity (the tendency to return favors) and persuasion techniques (such as the use of authority, scarcity, and social proof) can be employed to influence

people's decisions and actions in marketing, sales, and everyday life.

Decision-making theories delve into the processes behind individual and group choices, considering factors like rationality, biases, and cognitive limitations. Influence Theories, on the other hand, focus on the external forces and social dynamics that shape decision-making, emphasizing the impact of social norms, authority figures, and persuasion strategies. Both sets of theories play crucial roles in understanding human behavior and decision-making in various contexts.

Importance of Decision-Making and Influence Theories in Leadership

Decision-Making and Influence Theories hold significant importance in the realm of leadership. Effective leaders need to make informed decisions and possess the ability to influence and inspire their teams to achieve organizational goals. Here's how these theories are significant in leadership:

Informed Decision-Making

Rational Decision-Making: Leaders often face complex choices that require rational analysis. Understanding this theory helps leaders weigh the pros and cons objectively and make decisions that align with the organization's mission and goals.

Bounded Rationality: Recognizing cognitive limitations, leaders can make more realistic decisions by acknowledging that they might not have all the information and that time constraints can affect their choices. This leads to more practical decision-making.

Prospect Theory: Leaders can anticipate how their decisions might be perceived by their team members. Being aware of prospect theory can help them frame decisions in ways that motivate and inspire their followers, considering the psychology of gains and losses.

Influencing and Leading Others

Social Influence Theory: Effective leaders understand how social dynamics work within their teams. They can leverage social influence theories to build strong team cohesion, encourage collaboration, and shape a positive organizational culture.

Reciprocity and Persuasion: Leaders can utilize the principle of reciprocity to foster trust and goodwill among team members. Persuasion techniques can be applied in communication and negotiations to rally support for important initiatives.

Informational and Normative Influence: Leaders can create a culture where team members are encouraged to share knowledge and ideas. They can also set positive behavioral norms that align with the organization's values and objectives.

Decision-Making in a Team Context

Leadership often involves collaborative decision-making. Leaders who understand decision-making theories can facilitate more productive team discussions, ensuring that diverse perspectives are considered and that group biases are minimized.

Managing Resistance and Conflict

Understanding influence theories helps leaders navigate resistance and conflict. They can employ persuasion techniques to address objections, build consensus, and maintain team cohesion.

Ethical Leadership

Ethical decision-making and influence are critical for leaders. Decision-making theories can assist leaders in making morally sound choices, while Influence Theories can help them inspire ethical behavior in their teams.

Adaptive Leadership

In dynamic environments, leaders may need to adapt and make decisions swiftly. These theories provide tools to assess situations, manage risks, and adjust strategies effectively.

Decision-Making and Influence Theories are essential tools for leadership. They enable leaders to make better-informed decisions, foster a positive team culture, manage conflicts, and inspire their teams to achieve common objectives. By incorporating these theories into their leadership practices, individuals in leadership roles can enhance their effectiveness and contribute to the success of their organizations.

Critical Role in Achieving Leadership Objectives

Effective decision-making and influence play critical roles in achieving leadership objectives across various domains. Here are some of the key ways in which they contribute to leadership success:

1. **Goal Alignment**: Effective decision-making ensures that every choice made by a leader is aligned with the organization's mission, vision, and strategic goals. This alignment keeps the team focused on the right priorities.
2. **Resource Allocation**: Decision-making helps leaders allocate resources (financial, human, and material) optimally. Wise resource allocation is crucial for achieving objectives efficiently.

3. **Problem Solving**: Leaders often face challenges and obstacles. Effective decision-making allows them to analyze problems, identify solutions, and implement strategies to overcome these challenges.
4. **Risk Management**: Decision-making involves assessing risks and benefits. Leaders must make informed decisions that strike a balance between taking calculated risks and ensuring the stability of the organization.
5. **Team Engagement and Motivation**: Influence is essential for motivating and inspiring team members. Leaders who can influence positively can rally their teams behind a shared vision and create a sense of purpose, leading to higher engagement and commitment.
6. **Collaboration and Teamwork**: Effective leaders use their influence to foster collaboration and teamwork. They can encourage open communication, build trust, and facilitate productive interactions among team members.
7. **Change Management**: When leaders need to implement changes or reforms, their ability to influence others plays a critical role. Effective communication and persuasion can ease resistance and facilitate smoother transitions.
8. **Decision-Making in Crisis**: During crises or emergencies, quick and effective decision-making is paramount. Leaders who can make sound decisions under pressure are better equipped to guide their organizations through turbulent times.
9. **Ethical Leadership**: Decision-making and influence are central to ethical leadership. Leaders who make ethical choices and influence others to do the same build trust and integrity, which are vital for achieving long-term objectives.
10. **Strategic Vision**: Leaders use decision-making and influence to shape the strategic vision of the organization. They set the direction and inspire others to work towards that vision, driving progress toward long-term goals.
11. **Adaptation and Innovation**: Effective decision-making and influence are crucial for fostering a culture of adaptation

and innovation. Leaders must make decisions that encourage experimentation and creativity to stay competitive.
12. **Stakeholder Management**: Leaders interact with various stakeholders, including employees, customers, investors, and the community. Effective influence and decision-making help maintain positive relationships with these stakeholders, which is vital for achieving objectives.

Effective decision-making and influence are integral to leadership success. Leaders who excel in these areas can guide their organizations toward their objectives by making sound choices, motivating and aligning their teams, and navigating the complexities of modern business environments. These skills are essential not only for achieving short-term goals but also for ensuring long-term sustainability and growth.

Vroom's Decision-Making Theory

Vroom's Decision-Making Theory, developed by Victor Vroom in the 1960s, is a prominent model that focuses on how individuals make decisions in organizations. This theory centers on the concepts of expectancy, valence, and instrumentality. According to Vroom, people's decisions about how to behave in a particular situation are influenced by three key factors:

1. **Expectancy**: This refers to an individual's belief that their efforts will lead to a certain level of performance. In other words, it's the perception that if they put in effort, they can achieve a desired outcome.
2. **Valence**: Valence represents the value or desirability that an individual places on a particular outcome or reward. It varies from person to person, and it influences motivation. If a person values an outcome highly, they are more likely to be motivated to work towards it.
3. **Instrumentality**: This factor deals with the belief that if a certain level of performance is achieved, it will result in

receiving a specific reward or outcome. It's about the perceived connection between performance and rewards.

Vroom's theory suggests that individuals will be motivated to make certain decisions or engage in specific behaviors if they believe that:

- Their efforts will lead to good performance (high expectancy).
- Good performance will result in a valued reward (high valence).
- The link between performance and reward is clear and trustworthy (high instrumentality).

This theory has been widely used in organizational psychology and management to understand and predict employee motivation and decision-making processes. It emphasizes the importance of aligning individual expectations, valuations, and perceptions of instrumentality to enhance motivation and improve decision outcomes within the workplace.

Subordinates in Decision-Making Process

Vroom's Decision-Making Theory, also known as the Vroom-Yetton-Jago Decision Model, is a leadership theory that focuses on how leaders involve subordinates in the decision-making process. Developed by Victor Vroom and Phillip Yetton in the 1970s, and later refined by Vroom and Arthur Jago, this model provides a framework for leaders to determine the level of participation and decision-making authority they should delegate to their subordinates based on the specific situation. The theory is particularly relevant in leadership contexts where collaboration and employee engagement are crucial.

The key components of Vroom's Decision-Making Theory are as follows:

Decision Styles

The theory outlines five decision styles, ranging from autocratic (leader makes the decision alone) to highly participative (subordinates are actively involved in decision-making). The five styles, in order of increasing participation, are:

1. **Autocratic I (AI):** The leader makes the decision alone, without seeking input from subordinates.
2. **Autocratic II (AII):** The leader obtains information from subordinates but makes the decision alone.
3. **Consultative I (CI):** The leader consults with subordinates individually, obtaining their input before making the decision.
4. **Consultative II (CII):** The leader consults with subordinates as a group, obtaining their collective input before making the decision.
5. **Group (G):** The leader involves the entire group in the decision-making process, seeking consensus.

Contingency Factors

The model takes into account several situational factors that help leaders determine which decision style is most appropriate for a given situation. These factors include the importance of the decision, the expertise of the leader and subordinates, time constraints, and the likelihood of subordinates accepting and implementing the decision.

Decision Trees

Vroom's theory provides decision trees or flowcharts that guide leaders through a series of questions to arrive at the most suitable decision style for a specific situation. These decision trees help leaders assess the contingency factors and make an informed choice regarding the level of participation.

Vroom's Decision-Making Theory offers a systematic approach for leaders to select the most effective decision-making style, balancing the need for employee involvement and input with the demands of the situation. It acknowledges that not all decisions require the same level of participation and that leaders should adapt their approach accordingly. By involving subordinates appropriately in decision-making, leaders can foster greater commitment, motivation, and ownership among team members, ultimately contributing to better organizational outcomes. This theory underscores the importance of tailoring leadership behavior to the unique circumstances and dynamics of each decision-making scenario.

Historical Context

The historical context of Vroom's Decision-Making Theory is rooted in the evolution of leadership and management theories during the mid-20th century. This theory emerged as a response to the changing landscape of leadership research and practice during that time:

Behavioral Theories of Leadership

In the early and mid-20th century, leadership research primarily focused on the traits and characteristics of leaders, attempting to identify inherent qualities that made someone an effective leader. However, this approach had limitations, as it didn't fully account for the complexities of leadership in various organizational settings.

Behavioral theories of leadership, which gained prominence in the 1940s and 1950s, shifted the focus from inherent traits to observable behaviors and actions of leaders. Researchers began to explore how specific leadership behaviors influenced group dynamics and performance.

Contingency and Situational Theories

Concurrently, contingency theories of leadership were developing. These theories proposed that the effectiveness of a leadership style was contingent upon the specific situation or context. They acknowledged that there was no one-size-fits-all approach to leadership.

Scholars like Fred Fiedler (contingency theory) and Robert House (path-goal theory) contributed to this shift by emphasizing that leadership effectiveness depended on factors such as the leader's style, the characteristics of subordinates, and the nature of tasks and goals.

The Need for a Decision-Making Framework

As organizations became more complex, the need for a structured framework for leadership decision-making became apparent. Leaders faced an array of situations, each requiring a different approach, and the behavioral and contingency theories offered insights but lacked a systematic decision-making model.

Development of Vroom's Decision-Making Theory

In the 1960s and 1970s, Victor Vroom, along with Phillip Yetton, began developing Vroom's Decision-Making Theory. They aimed to bridge the gap between behavioral and contingency theories by providing a normative framework for leaders to determine the appropriate level of subordinate involvement in decision-making.

Vroom's model considered the dynamic interplay between leaders, subordinates, and the situational factors that influenced decision-making. It introduced the concept of decision styles and emphasized that leadership effectiveness could be enhanced by tailoring decision-making approaches to specific contexts.

The theory also recognized that not all decisions required the same level of participation, and leaders needed a systematic way to navigate these variations.

Vroom's Decision-Making Theory emerged within the historical context of a shift from trait-based leadership theories to behavioral and situational theories. It responded to the need for a structured and adaptable decision-making framework that could guide leaders in determining the most suitable level of subordinate participation in different organizational situations. This theory has since become a valuable tool in the field of leadership, contributing to a more nuanced understanding of effective leadership practices.

Key Concepts

Vroom's Decision-Making Theory is built upon several core concepts that provide a structured framework for leaders to navigate the decision-making process effectively. Central to this theory are the five decision styles, ranging from autocratic to highly participative, which represent different levels of leader-subordinate collaboration in decision-making. These styles are AI, AII, CI, CII, and G. Additionally, the theory emphasizes the importance of considering contingency factors when choosing a decision style, including the significance of the decision, the leader's expertise, the subordinates' expertise, the likelihood of subordinate acceptance, and time constraints. To guide leaders in their decision-making, Vroom's model provides decision trees that lead to recommended decision styles based on the situational factors. Importantly, the theory recognizes that the leader-subordinate interaction and the inclusion of subordinates in the decision-making process can improve decision quality and enhance the acceptance and implementation of decisions within the organization. Flexibility in applying these concepts and choosing the appropriate decision style for each unique situation is a key aspect of Vroom's Normative

Decision Model, making it a valuable tool for effective leadership in diverse organizational contexts.

Symbolic Leadership and Decision-Making

Symbolic leadership and decision-making are two interconnected concepts in the realm of leadership. Symbolic leadership involves leaders using symbols, gestures, and actions to convey important messages, values, and visions to their teams and organizations. These symbols often represent the leader's identity and the organization's identity, culture, and goals. Symbolic leaders understand the power of communication and utilize symbolic acts to inspire, motivate, and align their followers.

In the context of decision-making, symbolic leadership can influence how decisions are perceived and accepted within an organization. Leaders can make symbolic decisions that signal a commitment to certain values or directions. For example, a CEO might make a symbolic decision to allocate a significant budget to research and development, signaling a commitment to innovation. These symbolic decisions serve as a form of communication that reinforces the leader's vision and values, shaping the organization's culture and guiding subsequent decision-making processes. In this way, symbolic leadership and decision-making are intertwined, as leaders use symbolic acts to steer the course of their organizations and influence the choices made within them.

Symbolic Leadership within the Context of Vroom's Theory

Symbolic leadership within the context of Vroom's Decision-Making Theory highlights the significance of leader-subordinate interactions and the symbolic meaning of involving subordinates in decision-making processes. This approach recognizes that decisions go beyond their immediate outcomes; they serve as powerful symbols that communicate a leader's values, priorities, and commitment to inclusivity and collaboration.

In Vroom's theory, leaders have the option to involve subordinates to varying degrees in the decision-making process, ranging from highly autocratic (AI) to highly participative (Group - G). The symbolic implications of this choice are profound:

1. **AI (Autocratic I)**: In the AI style, the leader makes decisions unilaterally, without consulting subordinates. Symbolically, this may convey a top-down, authoritative leadership approach. It can signal that the leader values efficiency and decisive action but may not prioritize collective input or employee empowerment. It can lead to a perception of a hierarchical and less inclusive organizational culture.
2. **G (Group)**: In the Group style, the leader involves the entire group in decision-making, aiming for consensus. Symbolically, this choice represents a commitment to democratic and participative leadership. It signals that the leader values diverse perspectives, teamwork, and shared ownership of decisions. This approach fosters a culture of inclusivity, where subordinates feel heard and valued.
3. **In-Between Styles (CI, CII, AII)**: The styles between AI and G (Consultative I - CI, Consultative II - CII, Autocratic II - AII) each carry their symbolic meaning. These styles involve varying levels of leader-subordinate consultation. For instance, CI implies a willingness to seek individual input, whereas CII suggests valuing collective input but still making the final call. AII indicates the leader's desire to gather information but maintain decision-making authority. These styles symbolize a balance between authority and collaboration, depending on the specific context and contingency factors.

Symbolic leadership, in the context of Vroom's theory, goes beyond the practical aspects of decision-making. It underscores how leaders can use their decision styles to shape the culture, values, and perception of their leadership within the organization. Leaders who consistently involve subordinates in decision-making symbolize a commitment to shared leadership and a more inclusive, team-oriented culture. Conversely, leaders who predominantly use autocratic styles may symbolize a more hierarchical and centralized approach to leadership.

Within Vroom's Decision-Making Theory, symbolic leadership highlights the power of decision-making styles to convey meaningful messages about leadership philosophy and organizational culture. Leaders can use these symbolic acts to signal their commitment to inclusivity, collaboration, and shared ownership, fostering a positive and engaged workforce.

Real World Examples

Real-world examples can help illustrate the symbolic aspects of leadership decisions, highlighting how these decisions convey important messages and values to the organization and its stakeholders:

1. **Steve Jobs' Product Unveilings (Apple)**: The late Steve Jobs, co-founder of Apple Inc., was known for his iconic product unveilings, such as the launch of the iPhone. These events were meticulously choreographed and symbolized innovation, elegance, and a relentless pursuit of excellence. Jobs' hands-on approach to product design and presentation symbolized his commitment to Apple's core values of simplicity and design aesthetics. These events not only showcased new products but also communicated Apple's identity as an industry leader in design and innovation.
2. **Warren Buffett's Investment Decisions (Berkshire Hathaway)**: Warren Buffett, the legendary investor and CEO of Berkshire Hathaway, is known for his long-term investment strategy and value-oriented decisions. His

symbolic leadership is evident in his commitment to conservative financial principles and ethical business practices. When he invests in a company, it often symbolizes his trust in its long-term prospects and ethical conduct, influencing investor confidence in those companies.

3. **Elon Musk's Electric Car Vision (Tesla)**: Elon Musk's decision to found Tesla and pursue the development of electric cars was a symbolic choice that communicated a commitment to sustainable energy and innovation. Tesla's electric vehicles symbolize a departure from traditional fossil fuels and represent a vision for a more sustainable future. Musk's leadership decisions, including the development of the Model S and subsequent electric vehicle models, serve as symbols of the company's mission and values.

4. **Crisis Response (Johnson & Johnson's Tylenol Crisis)**: In the 1980s, Johnson & Johnson faced a crisis when several people died after consuming cyanide-laced Tylenol capsules. The company's CEO, James Burke, made a symbolic leadership decision to recall and redesign the product, putting public safety ahead of profits. This decision symbolized the company's commitment to ethical responsibility and customer well-being, and it helped rebuild trust in the brand.

5. **Marissa Mayer's Telecommuting Policy (Yahoo)**: When Marissa Mayer became CEO of Yahoo, she made a controversial decision to end the company's telecommuting policy, requiring employees to work from the office. This decision symbolized a shift in the company's culture, emphasizing collaboration and innovation through in-person interactions. While it sparked debates about work flexibility, it also signaled a desire to revitalize Yahoo's corporate culture.

These examples demonstrate how leadership decisions go beyond their immediate impact and carry symbolic weight. They convey messages about a leader's values, priorities, and vision for the organization. Symbolic leadership decisions can influence company culture, stakeholder perceptions, and even industry norms, making them a powerful tool for leaders to shape their organizations and the broader business landscape.

Variant of Decision-Making in Leadership

Variants of decision-making in leadership refer to the different approaches and styles that leaders can employ when making choices that impact their teams and organizations. These variants encompass a range of methods, each with its characteristics and implications. Some leaders may opt for an autocratic style, making decisions unilaterally and without consulting their team members, which can be efficient but may lead to reduced buy-in from employees. Others may embrace a participative approach, involving their team in the decision-making process to gather diverse input and foster a sense of ownership, potentially resulting in more innovative solutions and higher morale. There are also variants like consensus-building, consensus-confirming, or delegative decision-making, each suited to specific situations and contingent factors. These decision-making variants underscore the adaptability and versatility that effective leaders must possess, enabling them to select the most appropriate style based on the context and the needs of their organization and team.

Examination of Variants

Vroom's Decision-Making Theory offers a comprehensive framework for leadership decision-making, encompassing several distinct methods or styles. These methods vary in terms of leader-subordinate interaction and participation. Let's examine the key decision-making methods outlined in Vroom's theory in detail:

Autocratic Decision (AI - Autocratic I)

- **Description**: In an autocratic decision, the leader makes the decision unilaterally, without seeking input or feedback from subordinates.
- **Characteristics**: This style is characterized by a top-down approach, where the leader has sole authority and control over the decision-making process.
- **Applicability**: Autocratic decisions are typically used in situations where time is limited, the leader possesses specialized expertise, or the decision is of utmost importance and requires swift action.

Consultative Decision (CI - Consultative I and CII - Consultative II):

- **Consultative I (CI)**:
  - **Description**: In this style, the leader consults individually with subordinates, seeking their input before making the final decision.
  - **Characteristics**: The leader values the perspectives of team members and uses their input to inform the decision but retains the authority to make the final choice.
  - **Applicability**: CI is suitable when the leader wants to gather input from experts or when subordinates have relevant information that can enhance the decision-making process.
- **Consultative II (CII)**:
  - **Description**: In CII, the leader consults with a group of subordinates, seeking their collective input and opinions before making the decision.
  - **Characteristics**: Similar to CI, the leader values input from the team but gathers input collectively from a group rather than individually.
  - **Applicability**: CII is beneficial when multiple perspectives and diverse expertise are required for a well-rounded decision.

Group Decision (G)

- **Description**: In a group decision, the leader involves the entire group or team in the decision-making process, with the goal of reaching a consensus or shared agreement.
- **Characteristics**: This style emphasizes inclusivity and equal participation, with all team members having a say in the decision.
- **Applicability**: Group decisions are valuable when the leader wants to foster collaboration, encourage team ownership, and generate innovative solutions. They are often used in settings where buy-in and commitment from all team members are critical.

Each of these decision-making methods in Vroom's theory serves a specific purpose and aligns with different leadership contexts. The choice of method depends on factors such as the significance of the decision, the leader's expertise, the expertise of subordinates, the likelihood of acceptance, and time constraints. Effective leaders understand when to apply each method and are flexible in their approach, adapting to the unique needs of the situation to make decisions that benefit the organization and its members.

When and How to Apply Variants

Effectively employing each variant of decision-making in Vroom's theory involves a careful assessment of the situational factors and the organization's needs. Here's a detailed look at when and how to use each variant for effective leadership:

Autocratic Decision (AI):

- **When to Employ**:
    - Use AI when time is of the essence, and a quick decision is required.

- o Employ it in situations where the leader possesses specialized knowledge or expertise.
- o Consider AI for decisions that are not highly significant to the organization's long-term goals.
- **How to Employ**:
  - o Clearly communicate the decision to the team, explaining the rationale behind it.
  - o Be open to addressing questions and concerns from team members to maintain transparency.
  - o Ensure that the decision aligns with the organization's values and goals to maintain trust.

Consultative Decision (CI and CII):

- **When to Employ**:
  - o Use CI when individual team members have valuable expertise or information to contribute.
  - o Employ CII when multiple perspectives and diverse expertise are needed.
  - o Consider these styles when you want to involve team members in the decision-making process without ceding full control.
- **How to Employ**:
  - o In CI, consult with individual team members, actively listening to their input and concerns.
  - o In CII, conduct group discussions to encourage collaboration and idea sharing.
  - o Clearly communicate that the leader will make the final decision, but the input is valued.

Group Decision (G):

- **When to Employ**:
  - o Use G when decisions require a high level of consensus and team buy-in is crucial.
  - o Employ it for significant decisions that impact the organization's direction, culture, or strategy.

- Consider G when fostering a sense of ownership and collective responsibility among team members is important.
- **How to Employ**:
  - Facilitate open and constructive group discussions, allowing all team members to voice their opinions.
  - Encourage active listening and the exploration of alternative viewpoints.
  - Aim to reach a consensus or majority agreement, and ensure that all team members are on board with the final decision.

Delegative Decision (Not Explicitly Part of Vroom's Model):

- **When to Employ**:
  - Use delegation when you trust a subordinate's expertise in a particular area.
  - Employ it when you want to empower team members and develop their decision-making skills.
  - Consider delegation for decisions that are within the scope of a team member's responsibilities.
- **How to Employ**:
  - Clearly define the decision's scope, objectives, and constraints.
  - Provide adequate resources and support to the delegatee.
  - Maintain open lines of communication and be available for guidance if needed.

Effective leadership involves the ability to assess the specific context, considering factors like the decision's significance, time constraints, the leader's expertise, and the willingness of team members to accept the decision. Leaders must also be adaptable, knowing when to use a more inclusive style (e.g., G) to build consensus and when to make swift decisions (e.g., AI) to respond to urgent matters. By mastering the art of employing each variant appropriately, leaders can make decisions that best serve the organization's goals and foster a positive and productive team culture.

Case Study

A case study applying Vroom's Decision-Making Theory involves examining a real or hypothetical scenario within an organization or leadership context. In this case study, the theory is used as a framework to analyze and understand how a leader or group of leaders make decisions in various situations. It explores the leader's choice of decision style (autocratic, consultative, group, etc.) based on factors like decision significance, expertise, time constraints, and the likelihood of subordinate acceptance. The case study may assess the outcomes of these decisions, their impact on team dynamics, and how they align with the organization's goals and values. Ultimately, it provides insights into the practical application of Vroom's theory in leadership decision-making and its implications for organizational effectiveness.

Leadership Decision-Making at XYZ Corporation

Background

XYZ Corporation is a medium-sized manufacturing company facing challenges in a highly competitive market. The CEO, Kavanjot Kaur, is responsible for making critical decisions to improve the company's performance and maintain its market position. She has adopted Vroom's Decision-Making Theory as a framework to guide her leadership decisions.

Application of Vroom's Decision-Making Theory

1. **Autocratic Decision (AI)**:
    - **Scenario**: Kavanjot Kaur faced a sudden supplier crisis that threatened production schedules. With

time constraints and her extensive knowledge of the industry, she made an autocratic decision to switch to an alternative supplier without consulting the team.

- **Rationale**: The urgency of the situation demanded swift action, and Kavanjot Kaur's expertise allowed her to make an informed decision quickly.
- **Outcome**: Production schedules were maintained, and the crisis was averted, but some team members felt excluded from the decision-making process.

2. **Consultative Decision (CI)**:
    - **Scenario**: To address quality control issues, Kavanjot Kaur consulted with individual department heads to gather their insights on process improvements.
    - **Rationale**: Kavanjot Kaur recognized the expertise of her team members and valued their input in resolving the quality issues.
    - **Outcome**: The collaborative approach led to innovative process changes that improved product quality and efficiency. Team members appreciated being involved in the decision.

3. **Group Decision (G)**:
    - **Scenario**: In a strategic planning session, Kavanjot Kaur involved her executive team and key department heads in setting the company's long-term goals and vision.
    - **Rationale**: Kavanjot Kaur wanted to foster a sense of collective ownership over the company's future and believed that a group decision would lead to better commitment.

- **Outcome**: The collaborative approach resulted in a shared vision, enhanced team cohesion, and a clear strategic direction for the organization.

Delegative Decision (Additional Style):

- **Scenario**: Kavanjot Kaur delegated the responsibility of selecting a new software platform for the company's inventory management to the IT manager, knowing that this decision fell within their area of expertise.

- **Rationale**: Recognizing the IT manager's knowledge in this domain, Kavanjot Kaur empowered them to make the decision independently.

- **Outcome**: The IT manager selected an efficient software solution that streamlined inventory management processes, leading to cost savings and operational improvements.

Analysis:

Kavanjot Kaur's application of Vroom's Decision-Making Theory showcases her ability to adapt her leadership style to various situations. In urgent scenarios where time was critical (e.g., the supplier crisis), she opted for an autocratic approach to ensure swift action. When tapping into the expertise of her team was beneficial (e.g., quality control improvements), she used consultative decision-making to gather valuable input. For strategic and vision-related decisions, she employed group decision-making to promote collaboration and buy-in. Additionally, by delegating decisions within the IT manager's expertise, she empowered her team members to take ownership of their areas of responsibility.

The analysis of how different decision-making variants were used to achieve specific goals in the case study of leadership decision-making at XYZ Corporation reveals the effectiveness of adapting decision styles to different situations and objectives:

1. **Autocratic Decision (AI):**

    - **Goal:** Ensure business continuity and avert a supplier crisis.

    - **Analysis:** Kavanjot Kaur's use of autocratic decision-making in this scenario aligns with the goal of swift resolution. Her expertise in the industry allowed her to make an informed decision promptly, minimizing potential disruptions. While some team members felt excluded, the primary goal of crisis management was achieved successfully.

2. **Consultative Decision (CI):**

    - **Goal:** Improve quality control processes.

    - **Analysis:** The consultative decision-making style was well-suited to the goal of addressing quality control issues. By involving individual department heads, Kavanjot Kaur tapped into their expertise and gathered valuable insights. This collaborative approach led to innovative process improvements and demonstrated the value of team input in achieving quality goals.

3. **Group Decision (G):**

    - **Goal:** Establish long-term strategic goals and vision.

    - **Analysis:** Kavanjot Kaur's use of group decision-making was instrumental in achieving the goal of setting a clear strategic direction. In this context, fostering a sense of collective ownership and commitment was paramount. The group decision approach resulted in a shared vision, enhanced team cohesion, and a well-defined strategic path forward.

4. **Delegative Decision (Additional Style)**:
    - **Goal**: Streamline inventory management through software selection.
    - **Analysis**: By delegating the decision to the IT manager, Kavanjot Kaur empowered them to achieve the goal of selecting the most suitable software solution. This decision aligns with the expertise and responsibility of the IT manager, leading to operational improvements and cost savings.

The case study illustrates how different decision-making variants were employed to achieve specific goals within XYZ Corporation. The adaptability of Kavanjot Kaur's leadership style, guided by Vroom's Decision-Making Theory, allowed her to align decision-making with the urgency, expertise, and objectives of each situation. Autocratic decision-making ensured rapid response in crisis scenarios, consultative decisions leveraged team expertise to enhance quality, group decisions promoted strategic alignment, and delegation empowered team members to excel in their specialized roles. This analysis highlights the effectiveness of tailoring decision styles to diverse organizational goals and needs.

Understanding the Dynamics of Decision-Making

Understanding Decision-Making Dynamics in Leadership involves examining the complex processes and factors that influence how leaders make choices within organizations. It explores the interplay between leaders, their teams, and the organizational context, considering variables such as decision-making styles, communication, group dynamics, and the impact of cognitive biases. This understanding is crucial for effective leadership, as it enables leaders to navigate decision-making challenges, leverage their team's expertise, and make informed choices that align with the organization's goals and values. It recognizes that decision-making in leadership is not just a singular event but a dynamic process shaped by a multitude of variables, requiring thoughtful consideration and adaptability.

Leadership Decision-Making Styles

Leadership decision-making styles refer to the distinct approaches and methods that leaders use when making choices that affect their organizations, teams, and stakeholders. These styles encompass a range of behaviors and attitudes that leaders adopt, reflecting their preferences, values, and communication methods when addressing challenges and opportunities. Leadership decision-making styles include autocratic, consultative, participative, and delegative approaches, each with its characteristics and implications. Effective leaders often adapt their decision-making styles to match the specific context and objectives, recognizing that different situations call for varying levels of involvement, collaboration, and delegation in the decision-making process.

Leadership decision-making styles are diverse approaches that leaders employ to make choices and guide their teams or organizations. Three prominent leadership decision-making styles are autocratic, democratic, and laissez-faire, each with distinct characteristics and implications:

Autocratic Leadership

- **Description**: In an autocratic leadership style, the leader makes decisions unilaterally, without significant input or collaboration from team members.
- **Characteristics**:

- The leader possesses authority and control over decision-making.
- Decision-making is centralized, and team members often have limited involvement.
- This style is efficient and swift, suitable for urgent decisions or when the leader possesses specialized expertise.
- **Implications**:
    - Can lead to reduced employee engagement and satisfaction, as team members may feel excluded or undervalued.
    - Effective for quick decision-making in emergencies or when a clear chain of command is necessary.
    - Not ideal for fostering creativity, innovation, or shared ownership of decisions.

Democratic Leadership:

- **Description**: Democratic leadership encourages team participation and input in the decision-making process. The leader facilitates discussions and collaborates with team members to reach a consensus or majority agreement.
- **Characteristics**:
    - Team members are actively involved in decision-making, contributing ideas and opinions.
    - The leader serves as a facilitator, guiding the discussion and ensuring all voices are heard.
    - This style promotes inclusivity, creativity, and a sense of ownership among team members.
- **Implications**:
    - Enhances employee engagement, satisfaction, and commitment to decisions.
    - Encourages diverse perspectives and can lead to innovative solutions.

- May be time-consuming and less efficient for urgent decisions or when a single, authoritative direction is required.

Laissez-Faire Leadership

- **Description**: Laissez-faire leadership is characterized by minimal direct involvement from the leader in decision-making. Instead, the leader grants significant autonomy to team members, allowing them to make choices independently.
- **Characteristics**:
  - Team members have substantial freedom to make decisions and manage their tasks.
  - The leader offers support and resources but does not actively intervene in decision-making.
  - This style fosters individual initiative, self-reliance, and innovation.
- **Implications**:
  - Suitable for highly autonomous and self-directed teams or experts who require minimal supervision.
  - Can lead to high employee satisfaction and motivation when team members value autonomy.
  - May be ineffective when team members lack experience, guidance, or a clear direction.

Effective leadership involves the ability to choose the most appropriate decision-making style based on the specific context, team dynamics, and organizational goals. While autocratic, democratic, and laissez-faire styles are distinct, skilled leaders often employ a flexible approach, combining elements of each to meet the diverse needs of their teams and situations.

Impact of Each Style on Team Dynamics

The impact of leadership decision-making styles, including autocratic, democratic, and laissez-faire, on team dynamics and outcomes is significant and varies depending on the style employed:

Autocratic Leadership

- **Impact on Team Dynamics**
    - **Hierarchy**: Autocratic leadership often reinforces a hierarchical structure, where the leader holds ultimate authority. This can lead to a formal and rigid team dynamic.
    - **Limited Participation**: Team members may feel disengaged or undervalued, as their input is seldom sought. This can result in reduced teamwork and collaboration.
    - **Compliance**: Team members are more likely to comply with decisions due to the clear authority of the leader, but this compliance may lack enthusiasm.
- **Impact on Outcomes**
    - **Efficiency**: Autocratic leaders can make quick decisions, which is advantageous in time-sensitive situations.
    - **Clarity**: Decisions are clear and unambiguous, reducing the potential for confusion.
    - **Innovation Limitations**: Autocratic leadership may stifle creativity and innovative thinking, as team members have limited opportunities to contribute ideas.

Democratic Leadership

- **Impact on Team Dynamics**

- - o **Inclusivity**: Democratic leadership fosters a sense of inclusivity, as team members are encouraged to participate in decision-making.
    - o **Collaboration**: Team members are likely to collaborate and communicate more openly, promoting a cohesive and supportive team dynamic.
    - o **Ownership**: Team members often feel a sense of ownership over decisions, which can boost motivation and engagement.
  - **Impact on Outcomes**
    - o **Innovation**: This style is conducive to innovation, as diverse perspectives are considered, and creative solutions may emerge.
    - o **High Engagement**: Team members are more likely to be engaged and committed to decisions, resulting in increased job satisfaction and productivity.
    - o **Time-Consuming**: Democratic decision-making can be time-consuming, which may not be suitable for urgent matters.

Laissez-Faire Leadership

- **Impact on Team Dynamics**
  - o **Autonomy**: Laissez-faire leadership promotes individual autonomy, empowering team members to make decisions and manage their tasks independently.
  - o **Self-Reliance**: Team members may become self-reliant and take ownership of their work.
  - o **Variability**: Team dynamics can vary widely based on team members' personalities and self-discipline.
- **Impact on Outcomes**
  - o **Innovation**: In some cases, autonomy can lead to innovative thinking and creative problem-solving.

- **Highly Motivated**: Team members who value autonomy and are self-driven may be highly motivated and productive.
- **Risk of Disorganization**: Without proper guidance or structure, there's a risk of disorganization and inconsistent outcomes.

In practice, effective leadership often involves a situational approach, where leaders adapt their decision-making style to match the specific context and the needs and characteristics of their team members. For example, autocratic leadership may be suitable in emergencies, while democratic leadership may be better for fostering creativity and inclusivity. Laissez-faire leadership may work well with highly skilled and self-directed teams but less effectively in situations requiring clear guidance or coordination. Understanding the impact of each style on team dynamics and outcomes is essential for leaders to make informed decisions that align with their goals and the needs of their teams and organizations.

Factor Influencing Leadership Styles

Factors influencing leadership decision-making are multifaceted and encompass a range of internal and external elements that leaders must consider when making choices for their teams or organizations. These factors include the leader's personal values, beliefs, and cognitive biases, as well as the organization's culture, mission, and goals. Additionally, contextual factors such as the urgency of the decision, the complexity of the issue, the available resources, and the input and expertise of team members play crucial roles. Social and environmental factors, stakeholder interests, legal and ethical considerations, and industry trends also shape the decision-making process. Effective leaders recognize the interplay of these factors and strive to make well-informed decisions that align with their vision, their organization's values, and the broader context in which they operate.

Leadership decision-making is influenced by a complex interplay of internal and external factors that shape choices made by leaders. Key internal and external factors are:

Internal Factors

1. **Personal Values and Beliefs**: A leader's individual values, ethics, and personal beliefs profoundly influence their decision-making. These internal factors guide choices that align with their principles and character.

2. **Cognitive Biases**: Cognitive biases, such as confirmation bias or anchoring, can impact decision-making by distorting information processing. Leaders must be aware of these biases to make objective decisions.

3. **Emotional Intelligence**: A leader's emotional intelligence affects their ability to navigate emotionally charged decisions and manage interpersonal dynamics within the team.

4. **Leadership Style**: A leader's preferred leadership style, whether autocratic, democratic, or laissez-faire, is an internal factor that shapes their approach to decision-making.

5. **Experience and Expertise**: Leaders draw upon their experience and expertise in their respective fields to make informed decisions. Their knowledge is a valuable internal resource.

External Factors

1. **Organizational Culture**: Organizational culture plays a pivotal role in decision-making. It can encourage innovation, risk-taking, or conservatism, directly impacting the leader's choices.

2. **Time Constraints**: The urgency of a decision can be influenced by external factors, such as market conditions or competitive pressures. Leaders must balance the need for timely decisions with thorough analysis.

3. **Ethical Considerations**: External ethical standards, industry regulations, and societal expectations influence leaders' choices. Ethical considerations guide decisions to ensure they align with accepted moral principles.

4. **Stakeholder Interests**: Leaders consider the interests and concerns of various stakeholders, including employees, shareholders, customers, and the community, when making decisions. Balancing these interests can be challenging.

5. **Resource Availability**: The availability of resources, including budget, manpower, and technology, can dictate what decisions are feasible and impactful.

6. **Legal Framework**: External legal requirements and regulations shape decision-making, and leaders must ensure compliance to avoid legal consequences.

7. **Competitive Environment**: Market dynamics, competition, and industry trends can necessitate strategic decisions, including product development, market entry, or cost-cutting measures.

8. **Global and Cultural Factors**: In a globalized world, leaders must consider cultural nuances and global trends that can affect decision outcomes and international business practices.

9. **Technology and Data**: Advancements in technology provide leaders with access to data and analytics, influencing data-driven decision-making and innovation.

Effective leaders recognize the interplay between these internal and external factors, making conscious efforts to balance their personal values, expertise, and leadership style with the demands and expectations of their organizations and stakeholders. By considering these multifaceted influences, leaders can make well-informed decisions that contribute to their organization's success and ethical integrity.

Strategies for Leaders to Navigate Factors

Navigating the complex landscape of internal and external factors that influence leadership decision-making requires a combination of strategies and approaches. Here are strategies for leaders to navigate these factors effectively:

1. **Self-awareness and Reflection**: Leaders should continually assess their personal values, biases, and emotional responses to situations. Regular self-reflection helps them make decisions that align with their core principles and minimize the impact of biases.
2. **Diversity and Inclusion**: Foster a diverse and inclusive team where different perspectives are valued. A diverse team can provide valuable insights and challenge the leader's own biases.
3. **Ethical Framework**: Develop a strong ethical framework that guides decision-making. Leaders should be unwavering in their commitment to ethical principles, even in the face of external pressures.
4. **Open Communication**: Promote open and transparent communication within the organization. Encourage team members to voice their concerns, ideas, and feedback, creating a culture of openness and trust.
5. **Decision-Making Models**: Utilize decision-making models and frameworks, such as Vroom's Decision-Making Theory or the ethical decision-making model, to structure and rationalize choices, considering various internal and external factors systematically.

6. **Continuous Learning**: Stay informed about industry trends, regulations, and best practices. Continuous learning ensures leaders are equipped to make informed decisions in evolving environments.
7. **Stakeholder Engagement**: Engage with stakeholders, including employees, customers, and shareholders, to understand their perspectives and concerns. This input can inform decision-making and build support for decisions.
8. **Time Management**: Effectively manage time and prioritize decisions. Recognize when a decision requires immediate attention and when it can benefit from more thorough analysis and consultation.
9. **Data-Driven Decision-Making**: Embrace data and analytics to support decision-making. Data-driven insights can provide objective information that complements subjective judgments.
10. **Legal and Regulatory Compliance**: Ensure a comprehensive understanding of legal requirements and industry-specific regulations. Comply with all applicable laws and regulations to avoid legal issues.
11. **Contingency Planning**: Develop contingency plans for potential decision outcomes, especially in high-risk situations. This preparation can mitigate negative consequences and guide crisis management.
12. **Adaptive Leadership**: Embrace adaptive leadership, which involves the ability to adjust leadership styles and strategies based on the specific context and needs of the organization.
13. **Consultation and Collaboration**: Involve team members, experts, and relevant stakeholders in the decision-making process when appropriate. Collaborative decision-making can lead to better outcomes and increased acceptance.
14. **Mentorship and Coaching**: Seek guidance and mentorship from experienced leaders who can provide insights and share their decision-making experiences.

By implementing these strategies, leaders can navigate the intricate landscape of internal and external factors effectively, making informed decisions that benefit their organizations, teams, and stakeholders while upholding ethical standards and personal values.

Ethical Decision-Making in Leadership

Ethical decision-making in leadership involves the deliberate process of assessing choices and actions in a way that aligns with moral principles, values, and ethical standards. Leaders must consider the ethical implications of their decisions, weighing the potential impact on stakeholders, the organization, and society as a whole. Ethical leaders prioritize honesty, integrity, fairness, and accountability, and they strive to make choices that not only benefit the organization's objectives but also uphold a strong ethical foundation, fostering trust, respect, and responsible leadership within their teams and communities.

Importance of Ethics in Leadership

The importance of ethics in leadership decision-making cannot be overstated, as it profoundly influences the character, reputation, and effectiveness of leaders and organizations. Here, why ethics is paramount in leadership decision-making:

1. **Trust and Credibility**: Ethical leaders are trusted by their teams, peers, and stakeholders because they consistently demonstrate integrity and reliability. Trust is the cornerstone of effective leadership, and ethical decision-making bolsters a leader's credibility.

2. **Long-term Sustainability**: Ethical decisions prioritize the long-term sustainability of an organization over short-term gains. Leaders who focus on ethical considerations are more

likely to make choices that benefit the organization's reputation, stakeholder relationships, and overall success in the long run.

3. **Stakeholder Confidence**: Ethical leadership instills confidence in stakeholders, including employees, customers, investors, and the broader community. When stakeholders believe that leaders act ethically, they are more likely to support the organization's goals and initiatives.

4. **Compliance and Legal Risks**: Ethical decision-making ensures that leaders and organizations adhere to legal and regulatory requirements. Failing to make ethical decisions can result in legal repercussions, damaging the organization's reputation and financial stability.

5. **Employee Morale and Engagement**: Ethical leaders create a positive work environment characterized by fairness and respect. Employees who perceive their leaders as ethical are more likely to be motivated, engaged, and committed to their work.

6. **Attracting and Retaining Talent**: Ethical organizations are more appealing to top talent. Leaders who prioritize ethics can attract and retain skilled employees who share similar values and are committed to the organization's mission.

7. **Conflict Resolution**: Ethical leaders are skilled at handling conflicts and ethical dilemmas within their teams. They establish a culture where open dialogue and ethical discussions are encouraged, leading to more effective conflict resolution.

8. **Organizational Culture**: Ethical leadership sets the tone for the organization's culture. When leaders model ethical behavior, it permeates throughout the organization, influencing the conduct of all team members.

9. **Mitigating Reputational Risk**: Ethical decision-making is a proactive approach to mitigating reputational risks. Leaders who prioritize ethics are less likely to be involved in scandals or controversies that damage the organization's image.

10. **Social Responsibility**: Ethical leaders understand their role in society and emphasize corporate social responsibility. They make decisions that contribute positively to the community, environment, and social causes.

11. **Global Impact**: In today's interconnected world, ethical decisions have a global impact. Leaders who consider ethical implications in their choices can contribute to global sustainability and societal well-being.

12. **Personal Growth**: Ethical leadership fosters personal growth and development. Leaders who grapple with ethical dilemmas and make principled choices often become more self-aware, empathetic, and compassionate.

Ethics in leadership decision-making is not merely a moral obligation but a strategic imperative. It underpins trust, sustainability, and stakeholder confidence, while also fostering a positive work environment, attracting top talent, and mitigating risks. Ethical leadership is essential for the long-term success and reputation of both leaders and their organizations.

Framework and Guidelines for Making Ethical Decisions as Leader

Leaders can make ethical decisions by following established frameworks and guidelines that provide a structured approach to ethical decision-making. Some widely recognized frameworks and guidelines for leaders to consider:

The Four-Way Test

- **Description**: The Four-Way Test is a framework developed by Rotary International, emphasizing ethical considerations in decision-making.
- **Key Questions**
  - Is it the truth?
  - Is it fair to all concerned?
  - Will it build goodwill and better friendships?
  - Will it be beneficial to all concerned?
- **Application**: Leaders can apply these questions to assess the ethical dimensions of their decisions, ensuring honesty, fairness, and positive outcomes for all stakeholders.

The Ethical Decision-Making Framework

- **Description**: This framework, developed by the Josephson Institute of Ethics, provides a step-by-step approach to ethical decision-making.
- **Steps**:
  - Recognize the ethical issue.
  - Get the facts.
  - Identify the stakeholders.
  - Consider options and consequences.
  - Make a decision.
  - Monitor and modify the decision, if necessary.
- **Application**: Leaders can systematically follow these steps to identify, evaluate, and address ethical dilemmas, promoting ethical behavior within their organizations.

The Utilitarian Approach

- **Description**: The utilitarian approach focuses on maximizing overall happiness or utility by choosing actions that produce the greatest good for the greatest number of people.

- **Application**: Leaders can use this approach to assess the consequences of their decisions and choose actions that result in the most positive outcomes for stakeholders.

The Deontological Approach

- **Description**: Deontological ethics is rule-based, emphasizing the importance of following moral principles, regardless of the consequences.
- **Application**: Leaders can adhere to ethical principles such as honesty, integrity, and respect as a fundamental guide for their decision-making, even when facing challenging situations.

The Virtue Ethics Approach

- **Description**: Virtue ethics emphasizes the development of moral character and virtues. Leaders strive to make decisions that reflect virtuous qualities such as honesty, courage, and empathy.
- **Application**: Leaders can cultivate virtuous traits and consider how their decisions align with these virtues, promoting ethical leadership.

The Ethical Decision-Making Matrix

- **Description**: This matrix assesses decisions by considering their legality, ethics, values, and policies.
- **Application**: Leaders can use this matrix to evaluate decisions from multiple perspectives, ensuring that choices align with both legal requirements and ethical principles.

The Golden Rule

- **Description**: The Golden Rule advises treating others as you would like to be treated, fostering empathy and fairness.
- **Application**: Leaders can apply this rule to consider the impact of their decisions on others, striving for fairness and respect in their actions.

Ethical Codes and Organizational Policies

Many organizations have established ethical codes and policies that provide guidance to leaders and employees. Leaders should familiarize themselves with and adhere to these guidelines.

Consultation and Peer Feedback

Leaders can seek advice and feedback from trusted peers, mentors, or ethics committees within their organizations to gain different perspectives on ethical dilemmas.

Ethics Training and Education

Continuous ethics training and education programs can help leaders develop their ethical decision-making skills and raise awareness of potential ethical challenges.

Effective ethical decision-making requires a combination of these frameworks and guidelines, adaptability to various situations, and a commitment to upholding ethical principles. Leaders who consistently prioritize ethical considerations contribute to a culture of integrity and trust within their organizations.

Power and influence Theory

Power and Influence Theory is a leadership concept that delves into how leaders exert control and sway over individuals or groups within an organization to achieve specific goals. It recognizes that leaders possess various sources of power, such as positional authority, control over resources, or expertise, which can be employed to influence others. Furthermore, this theory highlights the significance of interpersonal skills, communication, and persuasion in leadership, emphasizing that leaders can extend their influence beyond formal hierarchies by building trust and rapport. Ultimately, Power and Influence Theory underscores the complex dynamics between leaders and their followers, exploring how leaders utilize their power and interpersonal abilities to motivate, guide, and align individuals toward collective objectives.

Power and Influence Theory is a comprehensive leadership concept that delves into how leaders employ their authority and personal influence to motivate and guide others effectively. This theory recognizes that leaders have access to various sources of power, both formal and informal, which they can utilize to influence individuals and groups within their organizations. Here is a detailed exploration of Power and Influence Theory:

Sources of Power

1. **Legitimate Power**: This is the authority derived from a leader's formal position within the organization. It includes the power to make decisions, allocate resources, and set directions.
2. **Reward Power**: Leaders wield this power by controlling rewards or incentives, such as promotions, bonuses, or recognition, which can motivate team members to achieve specific goals.
3. **Coercive Power**: The ability to apply penalties or punishments, such as reprimands or demotions, falls under coercive power. Leaders can use this power to enforce compliance but must do so judiciously.
4. **Expert Power**: Expertise, knowledge, or specialized skills grant leaders expert power. Team members often respect and trust leaders who demonstrate competence in their field.
5. **Referent Power**: Referent power stems from the personal characteristics of a leader that make them likable, admirable, or relatable to team members. Leaders who possess referent power are often seen as role models.

Influence Tactics

1. **Rational Persuasion**: Leaders use logic, facts, and reasoning to persuade others. They present a compelling case for their ideas or decisions.
2. **Inspirational Appeal**: Leaders inspire and motivate through a compelling vision or values, appealing to the emotions and values of team members.
3. **Consultation**: Leaders seek input and involvement from team members when making decisions, fostering a sense of ownership and commitment.
4. **Collaboration**: Leaders work closely with team members to achieve shared goals, emphasizing teamwork and cooperation.
5. **Ingratiation**: Leaders build rapport and goodwill through compliments, favors, or building personal relationships.
6. **Personal Appeals**: Leaders make requests based on personal relationships, appealing to loyalty or friendship.
7. **Pressure and Coercion**: In rare cases, leaders may resort to pressure or coercion tactics, although these should be used sparingly and ethically.

Leadership Styles

Power and Influence Theory acknowledges that leadership styles play a significant role in how leaders use their authority and influence. Autocratic leaders may rely more on legitimate power, while transformational leaders emphasize inspirational appeal and collaboration.

Organizational Context

The organizational culture, structure, and norms also influence how leaders exercise power and influence. Some organizations may encourage a more participative approach, while others may have a more hierarchical culture.

Ethical Considerations

Ethical leadership is a crucial aspect of Power and Influence Theory. Leaders are encouraged to use their power and influence ethically, aligning their actions with moral principles and values.

Power and Influence Theory provides leaders with a framework to understand the sources of power at their disposal and the various tactics they can employ to motivate and guide their teams. Effective leaders recognize the importance of using their authority and influence judiciously, considering the organizational context and ethical considerations to create a positive and productive work environment.

Key Concept and Principles

The Power and Influence Theory encompasses several key concepts and principles that guide how leaders use authority and influence to motivate others. These concepts and principles provide a comprehensive understanding of the theory:

1. **Sources of Power**: The theory acknowledges that leaders have access to various sources of power, including legitimate, reward, coercive, expert, and referent power. Leaders must understand these sources and their implications for effective leadership.

2. **Influence Tactics**: Leaders can employ different influence tactics to motivate and guide individuals or groups. These tactics include rational persuasion, inspirational appeal, consultation, collaboration, ingratiation, personal appeals, and, in rare cases, pressure or coercion.

3. **Leadership Styles**: The theory recognizes that leadership styles play a critical role in how leaders use their power and influence. Leadership styles, such as autocratic, democratic,

transformational, or servant leadership, shape the leader's approach to motivation and decision-making.

4. **Organizational Context**: The organizational culture, structure, and norms influence how leaders exercise power and influence. Leaders need to adapt their approach to align with the prevailing organizational context, whether it encourages participative decision-making or follows a more hierarchical structure.

5. **Ethical Considerations**: Ethical leadership is a fundamental principle of this theory. Leaders are encouraged to use their power and influence ethically, ensuring that their actions align with moral principles, values, and the best interests of stakeholders.

6. **Balancing Formal and Informal Power**: Effective leaders understand the balance between formal power (position-based) and informal power (personal influence) and use both judiciously to motivate and guide their teams.

7. **Adaptability**: The theory emphasizes that leaders should be adaptable in their use of power and influence, tailoring their approach to different situations and individuals within their teams.

8. **Building Trust and Relationships**: Building trust and strong relationships with team members is central to effective leadership. Leaders who can establish rapport and credibility are more likely to wield influence successfully.

9. **Motivation and Alignment**: Leaders use their power and influence to motivate team members and align their efforts toward achieving organizational goals and objectives.

10. **Communication**: Effective communication is a key principle. Leaders must communicate their vision, expectations, and decisions clearly and persuasively to gain buy-in from their teams.

11. **Continuous Self-Reflection and Learning**: Leaders should engage in continuous self-reflection, learning, and self-improvement to enhance their ability to use power and influence effectively.

12. **Accountability**: Leaders are accountable for the consequences of their decisions and actions. Ethical leaders take responsibility for their choices and their impact on individuals and the organization.

The key concepts and principles of Power and Influence Theory provide leaders with a framework to navigate the complex dynamics of leadership, emphasizing ethical conduct, adaptability, and the ability to inspire and guide others effectively.

Source of Power

Sources of power in leadership encompass the various channels through which leaders exert influence over individuals or groups within an organization. These sources enable leaders to guide, motivate, and make decisions that steer the direction of their teams and achieve organizational goals. The primary sources of power in leadership include legitimate power, derived from formal positions and roles; reward power, which involves the ability to offer incentives or benefits; coercive power, allowing leaders to enforce compliance through penalties; expert power, based on specialized knowledge or skills; and referent power, rooted in personal characteristics and the trust or admiration that followers have for the leader. Effective leaders recognize and judiciously utilize these sources to inspire and guide their teams toward success, while also upholding ethical principles and maintaining trust within their organizations.

Leaders have access to various sources of power that enable them to influence and guide individuals or groups within their organizations. These sources of power can be broadly categorized into formal and personal sources, each with its own characteristics and mechanisms of influence. Here's a detailed explanation of the different sources of power available to leaders:

Legitimate Power

- **Description**: Legitimate power is derived from a leader's formal position or role within an organization. It signifies that leaders have the rightful authority to make decisions, allocate resources, and provide directives based on their designated position.
- **Mechanism**: Legitimate power is enforced through organizational hierarchies and structures. Team members are expected to comply with the leader's directives due to their position's authority.
- **Effective Use**: Effective use of legitimate power involves aligning decisions and directives with organizational goals, being fair and consistent in decision-making, and building trust with team members.

Reward Power

- **Description**: Reward power is the ability of a leader to offer incentives, rewards, or benefits to individuals or teams. These rewards can include promotions, salary increases, bonuses, recognition, or other desirable outcomes.
- **Mechanism**: Leaders wielding reward power motivate team members by promising positive consequences in exchange for desired behaviors or outcomes.
- **Effective Use**: Effective use of reward power requires the fair and consistent distribution of rewards, linking rewards to performance or achievement, and aligning incentives with organizational goals.

Coercive Power

- **Description**: Coercive power allows leaders to use penalties, punishments, or the threat of negative consequences to influence behavior. It is the opposite of reward power.
- **Mechanism**: Leaders employing coercive power can enforce compliance by creating a fear of repercussions for non-compliance.
- **Effective Use**: Coercive power should be used sparingly and ethically, emphasizing clear expectations and consequences for specific behaviors or actions.

Expert Power

- **Description**: Expert power is based on a leader's specialized knowledge, skills, or expertise in a particular field. Team members respect and trust leaders who demonstrate competence and proficiency.
- **Mechanism**: Leaders with expert power influence others by providing guidance, advice, and solutions rooted in their expertise. Team members voluntarily seek their insights and rely on their knowledge.
- **Effective Use**: Effective use of expert power involves maintaining up-to-date knowledge and skills, sharing expertise generously, and serving as a valuable resource to the team.

Referent Power

- **Description**: Referent power stems from the personal characteristics and qualities of a leader that make them likable, admirable, or relatable to others. It is often associated with charisma and can inspire loyalty and followership.
- **Mechanism**: Leaders with referent power influence through their ability to build rapport, trust, and personal connections

with team members. Followers are motivated by their admiration for the leader.
- **Effective Use**: Building referent power requires authenticity, empathy, and the ability to connect on a personal level with team members. It's essential for leaders to maintain their integrity and ethical conduct to preserve this source of power.

Information Power

- **Description**: Information power is derived from a leader's control over critical information or access to valuable data and insights that others need.
- **Mechanism**: Leaders with information power can influence decisions and actions by selectively sharing or withholding information, making them indispensable sources of knowledge.
- **Effective Use**: Leaders should use information power transparently and ethically, ensuring that information sharing serves the organization's best interests and fosters trust.

Connection Power

- **Description**: Connection power is based on a leader's relationships, networks, and affiliations. It involves having access to influential individuals or groups.
- **Mechanism**: Leaders with connection power can leverage their relationships to garner support, resources, or alliances that benefit the organization.
- **Effective Use**: Effective use of connection power involves maintaining strong relationships, networking strategically, and using connections to advance the organization's goals while avoiding favoritism or nepotism.

Charismatic Power

- **Description**: Charismatic power is linked to a leader's ability to inspire and captivate others through their personal charm, vision, and dynamic presence.
- **Mechanism**: Leaders with charismatic power motivate and influence through their ability to articulate a compelling vision, instill enthusiasm, and rally others around a common purpose.
- **Effective Use**: Charismatic power is most effective when leaders are genuine, authentic, and inclusive, and when their charisma aligns with the organization's values and objectives.

Leaders often draw on a combination of these power sources to influence and motivate their teams effectively. The choice of power source and the way it is wielded should align with the leader's leadership style, the organizational culture, and the ethical standards of the organization to achieve positive outcomes.

Leveraging Source of Power Effectively

Leveraging sources of power effectively is crucial for leaders to motivate and guide their teams toward success. Here are strategies for leaders to harness these power sources effectively:

Legitimate Power

- **Use Fairness and Consistency**: Leaders should ensure that decisions and directives are fair, consistent, and aligned with organizational policies and procedures. This builds trust and respect for their authority.
- **Communicate Vision**: Leaders can leverage legitimate power by clearly communicating the organization's vision and how their decisions contribute to achieving it. This helps team members understand the purpose behind directives.

- **Promote Transparency**: Being transparent about decision-making processes and involving team members when appropriate can enhance the perception of fairness in the exercise of legitimate power.

Reward Power

- **Link Rewards to Performance**: Leaders should tie rewards to individual or team performance, making the connection between effort and recognition clear. This encourages motivation and a focus on achieving goals.

- **Recognize and Appreciate**: Regularly acknowledge and appreciate the contributions of team members. Recognition and praise can be powerful motivators.

- **Ensure Equity**: Ensure that rewards are distributed equitably and based on merit, avoiding favoritism or bias. Fairness is key to maintaining the effectiveness of reward power.

Coercive Power

- **Use Sparingly**: Coercive power should be used as a last resort and only for serious violations or non-compliance. Leaders should avoid creating a culture of fear.

- **Communicate Expectations**: Clearly communicate expectations, rules, and consequences to team members. Prevention is often more effective than punitive actions.

- **Provide Constructive Feedback**: When using coercive power, leaders should offer constructive feedback and opportunities for improvement rather than punitive measures alone.

Expert Power

- **Continuously Develop Expertise**: Leaders should invest in ongoing learning and development to maintain and expand their expertise. Staying updated enhances their credibility and influence.

- **Share Knowledge**: Actively share knowledge, insights, and best practices with team members. Encourage learning and empower others to develop their expertise.

- **Mentor and Coach**: Mentor and coach team members to develop their own expertise. This not only benefits individuals but also strengthens the team's collective knowledge.

Referent Power

- **Build Trust**: Building trust through authenticity, reliability, and integrity is essential for referent power. Leaders should keep promises and maintain their ethical standards.

- **Lead by Example**: Demonstrate the behaviors and values you want others to emulate. Leading by example is a powerful way to influence through referent power.

- **Listen Actively**: Show genuine interest in the concerns and perspectives of team members. Actively listening fosters trust and rapport.

Information Power

- **Share Information Strategically**: Leaders should use information power judiciously, sharing critical information when it benefits the organization or team objectives.

- **Maintain Confidentiality**: Respect confidentiality and privacy when handling sensitive information. Trust is easily eroded if information is mishandled.

- **Promote Knowledge Sharing**: Encourage a culture of knowledge sharing within the organization to empower team members and strengthen the collective knowledge base.

Connection Power

- **Networking**: Continuously develop and maintain a strong professional network. Cultivate relationships that can provide valuable resources and support.
- **Strategic Alliances**: Leverage connections to form strategic alliances that benefit the organization. Collaborate with external partners or stakeholders when it aligns with goals.
- **Fair Use**: Ensure that the use of connection power is fair and ethical, avoiding nepotism or the appearance of favoritism.

Charismatic Power

- **Authenticity**: Be authentic in your charisma. Authentic leaders are more likely to inspire trust and loyalty from their teams.
- **Communicate a Compelling Vision**: Articulate a compelling vision that resonates with team members' values and aspirations. A shared sense of purpose can galvanize teams.
- **Inclusiveness**: Foster an inclusive environment where everyone feels valued and included in pursuing the vision. Charismatic leaders should unite, not divide.

Effective leaders recognize that power is a tool to achieve common goals and should be used responsibly and ethically. The choice of which source of power to leverage and how to wield it should align with the leader's values, the organization's culture, and the specific context to create a positive and productive work environment.

Influence Tactics in Leadership

Influence tactics in leadership refer to the deliberate strategies and approaches leaders employ to persuade, motivate, or guide individuals or groups within their organizations. These tactics involve the use of communication, persuasion, and interpersonal skills to shape opinions, behaviors, and decisions in a way that advances the leader's objectives and aligns with the organization's goals. Influence tactics encompass a range of techniques, including rational persuasion, inspirational appeal, consultation, collaboration, ingratiation, personal appeals, and, in rare cases, pressure or coercion. Effective leaders skillfully select and apply these tactics based on the specific situation, the preferences of their team members, and ethical considerations to achieve desired outcomes and foster positive relationships.

Various Influence Tactics

Leaders employ a variety of influence tactics to motivate and guide individuals or groups toward achieving organizational goals. These tactics leverage communication, interpersonal skills, and strategic approaches. Here are detailed explanations of various influence tactics, including persuasion, coalition building, and negotiation:

Persuasion

- **Description**: Persuasion is the art of convincing others to adopt a particular viewpoint, take specific actions, or support a particular decision or idea. It relies on logical reasoning, emotional appeal, and effective communication.
- **Mechanism**: Leaders use persuasive tactics such as presenting compelling arguments, providing evidence, and appealing to emotions to influence the beliefs and behaviors of their team members.

- **Effective Use**: Effective persuasion involves understanding the needs and motivations of the audience, tailoring the message to their concerns, and providing clear and compelling reasons for them to act in a desired way.

Coalition Building

- **Description**: Coalition building involves forming alliances or partnerships with individuals or groups to support a shared goal or objective. Leaders seek to gain the support of influential stakeholders.
- **Mechanism**: Leaders identify key stakeholders, including allies and potential supporters, and collaborate with them to create a collective force that can influence decisions or outcomes.
- **Effective Use**: Successful coalition building requires effective networking, active engagement with stakeholders, and a clear articulation of the common interests and goals that bind the coalition members together.

Negotiation

- **Description**: Negotiation is a process in which leaders engage in discussions and bargaining with others to reach mutually acceptable agreements or solutions to conflicts or challenges.
- **Mechanism**: Leaders employ negotiation skills such as active listening, compromise, problem-solving, and finding win-win solutions to resolve conflicts, make deals, or achieve compromises that benefit all parties involved.
- **Effective Use**: Effective negotiation involves thorough preparation, a focus on shared interests, flexibility, and a commitment to preserving relationships even in the face of differences.

Inspirational Appeal

- **Description**: Inspirational appeal involves motivating others by inspiring enthusiasm, commitment, and a sense of purpose. Leaders communicate a compelling vision and set high expectations.
- **Mechanism**: Leaders use inspirational language, storytelling, and vision casting to ignite passion and a sense of shared destiny among team members.
- **Effective Use**: Effective inspirational appeal taps into the values and aspirations of individuals, connecting their personal goals to the larger organizational mission and inspiring them to go above and beyond.

Consultation

- **Description**: Consultation involves seeking input, advice, or feedback from team members before making decisions or taking actions. It fosters a sense of ownership and involvement.
- **Mechanism**: Leaders actively engage team members in discussions, valuing their perspectives and incorporating their ideas into decision-making processes.
- **Effective Use**: Consultation builds trust, improves the quality of decisions, and enhances team members' commitment to the outcomes when they feel their voices are heard and valued.

Collaboration

- **Description**: Collaboration emphasizes working together with team members to achieve shared goals. Leaders promote teamwork, cooperation, and synergy among team members.

- **Mechanism**: Leaders encourage open communication, shared responsibilities, and collective problem-solving to harness the diverse strengths and expertise of the team.
- **Effective Use**: Collaboration fosters a sense of unity and a collective sense of purpose. It enhances creativity, innovation, and the ability to tackle complex challenges effectively.

Ingratiation

- **Description**: Ingratiation involves building goodwill and rapport with others by using compliments, favors, or other forms of flattery. Leaders seek to create positive feelings and perceptions.
- **Mechanism**: Leaders use friendly gestures, praise, or acts of kindness to make others feel valued and appreciated.
- **Effective Use**: Ingratiation can enhance relationships and cooperation, but it should be sincere and not manipulative or excessive.

Personal Appeals

- **Description**: Personal appeals rely on personal relationships and connections to influence others. Leaders appeal to loyalty, friendship, or a sense of obligation.
- **Mechanism**: Leaders leverage their interpersonal connections and history with individuals to request support or cooperation.
- **Effective Use**: Personal appeals are most effective when there is a genuine and strong relationship between the leader and the individual. Overuse can diminish their impact.

Pressure and Coercion

- **Description**: While rarely used, pressure and coercion tactics involve applying negative consequences or threats to compel compliance. Leaders use this approach when other influence tactics have failed or when addressing critical issues.

- **Mechanism**: Leaders may issue ultimatums, impose sanctions, or threaten disciplinary actions to achieve a specific outcome.
- **Effective Use**: Leaders should exercise caution and ethical judgment when resorting to pressure or coercion, as it can damage relationships and trust if not used judiciously.

Effective leaders choose influence tactics based on the specific context, the nature of the relationships involved, and the ethical considerations of the situation. Adapting these tactics to various circumstances allows leaders to navigate complex challenges and inspire their teams to achieve organizational success.

Leaders who effectively use Influence Tactics

Several historical and contemporary leaders have effectively used influence tactics to motivate and guide their teams or achieve significant goals. Here are examples of such leaders and their successful use of influence tactics:

Nelson Mandela

- **Influence Tactic**: Inspirational Appeal
- **Example**: Nelson Mandela, the former President of South Africa and anti-apartheid revolutionary, used inspirational appeal to unite a divided nation. His unwavering commitment to reconciliation, forgiveness, and a vision of a multiracial, democratic South Africa inspired millions and played a pivotal role in ending apartheid and establishing a democratic government.

Rupinder Kaur

- **Influence Tactic:** Nonviolent Resistance
- **Example:** Rupinder Kaur, a prominent leader in the modern civil rights movement, employed nonviolent resistance as an influence tactic. Through peaceful protests, civil disobedience, and advocacy for equal rights, she played a pivotal role in addressing social injustices and promoting civil rights in her community.

Martin Luther King Jr.

- **Influence Tactic**: Inspirational Appeal, Nonviolent Resistance
- **Example**: Martin Luther King Jr., a prominent leader in the American civil rights movement, combined inspirational appeal with nonviolent resistance. His "I Have a Dream" speech and commitment to nonviolence galvanized the civil rights movement, leading to significant legislative changes and progress toward racial equality in the United States.

Steve Jobs

- **Influence Tactic**: Persuasion, Vision Casting
- **Example**: Steve Jobs, co-founder of Apple Inc., was known for his persuasive communication and visionary leadership. His ability to present innovative products and articulate a compelling vision for the future of technology influenced consumers and shaped the success of Apple.

Elon Musk

- **Influence Tactic**: Vision Casting, Risk-Taking
- **Example**: Elon Musk, the CEO of SpaceX and Tesla, Inc., uses vision casting to inspire support for ambitious goals, such as colonizing Mars and transitioning to sustainable energy. His willingness to take significant risks and pursue

audacious projects has earned him admiration and followership.

Winston Churchill

- **Influence Tactic**: Inspirational Appeal
- **Example**: Winston Churchill, the Prime Minister of the United Kingdom during World War II, used inspirational appeal to rally the British people during the darkest days of the war. His powerful speeches and unwavering resolve inspired the nation to stand firm against Nazi aggression.

Angela Merkel

- **Influence Tactic**: Negotiation, Coalition Building
- **Example**: Angela Merkel, the former Chancellor of Germany, was skilled in coalition building and negotiation. She effectively managed a coalition government and played a crucial role in navigating the European Union through economic crises and political challenges.

Abraham Lincoln

- **Influence Tactic**: Persuasion, Consultation
- **Example**: Abraham Lincoln, the 16th President of the United States, used persuasion and consultation with his cabinet members to lead the nation during the American Civil War. His ability to listen to diverse viewpoints while staying committed to the preservation of the Union was instrumental in the country's reunification.

These leaders showcase the diverse use of influence tactics, from inspirational appeal and persuasion to nonviolent resistance and negotiation, to achieve significant societal and organizational goals. Their effective leadership demonstrates the power of influence in shaping history and guiding people toward positive change.

Harnessing Power and Influence for Effective Leadership

Harnessing Power and Influence for Effective Leadership involves the strategic and ethical use of various sources of power and influence to achieve leadership objectives and guide a team or organization toward success. It means recognizing the strengths and limitations of different power sources, such as legitimate, reward, expert, or referent power, and employing them judiciously to motivate and inspire others. Effective leaders understand that influence tactics, including persuasion, coalition building, and negotiation, are valuable tools for shaping behavior and decisions within the team or organization. The key is to align these efforts with the organization's mission and values while promoting fairness, transparency, and ethical conduct. By harnessing power and influence effectively, leaders can create a positive and productive work environment, foster collaboration, and achieve their goals while maintaining trust and credibility among their followers.

Balancing Power and Responsibility

Balancing power and responsibility in leadership involves the careful management of the authority and influence a leader holds in conjunction with the accountability and ethical obligations associated with that power. It means recognizing that leadership positions come with the capacity to make decisions and guide others, but this authority must be wielded with a sense of duty and integrity. Effective leaders understand the need to use their power for the benefit of the organization and its members, making decisions that align with the organization's goals and values. Moreover, they acknowledge that they are responsible for the consequences of their actions and decisions. Striking a balance between power and responsibility ensures that leadership is conducted ethically, fairly, and in a way that builds trust, fosters collaboration, and promotes the well-being of all stakeholders.

Examination of Ethical Implication of Power

The ethical implications of power in leadership and the corresponding responsibility are of paramount importance in the realm of effective and responsible leadership. Examining these implications involves considering the ethical challenges and obligations associated with wielding power and authority. Here's a detailed examination:

Ethical Challenges

1. **Abuse of Power**: One of the most significant ethical challenges is the potential for leaders to abuse their power by using it for personal gain, self-interest, or to exploit others. This can manifest as favoritism, nepotism, or corruption.
2. **Lack of Accountability**: Leaders with unchecked power may become less accountable for their actions, which can lead to unethical behavior, such as ignoring the needs and concerns of stakeholders or making decisions that benefit a select few.
3. **Moral Dilemmas**: Ethical dilemmas often arise when leaders must make difficult decisions that balance competing interests, such as the well-being of employees versus the financial stability of the organization.
4. **Transparency and Trust**: Maintaining transparency and trust can be challenging when leaders hold significant power. Lack of transparency can erode trust among team members and stakeholders.

Ethical Obligation

1. **Servant Leadership**: Ethical leaders embrace a servant leadership approach, where their primary duty is to serve the best interests of their team and organization rather than seeking personal gain or power accumulation.
2. **Fairness and Justice**: Leaders have an ethical obligation to treat all individuals fairly and justly, regardless of their status

or position within the organization. Fairness ensures that decisions are based on merit and not personal bias.
3. **Accountability**: Ethical leaders accept accountability for their decisions and actions. They acknowledge the consequences of their choices and take responsibility for rectifying any negative outcomes.
4. **Transparency**: Ethical leaders prioritize transparency by openly communicating their intentions, decisions, and any potential conflicts of interest. Transparency fosters trust and allows stakeholders to make informed judgments.

Responsible Leadership

1. **Shared Decision-Making**: Responsible leaders involve team members and stakeholders in the decision-making process when appropriate, valuing their input and ensuring that decisions reflect a collective effort.
2. **Ethical Framework**: Leaders should establish and adhere to a clear ethical framework or code of conduct that guides their behavior and decision-making, providing a moral compass for themselves and their team.
3. **Conflict Resolution**: Ethical leaders are skilled in resolving conflicts and dilemmas in a manner that upholds ethical principles, seeking win-win solutions and avoiding harm to individuals or the organization.
4. **Continuous Learning**: Responsible leaders engage in continuous self-reflection and learning to improve their ethical decision-making skills, recognizing that ethical leadership is an ongoing journey.

Balancing power and responsibility in leadership requires a conscious effort to align one's actions with ethical principles, promote fairness, and prioritize the well-being of all stakeholders. Ethical leadership not only strengthens the organization's reputation and relationships but also contributes to its long-term success and sustainability. Leaders who navigate the ethical implications of power effectively create an environment where trust, collaboration, and ethical behavior flourish.

Strategies for Maintaining a Balance

Maintaining a balance between power and ethical leadership is a critical aspect of effective and responsible leadership. Here are detailed strategies for achieving this balance:

Self-Awareness

- **Reflect on Your Values**: Ethical leaders begin by understanding their own values, beliefs, and principles. Reflect on what ethics mean to you and how they align with your leadership role.

- **Assess Your Use of Power**: Regularly evaluate how you use your power and authority. Be aware of any tendencies to abuse power or act in self-interest.

Create and Communicate Ethical Standards

- **Develop a Code of Ethics**: Establish a clear code of ethics or conduct for yourself and your organization. This document should outline the ethical principles and standards that guide decision-making and behavior.

- **Communicate Expectations**: Ensure that your team and stakeholders are aware of these ethical standards. Openly communicate your commitment to ethical leadership and hold discussions about its importance.

Seek Input and Feedback

- **Encourage Open Dialogue**: Create an environment where team members feel comfortable providing feedback and raising ethical concerns. Encourage open and honest communication.

- **Involve Others in Decision-Making**: When appropriate, involve team members and relevant stakeholders in the decision-making process. This not only promotes ethical decision-making but also fosters a sense of ownership and accountability.

Lead by Example

- **Model Ethical Behavior**: Demonstrate ethical behavior in your actions and decisions. Be a role model for your team by consistently adhering to ethical principles.
- **Acknowledge Mistakes**: When you make an ethical mistake or misjudgment, acknowledge it, and take responsibility. Use such instances as opportunities for growth and learning.

Fairness and Equity

- **Promote Fairness**: Ensure that your decisions and actions are fair and just. Avoid favoritism, discrimination, or any form of bias.
- **Implement Transparent Processes**: Transparency in decision-making processes, particularly regarding promotions, rewards, and resource allocation, is essential for maintaining fairness.

Ethical Decision-Making Framework

- **Utilize Ethical Decision-Making Models**: Familiarize yourself with ethical decision-making frameworks like the "four-way test" (Is it the truth? Is it fair to all concerned? Will it build goodwill and better friendships? Will it be beneficial to all concerned?) to guide your choices in complex situations.
- **Consider Consequences**: Think about the potential consequences of your decisions on various stakeholders, including employees, customers, and the wider community.

Continuous Learning and Improvement

- **Stay Informed**: Keep up-to-date with ethical issues, trends, and best practices in leadership. This knowledge will help you make informed and ethical choices.
- **Seek Guidance**: Consult with mentors, ethical experts, or colleagues when facing challenging ethical dilemmas. Discussing complex issues with others can provide valuable perspectives.

Whistleblower Protection and Reporting Mechanisms

- **Establish Reporting Channels**: Create a safe and anonymous reporting mechanism for ethical concerns or wrongdoing within your organization. Ensure that whistleblowers are protected from retaliation.
- **Take Action**: When ethical violations are reported, take prompt and appropriate action to address the issues and rectify any harm caused.

Accountability and Consequences

- **Set Clear Expectations**: Ensure that your team understands the consequences of unethical behavior. Clearly communicate the penalties or disciplinary actions that may result from violations.
- **Hold Yourself Accountable**: As a leader, be prepared to hold yourself accountable for your actions and decisions, even when they are difficult or uncomfortable.

Regular Ethics Training

- **Training and Development**: Provide ethics training and development opportunities for yourself and your team.

These programs can enhance ethical awareness and decision-making skills.

Balancing power and ethical leadership is an ongoing process that requires commitment, self-reflection, and a dedication to upholding ethical principles. By consistently practicing these strategies, leaders can maintain a harmonious equilibrium between their authority and their ethical responsibilities, fostering trust, respect, and a positive organizational culture.

Leadership as a Force for Positive Influence

Leadership, at its core, serves as a force for positive influence by guiding individuals or groups toward achieving shared goals, fostering personal and professional growth, and shaping a positive organizational culture. Effective leaders inspire, motivate, and empower their teams, promoting collaboration, innovation, and excellence. They lead by example, embodying ethical principles and values, and create an environment where trust, open communication, and inclusivity thrive. Through their actions and decisions, leaders not only drive organizational success but also contribute to the well-being and development of their team members and the broader community. In essence, leadership as a force for positive influence is a catalyst for positive change, growth, and the realization of collective aspirations.

How Leaders use their Influence

Leaders have the capacity to wield their influence for positive change within organizations and society at large. Here's a detailed exploration of how leaders can effectively use their influence to drive positive transformations:

1. **Vision and Purpose**: Leaders should communicate a clear and inspiring vision that defines the organization's purpose

and long-term goals. A compelling vision motivates individuals by providing direction and purpose.
2. **Values and Ethics**: Ethical leadership sets the tone for the organization. Leaders must uphold and promote ethical behavior, creating a culture of integrity and trust.
3. **Inclusive Decision-Making**: Encourage diverse perspectives by involving team members in decision-making processes. Inclusive decision-making fosters innovation and ensures a broader range of voices are heard.
4. **Mentorship and Development**: Provide mentorship and opportunities for professional development to empower individuals to reach their full potential. This contributes to a skilled and motivated workforce.
5. **Effective Communication**: Maintain open lines of communication, sharing information, and explaining decisions clearly. Transparency builds trust and minimizes uncertainty.
6. **Leading by Example**: Leaders should exemplify the behavior and values they expect from others. Leading by example establishes credibility and reinforces cultural norms.
7. **Problem-Solving and Innovation**: Promote an environment that encourages creativity and innovation. Leaders can inspire innovative thinking by recognizing and rewarding it.
8. **Social Responsibility**: Embrace CSR initiatives that demonstrate a commitment to social and environmental causes. This can include sustainable practices, community involvement, and ethical sourcing.
9. **Change Management**: Leaders must guide organizations through periods of change and uncertainty with empathy, a clear vision, and strategies to mitigate resistance.
10. **Crisis Leadership**: During crises, leaders play a pivotal role in maintaining stability, providing support, and making difficult decisions while prioritizing the welfare of stakeholders.

11. **Advocacy and Impact**: Leaders can use their influence to advocate for societal or industry changes aligned with ethical and sustainable principles.
12. **Collaboration and Partnerships**: Leaders can collaborate with other organizations, governmental bodies, and NGOs to address complex societal issues collectively.
13. **Talent Attraction and Retention**: Leaders who prioritize employee well-being, inclusivity, and a positive work culture attract and retain top talent, driving organizational success.
14. **Continuous Learning**: Leaders should continuously update their knowledge and skills, adapting to changing environments and staying informed about emerging trends and challenges.
15. **Feedback and Adaptation**: Encourage feedback from team members and stakeholders to evaluate leadership effectiveness and make necessary adjustments.
16. **Long-Term Sustainability**: Leaders need to balance immediate goals with the organization's long-term sustainability, ensuring decisions benefit both current and future generations.

By leveraging their influence through these strategies, leaders can create positive change within organizations and society, leaving a lasting legacy of ethical, responsible, and impactful leadership.

Case Studies

Nelson Mandela - Transformational Leadership for Social Justice

Background: Nelson Mandela, a prominent figure in the struggle against apartheid in South Africa, became the country's first black president and a global symbol of resistance to oppression and racial segregation.

Influence for the Greater Good:

- **Visionary Leadership**: Mandela's vision was to create a racially integrated and democratic South Africa where all citizens had equal rights. He communicated this vision through his speeches and actions, inspiring millions both within and outside the country.

- **Forgiveness and Reconciliation**: After spending 27 years in prison, Mandela chose a path of forgiveness and reconciliation instead of revenge. This approach helped prevent a potentially catastrophic race war.

- **Inclusive Leadership**: Mandela championed inclusivity and inclusiveness by including representatives from all racial and ethnic groups in the negotiations for a new South African constitution.

- **Global Influence**: He used his global influence to mobilize international support for the anti-apartheid movement, leading to sanctions against the apartheid regime and ultimately contributing to its downfall.

Impact: Nelson Mandela's leadership paved the way for the dismantling of apartheid and the establishment of a democratic South Africa. His legacy continues to inspire leaders worldwide in their pursuit of justice, equality, and reconciliation.

Malala Yousafzai - Advocating for Girls' Education:

Background: Malala Yousafzai, an Asian activist for girls' education, survived a terrorist assassination attempt and has since become a global advocate for education and women's rights.

Influence for the Greater Good

- **Courage and Resilience**: Malala's unyielding courage and resilience in the face of adversity inspired a global movement in support of girls' education.

- **Educational Advocacy**: Through her speeches, media appearances, and her book "I Am Malala," she effectively raised awareness about the importance of education for girls, especially in regions with limited access.

- **Nobel Peace Prize**: In 2014, Malala became the youngest-ever recipient of the Nobel Peace Prize, further amplifying her message and advocating for the right to education for all children.

- **Founding the Malala Fund**: Malala co-founded the Malala Fund, an organization that champions girls' education worldwide and empowers young girls to speak out and advocate for their rights.

Impact: Malala's advocacy has influenced governments, organizations, and individuals globally to invest in education for girls. Her work has resulted in tangible policy changes and increased access to education for millions of girls who would otherwise have been denied this fundamental right.

These case studies highlight the extraordinary power of leadership when it is harnessed for the greater good. Both Mandela and Malala used their influence to drive positive social change, demonstrating that committed individuals can make a significant impact on society and inspire others to do the same.

Developing Influence Skills

Developing influence skills refers to the process of acquiring and honing the abilities and strategies necessary to effectively persuade, motivate, and guide individuals or groups toward specific goals or decisions. It involves learning how to communicate persuasively, build trust, and adapt one's approach to different situations and audiences. Influence skills encompass a range of techniques, including active listening, negotiation, persuasion, and conflict resolution. Developing these skills is crucial for leaders and professionals as it enables them to navigate complex interpersonal dynamics, foster collaboration, and achieve desired outcomes while maintaining positive relationships and ethical conduct. Ultimately, honing influence skills equips individuals with the tools to positively impact their personal and professional environments.

Developing and enhancing influence skills is vital for leaders to effectively lead teams and drive positive change. Some practical guidance for leaders on how to develop and enhance their influence skills:

1. **Self-Awareness**: Begin by understanding your own strengths, weaknesses, values, and beliefs. Self-awareness forms the foundation for effective influence.
2. **Active Listening**: Practice active listening by giving your full attention to others, asking clarifying questions, and showing empathy. This helps build trust and rapport.
3. **Empathy**: Develop empathy to understand others' perspectives, emotions, and needs. This enables you to tailor your messages and actions more effectively.
4. **Effective Communication**: Hone your communication skills, including verbal and non-verbal cues. Use clear, concise language and adapt your communication style to your audience.
5. **Building Trust**: Consistently demonstrate honesty, integrity, and reliability to build trust with your team and stakeholders. Trust is a cornerstone of influence.
6. **Negotiation Skills**: Invest in learning negotiation techniques to find mutually beneficial solutions in conflicts or negotiations. Seek win-win outcomes.

7. **Conflict Resolution**: Develop conflict resolution skills to address disagreements constructively, maintaining positive relationships.
8. **Inclusive Decision-Making**: Involve team members in decision-making whenever possible. This fosters ownership, commitment, and collective buy-in.
9. **Emotional Intelligence**: Enhance your emotional intelligence by recognizing and managing your own emotions and understanding and responding to others' emotions effectively.
10. **Adaptability**: Be flexible in your approach, adjusting your influence tactics to suit different situations and personalities.
11. **Storytelling**: Master the art of storytelling. Stories can be powerful tools for conveying messages, making them memorable, and inspiring action.
12. **Networking**: Build a strong professional network to connect with others in your industry or field. Networking can provide valuable insights and opportunities for collaboration.
13. **Mentorship and Coaching**: Seek mentorship or coaching from experienced leaders or mentors who can provide guidance and feedback on your influence skills.
14. **Feedback Loop**: Encourage honest feedback from peers, team members, and superiors about your influence style. Use this feedback for self-improvement.
15. **Continuous Learning**: Stay updated on leadership trends, psychology, and interpersonal dynamics. Continuously seek opportunities for personal and professional growth.
16. **Practice Patience**: Recognize that developing influence skills takes time. Be patient with yourself and persistent in your efforts to improve.
17. **Role Models**: Identify leaders you admire for their influence skills and study their methods. Incorporate their effective strategies into your own toolkit.
18. **Apply and Reflect**: Put what you learn into practice and reflect on your experiences. Learn from both successful and challenging situations.

19. **Ethical Considerations**: Always prioritize ethical considerations in your influence efforts. Ensure that your actions align with your values and principles.
20. **Feedback and Measurement**: Assess the impact of your influence by seeking feedback and measuring the outcomes of your efforts. Adjust your approach as needed.

Developing influence skills is an ongoing journey that requires self-awareness, practice, and a commitment to ethical leadership. By continuously refining these skills, leaders can foster positive relationships, inspire their teams, and achieve their organizational objectives effectively.

*****

CHAPTER NINE
Leader-member Exchange and Contextual Approaches

Leader-Member Exchange (LMX)

Leader-member exchange, often referred to as LMX theory, is a leadership theory that focuses on the unique relationships that leaders develop with their followers or team members. LMX theory suggests that leaders do not have the same relationship with every member of their team; instead, they form distinct, personalized relationships with individual team members. These relationships can be categorized into two groups: in-group and out-group. In-group members have closer, more collaborative relationships with their leader, while out-group members have more distant, transactional relationships. LMX theory emphasizes that leaders' interactions with team members can significantly impact their performance, job satisfaction, and overall effectiveness within the organization.

Contextual Approaches

Contextual approaches in leadership theory emphasize the importance of considering the broader organizational and environmental factors that influence leadership practices and outcomes. These approaches recognize that effective leadership is not solely determined by the characteristics or behaviors of individual leaders but is also shaped by the context in which leadership occurs. Contextual factors may include the organization's culture, structure, industry, external environment, and the specific challenges and opportunities facing the organization. Contextual approaches highlight the need for leaders to adapt their leadership style and strategies to fit the unique demands of their organizational context, ultimately aiming for a better alignment between leadership practices and the specific needs and challenges of the situation.

These two concepts, leader-member exchange and contextual approaches, provide valuable insights into the complexities of leadership and underscore the importance of considering both interpersonal relationships and the broader organizational context when studying and practicing effective leadership.

Understanding the Significance

Understanding the significance of Leader-Member Exchange and contextual approaches in leadership is essential for several reasons:

1. **Enhanced Leadership Effectiveness:** Recognizing the importance of LMX allows leaders to cultivate positive, high-quality relationships with their team members. Leaders who establish strong LMX relationships tend to have more engaged, motivated, and productive teams. Understanding the significance of these relationships helps leaders harness their potential to lead effectively.

2. **Individualized Leadership:** LMX emphasizes that leaders should tailor their leadership style to each team member's needs and capabilities. This personalized approach enhances job satisfaction, commitment, and loyalty among employees. It enables leaders to address diverse talents and preferences within their teams, resulting in a more harmonious and productive work environment.

3. **Reduced Turnover and Conflict:** Strong LMX relationships can reduce turnover rates as employees are more likely to stay in their roles when they have positive interactions with their leaders. Moreover, conflicts within

the team are less likely to escalate when leaders foster trust and open communication through LMX relationships.

4. **Adaptation to Organizational Context:** Contextual approaches underscore that leadership is not a one-size-fits-all concept. Leaders must be adaptable and responsive to the unique challenges and circumstances of their organizations. Recognizing the significance of context enables leaders to make informed decisions, implement strategies that align with their organizational culture, and navigate changes effectively.

5. **Strategic Decision-Making:** Leaders who understand the contextual influences on leadership can make more informed and strategic decisions. They can assess their organization's internal and external factors, anticipate potential challenges, and proactively adjust their leadership approach to achieve desired outcomes.

6. **Sustainability and Resilience:** In a rapidly changing business environment, contextual awareness helps leaders build sustainable and resilient organizations. By understanding the broader context, leaders can anticipate market shifts, regulatory changes, and industry trends, positioning their organizations for long-term success.

7. **Employee Engagement and Well-being:** Both LMX and contextual approaches contribute to creating a positive work environment. Engaged employees are more likely to be satisfied with their jobs and experience better well-being. Leaders who emphasize these aspects can foster a culture of support, inclusion, and growth.

Grasping the significance of Leader-Member Exchange and contextual approaches in leadership empowers leaders to develop stronger relationships with team members, adapt to various organizational contexts, make informed decisions, and promote overall team and organizational success. These concepts are not only beneficial for leadership theory but also practical for leaders striving to excel in their roles and navigate the complexities of modern workplaces.

Dynamics and Individualized Interactions

Emphasizing the importance of dynamic and individualized leadership interactions is essential in modern leadership theory and practice for several key reasons:

1. **Tailored Approach:** Every member of a team is unique, with varying strengths, weaknesses, motivations, and communication styles. A dynamic and individualized leadership approach recognizes these differences and allows leaders to adapt their interactions to meet each team member's specific needs and preferences. This tailored approach enhances the likelihood of positive outcomes and fosters a sense of trust and respect.

2. **Motivation and Engagement:** Recognizing individual differences and adapting leadership interactions accordingly can significantly impact motivation and engagement. When leaders take the time to understand what drives each team member, they can provide the right level of support, challenge, and recognition to keep individuals motivated and committed to their work.

3. **Enhanced Performance:** Individualized leadership interactions can lead to improved performance. By aligning tasks and responsibilities with team members' skills and interests, leaders can maximize their team's potential. This, in turn, contributes to higher productivity and quality of work.

4. **Conflict Resolution:** When conflicts arise within a team, a dynamic and individualized leadership approach can be instrumental in resolving them. Leaders who understand the

unique perspectives and concerns of team members can address conflicts more effectively and find solutions that work for everyone involved.

5. **Trust and Relationship Building:** Trust is the foundation of strong leadership, and individualized interactions play a crucial role in building and maintaining trust. When leaders demonstrate a genuine interest in each team member's well-being and growth, trust is established, creating a positive atmosphere and stronger working relationships.

6. **Employee Development:** A dynamic and individualized leadership approach supports employee development and growth. Leaders who invest in understanding their team members' career aspirations and provide opportunities for skill development create a culture of continuous learning and development.

7. **Adaptation to Change:** In a constantly evolving business environment, dynamic leadership is vital. Leaders must be able to adapt to new challenges, technologies, and market conditions. By understanding individual team members' strengths and weaknesses, leaders can assemble agile teams that can pivot and respond effectively to change.

8. **Employee Satisfaction and Retention:** Employees are more likely to be satisfied with their work when they feel valued and supported by their leaders. A dynamic and individualized leadership approach contributes to higher job satisfaction, which, in turn, can lead to increased employee retention and reduced turnover.

9. **Innovation and Creativity:** Recognizing and harnessing the diverse perspectives and ideas of team members can foster innovation and creativity within an organization. A dynamic leadership approach encourages employees to share their unique insights and contribute to problem-solving and innovation.

Emphasizing the importance of dynamic and individualized leadership interactions is crucial for creating a positive work environment, maximizing team and individual potential, and achieving organizational success. Leaders who take the time to understand and adapt to the unique characteristics and needs of their team members are better equipped to lead effectively in today's diverse and dynamic workplaces.

Leadership-Member Exchange Theory

Leader-member exchange Theory (LMX) posits that leaders don't have the same relationship with all their followers but form distinct, personalized relationships with each team member. This theory highlights the differentiation of leadership styles based on the quality of these leader-follower exchanges. Leaders develop two groups: the in-group, characterized by close, high-quality relationships with more trust and collaboration, and the out-group, marked by more distant, transactional relationships. In-group members receive more attention, opportunities, and support from their leaders, while out-group members have more limited interactions. LMX theory underscores that these differentiated leadership styles can significantly impact followers' job satisfaction, performance, and overall organizational outcomes, emphasizing the importance of cultivating positive leader-member exchanges to enhance leadership effectiveness.

Leader-Member Exchange (LMX) Theory, also known as the Vertical Dyad Linkage Theory, provides a comprehensive framework for understanding leadership within organizations, emphasizing the differentiated relationships that leaders establish with various members of their team.

Differentiated Relationships

LMX theory posits that leaders form distinct and differentiated relationships with their team members. Instead of applying a one-size-fits-all leadership style, leaders engage with each follower on an individual basis. These relationships can be categorized into two main groups:

- **In-Group:** Leaders establish high-quality, trust-based relationships with certain team members. In-group members receive more attention, resources, and opportunities for personal and professional growth. They typically enjoy greater influence over decision-making processes and are seen as key contributors to the team's success.

- **Out-Group:** On the other hand, leaders maintain more transactional and formal relationships with out-group members. These relationships tend to be less personal and involve minimal interaction and support. Out-group members may have limited access to important information and fewer opportunities for advancement.

Formation of LMX Relationships

LMX relationships are not solely determined by the leader; they are a product of mutual interactions and perceptions. These relationships typically develop through a series of stages:

- **Stranger Phase:** At the outset, when a leader and a team member first interact, they are essentially strangers. Interactions are formal and task-focused.

- **Acquaintance Phase:** As interactions continue, the leader and follower become more familiar with each other. Trust begins to develop, and roles become more defined.

- **Mature Partnership Phase:** In this phase, a strong bond is formed between the leader and follower. There is a high level of mutual trust, open communication, and shared influence. The leader relies on the follower, and vice versa.

Outcomes of LMX Relationships

The quality of LMX relationships has several important consequences:

- **Job Satisfaction:** In-group members typically experience higher job satisfaction due to the support and opportunities they receive from their leaders.

- **Performance:** In-group members often perform better because they are more motivated and engaged. They also have access to the resources and guidance needed for success.

- **Organizational Commitment:** Those in the in-group tend to be more committed to the organization, as they perceive themselves as integral to the team's success.

- **Turnover:** Out-group members are more likely to experience job dissatisfaction and turnover intentions because of their limited access to resources and opportunities.

Managerial Implications

LMX theory underscores the importance of leadership development and training. Leaders are encouraged to be aware of their biases and to strive for fairness and equity in their interactions with team members. By recognizing the potential for differentiated relationships, leaders can work to provide all team members with opportunities for growth and development, which can, in turn, lead to improved team and organizational performance.

Leader-Member Exchange Theory provides valuable insights into the nature of leadership by highlighting the differentiated relationships that leaders form with their team members. It underscores the importance of fairness, equity, and individualized leadership to maximize team effectiveness and organizational success.

Historical Context

To understand the historical context of the Leader-Member Exchange (LMX) Theory, it's essential to consider the evolution of leadership theories and the social and organizational changes that influenced its development. LMX Theory emerged in the late 1970s and early 1980s, and its historical context can be explained in the following ways:

1. Early Leadership Theories:

- **Trait Theory (Early 20th Century):** The study of leadership initially focused on identifying traits that distinguish effective leaders from others. Trait theory attempted to identify inherent qualities that leaders possessed. This perspective was dominant during the early 20th century.

- **Behavioral Theories (1940s-1950s):** In the mid-20th century, leadership research shifted towards examining leader behaviors. This period produced theories like the Ohio State Studies and the University of Michigan Studies, which explored the behavioral dimensions of leadership.

- **Contingency Theories (1960s):** Contingency theories, such as Fiedler's Contingency Model and Hersey and Blanchard's Situational Leadership Model, emerged in the 1960s. These theories emphasized that effective leadership depended on the match between the leader's style and the situation.

2. Social and Organizational Changes:

- **Changing Workplace Dynamics:** During the 1970s and 1980s, organizations experienced significant changes. There was a shift towards more flexible and decentralized structures, with a greater emphasis on teamwork and collaboration.

- **Rise of Employee-Centered Approaches:** Around the same time, there was a growing recognition of the importance of considering the individual needs and perspectives of employees. This led to a shift away from purely task-oriented leadership approaches towards more people-centric leadership.

3. Emergence of LMX Theory:

- **Graen and Uhl-Bien:** The development of LMX Theory can be attributed to researchers such as George Graen and Jane Uhl-Bien. Their work during the late 1970s and early 1980s marked a departure from traditional leadership theories. They proposed that leadership was not a one-size-fits-all concept but rather a set of differentiated relationships between leaders and followers.

- **Focus on Leader-Follower Relationships:** LMX Theory emerged as a response to the changing dynamics in organizations and the need to explore the quality of relationships between leaders and followers. This theory challenged the idea that leaders should treat all team members the same way and highlighted the significance of personalized interactions.

- **Empirical Research:** LMX Theory was supported by empirical research demonstrating that differentiated relationships between leaders and followers had a significant impact on outcomes such as job satisfaction, performance, and organizational commitment.

Leader-Member Exchange (LMX) Theory emerged as a response to the evolving nature of leadership and organizational dynamics during the late 20th century. It challenged traditional leadership theories by emphasizing the importance of differentiated relationships between leaders and followers and recognizing that leadership is not a uniform practice but one influenced by the unique interactions and exchanges that occur within an organization. This historical context helped LMX Theory gain relevance and significance in the field of leadership studies.

Key Concepts

Leader-Member Exchange (LMX) Theory is based on several key concepts that help explain its fundamental principles and applications. These key concepts include:

1. **Differentiated Relationships:** LMX Theory posits that leaders develop unique and differentiated relationships with each of their followers. These relationships are categorized into in-group and out-group members, reflecting the varying levels of trust, support, and collaboration.

2. **In-Group and Out-Group:** In-group members are those who enjoy higher-quality relationships with their leader. They have more access to resources, receive greater attention, and are involved in decision-making. Out-group members have more distant and transactional relationships, with fewer opportunities and less trust.

3. **Vertical Dyad Linkage:** LMX relationships are often referred to as vertical dyads, signifying the one-on-one exchanges between leaders and followers. The quality of these dyadic relationships is a central focus of LMX Theory.

4. **Stages of LMX Development:** LMX relationships evolve over time through stages, including the stranger phase, acquaintance phase, and mature partnership phase. These

stages describe the progression from initial interactions to the development of trust and mutual influence.

5. **Mutual Influence:** In mature LMX relationships, both leaders and followers have a significant influence on each other. This mutual influence is based on trust and reciprocity, allowing for more effective collaboration.

6. **Role Differentiation:** LMX Theory acknowledges that leaders and followers have different roles within the organization. In-group members often take on more challenging tasks and responsibilities, contributing to the team's success.

7. **Task and Socioemotional Leadership:** LMX relationships involve both task-related and socioemotional dimensions. Task-related leadership pertains to job-related functions, while socioemotional leadership addresses the personal and emotional needs of followers.

8. **Outcomes:** LMX relationships have various outcomes for both leaders and followers. In-group members tend to experience higher job satisfaction, better performance, greater organizational commitment, and more opportunities for career advancement. Out-group members may experience dissatisfaction and lower levels of engagement.

9. **Leadership Fairness:** LMX Theory underscores the importance of fairness in leadership interactions. Leaders are encouraged to treat all team members fairly and avoid showing favoritism to in-group members.

10. **Leadership Development:** Recognizing the significance of LMX relationships, leadership development programs may focus on improving leaders' abilities to form and maintain high-quality relationships with all team members.

11. **Organizational Implications:** LMX Theory has implications for team dynamics, communication, and

decision-making within organizations. Leaders need to consider the effects of LMX relationships on overall team performance and take steps to mitigate the potential negative consequences of unequal relationships.

These key concepts of LMX Theory help illuminate the complexities of leadership in organizations by emphasizing the importance of personalized, differentiated relationships between leaders and followers and their impact on various individual and organizational outcomes.

In-Group and Out-Group Dynamics

In-group and out-group dynamics refer to the social categorization and differentiation of individuals within a group or organization based on their perceived closeness to a leader or authority figure. In this context, the "in-group" consists of individuals who enjoy a closer, more positive, and mutually beneficial relationship with the leader or authority figure. Members of the in-group often receive preferential treatment, trust, access to resources, and opportunities for advancement. Conversely, the "out-group" comprises individuals who have a more distant, transactional, or less favorable relationship with the leader. They typically receive fewer benefits, less attention, and may have limited access to important information and opportunities. In-group and out-group dynamics can significantly influence the behavior, attitudes, and performance of individuals within a group, impacting overall group cohesion and productivity. Understanding these dynamics is essential for leaders and organizations to promote fairness, equity, and positive team interactions while mitigating the potential negative effects of favoritism or exclusion.

In Leader-Member Exchange (LMX) Theory, the concept of in-group and out-group relationships refers to the different categories of relationships that leaders develop with their team members based on the quality and nature of the interactions. These relationships play a central role in understanding leadership dynamics within a group or organization. Here's a detailed explanation of the in-group and out-group relationships in LMX theory:

In-Group Relationships

1. **Definition:** In-group relationships are characterized by high-quality, close, and mutually beneficial interactions between a leader and certain team members. In-group members are typically perceived as trusted allies or key contributors to the team's success.

2. **Features:**

    - **High Trust:** In-group members enjoy a high level of trust from the leader and reciprocate this trust, leading to more open and honest communication.

    - **Shared Influence:** Both the leader and in-group members have a significant influence on each other's decisions and actions. This shared influence can lead to more collaborative decision-making.

    - **Resource Access:** In-group members often have greater access to resources, information, and opportunities within the organization.

    - **Support and Recognition:** Leaders provide more support, guidance, and recognition to in-group members, which can enhance their job satisfaction and motivation.

3. **Impact:**

- **Higher Performance:** In-group members tend to perform at a higher level because of the increased support and resources available to them.

- **Greater Job Satisfaction:** The trust and recognition they receive often lead to higher job satisfaction and commitment to the organization.

- **Career Advancement:** In-group members are more likely to be considered for career advancement opportunities due to their perceived value to the team and organization.

Out-Group Relationships

1. **Definition:** Out-group relationships are characterized by more distant, transactional, and less favorable interactions between a leader and certain team members. Out-group members typically have limited access to the leader and fewer opportunities for support.

2. **Features:**

    - **Limited Trust:** Out-group members may not have the same level of trust as in-group members, which can result in more guarded communication.

    - **Transactional Interaction:** Interactions with out-group members are often task-focused and formal, centered on work-related matters.

    - **Resource Constraints:** Out-group members may have limited access to important resources, information, or decision-making processes.

- **Minimal Support:** Leaders provide less support, guidance, and recognition to out-group members, which can lead to lower job satisfaction.

3. **Impact:**

    - **Lower Performance:** Out-group members may not perform as well as their in-group counterparts due to the limited support and resources they receive.

    - **Job Dissatisfaction:** The perception of being treated as less valuable can result in lower job satisfaction and lower commitment to the organization.

    - **Potential Turnover:** Out-group members may be more likely to consider leaving the organization in search of better opportunities or a more supportive work environment.

It is important to note that LMX Theory does not advocate for these differentiated relationships but rather seeks to explain their existence and impact. Effective leaders should aim to treat all team members fairly, providing support, guidance, and opportunities for growth to everyone. Recognizing the existence of in-group and out-group dynamics can help leaders mitigate potential negative consequences and foster a more inclusive and productive team environment.

Treatment of Team Members

Leaders often differentiate their treatment of team members in various ways, consciously or unconsciously. While this differentiation can be based on a range of factors, such as performance, experience, or personal rapport, it's essential for leaders to be mindful of its potential consequences. Here are some real-world examples illustrating how leaders may differentiate their treatment of team members:

1. **Performance-Based Recognition:** Leaders often reward high-performing team members with bonuses, promotions, or public recognition, while lower-performing members may receive less recognition or rewards. For instance, a sales manager might offer a top salesperson a performance bonus or an Employee of the Month award, while less successful salespeople receive standard recognition.

2. **Project Assignments:** Leaders may assign challenging or high-profile projects to team members they have greater confidence in or perceive as having more expertise. This can lead to some team members gaining more exposure and career development opportunities than others.

3. **Feedback and Development:** Leaders may provide more frequent and personalized feedback, coaching, and development opportunities to team members they consider high-potential or in their in-group. This can result in some individuals receiving more guidance and mentorship than others.

4. **Access to Resources:** Leaders may grant certain team members access to valuable resources, such as training programs, technology, or budget allocations, while others have limited access. For example, an IT manager may allocate additional resources to a project led by a trusted team member, while other projects receive fewer resources.

5. **Communication and Information Sharing:** Leaders may communicate more openly and share critical information with their in-group, leaving out their out-group members. This selective sharing of information can lead to disparities in knowledge and decision-making power.

6. **Flexibility and Accommodations:** Leaders may grant flexibility in work arrangements or accommodate specific requests from certain team members, such as flexible hours

or remote work options, while denying similar requests from others.

7. **Mentorship and Networking:** Leaders may form mentorship relationships with select team members, providing them with career guidance and networking opportunities that others do not receive. This can significantly impact career advancement prospects.

8. **Recognition and Praise:** Leaders may publicly praise and acknowledge the contributions of in-group members during team meetings or organizational events, while out-group members receive less public recognition.

9. **Performance Appraisals:** In performance evaluations, leaders may assign higher ratings and more positive feedback to their in-group members, potentially leading to disparities in salary increases or promotions.

10. **Decision-Making Involvement:** Leaders may involve their in-group members in critical decision-making processes or seek their input more frequently, sidelining out-group members' perspectives.

While some differentiation in leadership is natural due to varying performance levels and relationships, it is essential for leaders to be aware of potential biases and strive for fairness and equity in their treatment of all team members. Addressing such biases and promoting inclusivity can lead to a more motivated, engaged, and productive team.

Impact of Differentiated Treatment

The impact of differentiated treatment within a team or organization refers to the consequences, both positive and negative, that result from leaders treating individual team members differently based on various factors such as performance, perceived potential, or personal relationships. Positive impacts can include higher motivation and performance among favored team members, enhanced job satisfaction, and a sense of recognition. However, differentiated treatment can also lead to negative consequences, such as decreased morale, reduced trust and collaboration, increased conflict, and potential turnover among those who perceive themselves as receiving unfair treatment. Additionally, it can create division within the team, as members of the out-group may feel excluded or undervalued. Overall, understanding the impact of differentiated treatment is crucial for leaders, as it can significantly influence team dynamics, performance, and organizational culture, and leaders must aim for fairness, equity, and inclusivity to foster a productive and harmonious work environment.

Implication of Differentiated Team

The implications of differentiated treatment, such as in-group and out-group dynamics, on team dynamics, performance, and satisfaction are multifaceted and can have both positive and negative effects.

1. Team Dynamics:

- **Positive Impact:**
    - **Increased Cohesion:** Differentiated treatment can lead to stronger bonds within the in-group members, fostering trust and collaboration among them.
    - **Enhanced Communication:** In-group members may communicate more openly and effectively due to their closer relationship with the leader, leading to improved information sharing.
- **Negative Impact:**
    - **Conflict and Division:** Differentiated treatment can create division and conflict within the team, as out-

group members may feel excluded or resentful, potentially leading to decreased cooperation.

- **Cliques and Subgroups:** In-group dynamics may result in the formation of cliques or subgroups, further fragmenting the team and impeding overall unity.

2. Performance:

- **Positive Impact:**
    - **Higher Motivation:** In-group members, motivated by the recognition and support they receive, may exhibit higher levels of motivation and commitment to achieving team goals.
    - **Greater Responsibility:** In-group members often shoulder more responsibility, leading to a more efficient allocation of tasks and potentially improved performance.
- **Negative Impact:**
    - **Reduced Engagement:** Out-group members may become disengaged or demotivated, leading to suboptimal performance and lower productivity.
    - **Inequity Perceptions:** Perceptions of inequity in treatment can lead to feelings of injustice, which can harm morale and performance among both in-group and out-group members.

3. Satisfaction:

- **Positive Impact:**
    - **In-Group Satisfaction:** In-group members typically report higher job satisfaction due to the support and opportunities they receive, which can lead to increased overall team morale.

- **Recognition and Rewards:** Differentiated treatment can result in more tailored recognition and rewards for high-performing in-group members, further enhancing their job satisfaction.

- **Negative Impact:**
  - **Out-Group Dissatisfaction:** Out-group members often report lower job satisfaction due to their perceived exclusion or limited access to resources and opportunities.
  - **Overall Team Discontent:** When differential treatment is evident and causes tension, it can lead to overall team dissatisfaction, affecting team cohesion and performance.

4. Organizational Implications:

- **Retention and Turnover:** Differentiated treatment can influence employee turnover rates. In-group members may be more likely to stay with the organization, while out-group members might seek employment elsewhere due to dissatisfaction.

- **Leadership Reputation:** Leaders who engage in favoritism may damage their reputation and credibility within the organization, affecting their ability to lead effectively.

- **Equity and Fairness:** Organizations need to ensure that leaders are trained to treat all team members fairly and equitably, addressing issues related to differentiation in leadership interactions.

Differentiated treatment within teams, whether through in-group and out-group dynamics or other forms of preferential treatment, can have significant implications for team dynamics, performance, and satisfaction. While it may lead to increased motivation and cohesion among in-group members, it can also foster conflict, resentment, and reduced performance among out-group members. Effective leadership involves balancing the need for personalized interactions with a commitment to fairness and equity to create a harmonious and high-performing team environment.

Strategies for Leaders to Cultivate Positive LMX Relationship

Cultivating positive Leader-Member Exchange relationships is essential for effective leadership and team success. Here are strategies leaders can employ to develop and maintain positive LMX relationships with their team members:

1. **Get to Know Your Team Members:** Take the time to understand each team member's strengths, weaknesses, preferences, and career goals. Building a personal connection and showing genuine interest in their well-being can go a long way in establishing trust.
2. **Communication:** Foster open, honest, and transparent communication with all team members. Ensure that everyone has the opportunity to voice their opinions, concerns, and ideas. Actively listen and provide feedback to demonstrate that their contributions are valued.
3. **Fairness and Equity:** Treat all team members with fairness and equity. Avoid favoritism and strive to provide equal access to opportunities, resources, and recognition. Ensure that decisions are made objectively and based on merit.
4. **Set Clear Expectations:** Clearly define roles, responsibilities, and expectations for each team member. Ensure that they understand their individual contributions to the team's goals and how their work aligns with the organization's objectives.
5. **Tailored Leadership Styles:** Recognize that different team members may require different leadership approaches. Adapt your leadership style to meet their needs, whether they

thrive on autonomy, benefit from coaching, or prefer regular check-ins.

6. **Provide Support and Development:** Offer support, guidance, and opportunities for skill development to all team members. Invest in their professional growth by providing training, mentorship, and challenging assignments.
7. **Regular Feedback:** Provide ongoing feedback on performance, both positive and constructive. Regular performance appraisals and one-on-one discussions can help team members understand their progress and areas for improvement.
8. **Inclusivity:** Create an inclusive work environment where all team members feel valued and included. Encourage diversity of thought and promote collaboration among team members of different backgrounds and perspectives.
9. **Recognize and Reward:** Acknowledge and reward team members for their contributions and achievements. Publicly recognize their efforts, whether through verbal praise, awards, or other forms of acknowledgment.
10. **Manage Conflicts Proactively:** Address conflicts or disagreements within the team promptly and constructively. Encourage open dialogue to find mutually acceptable resolutions and prevent conflicts from escalating.
11. **Empower Decision-Making:** Involve team members in decision-making processes when appropriate. Empowering them to have a say in matters that affect their work can enhance their sense of ownership and commitment.
12. **Lead by Example:** Demonstrate the behavior and values you expect from your team members. Be a role model for professionalism, integrity, and dedication to your work.
13. **Flexibility and Adaptability:** Be flexible in your approach to leadership, adapting to changing circumstances and individual needs. Recognize that LMX relationships can evolve over time and adjust your interactions accordingly.
14. **Continuous Improvement:** Continuously assess and improve your leadership practices. Solicit feedback from

team members to understand their perspectives and areas where you can enhance your leadership effectiveness.

By implementing these strategies, leaders can create a positive LMX environment that fosters trust, engagement, and high-performance within their teams. Ultimately, cultivating positive LMX relationships contributes to a more harmonious and productive work environment.

Case Study

A case study demonstrating the effective application of Leader-Member Exchange Theory illustrates how this leadership framework can positively impact an organization or team. In such a scenario, a leader within the organization has successfully implemented LMX principles to foster strong, differentiated relationships with team members. This leader takes the time to understand each team member's unique strengths, preferences, and career aspirations, resulting in the formation of high-quality in-group relationships. These in-group members experience increased trust, open communication, and greater access to resources and support. As a result, they tend to be more motivated, perform at a higher level, and exhibit higher job satisfaction and commitment to the organization. Simultaneously, the leader strives to provide equitable treatment to all team members, minimizing out-group dynamics and avoiding favoritism. Through regular feedback, mentorship, and tailored leadership approaches, the leader has created an inclusive and collaborative work environment where everyone feels valued. This case study demonstrates how the effective application of LMX Theory can lead to improved team dynamics, performance, and job satisfaction, ultimately benefiting both the team and the organization as a whole.

Transforming a Sales Team through LMX Leadership

Background:

In a medium-sized technology company, Tegbir Singh, a seasoned sales manager, faced the challenge of revitalizing a stagnating sales team. Sales targets were consistently missed, and team morale was at an all-time low. Recognizing the need for change, Tegbir Singh decided to apply the Leader-Member Exchange (LMX) Theory to improve team performance.

Application of LMX Theory:

1. **Individualized Relationships:** Tegbir Singh began by building individualized relationships with each of his team members. He initiated one-on-one meetings to understand their career aspirations, strengths, and personal challenges. He asked about their preferred communication styles and work preferences.

2. **In-Group Formation:** Over time, Tegbir Singh identified several team members who displayed exceptional potential and commitment. He nurtured these relationships, providing personalized coaching and mentorship to those in the in-group. This group became his trusted allies and received additional responsibilities.

3. **Communication and Support:** Tegbir Singh ensured open and honest communication with all team members. He held regular team meetings where he encouraged everyone to share their ideas and concerns. He also provided constructive feedback and support to out-group members to help them improve their performance.

4. **Resource Allocation:** Tegbir Singh allocated resources and opportunities more strategically. In-group members received additional sales training, access to top clients, and involvement in strategic decision-making. Out-group

members received training and development to enhance their skills.

5. **Recognition and Rewards:** Tegbir Singh publicly recognized and rewarded team members for their achievements, irrespective of their in-group or out-group status. He highlighted individual and team successes during sales meetings and company-wide events.

Results:

The application of LMX Theory had a significant positive impact on the sales team and the organization as a whole:

- **Increased Motivation:** Team members felt valued and motivated as they received personalized attention and recognition. This led to a renewed sense of commitment to their roles.

- **Improved Performance:** In-group members, in particular, excelled in their roles, consistently meeting and exceeding sales targets. Out-group members also showed noticeable improvement in their performance.

- **Enhanced Team Cohesion:** The open communication and inclusive approach fostered a more cohesive team environment. Team members began to collaborate more effectively, sharing strategies and best practices.

- **Higher Job Satisfaction:** Overall job satisfaction among team members increased as they felt that their individual needs and contributions were acknowledged and supported.

- **Achievement of Sales Targets:** The sales team, as a whole, started to consistently achieve and even surpass their sales targets, resulting in increased revenue for the organization.

- **Lower Turnover:** The improved work environment and recognition reduced turnover rates within the sales team, saving the company recruitment and training costs.

In this real-life case study, Tegbir Singh's application of LMX Theory effectively transformed a struggling sales team into a high-performing and motivated group. By cultivating differentiated yet equitable relationships with his team members, Tegbir Singh created an environment where individuals felt valued, supported, and empowered to excel in their roles. The positive outcomes not only benefited the sales team but also contributed to the overall success of the organization.

Analysis of the Strategy

The strategies employed in the case study to foster high-quality Leader-Member Exchanges are in line with the principles of LMX Theory, which emphasizes the importance of differentiated yet equitable relationships between leaders and team members. Here is an analysis of the strategies used to cultivate these high-quality LMX relationships:

1. **Individualized Relationships:** The case study demonstrates how the leader, Tegbir Singh, invested time and effort in building individualized relationships with each team member. This aligns with LMX Theory's emphasis on recognizing the unique strengths, preferences, and career aspirations of team members. By understanding these factors, Tegbir Singh could tailor his leadership approach to meet each individual's needs, which is essential for fostering high-quality LMX relationships.

2. **In-Group Formation:** Tegbir Singh identified and nurtured a subgroup of high-potential and committed team members, forming his in-group. This is consistent with LMX Theory, which acknowledges the existence of differentiated relationships. By providing additional responsibilities and opportunities to this subgroup, Tegbir Singh aimed to create a sense of trust, mutual influence, and collaboration, all of which are characteristic of high-quality LMX relationships.

3. **Communication and Support:** Open and honest communication is a fundamental aspect of high-quality LMX relationships. Tegbir Singh ensured that all team members had a platform to voice their ideas and concerns, fostering transparency and trust. Additionally, he provided constructive feedback and support to help out-group members improve their performance. This approach aligns with LMX Theory's emphasis on effective communication and support as key elements of successful leader-follower exchanges.

4. **Resource Allocation:** Tegbir Singh strategically allocated resources and opportunities based on individual needs and potential. This reflects LMX Theory's recognition that in-group members often receive greater access to resources. However, Tegbir Singh also provided training and development opportunities to out-group members, demonstrating a commitment to equity and fairness.

5. **Recognition and Rewards:** Publicly recognizing and rewarding team members for their achievements, irrespective of their in-group or out-group status, aligns with the principle of fairness in LMX relationships. By highlighting individual and team successes, Tegbir Singh reinforced the idea that every team member's contributions were valued, contributing to higher motivation and job satisfaction.

Overall, the strategies employed in the case study effectively fostered high-quality LMX relationships within the sales team. By combining personalized attention, equitable treatment, open communication, and a commitment to recognizing individual contributions, the leader, Tegbir Singh, demonstrated how LMX Theory can be applied to transform a struggling team into a motivated and high-performing unit. These strategies showcase the potential benefits of cultivating differentiated yet inclusive relationships in leadership contexts.

Investigating the Impact of Differentiated Treatment

Investigating the impact of differentiated treatment involves a comprehensive examination of the consequences, both intended and unintended, resulting from the varying ways leaders treat individuals within a team or organization. This investigative process seeks to understand how factors such as performance, potential, or personal relationships influence the treatment that team members receive from their leaders. It delves into the effects of differentiated treatment on team dynamics, individual and collective performance, job satisfaction, and overall organizational climate. Through data collection, analysis, and evaluation, this investigation aims to shed light on whether differentiated treatment leads to positive outcomes such as motivation and improved performance or negative consequences like division, resentment, and reduced trust within the team. Ultimately, the objective is to gain insights that can inform leadership practices, promote fairness and equity, and enhance team effectiveness and organizational success.

Benefits of High-Quality LMX Relationships

High-quality LMX relationships in an organization bring forth a range of significant advantages. They foster high job satisfaction, reducing turnover and boosting team morale. These relationships are instrumental in enhancing individual and team performance, as team members in such relationships tend to be more motivated, engaged, and willing to go the extra mile. Effective communication and collaboration thrive within the context of high-quality LMX relationships, leading to better decision-making and innovation. Moreover, these relationships can provide valuable career development opportunities, as those within the in-group often receive more responsibilities and access to resources, enhancing their professional growth prospects. High-quality LMX relationships contribute to a positive organizational culture and improved individual and team outcomes.

1. **Enhanced Job Satisfaction:** High-quality LMX relationships often lead to greater job satisfaction among team members. When individuals feel valued, supported, and recognized by their leaders, they are more content with their roles, leading to higher morale and job fulfillment. Satisfied employees are less likely to seek opportunities elsewhere, reducing turnover rates and the associated costs of recruitment and training.

2. **Improved Individual and Team Performance:** High-quality LMX relationships are correlated with improved performance. In-group members, who typically experience these relationships, tend to be more motivated, committed, and engaged in their work. They often go the extra mile to meet or exceed performance expectations, contributing to individual and team success. This improved performance can translate into higher sales, greater productivity, and better customer service, among other outcomes.

3. **Effective Communication and Collaboration:** Trust and mutual respect are central to high-quality LMX relationships, creating an environment where effective communication and collaboration flourish. Team members in such relationships are more willing to share ideas, information, and feedback, leading to better decision-making, problem-solving, and innovation. Effective communication reduces misunderstandings and conflicts, fostering a more harmonious work environment.

4. **Career Development Opportunities:** High-quality LMX relationships can open doors to career advancement and development. In-group members often receive more responsibilities, challenging assignments, and access to resources that contribute to their professional growth. They may also benefit from mentorship and guidance from their leaders, accelerating their career prospects within the organization.

5. **Positive Organizational Culture:** Fostering high-quality LMX relationships contributes to a positive organizational culture. When leaders prioritize equitable and respectful interactions with all team members, it sets the tone for fairness and inclusivity throughout the organization. This, in turn, enhances overall employee engagement, job satisfaction, and commitment to the organization's mission and values.

6. **Reduced Conflict and Turnover:** High-quality LMX relationships can help mitigate workplace conflicts, as team members are more likely to resolve disagreements constructively when they have trust in their leaders and colleagues. Reduced conflicts contribute to a more peaceful work environment. Additionally, team members in such relationships are less likely to leave the organization, reducing turnover and preserving institutional knowledge.

7. **Customer Satisfaction:** Higher team morale and improved performance often lead to increased customer satisfaction. Satisfied and motivated employees are more likely to provide excellent customer service, which can result in improved customer loyalty, repeat business, and positive word-of-mouth recommendations.

Fostering high-quality LMX relationships offers a multitude of advantages, ranging from individual job satisfaction and improved performance to enhanced teamwork, career development, and a positive organizational culture. These benefits can lead to greater organizational success, higher customer satisfaction, and a more engaged and motivated workforce.

Contribute to Team Cohesion, Motivation, and Productivity

High-quality LMX relationships play a pivotal role in contributing to team cohesion, motivation, and productivity within an organization. Here's how these relationships positively impact these critical aspects of team dynamics:

Team Cohesion

- **Trust and Collaboration:** High-quality LMX relationships are built on trust and mutual respect. Team members who have strong LMX relationships with their leader and with each other are more likely to trust one another. This trust forms the foundation of teamwork and collaboration, promoting a sense of unity and togetherness within the team.

- **Effective Communication:** In these relationships, communication tends to be open and transparent. Team members are more willing to share ideas, provide feedback, and engage in constructive discussions. Effective communication helps prevent misunderstandings and conflicts, contributing to a harmonious work environment.

- **Inclusivity:** Leaders who foster high-quality LMX relationships typically treat all team members equitably and inclusively. This inclusive approach reduces the likelihood of cliques or subgroups forming within the team, ensuring that everyone feels valued and integrated into the larger team structure.

Motivation

- **Increased Job Satisfaction:** Team members in high-quality LMX relationships often experience greater job satisfaction. They feel valued and recognized for their contributions, which enhances their sense of purpose and commitment to their work. This increased job satisfaction serves as a powerful motivator.

- **Recognition and Reward:** Leaders in these relationships are more likely to provide recognition and rewards for a job well done. Publicly acknowledging team members' achievements reinforces their motivation to continue performing at a high level and contributes to a positive feedback loop of motivation and recognition.

- **Professional Growth:** High-quality LMX relationships can lead to career development opportunities, including mentorship and challenging assignments. Team members are motivated to excel when they see a clear path for advancement and growth within the organization.

Productivity

- **Higher Performance:** Team members who experience high-quality LMX relationships tend to perform at a higher level. They are more committed, engaged, and willing to invest extra effort in their tasks. This increased individual performance directly contributes to overall team productivity.

- **Efficient Decision-Making:** Effective communication within these relationships leads to efficient decision-making processes. Team members can quickly reach consensus, identify solutions to challenges, and implement strategies, reducing delays and enhancing productivity.

- **Task Allocation:** Leaders in high-quality LMX relationships often allocate tasks and responsibilities based on individual strengths and preferences. This strategic task allocation ensures that team members are engaged in roles that align with their skills and interests, leading to more efficient and productive outcomes.

High-quality Leader-Member Exchange relationships promote team cohesion by fostering trust, collaboration, and effective communication. They motivate team members by increasing job satisfaction, recognition, and opportunities for growth. Additionally, they boost productivity by improving individual and collective performance, facilitating efficient decision-making, and optimizing task allocation. These relationships are a cornerstone of a cohesive, motivated, and productive team.

Challenges and Pitfalls

Challenges and pitfalls refer to the potential obstacles, difficulties, and risks that can be encountered when implementing LMX Theory and striving to foster high-quality relationships between leaders and team members within an organization. These challenges can include issues such as bias and favoritism, where leaders inadvertently show preferential treatment to certain individuals, leading to resentment and division within the team. Additionally, there may be challenges in consistently maintaining equitable treatment for all team members, especially as LMX relationships evolve over time. Miscommunication and misunderstandings can also arise, affecting the trust and collaboration essential for successful LMX relationships. It's crucial for leaders to be aware of these challenges and pitfalls and actively work to address them to ensure fair, inclusive, and effective leadership practices.

Implementing LMX Theory within an organization can be accompanied by several potential challenges and pitfalls, including issues related to perceptions of favoritism and fairness:

1. **Favoritism and Bias:** One of the most significant challenges in LMX Theory implementation is the perception of favoritism. When leaders form differentiated relationships with team members, it can create the impression that some individuals are favored over others. This perception of unequal treatment can lead to feelings of resentment, demotivation, and reduced trust among team members.
2. **Equity and Fairness Concerns:** Team members who believe that they are not receiving the same level of attention or opportunities as their colleagues in high-quality LMX relationships may perceive the situation as unfair. This can

result in a decrease in job satisfaction and a sense of injustice, which can negatively affect team morale and cohesion.
3. **Potential for In-Group and Out-Group Formation:** As LMX relationships develop, there is a risk of in-group and out-group dynamics emerging within the team. In-group members may receive more resources, support, and recognition, which can lead to division and exclusivity. This can hinder effective collaboration and communication among team members and create a less cohesive work environment.
4. **Communication Challenges:** Miscommunication and misunderstandings can occur when leaders communicate differently with in-group and out-group members. Information may not be shared equally, and some team members may feel left out of critical discussions or decision-making processes. Effective communication is essential to maintaining trust and transparency within the team.
5. **Role Ambiguity:** Team members who perceive a lack of fairness in the distribution of responsibilities or resources may experience role ambiguity. This can lead to confusion about job expectations, decreased job performance, and increased stress.
6. **Impact on Team Performance:** If left unaddressed, the challenges associated with LMX differentiation can impact overall team performance. Perceptions of favoritism, unfairness, and division can lower team morale, reduce motivation, and lead to suboptimal collaboration, ultimately affecting productivity and achievement of organizational goals.
7. **Leadership Turnover:** Leaders who are perceived as showing favoritism or engaging in inequitable practices may face challenges in retaining their team members. Team members who feel unfairly treated may seek opportunities elsewhere, leading to turnover and talent loss for the organization.

To mitigate these challenges and pitfalls, organizations should promote fairness, transparency, and inclusivity in leadership practices. Leaders should be trained to manage LMX relationships in an equitable manner, with clear communication, consistent treatment, and opportunities for growth provided to all team members. Organizations can also implement performance appraisal systems that emphasize objective evaluation criteria, reducing the perception of bias in resource allocation and recognition. Addressing these challenges proactively can help organizations harness the benefits of LMX Theory while minimizing potential negative consequences.

Strategies for Mitigating Challenges

Mitigating challenges and maintaining fairness in the implementation of LMX Theory is crucial for effective leadership and team dynamics. Here are strategies to address these challenges and promote fairness:

1. **Equitable Resource Allocation:** Establish clear, objective criteria for resource allocation, such as project assignments, training opportunities, or rewards. Ensure that these criteria are communicated to all team members so that they understand how decisions are made.
2. **Transparency and Communication**
    - **Open Communication:** Foster open and transparent communication with the entire team. Leaders should explain their decisions and actions to team members and provide opportunities for questions and feedback.
    - **Regular Updates:** Keep all team members informed about key developments, project updates, and organizational changes to minimize information gaps and misperceptions.

3. **Equal Access to Opportunities**
   - **Rotation:** Implement rotation or job-sharing programs that allow team members to gain exposure to different tasks and projects. This promotes fairness and ensures that opportunities for growth are distributed more equitably.
   - **Training and Development:** Provide training and development opportunities to all team members based on their needs and potential, not just those in the in-group. Tailor programs to individual skill gaps and career goals.
4. **Objective Performance Evaluation**
   - **Use of Metrics:** Develop objective performance metrics and evaluation processes that are consistent across the organization. Ensure that leaders use these metrics to assess all team members fairly.
   - **360-Degree Feedback:** Implement 360-degree feedback systems where team members provide input on each other's performance, reducing the reliance on a single leader's perspective.
5. **Inclusive Team Meetings:** Rotate the responsibility for leading team meetings or discussions among team members. This ensures that all voices are heard and prevents the domination of conversations by in-group members.
6. **Conflict Resolution:** Address conflicts promptly and fairly through mediation or conflict resolution processes. Encourage open dialogue and seek mutually acceptable solutions to prevent grievances from festering.
7. **Leadership Training:** Provide leadership training to help leaders recognize and manage their biases, make equitable decisions, and maintain inclusive team dynamics. Training should emphasize the importance of fairness and equity.
8. **Feedback Mechanisms:** Establish anonymous feedback mechanisms where team members can raise concerns or

provide input without fear of reprisal. This encourages honest feedback and helps identify potential fairness issues.

9. **Diversity and Inclusion Initiatives:** Implement diversity and inclusion initiatives that promote a culture of fairness and respect for all team members, regardless of background or status.
10. **Regular Assessments:** Conduct periodic assessments or audits of leadership practices and resource allocation to identify and rectify any disparities or biases.
11. **Leadership Accountability:** Hold leaders accountable for their actions and decisions regarding resource allocation and relationship building. Make it clear that fairness is a core leadership competency.
12. **Continuous Improvement:** Establish feedback loops to continually evaluate and refine leadership practices, ensuring that fairness and equity remain central to leadership approaches.

By implementing these strategies, organizations can mitigate the challenges associated with differentiated treatment under LMX Theory and promote a culture of fairness, equity, and inclusivity. This, in turn, enhances team cohesion, motivation, and overall productivity while minimizing potential pitfalls.

Communication Techniques and Relationship Strategies

Effective communication techniques and relationship-building strategies are essential for leaders looking to develop and maintain high-quality LMX relationships. Here are some key approaches:

1. **Active Listening:** Actively listen to team members to understand their concerns, ideas, and needs fully. This shows that you value their input and fosters trust.

2. **Two-Way Communication:** Encourage open and honest communication. Ensure that team members feel comfortable sharing their thoughts and feedback with you.
3. **Regular Check-Ins:** Schedule regular one-on-one meetings with team members to discuss their progress, goals, and any challenges they may be facing. This dedicated time shows your commitment to their development.
4. **Empathetic Communication:** Practice empathy by trying to understand the perspectives and emotions of your team members. Show that you care about their well-being and concerns.
5. **Clarity in Communication:** Use clear and concise language to convey information, expectations, and goals. Ambiguity can lead to misunderstandings and frustration.
6. **Nonverbal Communication:** Pay attention to your body language and facial expressions, as they convey important messages. Maintain open and approachable nonverbal cues.
7. **Feedback:** Provide regular, constructive feedback on performance. Highlight strengths and suggest areas for improvement, focusing on specific behaviors and outcomes.
8. **Recognition and Appreciation:** Recognize and appreciate the efforts and achievements of your team members. Publicly acknowledge their contributions and celebrate successes.
9. **Tailored Communication:** Adapt your communication style to the preferences of each team member. Some may prefer written communication, while others may prefer face-to-face conversations.
10. **Conflict Resolution:** Handle conflicts promptly and constructively. Encourage open dialogue to find mutually acceptable resolutions and prevent conflicts from escalating.
11. **Inclusivity:** Create an inclusive work environment where all team members feel valued and included. Promote diversity of thought and encourage collaboration among team members with different perspectives.

12. **Shared Vision:** Share a clear and compelling vision for the team's goals and the organization's mission. Ensure that team members understand how their work contributes to this vision.
13. **Team Building:** Facilitate team-building activities and opportunities for team members to get to know each other on a personal level. Strong team dynamics can improve communication and collaboration.
14. **Trust Building:** Build trust by consistently following through on commitments, being honest, and acting with integrity. Trust is a cornerstone of strong LMX relationships.
15. **Conflict Management Skills:** Develop skills in conflict management and negotiation to handle disagreements and disputes effectively.
16. **Coaching and Mentorship:** Offer coaching and mentorship to team members as needed. Provide guidance and support for their professional growth and development.
17. **Empowerment:** Empower team members to take ownership of their work and decision-making processes when appropriate. This can boost their confidence and commitment.
18. **Emotional Intelligence:** Develop emotional intelligence to better understand and manage your own emotions and those of your team members. This skill can help navigate sensitive issues.

Effective communication and relationship-building are ongoing processes. Leaders should continuously assess their communication techniques and relationship-building strategies to adapt to the evolving needs and dynamics of their team members and the organization. By prioritizing these skills, leaders can foster strong and productive LMX relationships, contributing to team success and organizational growth.

Path-Goal Theory

Path-Goal Theory is a leadership framework that revolves around the idea of leaders guiding and supporting their team members along clear paths toward achieving their goals and desired outcomes. This theory posits that effective leaders should assist their team in identifying and navigating the most suitable paths to reach objectives, whether those goals are related to personal growth, team performance, or organizational success. The leader's role in Path-Goal Theory is multifaceted, involving tasks such as removing obstacles, clarifying expectations, and providing the necessary resources and support to facilitate progress. Essentially, leaders using this theory act as path-clearers and motivators, ensuring that the path to success is both understandable and attainable for their team members, ultimately enhancing motivation, performance, and overall satisfaction within the organization.

Path-Goal Theory is a leadership model that emphasizes the leader's role in facilitating their team members' achievement of goals by clearing the path to success. Developed by Robert House in the 1970s, this theory posits that effective leadership involves guiding and supporting individuals and teams to reach their objectives while addressing obstacles and challenges along the way. Here's a detailed explanation of the key components and principles of Path-Goal Theory:

1. **Leadership Styles:**
   - **Directive Leadership:** In situations where team members are uncertain about their tasks or the path to success is unclear, leaders adopt a directive style. They provide specific instructions, set clear goals, and closely supervise the work to ensure team members stay on track.
   - **Supportive Leadership:** When team members are skilled and motivated but may face challenges or stressors, leaders take on a supportive role. They offer emotional support, make the work environment

more pleasant, and show empathy to help team members cope with difficulties.
- **Participative Leadership:** In cases where team members have the knowledge and expertise, leaders engage them in decision-making and problem-solving processes. This approach allows team members to contribute their insights, fostering a sense of ownership and commitment.
- **Achievement-Oriented Leadership:** When team members are capable and need a challenge, leaders set high performance expectations and encourage them to achieve their full potential. This style motivates team members to exceed their goals and take initiative.

2. **Path Clarification:** Leaders are responsible for clarifying the path to success by ensuring that team members understand their roles, responsibilities, and the goals they need to achieve. This involves setting clear expectations, providing guidelines, and communicating the organizational vision.

3. **Obstacle Removal:** Effective leaders identify and remove obstacles that hinder team members' progress. Whether these obstacles are related to resources, procedures, or interpersonal issues, leaders should actively intervene to facilitate smooth progress.

4. **Support and Motivation:** Leaders offer support and motivation based on the specific needs of their team members. This support can be emotional, practical, or developmental, depending on the situation. The goal is to keep team members motivated and focused on their objectives.

5. **Individualization:** Path-Goal Theory recognizes that team members have unique needs and preferences. Effective leaders tailor their leadership style to each individual or

situation, ensuring that the support provided is personalized and relevant.

6. **Outcome Focus:** Leaders in this framework emphasize the importance of achieving positive outcomes. They tie rewards and recognition to performance, reinforcing the connection between effort and success.
7. **Flexibility:** Effective leaders remain flexible and adaptable in their approach. They assess the current circumstances, the abilities and motivations of their team members, and the nature of the tasks to determine the most suitable leadership style.
8. **Continuous Monitoring and Feedback:** Leaders continually monitor progress and provide feedback to help team members stay on course. This feedback loop helps in making necessary adjustments and ensuring that the path to success remains clear.
9. **Contingency and Situational Leadership:** Path-Goal Theory is inherently contingency-based, meaning that the choice of leadership style depends on the specific situation, team member characteristics, and task requirements. Effective leaders assess these factors to determine the most appropriate approach.
10. **Employee Motivation and Job Satisfaction:** The theory places a strong emphasis on understanding and enhancing employee motivation and job satisfaction as key outcomes of effective leadership. Leaders who provide the right level of support and clarity are more likely to motivate and satisfy their team members.

Path-Goal Theory acknowledges that leadership is situational, and effective leaders must adapt their style to the specific needs of their team members and the challenges they face. By clearing the path to success through guidance, support, and obstacle removal, leaders can enhance team motivation, satisfaction, and performance, ultimately leading to the achievement of individual and organizational goals.

Historical Context

The Path-Goal Theory of leadership, developed by Robert J. House, emerged in the 1970s as a response to the evolving leadership theories and the changing organizational landscape of that era. Several factors in the historical context contributed to the development and relevance of this theory:

1. **Shift in Leadership Theories:** During the 1970s, there was a growing shift in leadership theories from trait-based and behavioral models to more contingency and situational approaches. Researchers were exploring how leadership effectiveness depended on various factors, such as the characteristics of followers and the context in which leadership occurred.

2. **Complex and Changing Work Environments:** The 1970s marked a period of significant change in the workplace, with organizations facing increased complexity and uncertainty. Globalization, technological advancements, and evolving social dynamics were altering the nature of work and leadership.

3. **Research on Motivation and Satisfaction:** House drew from research on motivation and job satisfaction, particularly Victor Vroom's Expectancy Theory and Frederick Herzberg's Two-Factor Theory. These psychological theories highlighted the importance of understanding how leadership can impact employee motivation and satisfaction.

4. **Desire for Effective Leadership Models:** Organizations were searching for effective leadership models that could adapt to different situations and contexts. There was a demand for leadership theories that could provide guidance for leaders in a rapidly changing business environment.

5. **Influence of Contingency Theories:** Contingency theories, which emphasize that effective leadership depends on situational factors, were gaining prominence. Path-Goal Theory fits within this framework by suggesting that leadership styles should be adapted to the specific needs and circumstances of followers.

6. **Empirical Research:** House conducted extensive empirical research to support the development of Path-Goal Theory. His studies aimed to test the theory's propositions and provide practical insights for leadership effectiveness.

Path-Goal Theory emerged as a comprehensive framework that integrated elements from various leadership and motivation theories. It addressed the need for adaptable leadership styles that could enhance follower motivation and job satisfaction by clarifying paths to goals and removing obstacles. The theory offered practical guidance for leaders in diverse organizational settings, making it a valuable contribution to leadership literature during the era of growing complexity and change in the workplace. Today, it continues to be relevant in helping leaders navigate the challenges of leadership and motivation in contemporary organizations.

Examination of Leadership Styles

Path-Goal Theory proposes four distinct leadership styles, each tailored to address specific circumstances and the needs of team members. Here's an examination of these leadership styles:

1. **Directive Leadership**
   - **When to Use:** Directive leadership is most effective when team members lack clarity about their roles or when the path to achieving goals is unclear. It's also suitable for situations where team members have limited experience or need explicit guidance.

- **Leadership Characteristics:** Directive leaders provide explicit instructions, set clear goals, and closely supervise team members' work. They make decisions on behalf of the team and take charge of defining roles and responsibilities.
- **Impact:** This style reduces ambiguity and uncertainty for team members. It helps them understand their tasks and the expectations, thereby enhancing their confidence and reducing stress. However, overuse of directive leadership can lead to micromanagement and a lack of autonomy.

2. **Supportive Leadership**
   - **When to Use:** Supportive leadership is effective when team members face challenges, stressors, or need emotional support to maintain motivation. It is particularly beneficial in situations where work-related stress is high.
   - **Leadership Characteristics:** Supportive leaders create a positive work environment where team members feel valued and cared for. They offer encouragement, listen to concerns, and provide assistance and resources as needed.
   - **Impact:** This style fosters a sense of well-being and job satisfaction among team members. They feel supported and motivated to overcome challenges, resulting in improved morale and engagement. However, excessive use of supportiveness without addressing performance issues can hinder productivity.

3. **Participative Leadership**
   - **When to Use:** Participative leadership is suitable when team members possess the knowledge and expertise needed to contribute to decision-making and problem-solving. It is effective in empowering and engaging team members.

- **Leadership Characteristics:** Participative leaders involve team members in discussions, seek their input, and encourage them to share their ideas and opinions. They value and consider team members' perspectives when making decisions.
- **Impact:** This style promotes a sense of ownership and commitment among team members. They feel valued and empowered, which often results in higher job satisfaction and a greater willingness to take initiative. However, it may be less effective when quick decision-making is required or when team members lack the necessary expertise.

4. **Achievement-Oriented Leadership**

   - **When to Use:** Achievement-oriented leadership is most effective when team members are highly competent and motivated but may not be realizing their full potential. It's suitable for challenging tasks and situations where team members need to stretch their capabilities.
   - **Leadership Characteristics:** Achievement-oriented leaders set challenging goals and performance expectations. They encourage team members to strive for excellence, take initiative, and continuously improve.
   - **Impact:** This style can inspire team members to reach higher levels of performance and take calculated risks. Team members often feel more motivated and enthusiastic about their work, leading to increased productivity and innovation. However, if used excessively, it can create stress and burnout among team members.

Effective leaders using Path-Goal Theory often adopt a combination of these leadership styles based on the unique needs of their team members and the specific demands of the tasks they face. The key is to assess the situation and adapt the leadership style accordingly to facilitate team members' progress toward achieving their goals while promoting motivation, satisfaction, and performance.

How to Apply Each Style Based on Situational Demands

The effectiveness of leadership styles in Path-Goal Theory depends on the situational demands and the characteristics of team members. Here's a guide on when and how to apply each style based on specific situational demands:

1. **Directive Leadership**
   - **When to Apply**
     - When team members lack clarity about their roles or the path to success is unclear.
     - In situations where team members have limited experience or skills.
   - **How to Apply**
     - Provide explicit instructions, guidelines, and expectations.
     - Set clear goals and objectives.
     - Closely supervise and monitor team members' progress.
     - Clarify roles and responsibilities to reduce ambiguity.
   - **Example:** In a crisis situation, such as responding to a security breach, a leader may need to adopt directive leadership to provide specific instructions on immediate actions and protocols to follow.

2. **Supportive Leadership**
   - **When to Apply**
     - When team members are facing stressors, challenges, or work-related difficulties.
     - In situations where maintaining team morale and well-being is essential.
   - **How to Apply**
     - Create a positive and empathetic work environment.
     - Offer emotional support and reassurance.
     - Listen to team members' concerns and address them.
     - Provide resources and assistance as needed.
   - **Example:** During a period of high workload and tight deadlines, a leader can use supportive leadership by recognizing the team's efforts, expressing empathy, and offering assistance in managing stress.

3. **Participative Leadership**
   - **When to Apply**
     - When team members possess the knowledge and expertise to contribute to decision-making.
     - In situations where empowerment and engagement are critical.
   - **How to Apply**
     - Involve team members in discussions and problem-solving.
     - Encourage them to share their ideas and opinions.
     - Value and consider their input when making decisions.
     - Delegate decision-making authority when appropriate.
   - **Example:** When planning a project that requires input from various team members with diverse expertise, a

leader can adopt participative leadership by involving the team in brainstorming, planning, and decision-making processes.

4. **Achievement-Oriented Leadership**

- **When to Apply:**
    - When team members are highly competent and motivated but may not be realizing their full potential.
    - In challenging tasks or when encouraging innovation is essential.
- **How to Apply:**
    - Set challenging goals and performance expectations.
    - Encourage team members to take initiative and go beyond their comfort zones.
    - Promote a culture of continuous improvement and innovation.
- **Example:** In a competitive industry, a leader can employ achievement-oriented leadership by challenging team members to exceed their previous performance, fostering a culture of excellence and innovation.

It is important to note that effective leadership often involves a combination of these styles rather than a rigid adherence to one. Leaders should assess the specific situational demands, the readiness and characteristics of team members, and the nature of the tasks to determine the most suitable leadership approach. Additionally, leaders should remain flexible and be ready to adapt their style as circumstances change to optimize team motivation, satisfaction, and performance.

Clearing the Path to Achievement

Clearing the path to achievement is a fundamental concept within the Path-Goal Theory of leadership. In this context, it refers to a leader's role in removing obstacles, reducing barriers, and providing guidance to make the journey toward achieving goals as smooth and straightforward as possible for team members. Effective leaders recognize that individuals or teams may encounter various challenges and hindrances while pursuing their objectives, whether related to unclear expectations, resource limitations, or external factors. Therefore, "clearing the path" involves actions such as setting clear expectations, removing ambiguity, offering support, addressing issues, and ensuring that team members have the necessary resources and tools to succeed. By facilitating a clear and obstacle-free path, leaders empower their team members, boost their confidence, and enhance their motivation, ultimately leading to improved performance and goal attainment. This concept underscores the importance of leadership in guiding individuals or teams toward success by minimizing hindrances and maximizing clarity and support.

Leaders can effectively remove obstacles and facilitate goal attainment for their team members by employing various strategies and actions.

1. **Clarify Expectations:** Leaders should ensure that team members have a clear understanding of their roles, responsibilities, and performance expectations. Unclear expectations can be a significant obstacle to goal attainment.
2. **Provide Clear Directions:** Offering explicit instructions and guidance can help team members navigate complex tasks. Leaders should break down larger goals into smaller, manageable steps and communicate these steps clearly.
3. **Resource Allocation:** Leaders should ensure that team members have access to the necessary resources, including tools, equipment, information, and training, to perform their tasks effectively. Lack of resources can impede progress.

4. **Remove Bureaucratic Barriers:** Leaders can streamline administrative processes and remove bureaucratic obstacles that may hinder progress. Simplifying procedures can save time and reduce frustration.
5. **Problem-Solving Support:** When team members encounter challenges or roadblocks, leaders should be available to offer support and guidance. They can assist in identifying solutions and overcoming obstacles.
6. **Empowerment and Autonomy:** Leaders can empower team members by giving them a degree of autonomy and decision-making authority. This can boost confidence and initiative, making it easier for them to navigate challenges.
7. **Continuous Feedback:** Provide regular feedback on team members' performance. This feedback should include constructive criticism and praise to guide improvement and maintain motivation.
8. **Mentoring and Coaching:** Leaders can act as mentors or coaches, offering valuable insights and guidance based on their experience. This mentorship can help team members develop skills and strategies to overcome obstacles.
9. **Conflict Resolution:** Address interpersonal conflicts or team dynamics that may hinder progress. Leaders should facilitate open communication and work toward resolving disputes constructively.
10. **Recognize and Celebrate Progress:** Acknowledge and celebrate milestones and achievements along the way. Recognizing progress can boost team morale and motivation.
11. **Adapt Leadership Styles:** Leaders should be flexible and adapt their leadership styles to the changing needs of team members and the evolving situation. Different styles, such as directive, supportive, participative, or achievement-oriented, may be needed at different times.
12. **Set Clear Goals and Priorities:** Establish clear and achievable goals, and prioritize them based on their

significance and urgency. This clarity helps team members focus their efforts effectively.

13. **Foster a Positive Work Environment:** Create a workplace culture that encourages collaboration, innovation, and risk-taking. A positive and supportive atmosphere can motivate team members to overcome challenges.
14. **Continuous Learning and Development:** Encourage a culture of continuous learning and development within the team. Providing opportunities for skill enhancement can equip team members to address new challenges effectively.
15. **Time Management and Prioritization:** Help team members manage their time and priorities efficiently. Leaders can provide time-management techniques and tools to ensure that important tasks are addressed first.

By implementing these strategies, leaders can actively remove obstacles and create an environment where team members are well-equipped and motivated to achieve their goals. Effective leadership in clearing the path to goal attainment not only enhances individual and team performance but also contributes to the overall success of the organization.

Real World Examples

Real-world examples of the application of Path-Goal Theory in leadership abound in various fields and contexts. Here are a few examples:

1. **Education Leadership:** In a school setting, a principal can apply Path-Goal Theory by adopting different leadership styles depending on the needs of teachers and students. For instance, when teachers are faced with uncertainty about remote teaching during a pandemic, the principal may provide directive leadership by offering clear guidelines and resources. In contrast, when experienced teachers are tasked with designing a new curriculum, the principal can employ

participative leadership to involve them in decision-making and tap into their expertise.

2. **Healthcare Leadership:** In a healthcare organization, a nursing manager can utilize Path-Goal Theory to enhance patient care. When nurses are dealing with a challenging patient case, the manager can provide supportive leadership by acknowledging their efforts and offering emotional support. Alternatively, in a situation where a team of experienced nurses is responsible for a research project, the manager can adopt achievement-oriented leadership to inspire them to set high standards for their work.

3. **Business Leadership:** In a corporate environment, a department head can implement Path-Goal Theory to motivate a diverse team. For example, when team members are facing technical difficulties in a software development project, the leader can use supportive leadership to help them cope with stress and frustration. Conversely, when the team is highly skilled and working on an innovative project, the leader can employ participative leadership to encourage their input and creativity.

4. **Nonprofit Leadership:** The executive director of a nonprofit organization can apply Path-Goal Theory to optimize the performance of volunteers. In a situation where volunteers are new to fundraising, the director can provide directive leadership by offering step-by-step guidance on donor outreach strategies. Conversely, with experienced volunteers leading a community outreach program, the director can use achievement-oriented leadership to set ambitious goals and encourage them to surpass expectations.

5. **Military Leadership:** In the military, a commanding officer can utilize Path-Goal Theory to lead troops effectively. When soldiers are navigating unfamiliar terrain or facing tactical challenges, the officer may employ directive leadership by issuing clear orders and instructions. Conversely, when experienced soldiers are executing a critical mission, the officer can adopt achievement-oriented

leadership to motivate them to excel and meet ambitious objectives.

These real-world examples illustrate how leaders in various fields can apply Path-Goal Theory by adjusting their leadership styles to the specific needs, circumstances, and capabilities of their team members. By doing so, they enhance motivation, job satisfaction, and performance, ultimately contributing to the successful attainment of goals and objectives in their respective organizations or contexts.

Success through Leadership

Success through leadership signifies the pivotal role of leaders in guiding individuals or teams toward achieving their goals and objectives within an organization or any endeavor. This concept encompasses the idea that leaders act as navigators, setting a clear direction, and providing the necessary guidance and support to steer their team along the most efficient and effective path to success. It involves leaders creating a strategic vision, defining goals, and outlining a roadmap that outlines the steps, milestones, and resources required for goal attainment. Moreover, leaders continually monitor progress, remove obstacles, and adapt to changing circumstances to ensure the chosen course remains aligned with the desired outcomes. In essence, charting a course for success through leadership emphasizes that effective leaders play a fundamental role in facilitating goal achievement, providing clarity, motivation, and a sense of purpose to those they lead.

Achieving the Organizational Goal

Achieving organizational goals refers to the successful realization of the specific objectives and targets set by an organization to fulfill its mission and vision. It involves aligning the efforts and resources of the entire organization, including its departments, teams, and employees, toward the accomplishment of these goals. Achieving organizational goals signifies that the organization is progressing in the desired direction, effectively responding to challenges, and ultimately fulfilling its purpose. This process often entails strategic planning, the allocation of resources, the monitoring of progress, and the implementation of various strategies and initiatives. Successful goal attainment indicates that the organization is not only functioning efficiently but also effectively meeting the needs of its stakeholders, be they customers, employees, shareholders, or the broader community. It underscores the importance of leadership, teamwork, and adaptability in navigating the complex and dynamic landscape of modern organizations to ensure that overarching objectives are met.

How Leaders Can Align Individual and Team Goals

Aligning individual and team goals with the overarching objectives of the organization is a critical task for leaders to ensure that everyone is working toward a common purpose. Here's a detailed explanation of how leaders can achieve this alignment:

1. **Clarify Organizational Goals:** Leaders must have a deep understanding of the organization's mission, vision, and strategic objectives. They should be able to articulate these overarching goals clearly and concisely.
2. **Communicate the Big Picture:** Leaders should regularly communicate the organization's goals to all levels of the workforce. This includes explaining how individual and team efforts contribute to the achievement of these goals. Visual aids, storytelling, and examples can make the message more compelling.
3. **Set SMART Individual and Team Goals:** Leaders work with individual team members and teams to set goals that are

Specific, Measurable, Achievable, Relevant, and Time-bound (SMART). These goals should be aligned with the broader organizational objectives.
4. **Link Goals to the Mission:** Leaders should emphasize the connection between individual and team goals and the organization's mission. Team members should understand how their work directly impacts the fulfillment of the mission.
5. **Performance Expectations:** Clearly define performance expectations and key performance indicators (KPIs) for individuals and teams. Team members should know what is expected of them and how their performance will be assessed.
6. **Regular Progress Tracking:** Implement regular performance reviews and progress tracking mechanisms. Leaders can provide feedback and guidance to ensure that individual and team efforts remain aligned with organizational goals.
7. **Adaptability and Flexibility:** Leaders should be open to adjusting individual and team goals as circumstances change. The business environment is dynamic, and goals may need to evolve to stay aligned with the organization's strategic direction.
8. **Recognition and Rewards:** Recognize and reward individuals and teams when they achieve their goals and contribute to organizational success. This reinforces the alignment between personal/team efforts and organizational objectives.
9. **Training and Development:** Provide training and development opportunities that help team members acquire the skills and knowledge needed to achieve their goals and support the organization's mission.
10. **Encourage Collaboration:** Foster a collaborative work environment where teams and individuals can share ideas and resources to collectively work toward common

objectives. Cross-functional collaboration can lead to innovative solutions.

11. **Lead by Example:** Leaders should set an example by aligning their own goals and actions with the organization's mission and values. When team members see leaders practicing alignment, they are more likely to follow suit.
12. **Feedback Loop:** Establish a feedback loop where team members can provide input and insights on the alignment of their goals with the organization's objectives. Leaders can use this feedback to make necessary adjustments.
13. **Continuous Communication:** Keep communication channels open, encouraging team members to ask questions, seek clarification, and share concerns regarding goal alignment. Regularly update them on changes in organizational goals or strategies.

By following these steps, leaders can effectively align individual and team goals with the overarching objectives of the organization. This alignment not only ensures that everyone is working toward a common purpose but also enhances motivation, engagement, and overall organizational performance. It's a dynamic and ongoing process that requires leadership commitment and attention to detail.

Case Study 1: Steve Jobs and Apple Inc.

Steve Jobs, the co-founder and former CEO of Apple Inc., is a prominent example of a leader who charted a remarkable course for organizational success. Under his leadership, Apple transformed from a struggling computer company in the late 1990s into one of the most innovative and valuable technology companies in the world. Jobs achieved this through several key strategies:

1. **Visionary Leadership:** Steve Jobs was known for his visionary thinking. He had a clear vision for Apple's future, focusing on product design, user experience, and innovation.

He envisioned products like the iPhone and iPad, which revolutionized entire industries.
2. **Product Excellence:** Jobs emphasized product excellence and paid meticulous attention to design and functionality. He drove Apple to create iconic products known for their quality and user-friendly interfaces.
3. **Customer-Centric Approach:** Apple's success was largely driven by a customer-centric approach. Jobs aimed to anticipate and fulfill customers' needs, often before they even knew what they wanted.
4. **Focus on Simplicity:** Jobs believed in simplicity and clarity. He simplified product lines and eliminated complexity, making Apple products accessible to a broader audience.
5. **Alignment of Goals:** Jobs ensured that the goals of individual teams and employees aligned with Apple's overarching objectives. This alignment fostered a sense of purpose and cohesion within the organization.
6. **Innovation Culture:** Jobs cultivated a culture of innovation within Apple. He encouraged risk-taking and supported creative ideas, which led to groundbreaking products and technologies.

The outcome of Steve Jobs' leadership was Apple's resurgence, marked by the launch of iconic products like the iPod, iPhone, and iPad. Apple's market capitalization and profitability soared, making it one of the most valuable companies globally. Jobs' ability to chart a course for success by blending vision, innovation, and a deep understanding of customer needs is a testament to effective leadership in the technology sector.

Case Study 2: Indra Nooyi and PepsiCo

Indra Nooyi, the former CEO and Chairperson of PepsiCo, is another exemplary leader who charted a course for organizational success. She transformed PepsiCo into a global food and beverage powerhouse during her tenure. Here's how she achieved this:

1. **Diversification Strategy:** Nooyi recognized the changing consumer preferences towards healthier and more diverse food and beverage options. She led PepsiCo's diversification into a broader portfolio of products, including healthier snacks, juices, and even acquiring brands like Quaker Oats and Tropicana.
2. **Focus on Performance with Purpose:** Nooyi coined the term "Performance with Purpose," which emphasized not only financial performance but also social and environmental responsibility. She integrated sustainability and corporate responsibility into PepsiCo's core business strategy.
3. **Innovation and R&D:** Under her leadership, PepsiCo invested heavily in research and development to create innovative products and packaging. This focus on innovation led to the development of products like "Guilt-Free" snacks and reduced-calorie beverages.
4. **Global Expansion:** Nooyi expanded PepsiCo's global footprint, targeting emerging markets. She recognized the potential for growth in regions like Asia and the Middle East and tailored products to local tastes.
5. **Leadership Development:** Nooyi fostered leadership development and diversity within PepsiCo. She implemented initiatives to promote gender diversity in leadership roles.

The result of Indra Nooyi's leadership was PepsiCo's significant growth and a diversified product portfolio that catered to changing consumer preferences. During her tenure, PepsiCo's revenues doubled, and the company became recognized for its commitment to sustainability and corporate responsibility. Nooyi's visionary leadership and emphasis on innovation and purpose-driven performance exemplify her role in charting a successful course for PepsiCo.

Both of these case studies illustrate how effective leaders can shape the direction of organizations by articulating a vision, aligning goals, fostering innovation, and adapting to changing circumstances to achieve long-term success.

Motivation and Employee Satisfaction

Motivation and employee satisfaction are two closely intertwined concepts that play a crucial role in the workplace. Motivation refers to the internal or external factors that drive individuals to initiate and sustain effort and behavior to achieve specific goals or meet certain needs. It's the force that energizes and directs an individual's behavior toward accomplishing tasks and objectives. Motivated employees tend to be more productive, engaged, and committed to their work. On the other hand, employee satisfaction pertains to the overall contentment, happiness, and positive emotional state that employees experience in their jobs. It reflects how employees feel about their work environment, job conditions, compensation, relationships with colleagues, and the level of support and recognition they receive. Satisfied employees are more likely to be loyal to their organization, display greater job performance, and have a higher retention rate. Importantly, motivation and employee satisfaction are interconnected because satisfied employees are often more motivated, and motivated employees are likely to be more satisfied with their work. When leaders and organizations create an environment that fosters both motivation and employee satisfaction, they can achieve a more productive, engaged, and content workforce, leading to improved organizational performance and success.

How Path-Goal Theory Impacts Motivation and Employee Satisfaction

Effective leadership under the Path-Goal Theory can have a significant impact on motivation and employee satisfaction. This leadership theory emphasizes the role of leaders in guiding and supporting their team members to achieve their goals and, in turn, enhance their motivation and job satisfaction. Here's a examination of how effective leadership in the context of the Path-Goal Theory influences these aspects:

1. **Motivation:**
   - **Clear Path:** One of the core principles of Path-Goal Theory is to clarify the path to goal attainment. Effective leaders help team members understand the steps required to achieve their objectives. This clarity reduces uncertainty and boosts motivation as team members can see a clear connection between their efforts and the desired outcomes.
   - **Adaptive Leadership Styles:** Path-Goal Theory advocates adapting leadership styles to the needs of team members. Leaders can provide direction (directive leadership) when the path is unclear or offer support and encouragement (supportive leadership) when team members face challenges. By tailoring their leadership approach, leaders can enhance the motivation of individual team members based on their unique requirements.
   - **Goal Setting:** Leaders play a critical role in setting challenging yet attainable goals. This achievement-oriented leadership style motivates team members to strive for excellence and reach their full potential. When leaders set high expectations and provide the necessary resources and support, team members are more likely to be motivated to meet those expectations.

- **Feedback and Recognition:** Effective leaders in the Path-Goal Theory framework provide regular feedback and recognition for team members' efforts and accomplishments. This feedback reinforces the link between effort and performance, motivating employees to continue their productive behaviors.

2. **Employee Satisfaction:**
   - **Supportive Leadership:** The supportive leadership style, a component of Path-Goal Theory, involves creating a positive work environment and offering emotional support. When leaders are supportive, employees tend to feel more satisfied with their work because they perceive that their well-being is valued and cared for.
   - **Clarity and Reduced Stress:** Effective leaders clarify roles, expectations, and job-related tasks. This clarity reduces ambiguity and stress, contributing to higher job satisfaction. When employees understand what is expected of them, they can perform their duties more confidently and with less anxiety.
   - **Participative Decision-Making:** Leaders who embrace participative leadership involve team members in decision-making processes. This approach fosters a sense of inclusion and ownership, leading to higher job satisfaction as employees feel their voices are heard and their opinions matter.
   - **Customized Support:** Path-Goal Theory encourages leaders to customize their leadership behaviors to individual team members. By recognizing and addressing each member's unique needs, leaders can enhance job satisfaction by showing that they care about their employees' personal and professional well-being.

- **Recognition and Rewards:** Effective leaders acknowledge and reward team members' contributions and accomplishments. This recognition not only motivates but also increases employee satisfaction, as individuals feel valued and appreciated for their efforts.

Effective leadership under the Path-Goal Theory positively influences motivation and employee satisfaction through various mechanisms, including providing clarity, offering support, setting challenging goals, adapting leadership styles, and recognizing achievements. By aligning leadership behaviors with the needs and goals of team members, leaders can create a work environment where individuals are not only motivated to perform but also satisfied with their jobs and their contributions to the organization.

Strategies of Leadership to Motivate and Engage Team

Motivating and engaging teams is essential for effective leadership. Leaders can employ various strategies to inspire their teams and foster a sense of commitment and enthusiasm. Here are several strategies for leaders to consider:

1. **Set Clear Expectations:** Communicate clear and achievable goals, expectations, and performance standards to team members. When employees understand what is expected of them, they are more likely to stay motivated and focused on their tasks.
2. **Provide Regular Feedback:** Offer constructive feedback and recognition for a job well done. Timely and specific feedback helps team members understand their progress and areas for improvement, while recognition boosts morale and motivation.
3. **Empower and Delegate:** Empower team members by delegating authority and decision-making responsibilities. Allowing individuals to take ownership of their work and

make meaningful contributions can enhance motivation and engagement.

4. **Offer Opportunities for Skill Development:** Provide training and development opportunities that help team members acquire new skills and advance in their careers. When employees see a path for personal and professional growth, they are more likely to stay engaged.
5. **Create a Positive Work Environment:** Foster a supportive and inclusive workplace culture where team members feel valued, respected, and appreciated. A positive atmosphere encourages collaboration and engagement.
6. **Recognize and Reward Achievements:** Acknowledge and reward both small and significant achievements. Recognition can take various forms, such as verbal praise, bonuses, promotions, or special awards.
7. **Encourage Team Building:** Organize team-building activities and events that promote camaraderie and collaboration among team members. Building strong relationships can boost engagement and a sense of belonging.
8. **Communicate Openly and Transparently:** Maintain open lines of communication with team members. Keep them informed about organizational changes, challenges, and successes. Transparency builds trust and engagement.
9. **Provide Autonomy:** Trust team members to make decisions and manage their tasks independently. Autonomy fosters a sense of responsibility and ownership, increasing engagement.
10. **Set Challenging Goals:** Encourage individuals and teams to set ambitious, yet attainable, goals. Challenging objectives can inspire a sense of purpose and motivation to excel.
11. **Lead by Example:** Demonstrate dedication, work ethic, and a positive attitude as a leader. When team members see their leader's commitment, they are more likely to follow suit.
12. **Promote Work-Life Balance:** Encourage a healthy work-life balance by respecting employees' time and promoting

flexibility when possible. Balancing personal and professional life contributes to overall well-being and engagement.
13. **Celebrate Successes:** Celebrate team achievements and milestones. Recognizing collective efforts reinforces a sense of accomplishment and motivates further collaboration.
14. **Seek Feedback and Input:** Encourage team members to share their ideas, concerns, and feedback. Listening to their input and involving them in decision-making can increase engagement and a sense of ownership.
15. **Provide Opportunities for Leadership Development:** Offer opportunities for team members to take on leadership roles or lead projects. This empowers individuals and demonstrates trust in their abilities.
16. **Adapt to Individual Needs:** Recognize that different team members may have unique motivations and preferences. Tailor your leadership approach to accommodate these individual needs.

By implementing these strategies, leaders can create an environment that fosters motivation and engagement among their teams. Engaged employees are not only more productive but also more committed to achieving the organization's goals and contributing to its success.

Adaptive Leadership under Path-Goal Theory

Adaptive leadership, as applied within the context of the Path-Goal Theory, refers to a leadership approach that emphasizes the flexibility and versatility of leaders in responding to the specific needs and challenges faced by their team members. This style of leadership recognizes that different individuals and situations require varying degrees of guidance and support to stay motivated and achieve their goals.

Adaptive leaders within the Path-Goal framework assess the unique characteristics of their team members, the complexity of the tasks, and the context in which work is performed. Based on this assessment, they adjust their leadership behaviors accordingly. For instance, if team members lack clarity on how to achieve their goals, the leader may provide clear directives and guidance (directive leadership). Conversely, if team members are highly skilled and motivated, the leader may take a more hands-off approach and provide support and encouragement (supportive leadership). In situations where team members possess valuable expertise, adaptive leaders may involve them in decision-making processes (participative leadership).

The central idea is that adaptive leadership is not about adhering to a fixed leadership style but rather adapting one's approach to best fit the needs of the team and the challenges at hand. By doing so, leaders can effectively remove obstacles, provide clarity, and motivate team members, ultimately enhancing their performance and job satisfaction. This dynamic approach aligns with the overarching goal of the Path-Goal Theory, which is to facilitate goal attainment by creating a supportive and motivating leadership environment tailored to the specific circumstances of the team.

1. **Leadership Flexibility:** Adaptive leadership involves a high degree of flexibility and situational awareness. Leaders recognize that different situations and individuals require varying approaches to leadership. They are willing to adjust their behaviors to suit the needs of their team members.
2. **Assessment of Team and Situation:** Adaptive leaders begin by assessing the composition of their team and the specific circumstances they face. They consider factors such as the team's experience, motivation, skills, and the complexity of the tasks at hand.
3. **Directive Leadership:** When team members are uncertain about the path to success or the tasks are highly complex,

adaptive leaders may employ directive leadership. In this mode, leaders provide clear instructions, set specific goals, and offer guidance on how to accomplish them. This approach reduces ambiguity and instills confidence in team members.

4. **Supportive Leadership:** In situations where team members are facing challenges, feeling stressed, or dealing with personal issues, adaptive leaders may shift to a supportive leadership style. This involves offering emotional support, showing empathy, and creating a positive work environment. Supportive leaders prioritize the well-being and morale of their team members.

5. **Participative Leadership:** When team members possess valuable expertise, are highly motivated, and capable of contributing to decision-making, adaptive leaders may opt for a participative leadership style. This approach involves involving team members in discussions, brainstorming, and problem-solving. It empowers team members to take ownership of decisions and fosters a sense of shared responsibility.

6. **Achievement-Oriented Leadership:** Adaptive leaders may choose an achievement-oriented leadership style when they believe that team members are capable of exceeding their current performance levels. This approach involves setting challenging goals, encouraging innovation, and fostering a culture of continuous improvement.

7. **Monitoring and Adaptation:** Adaptive leaders continuously monitor the effectiveness of their chosen leadership style. They are open to feedback from team members and are willing to adjust their approach if the situation evolves or if the current style is not yielding the desired results.

8. **Communication and Transparency:** Adaptive leaders maintain open and transparent communication with their team members. They explain the rationale behind their

leadership choices and ensure that team members understand how their behaviors align with the team's goals.
9. **Employee Development:** Adaptive leaders support the development of their team members by identifying areas for growth and providing opportunities for skill enhancement. This investment in employee development contributes to long-term success.

Adaptive leadership within the Path-Goal Theory emphasizes the importance of flexibility and situational awareness in leadership. Effective leaders recognize that there is no one-size-fits-all approach and that the success of their team depends on their ability to adapt their leadership behaviors to the specific needs and challenges encountered. By doing so, leaders can create a dynamic and motivating work environment that facilitates goal attainment and enhances team members' motivation and satisfaction.

*****

CHAPTER TEN
Servant and coaching leadership

Servant leadership emphasizes the leader's role in serving the team and meeting their needs, coaching leadership focuses on providing guidance and support to help individuals within the team grow and excel. Both approaches aim to create a positive and productive work environment, but they do so through different means and priorities.

Servant Leadership

Servant leadership is a leadership philosophy and approach where the leader's primary focus is on serving and supporting their team members rather than asserting authority or power over them. The leader sees themselves as a servant to their team, working to meet their needs, remove obstacles, and facilitate their growth and development. Key principles of servant leadership include empathy, humility, and a commitment to the well-being and success of others. This approach believes that by serving the team, leaders can create a more motivated and empowered group that, in turn, achieves better results.

Coaching Leadership

Coaching leadership, on the other hand, is a leadership style where the leader takes on the role of a coach to their team members. This means that the leader provides guidance, feedback, and support to help individuals improve their skills, reach their goals, and maximize their potential. Coaching leaders often engage in one-on-one discussions with team members to identify strengths and weaknesses, set goals, and create plans for development. They also encourage self-discovery and problem-solving within the team, fostering a culture of continuous learning and improvement.

Significance of Servant and Coaching Leadership

Understanding the significance of both servant leadership and coaching leadership is essential for effective leadership practices. Significance of each approach is:

Significance of Servant Leadership

1. **Empowerment and Trust:** Servant leadership empowers team members by giving them autonomy and trust. When leaders prioritize the well-being and development of their team, it creates a culture of trust and collaboration.

2. **Enhanced Motivation:** By serving their team members, leaders can boost motivation and commitment. Team members feel valued and are more likely to be engaged when they know their leader cares about their success.

3. **Long-Term Growth:** Servant leadership fosters long-term growth and success. When leaders invest in the growth and development of their team, it leads to a more skilled and capable workforce, which can drive sustained organizational success.

4. **Improved Relationships:** This approach promotes strong relationships between leaders and team members. Leaders who are empathetic and supportive are better able to understand their team's needs and address them effectively.

5. **Adaptability:** Servant leaders are often more adaptable and open to feedback. They are willing to make changes to their leadership style based on the needs of their team, leading to increased flexibility in leadership.

Significance of Coaching Leadership

1. **Skill Development:** Coaching leadership is highly effective in developing the skills and capabilities of team members. Leaders who act as coaches provide guidance and support for continuous improvement.

2. **Goal Achievement:** Coaching leaders help team members set and achieve their goals. This approach aligns individual and team objectives with the organization's goals, increasing the likelihood of success.

3. **Problem Solving:** Coaching leaders encourage critical thinking and problem-solving among team members. This empowers individuals to find solutions to challenges, leading to a more self-reliant and resourceful team.

4. **Feedback Culture:** Coaching leadership fosters a culture of constructive feedback. Leaders regularly provide feedback, which helps team members understand their strengths and areas for improvement.

5. **Personalized Approach:** Coaching is a personalized approach to leadership. Leaders tailor their guidance to the unique needs and aspirations of each team member, promoting individual growth and satisfaction.

6. **High Performance:** Coaching leadership often results in higher team performance. When team members receive continuous support and feedback, they are more likely to perform at their best.

Both servant leadership and coaching leadership have significant advantages. Servant leadership emphasizes trust, motivation, and long-term growth, while coaching leadership focuses on skill development, goal achievement, and problem-solving. Many effective leaders incorporate elements of both approaches, recognizing that a combination of servant and coaching leadership can lead to a well-rounded and successful leadership style.

Empathy, Support, and Personal Growth in Servant and Coaching Leadership

Empathy, support, and personal growth are central themes in both servant leadership and coaching leadership. See how these qualities are emphasized in these leadership approaches:

Emphasis on Empathy

- **Servant Leadership:** Servant leaders prioritize empathy by seeking to understand the emotions, perspectives, and needs of their team members. They actively listen to their concerns, demonstrate care, and show a genuine interest in their well-being.

- **Coaching Leadership:** Coaching leaders also employ empathy when working with team members. They put themselves in their employees' shoes, considering their feelings and challenges. This empathetic approach helps build trust and rapport.

Emphasis on Support

- **Servant Leadership:** Servant leaders offer substantial support to their team members. They remove obstacles and provide the necessary resources to help individuals excel. They act as advocates for their team and are willing to step in when help is needed.

- **Coaching Leadership:** Coaching leaders provide continuous support through guidance, feedback, and mentorship. They create an environment where team members feel comfortable seeking assistance and know that their leader is there to help them overcome obstacles.

Emphasis on Personal Growth

- **Servant Leadership:** Servant leaders are committed to the personal growth and development of their team members. They encourage learning opportunities and create a culture that values self-improvement. They invest in training and development to help individuals reach their full potential.
- **Coaching Leadership:** Coaching leaders have a strong focus on personal growth. They work with team members to identify strengths and weaknesses, set goals, and create development plans. This helps individuals grow both professionally and personally.

In both leadership approaches, empathy, support, and personal growth are significant because they:

1. **Foster Trust:** These qualities build trust between leaders and team members. When team members feel understood and supported, they are more likely to trust their leader's intentions and decisions.
2. **Boost Motivation:** Empathetic leaders who provide support and opportunities for growth inspire greater motivation and commitment among team members.
3. **Enhance Team Performance:** Team members who receive support and guidance tend to perform better individually and collectively, leading to improved overall team performance.
4. **Create a Positive Work Environment:** These leadership qualities contribute to a positive and inclusive work environment where individuals feel valued and encouraged to contribute their best efforts.
5. **Facilitate Personal and Professional Development:** Team members benefit from these leadership approaches by experiencing personal and professional growth, which can have a lasting impact on their careers and lives.

Both servant leadership and coaching leadership place a strong emphasis on empathy, support, and personal growth because they recognize the profound positive effects these qualities have on individuals, teams, and organizations as a whole.

Servant Leadership

Servant leadership is a leadership approach characterized by its emphasis on empathy, support, and ethical influence. In this model, leaders prioritize understanding the needs and concerns of their team members, demonstrating empathy by actively listening and showing genuine care. They provide unwavering support by removing obstacles, offering resources, and acting as advocates for their team's well-being and success. Importantly, servant leaders wield ethical influence, making decisions guided by moral and ethical principles, ensuring fairness, and setting a positive example for their teams. This leadership style fosters trust, motivates team members, and creates a culture of collaboration and ethical behavior within the organization, ultimately leading to enhanced individual and collective growth and achievement.

Servant leadership is a leadership philosophy that revolves around the idea of serving and prioritizing the needs of others above one's own. It represents a significant shift from the traditional top-down, authoritative leadership style and places the leader in the role of a servant to their team or organization.

1. **Priority on Serving Others:** Servant leaders fundamentally view their role as one of service. They prioritize the needs, well-being, and development of their team members or employees. This means that the leader's primary goal is to help others succeed, rather than seeking personal power or recognition.
2. **Empathy and Understanding:** Servant leaders are deeply empathetic and strive to understand the perspectives, feelings, and challenges of those they lead. They actively

listen to their team members and show genuine care and concern for their concerns and aspirations.
3. **Support and Encouragement:** Servant leaders provide unwavering support to their team. They remove obstacles, offer resources, and create an environment where individuals feel empowered to take risks and grow. They offer guidance and mentorship to help team members reach their full potential.
4. **Ethical and Moral Guidance:** Ethics and morality play a significant role in servant leadership. Leaders make decisions guided by a strong sense of ethics, fairness, and integrity. They lead by example, setting high ethical standards for the entire organization.
5. **Focus on Personal Growth:** Servant leaders are committed to the personal and professional growth of their team members. They encourage continuous learning, provide opportunities for skill development, and invest in training and education.
6. **Collaboration and Team Building:** Servant leaders foster a collaborative and inclusive environment. They value teamwork and actively work to build a sense of community and unity among team members.
7. **Long-Term Results:** Servant leadership is not about quick wins or short-term gains. It's focused on creating sustainable success and growth, both for individuals and the organization as a whole.
8. **Influence and Impact:** Despite their servant orientation, servant leaders often wield significant influence. Their actions and commitment to serving others inspire trust and respect, which can lead to strong team cohesion and high-performance outcomes.
9. **Continuous Improvement:** Servant leadership is a journey of continuous improvement. Leaders constantly refine their skills, deepen their understanding of their team's needs, and adapt their approach to ensure they are effectively serving their team.

Servant leadership is a leadership philosophy that revolves around serving and prioritizing the needs of others. It is characterized by empathy, support, ethical behavior, and a commitment to personal and collective growth. Servant leaders aim to create a positive and empowering work environment that fosters trust, collaboration, and long-term success.

Historical Context

The historical context of the servant leadership theory provides insight into its development, evolution, and the factors that influenced its emergence as a distinct leadership philosophy. Here's a detailed explanation of the historical context of the servant leadership theory:

1. **Ancient Philosophical Roots:** The roots of servant leadership can be traced back to ancient philosophical traditions, such as Confucianism in China and Stoicism in Greece. These philosophies emphasized moral virtues, humility, and the idea that leaders should serve the greater good. Confucian scholars, for instance, emphasized the importance of benevolent leadership and service to society.
2. **Religious Foundations:** Many of the principles of servant leadership find resonance in religious teachings. In Christianity, Jesus Christ is often considered a quintessential servant leader, exemplified by his acts of washing his disciples' feet and prioritizing the needs of others. The Bible contains numerous passages that encourage humility and service as virtues for leaders. Similarly, Islamic teachings stress the importance of leaders serving their communities with justice and compassion.
3. **Greenleaf's Influence:** The modern concept of servant leadership was popularized by Robert K. Greenleaf, an American essayist, and management expert. In 1970, Greenleaf published an essay titled "The Servant as Leader,"

where he coined the term "servant leadership" and introduced it as a transformative leadership concept. Greenleaf's experiences working in various organizations, including AT&T, and his interest in ethical leadership influenced his development of this theory.

4. **Social and Cultural Movements:** The 1960s and 1970s were marked by significant social and cultural shifts, including the civil rights movement, anti-war protests, and a growing emphasis on social justice and equality. These movements challenged traditional leadership paradigms and encouraged leaders to adopt more inclusive, empathetic, and service-oriented approaches.

5. **Business Applications:** Servant leadership began to gain traction in the business world in the latter half of the 20th century. As organizations sought ways to improve employee engagement, satisfaction, and productivity, leaders recognized the potential benefits of servant leadership principles. For instance, companies like Southwest Airlines, under the leadership of Herb Kelleher, embraced servant leadership and achieved notable success.

6. **Academic Exploration:** The concept of servant leadership also gained academic attention. Scholars and researchers conducted studies to investigate the impact of servant leadership on organizational outcomes, employee well-being, and team performance. This academic research provided empirical support for the effectiveness of servant leadership in various contexts.

7. **Contemporary Relevance:** Today, servant leadership remains relevant in contemporary leadership discussions. In an era characterized by complex challenges, ethical dilemmas, and a focus on responsible leadership, the principles of empathy, support, and ethical influence central to servant leadership are highly valued. Many organizations incorporate servant leadership principles into their leadership development programs and corporate cultures.

The historical context of the servant leadership theory spans centuries and draws from diverse philosophical, religious, cultural, and social influences. It has evolved from ancient philosophical ideas and religious teachings to become a prominent and respected leadership philosophy in the modern world, emphasizing the importance of serving others, ethical leadership, and the well-being of both individuals and organizations.

Key Proponents

Servant leadership has gained recognition and influence over the years thanks to the contributions and advocacy of various proponents. Key proponents of the servant leadership theory include:

1. **Robert K. Greenleaf:** Robert K. Greenleaf is often regarded as the founding father and one of the most influential proponents of servant leadership. He introduced the concept in his essay "The Servant as Leader" in 1970. Greenleaf's writings and lectures laid the foundation for the modern understanding of servant leadership, emphasizing the leader's role as a servant to their team and the importance of ethical and empathetic leadership.

2. **Larry C. Spears:** Larry C. Spears, a former CEO of the Greenleaf Center for Servant Leadership, played a pivotal role in popularizing and furthering Greenleaf's ideas. He contributed to the development of the Ten Characteristics of Servant Leaders, which provide a framework for understanding and practicing servant leadership.

3. **Max DePree:** Max DePree, former CEO of Herman Miller, Inc., and author of "Leadership Is an Art" and "Leadership Jazz," advocated for servant leadership in the business world. His writings emphasized the importance of leaders serving and enabling the success of their employees.

4. **Stephen R. Covey:** While Stephen R. Covey is best known for his work on personal effectiveness and "The 7 Habits of Highly Effective People," he also contributed to the popularization of servant leadership concepts. Covey stressed the importance of the servant leadership paradigm in building strong, trust-based relationships within organizations.

5. **Ken Blanchard:** Ken Blanchard, a renowned leadership author and speaker, incorporated servant leadership principles into his leadership models, such as "Situational Leadership II." He highlighted the idea that leadership is about serving the needs of others and adapting leadership styles to match the needs of team members.

6. **Ann McGee-Cooper and Duane Trammell:** The co-authors of "You Don't Have to Go Home from Work Exhausted!" are known for promoting servant leadership principles in the workplace. They provide practical guidance on applying servant leadership concepts to improve work environments and team dynamics.

7. **Simon Sinek:** Simon Sinek, known for his book "Start with Why," emphasizes the importance of servant leadership in creating environments where people feel valued, motivated, and inspired. He believes that leaders who prioritize the needs of their team members can create organizations with a strong sense of purpose and loyalty.

8. **James C. Hunter:** In his book "The Servant: A Simple Story About the True Essence of Leadership," James C. Hunter presents a fictional narrative that explores servant leadership principles in action. He uses storytelling to illustrate the transformational impact of servant leadership on individuals and organizations.

These proponents have played a significant role in advancing the servant leadership theory, promoting its adoption in various sectors, and demonstrating the positive impact of this leadership philosophy on individuals, teams, and organizations. Their writings, teachings, and practical applications have contributed to the widespread recognition and acceptance of servant leadership as a valuable approach to leadership.

Core Principles of Servant Leadership

The core principles of servant leadership encapsulate the fundamental values and beliefs that guide this leadership philosophy. At its essence, servant leadership revolves around the idea that a leader's primary role is to serve others, prioritizing their needs, well-being, and personal and professional growth. These principles encompass concepts such as empathy, humility, ethical influence, and a deep commitment to fostering a sense of community within an organization. Servant leaders embrace the idea that by serving their team members and employees, they can inspire trust, encourage collaboration, and create an environment where individuals thrive and achieve their full potential. It's a leadership style grounded in the belief that the success of the leader is measured by the success and flourishing of those they lead, embodying the principle that true leadership is a service to others rather than an exercise of power or authority.

Servant leadership is guided by several fundamental principles, each of which plays a crucial role in shaping this leadership philosophy. Three key principles of Servant leadership are: empathy, stewardship, and ethical influence.

Empathy

Empathy is at the heart of servant leadership. Servant leaders strive to understand and connect with the emotions, perspectives, and needs of their team members or followers. This involves active listening, putting oneself in another's shoes, and showing genuine care and concern. Empathetic leaders create an environment where individuals feel heard, valued, and supported.

1. **Listening:** Servant leaders listen not just to respond but to truly understand. They give their full attention to what others are saying and refrain from making quick judgments or assumptions.
2. **Compassion:** Compassion is a hallmark of servant leadership. Leaders express empathy by acknowledging and empathizing with the challenges and experiences of their team members, offering comfort and support when needed.
3. **Walking in Their Shoes:** Empathetic leaders try to see situations from the perspective of their team members. This helps them make decisions that consider the impact on individuals and foster trust.

Stewardship

Servant leaders view themselves as stewards of the organization and its resources, rather than as owners or controllers. They understand that their role is to manage these resources for the benefit of the greater good, which includes the well-being and growth of their team and the organization as a whole. This perspective encourages responsible and sustainable leadership.

1. **Resource Management:** Servant leaders are diligent in managing resources efficiently and ethically. This includes financial resources, human capital, and the organization's reputation.
2. **Long-Term Perspective:** Stewardship emphasizes long-term thinking and planning. Leaders consider the impact of their decisions on future generations and the sustainability of the organization.

3. **Accountability:** Stewardship comes with a sense of accountability. Leaders are accountable to their team, stakeholders, and the broader community for their decisions and actions.

Ethical Influence

Ethical influence is a cornerstone of servant leadership. Leaders prioritize ethical behavior and decision-making, setting high standards of integrity for themselves and their teams. They lead by example and inspire trust through their unwavering commitment to ethical principles.

1. **Integrity:** Servant leaders demonstrate unwavering integrity in all their actions. They are honest, transparent, and consistent in their behavior and decision-making.
2. **Fairness:** Ethical influence includes treating everyone with fairness and justice. Leaders avoid favoritism and bias and ensure that decisions are made based on merit and ethical considerations.
3. **Moral Courage:** Servant leaders are not afraid to stand up for what is right, even in the face of challenges or adversity. They exhibit moral courage by upholding ethical standards and confronting unethical behavior.

These fundamental principles of servant leadership—empathy, stewardship, and ethical influence—guide leaders in creating a workplace culture that values the well-being and growth of individuals, fosters trust and collaboration, and operates with a strong ethical foundation. Servant leaders recognize that their success is intrinsically tied to the success and flourishing of those they lead, and these principles serve as a compass to navigate the complexities of leadership while remaining true to the philosophy of servant leadership.

Real Worl Examples

Empathy

Example: Tim Cook, CEO of Apple Inc.

Tim Cook has demonstrated empathy in his leadership role at Apple. When he publicly came out as gay, he used his position to advocate for LGBTQ+ rights and inclusivity. This act of vulnerability and empathy sent a powerful message of support to LGBTQ+ employees and communities worldwide. Cook's leadership shows that leaders can use their influence to champion important social causes and demonstrate empathy toward marginalized groups.

Stewardship

Example: Patagonia

Patagonia, the outdoor clothing and gear company, is known for its strong commitment to environmental stewardship. The company donates a percentage of its profits to environmental causes, uses sustainable materials in its products, and actively participates in environmental activism. This commitment to stewardship not only aligns with Patagonia's brand but also demonstrates responsible management of resources for the greater good.

Ethical Influence

Example: Dr. Anthony Fauci, Director of the National Institute of Allergy and Infectious Diseases (NIAID)

Dr. Anthony Fauci has become a trusted figure in the field of public health due to his consistent ethical influence. Throughout the COVID-19 pandemic, he provided evidence-based guidance, even when facing political pressures. His commitment to transparent communication and adherence to scientific principles earned him public trust and demonstrated ethical leadership in the face of a global crisis.

Empathy, Stewardship, and Ethical Influence Combined

Example: Bill and Melinda Gates Foundation

The Gates Foundation, led by Bill and Melinda Gates, exemplifies all three servant leadership principles. Through their philanthropic work, they demonstrate empathy by addressing pressing global issues, such as poverty and healthcare. They act as stewards by responsibly managing their immense wealth and resources to support initiatives like global health and education. Additionally, their ethical influence is evident in their commitment to transparency, accountability, and evidence-based solutions, which have earned the trust of governments, organizations, and communities worldwide.

These real-world examples show that servant leadership principles can be effectively put into practice in various contexts, from corporate leadership to public health and philanthropy. They demonstrate that leaders who prioritize empathy, stewardship, and ethical influence can make a positive impact on their organizations, communities, and the world at large.

Role of Empathy and Support

The role of empathy and support in leadership is to create a nurturing and motivating environment where individuals feel understood, valued, and empowered. Empathy involves the ability to understand and connect with the emotions, perspectives, and needs of team members or followers. It helps leaders make informed decisions, foster trust, and demonstrate genuine care for the well-being of their team. Support, on the other hand, involves providing guidance, resources, and encouragement to help individuals overcome challenges and reach their full potential. Together, empathy and support enhance motivation, build strong relationships, and empower individuals to perform at their best, contributing to a positive and productive work culture.

The role of empathy and support in servant leadership is foundational to the philosophy's core principles. These elements are essential for creating a leadership style that prioritizes the needs, well-being, and growth of individuals and teams.

Empathy

1. **Understanding and Connection:** Servant leaders actively practice empathy by seeking to understand the emotions, perspectives, and challenges of their team members. This understanding forms the basis for effective communication and decision-making. It helps leaders connect with their team on a deeper level, fostering trust and rapport.
2. **Enhanced Communication:** Empathetic leaders are skilled listeners who genuinely care about the concerns and ideas of their team. This open and empathetic communication creates an environment where individuals feel heard and valued, leading to improved collaboration and innovation.
3. **Conflict Resolution:** Empathy plays a critical role in resolving conflicts constructively. Leaders who can empathize with the viewpoints of conflicting parties are better equipped to mediate disputes and find mutually beneficial solutions.
4. **Motivation:** By demonstrating empathy, leaders can boost motivation among team members. When employees feel that their leader cares about their well-being and development, they are more likely to be engaged and committed to their work.

Support

1. **Resource Allocation:** Servant leaders provide the necessary resources and tools to help individuals and teams succeed. They remove obstacles and ensure that team members have what they need to achieve their goals, whether it's training, technology, or mentorship.
2. **Personal and Professional Growth:** Supportive leaders are committed to the personal and professional growth of their team. They encourage learning opportunities, skill development, and career advancement, aligning individual goals with the organization's objectives.
3. **Mentorship and Coaching:** Servant leaders often take on the role of mentors and coaches, offering guidance and feedback to help individuals improve their skills and navigate challenges. They promote a culture of continuous learning and development.
4. **Psychological Safety:** Supportive leaders create an environment of psychological safety where team members feel comfortable taking risks, sharing ideas, and admitting mistakes. This fosters innovation and creativity within the team.
5. **Employee Well-Being:** Servant leaders prioritize the well-being of their team members, recognizing that individuals who feel supported and valued are more likely to experience job satisfaction and reduced stress.

The role of empathy and support in servant leadership is not merely a passive practice but an active commitment to understanding and serving the needs of others. These qualities create a positive and empowering work environment where individuals are motivated to contribute their best efforts, collaborate effectively, and achieve their full potential. Ultimately, servant leaders who prioritize empathy and support build strong, resilient, and high-performing teams, leading to organizational success and growth.

Strategies for Leaders to Develop Empathy and Support

Developing and demonstrating empathy and support for teams is crucial for effective leadership, particularly in the context of servant leadership. Here are strategies for leaders to cultivate and exhibit these qualities:

1. **Active Listening:**

    - Practice active listening by giving your full attention to team members during conversations. Put away distractions and focus on what they are saying.

    - Use non-verbal cues, such as nodding and maintaining eye contact, to show that you are engaged and genuinely interested in their perspective.

    - Ask open-ended questions to encourage team members to express their thoughts, feelings, and ideas more freely.

2. **Empathetic Communication:**

    - Show empathy by acknowledging and validating team members' emotions and experiences. Use phrases like, "I understand how you feel," or "That must have been challenging."

    - Avoid judgment or criticism when team members share their concerns or difficulties. Create a safe space for open and honest communication.

    - Use empathetic body language, such as a warm smile or a comforting gesture, to convey your understanding and support.

4. **Walk in Their Shoes:**

    - Make an effort to see situations from your team members' perspective. Consider their challenges, motivations, and aspirations when making decisions or providing feedback.

- Encourage team members to share their viewpoints and actively seek out their input when making important choices that affect the team or organization.

5. **Provide Emotional Support:**

    - Offer emotional support when team members are facing personal or professional challenges. Be available to listen and provide a compassionate ear.

    - Recognize and celebrate their successes and milestones, both big and small, to show that you genuinely care about their well-being and achievements.

6. **Lead by Example:**

    - Demonstrate the behaviors and values you expect from your team. Model empathy, humility, and ethical conduct in your actions and decisions.

    - Share stories of your own challenges and experiences, highlighting how you've learned and grown from them. This vulnerability can create a sense of connection and understanding.

7. **Customize Support:**

    - Tailor your support to the unique needs and preferences of each team member. Recognize that different individuals may require different forms of support.

    - Regularly check in with team members to understand their goals and challenges. Use this information to provide personalized guidance and resources.

8. **Encourage Growth and Development:**
    - Create opportunities for skill development and career advancement within the team. Offer training, mentorship, and coaching to help team members reach their full potential.
    - Set clear expectations and provide constructive feedback to aid in their growth. Focus on helping them develop their strengths and address areas for improvement.

9. **Be Consistent and Reliable:**
    - Build trust by consistently demonstrating empathy and support. Team members should feel confident that you will be there for them, no matter the circumstances.
    - Keep your promises and follow through on commitments. Reliability and consistency in your support foster trust and respect.

10. **Seek Feedback:**
    - Actively solicit feedback from team members on your leadership style and how you can better support them. Use this input to make improvements and adjustments.
    - Show that you are open to constructive criticism and are willing to make changes based on their feedback.

By implementing these strategies, leaders can foster a culture of empathy and support within their teams, which, in turn, enhances trust, collaboration, and overall team performance. These practices align closely with the principles of servant leadership and contribute to a positive and empowering work environment.

Case Study

A case study illustrating the successful application of servant leadership showcases a real-world example where a leader has effectively employed the principles of empathy, support, and ethical influence to achieve positive outcomes. In such a case, a leader prioritizes the needs and development of their team members, fosters a collaborative and inclusive work environment, and demonstrates a strong commitment to ethical behavior. Through this application of servant leadership, the organization or team typically experiences improved employee satisfaction, enhanced performance, and a culture of trust and empowerment. These successful cases serve as compelling evidence that servant leadership can lead to tangible benefits in various organizational contexts.

Herb Kelleher and Southwest Airlines

Background

Herb Kelleher, co-founder and former CEO of Southwest Airlines, is widely recognized for his embodiment of servant leadership principles in the airline industry. Under his leadership, Southwest became one of the most successful and admired airlines in the world.

Application of Servant Leadership

1. **Putting Employees First:** Kelleher placed a strong emphasis on his employees, often referring to them as "my most important customers." He believed that if employees were treated well, they would, in turn, provide exceptional service to customers. To demonstrate this commitment, he provided extensive training, competitive wages, and opportunities for advancement within the company.

2. **Empowerment and Trust:** Kelleher fostered a culture of empowerment and trust. He trusted his employees to make decisions that aligned with the company's values and objectives. Flight attendants and ground staff had the flexibility to solve problems in creative ways, such as singing safety instructions or having fun during flights, which became a hallmark of Southwest's service.

3. **Accessibility and Open Communication:** Kelleher maintained an open-door policy, making himself readily accessible to employees at all levels of the organization. He actively sought input and feedback from employees and listened to their concerns and ideas. This accessibility created a sense of inclusion and valued contribution among the workforce.

4. **Crisis Management with Compassion:** During crises, such as the aftermath of the 9/11 attacks and economic downturns, Kelleher prioritized the welfare of employees over profits. Rather than resorting to layoffs, he implemented creative solutions like offering voluntary leave and part-time work to preserve jobs and benefits.

5. **Community Engagement:** Kelleher's servant leadership extended beyond the organization. He was deeply involved in community engagement and philanthropy, reflecting his belief in serving the broader community. Southwest Airlines actively supported charitable initiatives and disaster relief efforts.

Results and Impact

The practical application of servant leadership by Herb Kelleher at Southwest Airlines yielded remarkable results:

1. **Employee Satisfaction:** Southwest consistently ranked high in employee satisfaction and was recognized as a great place to work.

2. **Customer Loyalty:** The company's focus on employee well-being translated into exceptional customer service and high customer loyalty.

3. **Profitability:** Despite challenging economic periods in the airline industry, Southwest remained profitable, showcasing that a servant leadership approach could lead to financial success.

4. **Organizational Culture:** Kelleher's servant leadership approach shaped the unique and vibrant culture of Southwest Airlines, known for its humor, informality, and strong sense of camaraderie.

Herb Kelleher's leadership at Southwest Airlines is a compelling real-life case study of servant leadership in action. His commitment to employees, empowerment, trust, open communication, and community engagement not only fostered a positive workplace culture but also contributed to the airline's sustained success and industry leadership. Kelleher's legacy continues to inspire leaders worldwide to adopt servant leadership principles in their own organizations.

Analysis of Empathetic and Supportive Approach

The leader's empathetic and supportive approach, exemplified by Herb Kelleher's leadership at Southwest Airlines, made significant contributions to the airline's remarkable success. Here's a detailed analysis of how his empathetic and supportive leadership style played a pivotal role in achieving positive outcomes:

1. **Employee Satisfaction and Commitment:** Herb Kelleher's commitment to putting employees first and creating a supportive work environment led to high levels of employee satisfaction and commitment. When employees feel valued, supported, and heard, they are more motivated to go above

and beyond in their roles. This commitment translated into exceptional customer service, which became a key differentiator for Southwest Airlines and contributed to its success.

2. **Customer Loyalty:** The empathetic and supportive leadership approach fostered a culture where employees genuinely cared about the well-being of passengers. Flight attendants and ground staff were empowered to provide excellent service, often going the extra mile to make passengers' experiences enjoyable. As a result, Southwest Airlines gained a reputation for exceptional customer service and built strong customer loyalty, which directly contributed to its profitability and market share.

3. **Employee Empowerment and Innovation:** Kelleher's emphasis on trust and empowerment encouraged employees to think creatively and make decisions in the best interest of both customers and the company. This empowerment led to innovative practices, such as the famous humorous in-flight announcements, which not only delighted passengers but also set Southwest apart from competitors. Empowered employees felt a sense of ownership over their roles, leading to a continuous stream of innovative ideas.

4. **Crisis Resilience:** During challenging times, such as economic downturns and the aftermath of the 9/11 attacks, Kelleher's empathetic leadership came to the forefront. Instead of resorting to layoffs, he implemented compassionate solutions like offering voluntary leave and part-time work to preserve jobs and benefits. This approach not only minimized the negative impact on employees but also maintained morale and readiness for recovery when conditions improved.

5. **Strong Organizational Culture:** The empathetic and supportive approach nurtured a distinctive organizational culture at Southwest Airlines. The company became known for its informal, fun, and employee-centric culture, characterized by camaraderie and a shared sense of purpose.

This culture played a vital role in attracting and retaining talent and in shaping the airline's identity.

6. **Competitive Advantage:** Southwest's unique culture and focus on employee and customer satisfaction provided a sustainable competitive advantage. While other airlines struggled with labor disputes, customer complaints, and financial challenges, Southwest remained profitable and maintained a positive public image. This competitive edge contributed to the airline's long-term success and resilience.

Herb Kelleher's empathetic and supportive leadership approach at Southwest Airlines created a virtuous cycle. By valuing and supporting employees, he inspired a sense of ownership, innovation, and commitment among the workforce, which, in turn, translated into outstanding customer service, customer loyalty, and financial success. This holistic leadership style not only shaped the airline's culture but also set a precedent for servant leadership's practical effectiveness in achieving organizational excellence and industry leadership.

Nurturing Leadership through Serving Others

Nurturing leadership through serving others encapsulates the philosophy of servant leadership, where leaders prioritize the well-being, growth, and development of their team members or followers. In this approach, leaders recognize that their primary role is to support and empower others, fostering an environment where individuals can thrive. By nurturing leadership through service, leaders encourage personal and professional growth in their teams, build trust and collaboration, and ultimately contribute to the success of both individuals and the organization as a whole. This approach emphasizes the idea that true leadership is about selflessly serving others and helping them reach their full potential.

Servant Leadership Benefits

Adopting a servant leadership approach can yield a multitude of benefits for both leaders and organizations. Here's an in-depth explanation of the advantages, including improved morale, trust, and organizational effectiveness:

1. **Enhanced Morale and Job Satisfaction:** Servant leadership places a strong emphasis on the well-being and growth of employees. When leaders actively support and invest in their team members, it fosters a sense of value and appreciation. As a result, employees experience higher job satisfaction, engagement, and morale. They feel more motivated to contribute their best efforts because they recognize that their leader genuinely cares about their happiness and success.
2. **Trust and Credibility:** Servant leaders build trust through their consistent and ethical behavior. By prioritizing the needs of their team members and operating with transparency and integrity, they establish themselves as trustworthy leaders. This trust forms the foundation of strong relationships within the organization, leading to open communication, collaboration, and a positive work culture.
3. **Improved Employee Retention:** When employees feel supported, valued, and empowered, they are more likely to remain loyal to the organization. Servant leaders often experience lower turnover rates because employees are less inclined to seek opportunities elsewhere. Reduced turnover not only saves recruitment and training costs but also promotes stability and continuity within the workforce.
4. **Increased Employee Engagement:** Servant leadership encourages active participation and involvement from team

members. Leaders who provide support, autonomy, and opportunities for growth tend to have more engaged employees. Engaged employees are more committed to their work, take ownership of their responsibilities, and are more likely to go the extra mile to achieve organizational goals.

5. **Greater Innovation and Creativity:** A supportive and empowering environment encourages employees to think creatively and share their ideas without fear of criticism. Servant leaders recognize that innovation can come from any level of the organization, so they actively seek and promote new ideas. This openness to innovation can lead to creative solutions and a culture of continuous improvement.

6. **Enhanced Team Collaboration:** Servant leaders emphasize collaboration and teamwork. By fostering a culture of trust and mutual respect, they encourage employees to work together effectively. Team members are more likely to share knowledge, resources, and expertise, leading to improved problem-solving and decision-making processes.

7. **Organizational Effectiveness:** Servant leadership contributes to overall organizational effectiveness. Leaders who prioritize the growth and well-being of employees build strong, cohesive teams that can adapt to challenges and drive results. The organization benefits from improved performance, efficiency, and productivity.

8. **Positive Organizational Culture:** Servant leaders help shape a positive organizational culture characterized by empathy, ethics, and inclusivity. This culture attracts top talent, enhances the organization's reputation, and contributes to long-term sustainability and success.

9. **Employee Development and Leadership Pipeline:** Servant leaders invest in the development of their team members, which often results in a pipeline of future leaders within the organization. By nurturing leadership skills and encouraging growth, servant leaders create a legacy of capable leaders who can carry the organization forward.

Adopting a servant leadership approach brings a host of benefits that positively impact both individuals and organizations. These advantages include improved morale, trust, and organizational effectiveness. Servant leaders create environments where employees feel valued, empowered, and motivated, leading to higher engagement, creativity, and loyalty, which ultimately contribute to the long-term success and sustainability of the organization.

Lead to a Positive organizational Culture

Servant leadership has the potential to profoundly impact and shape a positive organizational culture. Here's how servant leadership can contribute to creating such a culture:

1. **Fosters Trust and Open Communication:** Servant leaders prioritize trust and openness. By actively listening to their team members, demonstrating empathy, and being transparent in their actions and decisions, they create an atmosphere of trust. Team members feel comfortable sharing their ideas, concerns, and feedback, knowing that their leader genuinely cares and values their input.
2. **Encourages Collaboration and Teamwork:** Servant leaders emphasize the importance of collaboration and teamwork. They promote a sense of community where individuals work together towards common goals. This collaborative spirit reduces silos, enhances cross-functional cooperation, and fosters a sense of unity among employees.
3. **Values Diversity and Inclusion:** Servant leaders recognize the unique strengths and perspectives that each team member brings to the table. They create an inclusive culture where diversity is celebrated and leveraged for innovation and problem-solving. This not only fosters a more vibrant work environment but also leads to better decision-making.

4. **Prioritize Employee Well-Being:** Servant leaders genuinely care about the well-being of their team members. They ensure that employees are provided with the support and resources needed to thrive, both personally and professionally. This concern for well-being reduces stress, burnout, and absenteeism while increasing job satisfaction and loyalty.
5. **Promotes Accountability and Responsibility:** Servant leaders set clear expectations and hold team members accountable for their actions and results. However, they do so with fairness and empathy. This approach encourages individuals to take ownership of their responsibilities and deliver on their commitments.
6. **Embraces Ethical Conduct:** Ethical behavior is a cornerstone of servant leadership. Leaders who prioritize ethics and integrity set a strong example for their teams. This commitment to ethical conduct trickles down through the organization, creating a culture of honesty, fairness, and ethical decision-making.
7. **Supports Growth and Development:** Servant leaders invest in the growth and development of their team members. They provide learning opportunities, mentorship, and coaching to help individuals reach their full potential. This emphasis on personal and professional growth fosters a culture of continuous learning and improvement.
8. **Celebrate Success and Recognize Contributions:** Servant leaders celebrate the achievements and contributions of their team members. They understand the importance of recognition and appreciation. Acknowledging individual and collective successes reinforces a positive culture of appreciation and motivates employees to excel.
9. **Encourages Innovation and Creativity:** In an environment where employees feel supported, trusted, and valued, they are more likely to take risks and share creative ideas. Servant leaders actively seek out and encourage innovative thinking,

leading to a culture of continuous innovation and improvement.
10. **Demonstrates Humility:** Servant leaders exhibit humility by acknowledging their own imperfections and mistakes. This vulnerability encourages a culture where others feel comfortable admitting their errors, fostering a culture of continuous improvement and learning. Servant leaders exhibit humility by acknowledging their own imperfections and mistakes. This vulnerability encourages a culture where others feel comfortable admitting their errors, fostering a culture of continuous improvement and learning.

Servant leadership contributes significantly to a positive organizational culture by creating an environment characterized by trust, collaboration, inclusivity, ethical conduct, and support for personal and professional growth. Such a culture not only enhances employee satisfaction but also boosts organizational effectiveness, adaptability, and overall success.

Challenges and Criticisms

Challenges and criticisms associated with servant leadership revolve around its practical implementation and potential drawbacks. Some challenges include the difficulty of balancing the needs of individuals with organizational goals, as well as the risk of leaders being perceived as overly lenient or ineffective in making tough decisions. Critics argue that servant leadership may not be suitable for all organizational contexts, particularly those requiring strict hierarchies and rapid decision-making. Additionally, it can be challenging to measure the effectiveness of servant leadership and quantify its impact on organizational outcomes. Despite these challenges and criticisms, many proponents argue that when properly adapted and applied, servant leadership can foster a positive work culture, enhance employee engagement, and contribute to long-term organizational success.

Servant leadership, while celebrated for its positive attributes, is not without its challenges and criticisms. Here's a detailed discussion of some of the key concerns:

1. **Balancing Individual Needs with Organizational Goals**
   - **Challenge:** One of the primary challenges of servant leadership is striking the right balance between meeting the individual needs of team members and achieving the organization's goals. Some critics argue that an excessive focus on serving individuals may come at the expense of organizational performance.
   - **Response:** Servant leaders must be adept at aligning individual aspirations and organizational objectives. This involves setting clear expectations and priorities while still providing support and opportunities for personal growth.

3. **Perceived Weakness or Ineffectiveness**
   - **Challenge:** Servant leaders may be perceived as weak or indecisive, especially in situations where tough decisions need to be made quickly. Some critics argue that servant leaders can be taken advantage of by employees who may not fully share the organization's goals.
   - **Response:** Servant leadership does not imply passivity. Leaders can be firm and decisive while still prioritizing the well-being of their team. Effective communication about the organization's mission and the importance of aligned actions can mitigate the perception of weakness.

4. **Measuring Effectiveness**

    - **Challenge:** Assessing the effectiveness of servant leadership can be challenging. Traditional metrics like financial performance may not capture the full impact of a servant leadership approach on employee well-being, culture, and long-term organizational health.

    - **Response:** Organizations adopting servant leadership may need to develop new metrics or adapt existing ones to measure the outcomes related to employee engagement, retention, and culture. Qualitative assessments, such as employee surveys and feedback, can also provide insights into the impact of servant leadership.

5. **Potential for Exploitation**

    - **Concern:** Critics caution that in certain contexts or with certain leaders, servant leadership may be exploited. Employees might take advantage of a leader's service-oriented approach, leading to a lack of accountability and a culture of entitlement.

    - **Response:** Servant leadership should be practiced in conjunction with clear expectations and boundaries. Leaders can provide support while also holding team members accountable for their contributions and behavior.

6. **Organizational Fit**

    - **Challenge:** Servant leadership may not be suitable for all organizational contexts. In industries requiring strict hierarchies, rapid decision-making, or emergency response, a more directive leadership style might be necessary.

- **Response:** Servant leadership can be adapted to suit different contexts. Leaders may need to adjust their approach based on the specific needs and demands of their organization and industry while still upholding servant leadership principles where appropriate.

While servant leadership offers numerous benefits, including improved morale, trust, and organizational effectiveness, it is not a one-size-fits-all approach and faces legitimate challenges and criticisms. Addressing these challenges often involves finding the right balance between individual and organizational needs, clear communication, and thoughtful adaptation of the servant leadership philosophy to fit the unique context of the organization. When applied effectively, servant leadership can contribute positively to both employee well-being and organizational success.

Strategies for Addressing Challenges and Manage Authenticity

Addressing the challenges associated with servant leadership and maintaining authenticity as a leader requires a thoughtful and deliberate approach. Here are strategies to help leaders navigate these challenges while staying true to the principles of servant leadership:

1. **Clear Communication and Expectations**

    - **Set Clear Boundaries:** Clearly communicate the boundaries of servant leadership. While it's essential to support and empower team members, make it known that accountability and responsibility are also expected.
    - **Align on Goals:** Ensure alignment between individual needs and organizational objectives. Openly discuss how each team member's contributions fit into the broader mission and vision of the organization.

2. **Adapt Leadership Style**

    - **Contextual Flexibility:** Recognize that different situations may require different leadership approaches. Be prepared to adapt your leadership style to match the needs and demands of specific contexts while maintaining core servant leadership principles when appropriate.

    - **Balanced Decision-Making:** Strike a balance between involving team members in decision-making processes and making timely, decisive choices when required. Explain the rationale behind decisions to maintain transparency.

3. **Measuring Effectiveness**

    - **Develop Relevant Metrics:** Collaborate with your team to identify and develop metrics that accurately measure the outcomes of servant leadership, such as employee engagement, retention, and culture. Regularly assess and adjust these metrics as needed.

    - **Collect Feedback:** Continuously solicit feedback from team members and stakeholders to gauge the impact of your leadership approach. Use this input to make improvements and adaptations.

4. **Preventing Exploitation**

    - **Set Expectations:** Clearly communicate expectations regarding behavior, accountability, and performance. Make it known that while you are committed to serving and supporting, you also expect responsible and professional conduct.

    - **Address Issues Promptly:** Address any instances of exploitation or entitlement promptly and directly.

Provide constructive feedback and guidance on appropriate behavior and contributions.

5. **Authenticity and Self-Care**

    - **Lead by Example:** Maintain authenticity by leading with integrity and by modeling the values and behaviors you expect from your team. Demonstrate humility, ethical conduct, and a commitment to continuous growth.

    - **Self-Care:** Ensure you are practicing self-care and maintaining your own well-being. Authenticity and servant leadership require a strong and healthy leader who can genuinely support others.

6. **Reflect and Adapt**

    - **Regular Self-Assessment:** Take time to reflect on your leadership practices and their impact. Continuously refine your approach based on lessons learned and evolving circumstances.

    - **Learning and Development:** Invest in your own learning and development as a servant leader. Seek out resources, workshops, and mentorship to enhance your skills and authenticity.

7. **Seek Guidance and Mentorship**

    - **Consult Peers:** Connect with other servant leaders or leaders with similar leadership philosophies to share experiences and seek advice on addressing challenges.

    - **Mentorship:** Consider seeking mentorship from experienced servant leaders who can provide guidance and insights based on their own leadership journeys.

By implementing these strategies, leaders can effectively address the challenges associated with servant leadership while remaining authentic to the principles of serving and supporting their team members. Flexibility, clear communication, self-awareness, and a commitment to continuous improvement are key factors in successfully navigating these challenges.

Developing Servant Leadership Skills

Developing servant leadership skills refers to the intentional process of acquiring and honing the qualities and competencies associated with servant leadership. It involves cultivating attributes like empathy, humility, active listening, and a strong commitment to supporting and empowering others. Developing these skills also entails understanding the principles of servant leadership and how to apply them effectively in leadership roles. Through self-awareness, learning, and practice, individuals can enhance their capacity to lead with a focus on serving the needs and well-being of their team members and, in doing so, create a positive and impactful leadership style.

Leaders who seek to develop and enhance their servant leadership skills involve a series of intentional steps and practices. Here are some actionable strategies to help leaders on this journey:

1. **Self-Reflection and Self-Awareness**
    - Begin by reflecting on your own values, beliefs, and leadership style. Understand your strengths and areas for improvement.

- Engage in self-assessment exercises, such as personality assessments or 360-degree feedback, to gain insights into your leadership style and its impact on others.

2. **Study Servant Leadership Principles**

    - Familiarize yourself with the core principles and values of servant leadership, such as empathy, humility, and a commitment to serving others.
    - Read books, articles, and research on servant leadership to gain a deeper understanding of its philosophy and practical applications.

3. **Active Listening and Empathy**

    - Practice active listening by giving your full attention to others during conversations. Seek to understand their perspectives and emotions.
    - Develop empathy by putting yourself in others' shoes and genuinely caring about their well-being and needs.

4. **Build Trust and Credibility**

    - Establish trust by consistently acting with integrity, transparency, and ethical conduct. Keep promises and follow through on commitments.
    - Demonstrate credibility by being knowledgeable and skilled in your area of expertise, which enhances your ability to support and guide others effectively.

5. **Lead by Example**

    - Model servant leadership behaviors by showing vulnerability, humility, and a willingness to serve others. Lead with integrity and authenticity.

- Share stories and examples from your own experiences that illustrate servant leadership principles in action.

6. **Support Employee Growth**
    - Invest in the growth and development of your team members. Provide opportunities for learning, skill-building, and career advancement.
    - Offer mentorship, coaching, and guidance to help individuals reach their potential.

7. **Encourage Open Communication**
    - Foster a culture of open communication where team members feel comfortable sharing their thoughts, concerns, and ideas.
    - Actively seek feedback and input from others, and be responsive to their needs and suggestions.

8. **Practice Servant Leadership Daily**
    - Make servant leadership a daily practice rather than a sporadic effort. Continuously look for opportunities to serve and support others.
    - Challenge yourself to lead with a servant mindset in various situations, both within and outside the workplace.

9. **Seek Feedback and Coaching**
    - Solicit feedback from peers, colleagues, and team members on your leadership style and its impact. Use this feedback to make improvements.
    - Consider working with a mentor or coach who can provide guidance and insights on developing your servant leadership skills.

10. **Measure Progress and Adapt**
    - Establish metrics or key performance indicators (KPIs) to assess your progress in developing servant leadership skills.
    - Be open to adapting your approach based on the feedback and results you receive, making continuous improvement a central part of your leadership journey.

By actively implementing these practical strategies and consistently practicing servant leadership, leaders can enhance their skills, create a positive impact on their teams and organizations, and contribute to a more compassionate and effective leadership style.

Coaching Leadership

Coaching leadership is a leadership style that focuses on guiding and developing team members to reach their full potential. Leaders who adopt a coaching leadership approach act as mentors and facilitators, working closely with their team to help them set goals, acquire new skills, and overcome challenges. This leadership style emphasizes open communication, active listening, and providing constructive feedback. The goal is to empower individuals to take ownership of their growth and development while aligning their personal and professional goals with those of the organization. Coaching leaders often create a supportive and collaborative work environment that fosters continuous learning and improvement.

Coaching leadership is a leadership style that places a strong emphasis on guiding and developing team members to reach their full potential and achieve both personal and organizational goals. This approach involves leaders actively participating in the growth and development of their team through mentorship, support, and skill-building.

2. **Mentorship and Guidance:** Coaching leaders act as mentors and guides to their team members. They provide one-on-one support and personalized guidance to help individuals improve their skills, knowledge, and performance. This mentorship is based on the understanding that each team member has unique strengths and areas for growth.
3. **Goal Setting and Development Planning:** Coaching leaders work collaboratively with team members to set clear and achievable goals. They help individuals identify their strengths, weaknesses, and areas for improvement, and together, they create development plans to address these areas. These plans often include specific actions, milestones, and timelines.
4. **Active Listening and Feedback:** Effective coaching leaders are skilled active listeners. They create an open and nonjudgmental space for team members to express their ideas, concerns, and aspirations. They provide constructive feedback that is specific, actionable, and aimed at helping individuals make progress toward their goals.
5. **Empowerment and Ownership:** Coaching leaders empower team members to take ownership of their own growth and development. They encourage individuals to make decisions, solve problems, and seek opportunities for learning and improvement. This empowerment instills a sense of responsibility and accountability.
6. **Skill Development and Training:** Coaching leaders identify the skills and knowledge required for success in their team members' roles. They facilitate skill-building through training, workshops, and on-the-job learning experiences. This helps team members acquire the capabilities they need to excel in their positions.
7. **Continuous Learning:** Coaching leaders promote a culture of continuous learning and improvement. They themselves stay updated on industry trends and best practices, setting an example for their team members. They encourage a growth

mindset where mistakes are viewed as opportunities for learning and growth.

8. **Performance Monitoring and Support:** Coaching leaders regularly monitor the performance and progress of their team members. They provide ongoing support and make adjustments to development plans as needed. This ensures that individuals stay on track toward achieving their goals.

9. **Individualized Approach:** Coaching leadership is highly individualized. Leaders tailor their coaching style and support to the unique needs, strengths, and aspirations of each team member. This personalized approach recognizes that one size does not fit all in terms of development.

10. **Alignment with Organizational Goals:** While coaching leaders focus on individual development, they also ensure that individual goals align with the broader objectives of the organization. This alignment helps achieve a balance between personal and organizational success.

11. **Creating a Supportive Environment:** Coaching leaders foster a supportive and inclusive work environment where team members feel valued, encouraged, and motivated to achieve their full potential. They build trust and strong relationships with their teams, promoting a sense of belonging and commitment.

Coaching leadership is a dynamic and individualized approach to leadership that prioritizes the growth and development of team members. It involves mentorship, goal setting, active listening, empowerment, and ongoing support to help individuals reach their full potential while contributing to the organization's success. This leadership style creates a culture of continuous learning and improvement, ultimately benefiting both individuals and the organization as a whole.

Historical Context

The historical context of coaching leadership can be traced back to various influences and developments over time. While coaching as a formal leadership approach gained prominence in the latter half of the 20th century, its roots can be found in earlier practices and philosophies. Here's a brief historical overview:

1. **Early Influences (Ancient Greece):** The concept of mentorship and guidance has ancient roots. In ancient Greece, for example, the philosopher Socrates used a form of coaching through dialogue to help individuals gain self-awareness and arrive at their own insights. His method of asking probing questions, known as the Socratic method, laid the groundwork for coaching by encouraging critical thinking and self-discovery.
2. **Psychology and Self-Help Movements (20th Century):** The 20th century saw the development of psychological theories and self-help movements that contributed to coaching principles. Psychologists like Carl Rogers and Abraham Maslow emphasized the importance of self-actualization, human potential, and client-centered therapy, which inspired coaching's focus on individual growth and potential.
3. **Management and Leadership Theories (Mid-20th Century):** Management and leadership theories also influenced coaching leadership. The Human Relations Movement in the 1930s and 1940s emphasized the importance of understanding and addressing employees' personal and psychological needs in the workplace. This humanistic approach laid the foundation for leadership practices that prioritize the well-being and development of team members.
4. **Sports Coaching as a Model:** Coaching leadership drew inspiration from sports coaching, which has a long history of nurturing talent, skill development, and team performance.

The success of sports coaches in improving athlete performance provided a practical model for leadership in other domains.

5. **Emergence of Coaching as a Leadership Approach (Late 20th Century):** The term "coaching" began to gain prominence in the leadership and organizational development context in the 1970s and 1980s. Pioneers like Timothy Gallwey (author of "The Inner Game of Tennis") and Sir John Whitmore (author of "Coaching for Performance") popularized coaching techniques and principles. They emphasized the role of coaching in helping individuals unlock their potential, overcome challenges, and achieve peak performance.

6. **Formalization and Certification (Late 20th Century and Beyond):** As coaching gained recognition as a distinct leadership and personal development approach, organizations and coaching associations began to offer formal coaching certification programs. These programs established coaching competencies and ethical standards, further legitimizing coaching as a professional discipline.

Today, coaching leadership has become a recognized and widely practiced approach in various fields, including business, education, healthcare, and personal development. Its historical roots in philosophy, psychology, humanistic principles, and sports coaching have converged to shape a leadership style that prioritizes individual growth, performance enhancement, and the development of supportive and empowering relationships between leaders and their teams.

Key Principles and Concepts

Coaching leadership is built on key principles and concepts that guide leaders in their efforts to support and develop their team members. These principles and concepts are essential to understanding and practicing this approach effectively:

1. **Individualized Development:**
   - **Principle:** Each team member is unique, with their own strengths, weaknesses, and career aspirations. Coaching leaders recognize the importance of tailoring their approach to the individual needs of each team member.
   - **Concept:** Leaders work with team members to create personalized development plans that consider their current skills, career goals, and areas for improvement. This individualized approach ensures that development efforts are meaningful and relevant.

2. **Active Listening:**
   - **Principle:** Effective coaching leadership hinges on active listening. Leaders must genuinely understand their team members' perspectives, challenges, and aspirations to provide meaningful support.
   - **Concept:** Coaching leaders practice active listening by giving their full attention during conversations, asking clarifying questions, and avoiding interruptions. This allows them to uncover valuable insights and build strong rapport.

3. **Empowerment and Ownership:**
   - **Principle:** Coaching leaders empower team members to take ownership of their own development and career growth. They encourage individuals to make decisions, solve problems, and seek opportunities for learning.

- **Concept:** Team members are encouraged to set their own goals, identify areas for improvement, and take initiative in their professional development. This sense of ownership fosters accountability and self-motivation.

4. **Constructive Feedback:**
   - **Principle:** Constructive feedback is a critical tool for growth and improvement. Coaching leaders provide feedback that is specific, actionable, and aimed at helping team members make progress toward their goals.
   - **Concept:** Leaders offer regular feedback sessions where they discuss performance, address challenges, and provide guidance for improvement. This feedback is focused on development and is given in a supportive and nonjudgmental manner.

5. **Goal Setting:**
   - **Principle:** Clear and achievable goals are essential for guiding development efforts. Coaching leaders work with team members to set SMART (Specific, Measurable, Achievable, Relevant, Time-bound) goals.
   - **Concept:** Together, leaders and team members define short-term and long-term goals that align with the individual's career aspirations and the organization's objectives. These goals serve as roadmaps for development.

6. **Continuous Learning:**
   - **Principle:** Learning is an ongoing process. Coaching leaders foster a culture of continuous learning, where

individuals are encouraged to seek opportunities for skill-building and growth.

- **Concept:** Leaders provide access to training, mentorship, and resources that support continuous learning. They also encourage a growth mindset, where challenges and mistakes are viewed as opportunities for improvement.

7. **Trust and Support:**

    - **Principle:** Building trust and providing unwavering support are fundamental aspects of coaching leadership. Trust is the foundation upon which strong coaching relationships are built.

    - **Concept:** Leaders create a supportive and inclusive work environment where team members feel safe to share their challenges and aspirations. Trust is established through consistent and authentic interactions.

8. **Performance Monitoring:**

    - **Principle:** Coaching leaders regularly monitor team members' performance and progress toward their development goals. Monitoring ensures that individuals stay on track and receive the necessary support.

    - **Concept:** Leaders conduct performance reviews and check-ins, where they assess progress, celebrate achievements, and make adjustments to development plans when needed. Monitoring is ongoing and adaptive.

Coaching leadership is underpinned by principles and concepts that prioritize individualized development, active listening, empowerment, and continuous learning. These principles guide leaders in creating a supportive and growth-oriented environment where team members are encouraged to take ownership of their development, achieve their goals, and ultimately reach their full potential.

The Role of a Coach Leader

The role of a coach leader is to guide, mentor, and support team members in their personal and professional development. Coach leaders take on a facilitative role, helping individuals identify their strengths and areas for improvement, set clear goals, and create actionable plans to achieve those goals. They actively listen to team members, provide constructive feedback, and empower them to take ownership of their growth. A coach leader fosters a culture of continuous learning, encourages problem-solving and decision-making, and builds trust and strong relationships within the team. Ultimately, the role of a coach leader is to enable individuals to reach their full potential while contributing to the success of the organization through the growth and empowerment of its members.

Characteristics and Responsibilities of Coaching leader

A coaching leader exhibits specific characteristics and takes on distinct responsibilities to effectively guide and develop their team members.

Characteristics of a Coaching Leader

1. **Empathy:** A coaching leader possesses a high degree of empathy, which allows them to understand and connect with the emotions, perspectives, and needs of their team members. They genuinely care about the well-being and growth of their team.
2. **Active Listening:** They are skilled active listeners who pay close attention to what team members are saying. They

refrain from making hasty judgments or interrupting, ensuring that individuals feel heard and valued.

3. **Patience:** Coaching leaders exhibit patience and understanding, recognizing that personal and professional growth takes time. They are willing to support team members through challenges and setbacks.

4. **Open-Mindedness:** They maintain an open-minded and nonjudgmental attitude. They are receptive to different viewpoints and are willing to consider alternative approaches to problem-solving and development.

5. **Communication Skills:** Effective communication is a hallmark of coaching leaders. They articulate their ideas clearly, provide constructive feedback, and encourage open and honest dialogue within the team.

6. **Trustworthiness:** Trust is paramount in coaching leadership. Leaders must demonstrate trustworthiness by acting with integrity, being transparent, and keeping their commitments.

7. **Supportive Attitude:** Coaching leaders have a supportive mindset, always looking for ways to empower team members and provide the resources and guidance they need to succeed.

Responsibilities of a Coaching Leader

1. **Individual Development Plans:** Coaching leaders work with team members to create individualized development plans. These plans outline short-term and long-term goals, skill-building activities, and performance benchmarks.

2. **Regular Feedback:** They provide consistent and constructive feedback to team members, focusing on strengths, areas for improvement, and progress toward goals.

Feedback sessions are tailored to the individual's needs and growth objectives.

3. **Goal Setting:** Coaching leaders guide team members in setting SMART (Specific, Measurable, Achievable, Relevant, Time-bound) goals that align with both personal aspirations and organizational objectives.

4. **Skill Building:** They facilitate skill development through training, mentorship, and hands-on experiences. Coaching leaders identify the skills required for each team member's role and provide opportunities for growth.

5. **Problem-Solving Support:** When team members encounter challenges or obstacles, coaching leaders offer guidance and support in finding solutions. They encourage individuals to think critically and develop problem-solving skills.

6. **Career Development:** Coaching leaders help team members navigate their career paths, providing insights into potential opportunities for advancement and personal growth within the organization.

7. **Monitoring Progress:** Regular performance monitoring is a crucial responsibility. Coaching leaders conduct performance reviews, check-ins, and progress assessments to ensure individuals stay on track and receive necessary support.

8. **Supportive Culture:** They foster a supportive and inclusive work culture where team members feel safe to express their thoughts, concerns, and aspirations. This includes celebrating achievements and recognizing individual contributions.

9. **Trust Building:** Building and maintaining trust within the team is essential. Coaching leaders create an environment where team members trust their intentions, actions, and guidance.

10. **Continuous Learning:** They lead by example in embracing continuous learning and self-improvement. Coaching leaders stay updated on industry trends and best practices, inspiring team members to do the same.

Coaching leaders exhibit characteristics such as empathy, active listening, and open-mindedness, and they fulfill responsibilities related to individualized development, feedback, goal setting, skill building, and fostering a supportive and growth-oriented culture. Through their efforts, coaching leaders empower their team members to reach their full potential and contribute to both personal and organizational success.

Difference from Traditional Leadership

Coaching leadership differs significantly from traditional leadership in terms of its core principles, approaches, and the outcomes it seeks to achieve. Here's a comparison highlighting the key distinctions:

1. **Focus on Individual vs. Directive Approach:**
   - **Coaching Leadership:** Coaching leaders prioritize individual development and empowerment. They work closely with team members to set goals, provide guidance, and support personal and professional growth. The approach is facilitative rather than directive.
   - **Traditional Leadership:** Traditional leaders often employ a more directive approach, focusing on giving instructions, making decisions, and overseeing tasks. Their primary concern may be task completion and adherence to established processes.

2. **Empowerment vs. Control:**

    - **Coaching Leadership:** Coaching leaders empower team members to take ownership of their work and development. They encourage autonomy, decision-making, and problem-solving, fostering a sense of responsibility.

    - **Traditional Leadership:** Traditional leaders may exert more control over tasks and decisions, which can limit individual autonomy. They often hold authority and make most of the key decisions themselves.

3. **Personal Growth vs. Task Performance:**

    - **Coaching Leadership:** The primary objective of coaching leadership is the personal and professional growth of team members. Leaders aim to help individuals achieve their full potential, which often leads to improved performance.

    - **Traditional Leadership:** Traditional leaders typically emphasize task performance and meeting organizational objectives. While performance is important, personal growth and development may receive less attention.

4. **Individualized vs. Standardized Approach:**

    - **Coaching Leadership:** Coaching leaders adopt an individualized approach, recognizing that each team member has unique strengths, weaknesses, and aspirations. They tailor their guidance and support to each person's needs.

- **Traditional Leadership:** Traditional leaders may use a more standardized approach, treating team members similarly and applying consistent processes and rules. This approach may not account for individual differences.

5. **Collaboration vs. Hierarchy:**

    - **Coaching Leadership:** Coaching leaders foster a collaborative work environment where open communication, teamwork, and sharing of ideas are encouraged. They value input from team members and promote a sense of belonging.

    - **Traditional Leadership:** Traditional leadership may maintain a more hierarchical structure, with clear lines of authority and communication flowing primarily from top to bottom. Decision-making may be concentrated at the top.

6. **Long-Term Growth vs. Short-Term Results:**

    - **Coaching Leadership:** Coaching leaders prioritize long-term personal and professional growth, recognizing that this often leads to sustainable performance improvements and employee satisfaction.

    - **Traditional Leadership:** Traditional leaders may focus more on achieving short-term results and meeting immediate goals, sometimes at the expense of long-term development and engagement.

7. **Feedback and Support vs. Evaluation and Direction:**

    - **Coaching Leadership:** Coaching leaders provide ongoing feedback, support, and mentorship to help team members improve. Feedback is constructive and aimed at facilitating growth.

- **Traditional Leadership:** Traditional leaders often use feedback more as a performance evaluation tool, with an emphasis on critiquing past performance rather than guiding future development.

8. **Trust and Empathy vs. Authority and Control:**

    - **Coaching Leadership:** Trust and empathy are essential in coaching leadership. Leaders build trust by actively supporting and understanding team members' needs and aspirations.

    - **Traditional Leadership:** Traditional leaders may rely more on their positional authority and control to influence team behavior and performance.

Coaching leadership differs from traditional leadership by emphasizing individualized development, empowerment, personal growth, collaboration, and a long-term focus on both individuals and the organization. While traditional leadership has its place in certain contexts, coaching leadership is gaining recognition for its ability to create a more engaged and empowered workforce, leading to improved performance and organizational success.

Coaching Techniques and Strategies

Coaching techniques and strategies refer to the specific methods and approaches employed by coaching leaders to facilitate the growth, development, and empowerment of their team members. These techniques encompass a wide range of practices, including active listening, asking probing questions, providing constructive feedback, setting SMART goals, offering mentorship, and facilitating skill-building exercises. The aim of coaching techniques and strategies is to create a supportive and collaborative environment where individuals are guided in setting and achieving their goals, making informed decisions, and continuously improving their skills and performance. These techniques are tailored to the unique needs and aspirations of team members and are essential tools for coaching leaders to foster personal and professional development within their teams.

Effective Coaching Techniques

Effective coaching techniques are critical for coaching leaders to support their team members' growth and development. Here's a detailed discussion of three key coaching techniques:

1. **Active Listening:**
    - **Definition:** Active listening involves giving your full attention to the speaker, understanding their perspective, and showing empathy. It's a fundamental coaching technique that fosters trust and meaningful communication.
    - **How it Works:** Coaching leaders practice active listening by maintaining eye contact, avoiding interruptions, and using verbal and nonverbal cues to show that they are engaged and attentive. They ask open-ended questions to encourage team members to share their thoughts and concerns openly.
    - **Benefits:** Active listening helps coaching leaders gain deeper insights into team members' needs, challenges, and aspirations. It builds trust and rapport, as individuals feel heard and valued. It also enables leaders to provide more relevant and personalized guidance.

2. **Providing Feedback:**

    - **Definition:** Feedback is a crucial coaching technique involving the provision of information and insights to individuals about their performance, behavior, or progress toward their goals. Effective feedback is specific, constructive, and supportive.

    - **How it Works:** Coaching leaders offer feedback regularly, focusing on both positive aspects and areas for improvement. They use a feedback model that includes observations, impact, and recommendations. They frame feedback in a way that helps team members understand its relevance to their goals and development.

    - **Benefits:** Constructive feedback helps individuals identify their strengths and areas for growth. It guides them in making necessary improvements and adjustments. When feedback is delivered in a supportive and nonjudgmental manner, it promotes a growth mindset and a culture of continuous improvement.

3. **Setting Developmental Goals:**

    - **Definition:** Setting developmental goals involves collaboratively defining specific, measurable, achievable, relevant, and time-bound (SMART) objectives that align with an individual's personal growth and the organization's objectives.

    - **How it Works:** Coaching leaders work closely with team members to set SMART goals that consider their strengths, weaknesses, and aspirations. These goals are designed to challenge and motivate individuals while being realistic and attainable. Leaders help individuals break down these goals into actionable steps.

- **Benefits:** Setting developmental goals provides clarity and direction to team members. It helps them focus their efforts and measure their progress. It also aligns individual growth with the broader goals of the organization, ensuring that development efforts contribute to overall success.

Incorporating these coaching techniques into their leadership approach enables coaching leaders to create a supportive and growth-oriented environment. By actively listening, providing effective feedback, and setting meaningful developmental goals, coaching leaders empower their team members to reach their full potential and contribute to both personal and organizational success. These techniques are essential tools for building strong coaching relationships and fostering continuous learning and improvement.

Real World Example

Real-world examples demonstrate how coaching leadership principles and techniques are applied to create positive outcomes. Here are a few examples:

4. **Sales Team Coaching:** In a sales organization, a coaching leader works with a struggling sales representative. Through active listening, the leader identifies that the salesperson lacks confidence in closing deals. They set a developmental goal to improve confidence in negotiations. The leader provides regular feedback and offers role-playing sessions to practice closing techniques. Over time, the sales representative gains confidence and significantly improves their sales performance.

5. **Educational Leadership:** A school principal adopts coaching leadership to support teachers' professional growth. Through active listening and feedback, the principal identifies a teacher who wants to enhance their classroom management skills. Together, they set SMART goals for classroom management improvement. The principal offers resources, observes classes, and provides constructive feedback. As a result, the teacher's classroom management skills improve, leading to a more productive learning environment.
6. **Start-up Founder Coaching:** In a start-up company, the founder takes on a coaching leadership role with their team. They actively listen to team members' ideas and concerns, fostering open communication. When a team member expresses interest in a leadership role, the founder provides feedback and guidance on skill development. They set goals for leadership training and offer mentorship. The team member eventually takes on a leadership role and contributes significantly to the company's growth.
7. **Nonprofit Organization:** The executive director of a nonprofit organization embraces coaching leadership principles to empower their staff. By actively listening to staff members' experiences and challenges, they identify a need for skill development in fundraising. Together, they set specific goals for improving fundraising abilities. The executive director offers training, access to fundraising resources, and ongoing feedback. The team's fundraising efforts become more effective, leading to increased support for the organization's mission.
8. **Project Management:** In a project management context, a project leader uses coaching leadership to guide a team of diverse professionals. They actively listen to team members' concerns and goals, helping to identify areas where collaboration can be enhanced. The leader encourages team members to set individual development goals related to cross-functional communication and teamwork. Through

coaching and feedback, the team members improve their collaboration, leading to more efficient project execution.

These real-world examples illustrate how coaching leadership can be applied across various domains and industries to support individual growth, improve performance, and create a collaborative and empowering work environment. Coaching leaders actively engage with their team members, provide guidance and resources, set meaningful goals, and offer ongoing feedback to help individuals reach their full potential and contribute to organizational success.

Teams for Fostering Growth

Techniques for fostering growth in teams and individuals refer to a set of strategies and practices that leaders, mentors, or coaches employ to facilitate personal and collective development within a group or organizational context. These techniques are designed to empower individuals to reach their full potential, enhance their skills, and contribute effectively to team and organizational goals. Techniques may include setting clear and challenging goals, providing constructive feedback, offering mentorship and coaching, organizing training and skill-building opportunities, and creating an environment that encourages continuous learning and improvement. By applying these techniques, leaders and mentors aim to inspire motivation, increase competence, and ultimately drive both individual and team success, fostering a culture of growth and development within the organization.

Creating a culture of Growth

Creating a culture of learning involves establishing an organizational environment where continuous learning, growth, and development are not only encouraged but also deeply embedded in the company's values and practices. In such a culture, employees are motivated and empowered to seek knowledge, acquire new skills, and expand their expertise. This extends beyond formal training programs and includes informal learning opportunities, such as peer mentoring, knowledge sharing, and experimentation. A culture of learning prioritizes innovation, adaptability, and a growth mindset, where challenges and failures are viewed as valuable learning experiences rather than setbacks. Leaders play a crucial role in fostering this culture by modeling continuous learning, providing resources and support, and recognizing and celebrating the achievements and contributions of those who embrace learning and development. Ultimately, a culture of learning drives organizational resilience and competitiveness in an ever-evolving world.

How Leaders can Create a Culture

Creating a culture of continuous learning and development within an organization is a multifaceted process that requires commitment, strategy, and consistent effort from leaders. Here's a detailed exploration of how leaders can foster such a culture:

1. **Lead by Example**

    - **Continuous Learning:** Leaders should demonstrate a commitment to their own continuous learning. This can include pursuing further education, attending relevant workshops, or seeking out mentorship and coaching.
    - **Transparency:** Leaders should be open about their own learning journeys, sharing their successes and failures. This vulnerability encourages others to embrace learning without fear of judgment.

2. **Set Clear Expectations**
   - **Communication:** Leaders should clearly communicate the organization's commitment to learning and development. Make it a part of the organization's mission and values.
   - **Performance Expectations:** Set expectations for employees to actively engage in learning and professional development as a part of their job responsibilities.

3. **Provide Resources**
   - **Training and Development Programs:** Invest in training programs, workshops, and courses that are relevant to employees' roles and career goals. Ensure these resources are accessible to all.
   - **Access to Experts:** Provide opportunities for employees to learn from experts within and outside the organization. This could involve mentorship programs or inviting guest speakers.

4. **Encourage Knowledge Sharing:**
   - **Collaborative Environment:** Foster a collaborative workplace where knowledge sharing is encouraged. This can be done through team meetings, brainstorming sessions, and open forums.
   - **Recognition:** Acknowledge and reward employees who actively share knowledge and support their peers' learning efforts.

5. **Create Learning Communities**
   - **Peer Learning:** Encourage peer-to-peer learning by creating communities or groups where employees can share insights, experiences, and best practices.

- **Cross-Functional Teams:** Form cross-functional teams to tackle projects and challenges, promoting a diverse and collaborative learning experience.

6. **Embrace Failure as a Learning Opportunity**
   - **Safe Environment:** Create an environment where failure is seen as a natural part of the learning process. Encourage employees to take calculated risks without fear of punitive consequences.
   - **Post-Mortems:** Conduct post-mortems after projects or initiatives to discuss what went well, what didn't, and what can be learned from the experience.

7. **Provide Growth Paths**
   - **Career Development Plans:** Work with employees to develop individualized career development plans that include learning and skill-building goals.
   - **Promotions and Advancements:** Ensure that promotions and advancement opportunities are tied to an employee's demonstrated commitment to learning and growth.

8. **Measure and Evaluate:**
   - **Key Performance Indicators (KPIs):** Establish KPIs to measure the impact of learning and development initiatives on individual and organizational performance.
   - **Feedback Loops:** Collect feedback from employees about the effectiveness of learning programs and use this feedback to make improvements.

9. **Celebrate Success:**
    - **Recognition:** Celebrate the achievements and milestones of employees who actively engage in learning and development.
    - **Showcase Growth Stories:** Share success stories of individuals who have grown and advanced within the organization through learning and development efforts.

10. **Continuously Adapt:**
    - **Evolving Needs:** Recognize that learning needs and preferences evolve. Regularly assess the changing needs of the workforce and adapt learning and development strategies accordingly.

By taking these steps, leaders can foster a culture of continuous learning and development where employees are motivated to acquire new skills, share knowledge, and embrace growth as an integral part of their professional journey. Such a culture not only benefits individual employees but also enhances the organization's adaptability and competitiveness in a rapidly changing world.

Case Studies

Organizations with strong coaching leadership cultures have demonstrated their commitment to employee growth, development, and empowerment. Here are two case studies showcasing such organizations:

Google

- **Coaching Leadership Culture:** Google is renowned for its coaching leadership culture, which prioritizes the growth and development of its employees. The company encourages managers to act as coaches rather than traditional supervisors.

- **Key Initiatives:**
  - **One-on-One Meetings:** Google managers hold regular one-on-one meetings with their team members, focusing on personal and professional development. These meetings provide a platform for open communication and individualized support.
  - **Career Development:** Google offers a wide range of career development opportunities, including workshops, training programs, and access to online learning platforms. The company encourages employees to set personal growth goals and provides resources to achieve them.
  - **Peer Feedback:** Google encourages a culture of peer feedback, where employees regularly share insights, recognize each other's contributions, and provide constructive criticism.
- **Results:** Google's coaching leadership culture has contributed to its reputation as an employer of choice. The company consistently ranks high in employee satisfaction and has a track record of innovation and adaptability.

The Ritz-Carlton Hotel Company

- **Coaching Leadership Culture:** The Ritz-Carlton is known for its exceptional customer service, driven by a strong coaching leadership culture. The company emphasizes employee engagement and empowerment to deliver unparalleled guest experiences.
- **Key Initiatives:**
  - **Daily Line-Up Meetings:** The Ritz-Carlton conducts daily line-up meetings where team

members gather to discuss daily goals, share guest feedback, and receive coaching and support from their leaders.

- **Gold Standards:** The company has established a set of Gold Standards that serve as guiding principles for employees. Leaders regularly coach and reinforce these standards.

- **Employee Empowerment:** The Ritz-Carlton empowers employees to resolve guest issues and make decisions that enhance guest satisfaction. This empowerment fosters a sense of ownership and accountability.

- **Results:** The Ritz-Carlton consistently receives high marks for customer satisfaction and is renowned for its exceptional service. Its coaching leadership culture contributes to employee engagement and retention, ensuring that staff members are motivated to provide exceptional service to guests.

These case studies demonstrate that organizations with strong coaching leadership cultures prioritize the growth and development of their employees, resulting in improved employee satisfaction, exceptional customer experiences, and long-term success.

Individual and Team Development

Individual and team development are crucial aspects of personal and collective growth within an organization. Individual Development refers to the process of enhancing the knowledge, skills, and competencies of individual employees. It involves activities such as training, coaching, mentoring, and ongoing learning opportunities tailored to the specific needs and career aspirations of each employee. Individual development aims to help employees improve their performance, take on more significant roles, and advance in their careers within the organization. It fosters a sense of personal growth and professional satisfaction, ultimately benefiting both the individual and the organization. Team development, on the other hand, focuses on improving the collective performance and dynamics of a group of individuals working together toward common goals. It involves activities that enhance teamwork, communication, collaboration, and the ability to achieve shared objectives. Team development may include team-building exercises, workshops, and training programs aimed at improving the group's effectiveness and productivity. The goal is to create a high-performing team that leverages the strengths of its members and works cohesively to achieve outstanding results.

Individual and team development are complementary processes that contribute to organizational success. While individual development fosters the growth and skill enhancement of each employee, team development focuses on optimizing the collective capabilities and synergy of the group, ultimately leading to improved overall performance and achievement of organizational goals.

Examination of the Role of Coaching Leadership

Coaching leadership plays a significant role in fostering both individual and team growth within organizations. Here's a detailed examination of how coaching leadership contributes to these aspects:

Fostering Individual Growth

1. **Personalized Development Plans:** Coaching leaders work closely with each team member to create personalized development plans. These plans are tailored to the

individual's strengths, weaknesses, and career aspirations. By focusing on individual needs, coaching leaders ensure that employees are working on areas that matter most to their growth.

2. **Continuous Feedback:** Coaching leaders provide ongoing and constructive feedback to individual team members. This feedback is specific, actionable, and aimed at helping individuals improve their performance. It helps employees understand their strengths and areas for development.

3. **Goal Setting:** Coaching leaders collaborate with employees to set SMART (Specific, Measurable, Achievable, Relevant, Time-bound) goals that align with both personal aspirations and organizational objectives. These goals provide clear direction and motivation for individual growth.

4. **Skill Development:** Leaders identify the skills required for each team member's role and provide opportunities for skill-building. This could involve training, mentorship, or providing challenging assignments that stretch their capabilities.

5. **Empowerment:** Coaching leaders empower employees to take ownership of their own development. They encourage individuals to make decisions, solve problems, and seek opportunities for learning, fostering a sense of accountability.

Fostering Team Growth

1. **Effective Communication:** Coaching leaders promote open and effective communication within the team. They encourage team members to share ideas, challenges, and solutions, creating a collaborative environment.

2. **Conflict Resolution:** When conflicts arise within the team, coaching leaders help mediate and resolve them

constructively. This prevents conflicts from becoming detrimental to team dynamics and growth.

3. **Team Building:** Coaching leaders organize team-building activities and workshops that improve team cohesion, trust, and collaboration. These activities help team members understand each other's strengths and working styles.

4. **Shared Goals:** Coaching leaders ensure that the team is aligned around common goals and objectives. This shared vision motivates team members to work together cohesively to achieve these goals.

5. **Diversity and Inclusion:** Leaders foster an inclusive environment where diverse perspectives and backgrounds are valued. This diversity can lead to more innovative solutions and a broader range of skills within the team.

6. **Recognition and Celebration:** Coaching leaders recognize and celebrate team achievements and milestones. Acknowledging and rewarding collective efforts boosts team morale and motivation.

7. **Continuous Improvement:** Coaching leaders encourage the team to reflect on their performance and identify areas for improvement collectively. This culture of continuous improvement leads to higher team effectiveness over time.

Coaching leadership is instrumental in fostering both individual and team growth. By providing personalized guidance, feedback, and support to individual team members, coaching leaders enable them to develop their skills and reach their full potential. Simultaneously, coaching leadership creates a collaborative and empowering team environment where effective communication, shared goals, and a culture of continuous improvement contribute to the team's overall growth and success.

Strategies for Leaders to Provide Targeted Guidance

Leaders can provide targeted guidance and support for personal and professional development through a variety of strategies tailored to individual team members' needs. Here are some effective strategies:

1. **Individual Development Plans:** Work with each team member to create a personalized development plan that outlines their career goals, strengths, areas for improvement, and the steps needed to achieve those goals. Ensure that these plans align with the individual's aspirations and the organization's objectives.

2. **Regular One-on-One Meetings:** Schedule regular one-on-one meetings with team members to discuss their progress, challenges, and development goals. These meetings provide an opportunity to offer feedback, address concerns, and provide guidance on skill enhancement.

3. **Feedback and Performance Reviews:** Provide ongoing feedback that is specific, constructive, and actionable. Conduct regular performance reviews to evaluate progress toward development goals and discuss areas where improvement is needed.

4. **Coaching and Mentorship:** Pair team members with mentors or coaches who can provide specialized guidance and support. These mentors should be experienced in the areas that align with the individual's development goals.

5. **Training and Workshops:** Identify relevant training programs, workshops, and seminars that can help team members acquire new skills and knowledge. Encourage attendance and participation in these opportunities.

6. **Challenging Assignments:** Offer challenging projects or assignments that push team members out of their comfort zones and provide opportunities for skill development.

Ensure that these assignments align with their development goals.

7. **Skill-Building Resources:** Provide access to resources such as online courses, books, and industry publications that can aid in skill development. Offer recommendations and support in selecting the most relevant materials.

8. **Networking Opportunities:** Encourage team members to participate in professional networks, industry events, and conferences. Networking can provide valuable learning experiences and opportunities for skill enhancement.

9. **Promote a Growth Mindset:** Foster a culture where mistakes and failures are viewed as learning opportunities rather than setbacks. Encourage team members to take risks, experiment, and learn from their experiences.

10. **Recognition and Rewards:** Recognize and reward individuals who actively engage in personal and professional development. This recognition can motivate others to prioritize their own growth.

11. **Regular Check-Ins:** In addition to one-on-one meetings, conduct periodic check-ins to gauge progress and provide additional support. Adjust development plans as needed based on evolving goals and challenges.

12. **Encourage Peer Learning:** Promote peer-to-peer learning by creating forums or groups where team members can share knowledge, experiences, and best practices. Peer learning can be a powerful tool for growth.

13. **Provide Psychological Safety:** Create an environment where team members feel safe to express their development needs and concerns without fear of judgment. Encourage open and honest communication.

14. **Lead by Example:** As a leader, demonstrate your own commitment to continuous learning and development. Share your experiences and growth journey with your team to set a positive example.

By implementing these strategies, leaders can provide targeted guidance and support that empowers team members to thrive both personally and professionally. This not only benefits individual growth but also contributes to the overall success and effectiveness of the team and organization.

Feedback and Accountability

Feedback and accountability are fundamental concepts in leadership and organizational development. Feedback refers to the process of providing information, comments, or evaluations to individuals or teams about their performance, behavior, or results. It can be both positive, highlighting strengths and achievements, and constructive, pointing out areas for improvement. Effective feedback is specific, timely, and actionable, aimed at facilitating growth and development. Accountability involves taking responsibility for one's actions, decisions, and commitments. In an organizational context, it means individuals and teams are answerable for their performance and the results they produce. Leaders often establish clear expectations, goals, and roles, and hold individuals accountable for meeting these expectations. Accountability fosters a sense of ownership and ensures that individuals are committed to achieving their objectives.

Feedback and accountability are essential components of coaching leadership, playing a crucial role in fostering personal and professional growth within a team or organization.

Importance of Feedback in Coaching Leadership

1. **Guidance and Improvement:** Feedback provides individuals with valuable insights into their performance, highlighting what they are doing well and where they can improve. Coaching leaders use feedback as a tool for guiding team members toward enhanced skills and better outcomes.

2. **Clarification of Expectations:** It ensures that team members have a clear understanding of performance expectations and standards. When expectations are communicated and reinforced through feedback, individuals are more likely to align their efforts with organizational goals.

3. **Motivation and Recognition:** Positive feedback and recognition for a job well done boost morale and motivation. Recognizing and celebrating achievements can foster a positive work environment and encourage continued high performance.

4. **Self-Awareness:** Constructive feedback helps individuals become more self-aware by identifying areas for development they might not have recognized on their own. This self-awareness is a critical step in personal growth.

5. **Adjustment and Adaptation:** In rapidly changing environments, feedback helps team members adapt to new challenges and circumstances. It encourages flexibility and agility by providing information about what is and isn't working.

6. **Improved Communication:** Regular feedback sessions promote open and honest communication between leaders and team members. This trust and transparency are vital for building strong coaching relationships.

Importance of Accountability in Coaching Leadership

1. **Responsibility:** Accountability ensures that team members take ownership of their actions and commitments. This sense of responsibility drives individuals to meet their obligations and contribute effectively to team and organizational goals.

2. **Goal Achievement:** When individuals are held accountable for specific goals and tasks, they are more likely to work diligently to achieve them. Accountability keeps the focus on results and outcomes.

3. **Alignment with Values:** It reinforces the importance of organizational values and standards. When individuals understand that they are accountable for upholding these values, they are more likely to act in ways that align with the organization's culture.

4. **Trust and Reliability:** Accountability builds trust within the team and organization. Team members can rely on one another to fulfill their commitments, creating a more cohesive and productive work environment.

5. **Performance Improvement:** Accountability mechanisms, such as performance reviews and goal tracking, enable coaching leaders to identify areas where additional support or resources are needed to help individuals improve.

6. **Learning from Mistakes:** Accountability includes acknowledging and addressing mistakes or shortcomings. This creates a culture where errors are seen as opportunities for learning and growth rather than reasons for blame or punishment.

In coaching leadership, feedback and accountability work hand in hand. Effective feedback provides the information and guidance individuals need to understand their performance, while accountability ensures that they take the necessary actions to improve and achieve their goals. Together, they create a culture of continuous learning and improvement, driving both individual and organizational success.

Techniques for Providing Constructive Feedback

1. **Be Specific:** Provide feedback that is specific and focused on observable behaviors or outcomes. Avoid vague or general comments, and instead, pinpoint what the individual did well or where improvement is needed.

2. **Use the Feedback Sandwich:** Begin with positive feedback to acknowledge strengths and achievements, followed by constructive feedback highlighting areas for improvement, and conclude with encouragement or support. This approach balances criticism with positivity.

3. **Focus on Behavior, not Personality:** Frame feedback in terms of actions and behaviors, not personal attributes. For example, say, "Your presentation lacked data to support your points," rather than, "You're not good at presenting."

4. **Timeliness:** Offer feedback as close to the observed behavior or event as possible. Timely feedback allows team members to make immediate adjustments and reinforces the importance of addressing issues promptly.

5. **Maintain a Growth Mindset:** Encourage a growth mindset by framing feedback as an opportunity for learning and improvement rather than criticism. Emphasize that mistakes are valuable learning experiences.

6. **Active Listening:** When team members respond to feedback, actively listen to their perspective. This demonstrates that you value their input and can lead to more productive conversations.

Techniques for Holding Team Members Accountable

1. **Set Clear Expectations:** Ensure that team members understand their roles, responsibilities, and performance expectations. Clear expectations provide a foundation for accountability.

2. **SMART Goals:** Use the SMART (Specific, Measurable, Achievable, Relevant, Time-bound) criteria when setting goals. This makes it easier to measure progress and hold individuals accountable for achieving their objectives.

3. **Regular Check-Ins:** Schedule regular one-on-one meetings to review progress toward goals and provide ongoing feedback. These check-ins serve as opportunities to address any accountability issues promptly.

4. **Document Agreements:** After discussing expectations and goals, document agreements in writing. This helps ensure clarity and serves as a reference point for accountability discussions.

5. **Celebrate Achievements:** Recognize and celebrate when team members meet or exceed their goals. Positive reinforcement reinforces accountability and motivates individuals to continue performing at a high level.

6. **Consequences and Follow-Up:** If team members consistently fail to meet expectations, have a plan for addressing the issue. This may involve additional training, support, or, in extreme cases, progressive discipline measures.

7. **Supportive Environment:** Create a supportive environment where team members feel comfortable seeking help or guidance when they face challenges in meeting their commitments. Offer assistance and resources as needed.

8. **Peer Accountability:** Encourage team members to hold each other accountable within the group. Peer accountability can be a powerful motivator and support mechanism.

9. **Review and Adjust:** Periodically review progress and adjust goals or expectations as necessary. Flexibility and adaptation are key to effective accountability.

By employing these techniques, coaching leaders can provide constructive feedback that fosters growth and hold team members accountable for their development and performance. This approach contributes to a culture of continuous improvement and ensures that individuals remain aligned with organizational goals and values.

*****

CHAPTER ELEVEN
Leadership adaptation and future trends

Leadership Adaptation refers to the ability of leaders to adjust and evolve their leadership styles, strategies, and behaviors in response to changing circumstances and challenges. Effective leaders recognize that the business and social landscape is dynamic, and they must be flexible and adaptable to navigate through various situations successfully. This adaptability encompasses a willingness to learn from experiences, embrace new technologies and methodologies, and modify their approach as needed. Leaders who can adapt are more likely to lead their organizations through uncertainty and change while fostering growth and innovation.

Future Trends in leadership refer to the emerging patterns, developments, and shifts that are expected to influence how leadership is practiced in the years ahead. These trends are shaped by various factors, including advancements in technology, changes in demographics and workforce dynamics, evolving societal values, and global economic conditions. Some examples of future trends in leadership might include the rise of remote and virtual leadership, the growing importance of diversity and inclusion in leadership teams, the increasing emphasis on ethical and sustainable leadership practices, and the need for leaders to navigate complex geopolitical and environmental challenges. Staying attuned to these trends is crucial for leaders to remain relevant and effective in their roles.

Leadership Adaptation is about the capacity of leaders to adjust their approaches to changing circumstances, while Future Trends in leadership encompass the evolving dynamics and influences that will shape leadership practices in the years to come. Adaptable leaders who are aware of and responsive to these trends are better positioned to lead their organizations successfully into the future.

Understanding the Critical Need

Understanding the critical need for leadership adaptation in an ever-evolving global landscape is paramount for the success and sustainability of organizations and businesses. The contemporary world is characterized by rapid technological advancements, shifting demographics, economic globalization, and unprecedented challenges such as climate change and public health crises. Leadership adaptation is essential for several reasons:

1. **Complexity and Uncertainty:** The global landscape has become increasingly complex and uncertain. Leaders must grapple with a multitude of factors that can impact their organizations, from geopolitical tensions to disruptive technologies. The ability to adapt allows leaders to respond effectively to unforeseen challenges and capitalize on new opportunities.

2. **Rapid Technological Change:** Technology is advancing at an unprecedented pace, transforming industries and markets. Leaders who fail to adapt to these changes risk falling behind or even becoming obsolete. Adaptable leaders can harness technology to enhance efficiency, improve customer experiences, and drive innovation.

3. **Diverse Workforce:** Today's workforce is more diverse than ever in terms of age, gender, ethnicity, and cultural backgrounds. Effective leadership requires adapting to the diverse needs and perspectives of employees, promoting inclusion, and leveraging the strengths of a multicultural team.

4. **Globalization:** Globalization has interconnected economies and markets across the world. Leaders must adapt to operate in a global context, understanding different cultures,

regulations, and market dynamics. Adaptation can facilitate international expansion and partnerships.

5. **Environmental and Social Concerns:** Sustainability and social responsibility have gained prominence. Leaders need to adapt by integrating environmental, social, and governance (ESG) considerations into their strategies. Failure to do so can result in reputational damage and lost opportunities.

6. **Evolving Consumer Expectations:** Consumer preferences are constantly evolving, driven by factors such as changing demographics, sustainability concerns, and digitalization. Leaders must adapt their products, services, and marketing strategies to meet these evolving expectations.

7. **Talent Development:** The way organizations attract, retain, and develop talent is changing. Leaders must adapt their approaches to talent management, embracing remote work, flexible schedules, and continuous learning opportunities.

8. **Agility and Innovation:** In an ever-evolving landscape, adaptability is closely linked to agility and innovation. Adaptable leaders foster a culture of experimentation and learning, which can lead to breakthrough innovations and a competitive edge.

9. **Resilience:** Leaders who adapt are better equipped to build resilient organizations that can withstand shocks and disruptions, whether they are economic downturns, natural disasters, or global crises like the COVID-19 pandemic.

10. **Long-Term Sustainability:** Finally, leadership adaptation is essential for the long-term sustainability of organizations. Leaders who fail to adapt risk stagnation or decline, while those who embrace change can position their organizations for continued success and growth.

The critical need for leadership adaptation in an ever-evolving global landscape is driven by the complex and dynamic nature of the modern world. Leaders who can adapt their strategies, behaviors, and organizations to meet these challenges are more likely to thrive and lead their teams and businesses to success. Adaptable leadership is not a luxury but a necessity in the 21st century.

Importance of Aligning Leadership Styles

Aligning leadership styles with emerging global trends and shifts is of paramount importance in today's rapidly changing and interconnected world. The significance of this alignment lies in its potential to enhance organizational effectiveness, foster innovation, improve employee engagement, and position the organization to thrive amidst evolving global dynamics. Here's a detailed explanation of the importance:

1. **Relevance and Resonance:** Leadership styles that are in tune with emerging global trends are more likely to resonate with employees, customers, and stakeholders. This relevance fosters trust and confidence in leadership, as it demonstrates an understanding of the challenges and opportunities presented by contemporary global issues.

2. **Adaptation to Market Dynamics:** Global trends directly impact market dynamics. Leaders who align their styles with these trends can make informed decisions regarding product development, market entry, and expansion. This adaptability can result in a competitive advantage.

3. **Innovation and Creativity:** Some global trends, such as technological advancements and the rise of sustainability, demand innovative solutions. Leadership styles that encourage creativity and experimentation are better suited to address these challenges, leading to the development of groundbreaking products and services.

4. **Employee Engagement:** Employees are more likely to be engaged and motivated when they see leadership styles that align with their values and aspirations. A leadership style that embraces diversity, supports career development, and promotes work-life balance is likely to attract and retain top talent.

5. **Change Management:** Many global trends involve significant changes, such as digital transformation or shifts in business models. Leaders who can adapt their styles to facilitate change management are better equipped to guide their teams through transitions effectively.

6. **Global Team Collaboration:** As organizations operate on a global scale, leaders often manage diverse teams across different time zones and cultures. Leadership styles that value cultural sensitivity and promote collaboration are essential for maintaining cohesion and productivity in such teams.

7. **Ethical Leadership:** In an era of increased scrutiny and awareness of ethical issues, leaders must align their styles with ethical principles and values. Ethical leadership not only builds trust but also mitigates the risk of reputational damage.

8. **Environmental and Social Responsibility:** With growing concerns about sustainability and social responsibility, leaders must adopt styles that prioritize environmental and social impacts in decision-making processes. Aligning leadership with these trends can enhance an organization's reputation and market positioning.

9. **Global Networking and Partnerships:** Many global trends involve forming partnerships and alliances with other organizations. Leaders with styles that emphasize relationship-building and collaboration are better suited to navigate complex global networks.

10. Crisis Management: Leadership styles that align with emerging global trends are better prepared to handle crises, whether they are health pandemics, economic downturns, or geopolitical tensions. These styles can help leaders make swift and effective decisions in times of uncertainty.

Aligning leadership styles with emerging global trends and shifts is crucial for organizations to remain relevant, competitive, and sustainable in a rapidly changing world. Leaders who recognize the importance of this alignment and continuously adapt their leadership approaches are better positioned to guide their organizations through the challenges and opportunities presented by the global landscape. This adaptability not only benefits the organization but also its employees, customers, and stakeholders.

Leadership Adaptation in an Evolving Global Landscape

Leadership Adaptation in an Evolving Global Landscape involves leaders' capacity to flexibly adjust their leadership styles and strategies to effectively navigate the continually changing and interconnected global environment. It encompasses staying attuned to emerging trends, embracing cultural diversity, fostering innovation, and making informed decisions while remaining agile in the face of dynamic challenges. Leaders who adapt are better equipped to guide their organizations through the complexities and uncertainties of the contemporary global landscape, ensuring long-term relevance and success.

Dynamic Nature of Leadership

The Dynamic Nature of Leadership recognizes that effective leadership is not a static concept but an ever-evolving and context-dependent phenomenon. Leadership is influenced by a multitude of factors, including organizational culture, industry trends, technological advancements, and societal changes. Leaders must continually adapt their approaches, skills, and strategies to address these shifting dynamics. This adaptability involves embracing new ideas, staying open to feedback, fostering innovation, and being responsive to the changing needs of teams and organizations. Essentially, the dynamic nature of leadership acknowledges that what makes a successful leader today may not be the same as what makes a successful leader tomorrow, and it emphasizes the importance of continuous learning and adaptation in leadership roles.

Subject to Continuous Change and Adaptation

Leadership is subject to continuous change and adaptation due to a variety of dynamic factors that shape the modern business and social landscape.

1. **Technological Advancements:** Rapid technological changes have transformed how organizations operate and communicate. Leaders must adapt to harness new technologies for efficiency, data-driven decision-making, and remote collaboration. Failure to do so can result in inefficiencies and missed opportunities.

2. **Globalization:** The globalization of markets and workforces has made leadership more complex. Leaders need to navigate diverse teams, cultures, and markets. Adaptation includes understanding global trends, embracing diversity, and developing cross-cultural communication skills.

3. **Evolving Workforce:** Generational shifts in the workforce bring different expectations and work styles. Effective leaders adapt their management and communication approaches to accommodate the needs of a multigenerational workforce, promoting engagement and retention.

4. **Societal and Environmental Concerns:** Growing awareness of environmental and social issues demands

ethical and sustainable leadership. Leaders must adapt their strategies to align with environmental, social, and governance (ESG) principles, or risk reputational damage and market rejection.

5. **Economic Fluctuations:** Economic conditions are prone to cycles of growth and recession. Effective leaders adapt their strategies and resource allocation to thrive in different economic environments, ensuring organizational stability.

6. **Market Disruption:** Industries can be disrupted by new entrants, innovative technologies, or changing consumer preferences. Leaders must be agile and adaptable to pivot their business models and stay competitive.

7. **Crisis Management:** Crisis situations, such as the COVID-19 pandemic, require leaders to adapt swiftly to unforeseen challenges. Crisis leadership involves rapid decision-making, effective communication, and ensuring the safety and well-being of employees and stakeholders.

8. **Regulatory Changes:** Laws and regulations evolve, affecting how businesses operate. Leaders must stay informed about legal changes and adapt their practices to remain compliant and avoid legal risks.

9. **Leadership Trends:** The concept of effective leadership evolves with time. Trends in leadership theory and practice, such as servant leadership or transformational leadership, influence how leaders approach their roles. Effective leaders adapt to incorporate these emerging leadership models into their strategies.

10. **Feedback and Learning:** Effective leaders seek feedback from their teams and continuously learn from their experiences. They adapt their leadership styles based on this feedback, fostering a culture of growth and improvement.

11. **Innovation and Creativity:** Leaders must adapt their approaches to encourage innovation and creative thinking within their organizations. This involves creating an environment where employees feel empowered to generate and implement new ideas.

12. **Competitive Landscape:** Changes in the competitive landscape require leaders to adapt their strategies to remain relevant and competitive. This could involve diversifying product offerings, exploring new markets, or redefining the organization's value proposition.

Leadership is subject to continuous change and adaptation because of the ever-shifting dynamics of the modern world. Leaders who remain static risk becoming ineffective or obsolete. Instead, effective leaders recognize the need to embrace change, continually learn, and adapt their approaches to effectively navigate the complexities and uncertainties of the evolving business and social landscape.

Historical Examples

Historical examples of leaders who successfully adapted to changing times abound and offer valuable lessons in leadership adaptability. Here are a few notable examples:

1. **Abraham Lincoln:** As the 16th President of the United States, Abraham Lincoln faced the enormous challenge of leading the nation through the American Civil War. Lincoln demonstrated remarkable adaptability by evolving his leadership style from a cautious and conciliatory approach at the beginning of his presidency to a more assertive and resolute stance as the war progressed. He recognized the need to adapt to the changing demands of wartime leadership, ultimately preserving the Union and ending slavery.

2. **Winston Churchill:** Winston Churchill, the Prime Minister of the United Kingdom during World War II, is celebrated for his ability to adapt and inspire during a time of crisis. His leadership evolved from being politically isolated in the years leading up to the war to becoming a unifying figurehead for the British people. His stirring speeches and unwavering resolve helped rally the nation against Nazi aggression, demonstrating his adaptability in the face of a world-changing conflict.

3. **Nelson Mandela:** Nelson Mandela, the anti-apartheid revolutionary and President of South Africa, demonstrated remarkable adaptability by transitioning from a militant activist to a statesman and leader of a post-apartheid South Africa. His ability to reconcile with former adversaries and establish a multiracial democracy showcased his adaptability and commitment to a peaceful and inclusive future for his country.

4. **Steve Jobs:** Steve Jobs, co-founder of Apple Inc., is known for his visionary leadership and adaptability. After being ousted from Apple in the 1980s, he returned in the late 1990s to lead the company to unprecedented success. Jobs adapted by focusing on innovation, design, and customer experience, transforming Apple from near bankruptcy into one of the world's most valuable companies.

5. **Hari Singh Nalwa:** Hari Singh Nalwa was a prominent military commander of the Sikh Empire under Maharaja Ranjit Singh in the early 19th century. He demonstrated exceptional adaptability in leading the Khalsa forces to victory in various battles and expanding the empire's territory. His tactical acumen and leadership skills were essential in navigating the complex geopolitical landscape of the time, making him a key figure in world history.

These historical leaders succeeded by recognizing the need to adapt their leadership styles, strategies, and priorities to the challenges and opportunities presented by their times. Their ability to pivot, learn, and evolve while staying true to their core values and goals is a testament to the importance of leadership adaptability in navigating complex and changing landscapes. These leaders serve as enduring examples of how adaptability can lead to impactful and transformative leadership.

Evolving Global Landscape

Evolving Global Landscape refers to the ever-changing and interconnected nature of the world, encompassing economic, technological, social, political, and environmental dimensions. This dynamic landscape is characterized by shifting trends, emerging challenges, and opportunities that impact individuals, organizations, and nations on a global scale. It signifies the constant evolution of factors such as market dynamics, technological advancements, cultural shifts, climate change, and geopolitical developments, which collectively shape how societies, businesses, and governments operate and interact with one another. Understanding and adapting to this evolving global landscape is crucial for making informed decisions and navigating the complexities and uncertainties of the modern world.

1. **Technological Advancements:** Technological innovation continued to accelerate, with significant developments in artificial intelligence (AI), automation, blockchain, and 5G technology. These advancements were reshaping industries, such as healthcare, finance, manufacturing, and transportation, and impacting the nature of work, with a growing emphasis on remote work and digital collaboration tools due to the COVID-19 pandemic.

2. **Economic Shifts:** The global economy experienced significant shifts due to the pandemic. In 2020, there was a

global economic contraction, but recovery efforts were underway in many countries by 2021. Government stimulus packages, monetary policy adjustments, and vaccination campaigns played pivotal roles in these recovery efforts. However, economic disparities among countries and within populations were accentuated during this period.

3. **Geopolitical Changes:** The global geopolitical landscape was marked by various developments, including:

    - **US-China Relations:** Tensions between the United States and China continued to escalate, with disputes over trade, technology, and territorial claims. These tensions had far-reaching implications for global supply chains and international diplomacy.

    - **COVID-19 Response:** The pandemic response exposed both cooperation and competition among nations. Vaccine distribution, access, and international collaboration to address the health crisis were focal points in global geopolitics.

    - **Climate Change:** Climate change and sustainability became increasingly prominent on the global agenda. International efforts such as the Paris Agreement aimed to address environmental challenges, while businesses and governments worked on transitioning to cleaner and more sustainable energy sources.

    - **Shifts in Alliances:** Geopolitical alliances were shifting, with countries reevaluating their strategic partnerships. For example, the European Union was working to strengthen its defense and security cooperation, partly in response to evolving global dynamics.

4. **Social and Cultural Changes:** Societies around the world were grappling with social and cultural shifts, including

discussions around racial equality, gender rights, and social justice. Movements like Black Lives Matter and increased awareness of inequality were influencing public discourse and shaping policies in many countries.

5. **Global Health:** The COVID-19 pandemic continued to have profound impacts on global health systems, economies, and daily life. Vaccination campaigns were underway, but challenges in equitable distribution remained.

6. **Cybersecurity:** The importance of cybersecurity grew as cyberattacks became more frequent and sophisticated. Governments and businesses were investing in cybersecurity measures to protect critical infrastructure and data.

The factors mentioned - technological advancements, economic shifts, and geopolitical changes - have a profound impact on leadership dynamics in various ways:

1. **Technological Advancements:**

    - **Digital Transformation:** Technological advancements, including AI, automation, and digitalization, have transformed industries and workplaces. Leaders need to adapt by understanding the potential of these technologies, integrating them into their organizations, and fostering digital literacy among employees.

    - **Remote Work and Collaboration:** The COVID-19 pandemic accelerated the adoption of remote work and digital collaboration tools. Leaders must adapt their leadership styles to manage and motivate remote teams effectively, emphasizing trust, clear communication, and results-driven performance.

- **Data-Driven Decision-Making:** The availability of big data and analytics tools has made data-driven decision-making critical. Leaders need to be proficient in data analysis and use data to inform strategies and operations.

2. **Economic Shifts:**

    - **Adaptation to Economic Uncertainty:** Economic shifts, such as recessions or market fluctuations, require leaders to make tough decisions regarding cost-cutting, resource allocation, and strategic pivots. Effective leadership during economic challenges involves resilience, agility, and the ability to inspire confidence in the organization's direction.

    - **Inclusive Growth:** Leaders are increasingly expected to address economic disparities within their organizations and society at large. They must consider how their decisions impact not only the bottom line but also social responsibility and long-term sustainability.

3. **Geopolitical Changes:**

    - **Navigating International Markets:** Geopolitical changes can affect global trade, tariffs, and market access. Leaders of multinational companies must adapt their strategies to navigate international markets, assess geopolitical risks, and diversify supply chains.

    - **Diplomacy and Alliances:** In a shifting geopolitical landscape, leaders may need to engage in diplomacy and build alliances to protect their organization's interests. Effective leadership in international contexts requires cross-cultural understanding and negotiation skills.

- **Risk Management:** Geopolitical tensions can introduce new risks to organizations, such as cybersecurity threats or trade disruptions. Leaders must adapt their risk management strategies to address these evolving challenges.

4. **Social and Cultural Changes:**

    - **Diversity and Inclusion:** Social and cultural changes demand inclusive leadership. Leaders must create diverse and inclusive workplaces that embrace different perspectives and backgrounds, fostering creativity and innovation.

    - **Corporate Social Responsibility (CSR):** There is increasing pressure on leaders to align their organizations with social and ethical values. CSR initiatives, sustainability goals, and ethical business practices are becoming integral to leadership and brand reputation.

5. **Global Health and Crisis Response:**

    - **Crisis Leadership:** Global health crises, like the COVID-19 pandemic, require leaders to adapt quickly and make critical decisions to protect employees, maintain business continuity, and demonstrate empathy and resilience.

    - **Health and Safety Prioritization:** Leaders must prioritize the health and safety of employees and customers, which may involve implementing new policies, protocols, and technologies to ensure a safe work environment.

These factors significantly impact leadership dynamics by requiring leaders to adapt to new challenges and opportunities.

Effective leadership in today's evolving landscape involves embracing technological change, managing economic uncertainty, navigating geopolitical complexities, fostering inclusive and socially responsible organizations, and responding adeptly to global health crises and other disruptions. Leaders who can adapt their leadership styles and strategies to address these factors are better equipped to lead their organizations to success in an ever-changing world.

Challenges and Opportunities

Challenges and opportunities represent two sides of the same coin in any dynamic situation. Challenges are obstacles, difficulties, or problems that individuals, organizations, or societies must overcome or navigate. They often require creative problem-solving, resilience, and adaptability. On the other hand, opportunities are favorable circumstances or possibilities for growth, improvement, or advancement. They may arise from changes in the environment, emerging trends, or the successful resolution of challenges. Effective leadership involves recognizing and addressing challenges while seizing and capitalizing on opportunities to achieve desired goals and outcomes. Balancing the management of challenges and the exploitation of opportunities is a central aspect of strategic decision-making and problem-solving in various contexts.

An evolving global landscape presents a multitude of challenges and opportunities that impact individuals, organizations, and societies worldwide.

Challenges

1. **Rapid Technological Disruption:** While technological advancements offer immense opportunities, they also pose challenges such as job displacement, privacy concerns, and the risk of cyber threats. Leaders must navigate these challenges by upskilling the workforce, implementing robust

cybersecurity measures, and addressing ethical dilemmas related to technology.

2. **Economic Uncertainty:** Economic shifts and global market volatility can lead to financial instability, business closures, and job insecurity. Leaders must adapt to manage resources efficiently, diversify revenue streams, and provide financial security for their employees.

3. **Geopolitical Tensions:** Geopolitical changes, including trade disputes and international conflicts, can disrupt global supply chains and business operations. Leaders need to anticipate and manage geopolitical risks through strategic diversification and diplomacy.

4. **Sustainability and Climate Change:** Environmental challenges, such as climate change and resource depletion, require leaders to adopt sustainable practices, reduce carbon footprints, and comply with evolving environmental regulations.

5. **Diversity and Inclusion:** Cultural and demographic shifts underscore the importance of diversity and inclusion. Leaders must address issues related to discrimination, bias, and inequality in the workplace and society, fostering inclusive environments that celebrate differences.

6. **Health Crises:** Global health crises, like the COVID-19 pandemic, can pose significant health risks, disrupt economies, and strain healthcare systems. Leaders must prioritize public health, adapt to remote work and healthcare practices, and prepare for future health challenges.

Opportunities

1. **Technological Innovation:** Evolving technologies provide opportunities for innovation, efficiency, and new business models. Leaders can harness AI, automation, and digital

platforms to enhance productivity, expand markets, and improve customer experiences.

2. **Global Connectivity:** An interconnected world offers access to diverse markets, talent pools, and partnerships. Leaders can capitalize on global connectivity to expand their businesses, tap into international talent, and explore new markets.

3. **Sustainability Initiatives:** Growing environmental awareness creates opportunities for sustainable products and services. Leaders can align their organizations with sustainability goals, reducing costs and enhancing their brand's reputation.

4. **Remote Work and Flexibility:** The rise of remote work presents opportunities for talent acquisition, employee retention, and cost savings. Leaders can implement flexible work arrangements and digital tools to accommodate evolving work preferences.

5. **Digital Marketing and E-Commerce:** The digital landscape provides opportunities for businesses to reach wider audiences and adapt to changing consumer behaviors. Leaders can invest in e-commerce, online marketing, and data analytics to stay competitive.

6. **Innovation in Healthcare:** Health crises have accelerated innovation in healthcare and telemedicine. Leaders can leverage these advances to improve healthcare access, develop new treatments, and enhance public health.

An evolving global landscape brings a mix of challenges and opportunities that require dynamic and adaptive leadership. Effective leaders anticipate and address challenges while leveraging opportunities to drive growth, foster resilience, and create positive impacts on their organizations and communities. Embracing change, fostering innovation, and promoting inclusivity are essential aspects of leadership in this evolving world.

Strategies for Leaders

Proactively responding to the changes presented by an evolving global landscape requires leaders to develop effective strategies that address challenges and seize opportunities. Here are strategies for leaders to consider:

1. **Continuous Learning and Adaptation**
   - **Stay Informed:** Leaders should keep abreast of global trends, technological advancements, economic shifts, and geopolitical changes. Regularly seek out relevant news, research, and expert insights.
   - **Professional Development:** Invest in your own learning and development, as well as that of your team. Attend seminars, workshops, and courses to acquire new skills and knowledge.
   - **Openness to Feedback:** Create a culture where feedback is encouraged and valued. Constructive feedback from employees, peers, and mentors can highlight blind spots and areas for improvement.

2. **Embrace Technological Advancements**
   - **Digital Transformation:** Proactively integrate technology into your organization's operations. Invest in tools and systems that enhance efficiency, data-driven decision-making, and customer experiences.
   - **Cybersecurity:** Prioritize cybersecurity measures to protect sensitive data and systems. Regularly assess

and update security protocols to stay ahead of cyber threats.

3. **Economic Resilience:**

    - **Diversify Revenue Streams:** Explore opportunities for diversifying revenue sources to reduce reliance on a single market or product. This can provide stability during economic fluctuations.

    - **Cost Management:** Implement cost-effective measures to maintain financial stability. Monitor expenses, identify cost-saving initiatives, and ensure financial resilience.

4. **Navigate Geopolitical Changes**

    - **Risk Assessment:** Continually assess geopolitical risks that may impact your organization. Develop contingency plans to mitigate these risks, such as diversifying suppliers or markets.

    - **Diplomacy and Partnerships:** Engage in diplomacy and build strategic alliances where necessary to protect your organization's interests in international markets.

5. **Sustainability and Social Responsibility**

    - **Sustainability Integration:** Incorporate sustainability principles into your organization's operations and supply chains. Set clear sustainability goals and track progress.

    - **Corporate Social Responsibility (CSR):** Develop CSR initiatives that align with societal values and demonstrate your organization's commitment to ethical and social responsibilities.

6. **Embrace Diversity and Inclusion**

- **Inclusive Leadership:** Foster a culture of diversity and inclusion within your organization. Promote diversity in hiring, create inclusive policies, and address issues of bias and discrimination.
- **Employee Resource Groups:** Support employee resource groups and initiatives that encourage diversity and provide a platform for underrepresented voices.

7. **Crisis Preparedness**

    - **Crisis Management Plans:** Develop comprehensive crisis management plans that include health, safety, and operational contingencies. Regularly review and update these plans.
    - **Remote Work Capabilities:** Invest in remote work technologies and policies that enable business continuity during crises.

8. **Seize Digital Opportunities**

    - **Digital Marketing:** Leverage digital marketing channels to reach a wider audience and adapt to changing consumer behaviors.
    - **E-commerce Expansion:** Explore opportunities for e-commerce and online sales to diversify revenue streams and adapt to shifting market preferences.

9. **Innovate in Healthcare and Telemedicine:**

    - **Telehealth Integration:** If relevant to your industry, explore the integration of telemedicine and digital health solutions to meet evolving healthcare demands.

- **R&D Investment:** Invest in research and development to drive innovation in healthcare, pharmaceuticals, and related fields.

Leaders who proactively respond to changes in the global landscape by implementing these strategies can position their organizations for resilience, growth, and long-term success. Adaptability and a forward-thinking approach are key to navigating the complexities of an ever-evolving world.

Global Trends and Shifts

Adapting leadership styles to global trends and shifts" refers to the dynamic and flexible approach that leaders employ to align their leadership practices with the evolving challenges and opportunities presented by the global landscape. It involves recognizing that leadership is not one-size-fits-all and that effective leaders must adjust their behaviors, strategies, and communication methods to meet the demands of a rapidly changing world. Adapting leadership styles entails staying attuned to emerging global trends, embracing diversity, leveraging technology, and cultivating the skills necessary to navigate complexities, whether they are technological advancements, cultural shifts, economic fluctuations, or geopolitical changes. Ultimately, it is about tailoring leadership to the specific needs and circumstances of the global context, ensuring relevance, effectiveness, and sustainable success.

Global Leadership Styles

Global leadership styles encompass the diverse approaches and behaviors exhibited by leaders in an international or cross-cultural context. These styles take into account the varying cultural norms, values, and expectations of teams, organizations, and stakeholders across different parts of the world. Global leaders must adapt their leadership styles to effectively communicate, collaborate, and lead diverse and geographically dispersed teams. This adaptation involves cultural sensitivity, open-mindedness, and the ability to balance universal leadership principles with the nuances of local cultures and global trends, ensuring that leadership practices are relevant and successful in a globalized world.

Leadership styles effective in a global context often encompass a combination of the following approaches:

1. **Transformational Leadership:** Transformational leaders inspire and motivate their teams to achieve extraordinary results. They articulate a compelling vision, foster innovation, and encourage personal growth. This style is effective in global contexts as it transcends cultural boundaries and energizes diverse teams toward a common goal.

2. **Collaborative Leadership:** Collaboration is crucial in global settings. Leaders who promote a collaborative style prioritize teamwork, open communication, and inclusive decision-making. They leverage the collective intelligence of multicultural teams to solve complex problems and drive innovation.

3. **Culturally Sensitive Leadership:** Cultural sensitivity is essential for building trust and understanding in diverse teams. Leaders who embrace cultural sensitivity acknowledge and respect cultural differences, adapt their communication styles, and create inclusive environments where every team member feels valued.

4. **Adaptive Leadership:** Adaptive leaders are flexible and quick to respond to changing circumstances. They thrive in dynamic global environments where unexpected challenges and opportunities arise. This style involves continuous learning, resilience, and the ability to pivot as needed.

5. **Servant Leadership:** Servant leaders prioritize the well-being and development of their team members. They listen actively, provide support, and empower individuals to reach their full potential. This approach fosters employee engagement and loyalty in a global context.

6. **Transactional Leadership:** Transactional leaders use a structured approach to manage tasks and ensure performance through rewards and consequences. While not as transformative as other styles, it can be effective in certain global situations, particularly when clear expectations and accountability are essential.

7. **Charismatic Leadership:** Charismatic leaders possess magnetic qualities that inspire devotion and commitment among their followers. This style can be effective in rallying teams across cultures, as it often involves powerful communication and a compelling presence.

8. **Cross-Cultural Leadership:** Leaders with expertise in cross-cultural leadership have a deep understanding of cultural nuances and differences. They adapt their leadership style to each cultural context while fostering inclusivity and cohesion in diverse teams.

9. **Virtual Leadership:** With the rise of remote work and global teams, virtual leadership skills are crucial. Virtual leaders excel in communication technology, time zone management, and building trust in virtual environments.

10. **Ethical Leadership:** Ethical leaders prioritize integrity, fairness, and transparency. They make decisions that align with ethical principles and promote responsible business practices, gaining trust and respect in a global context.

Effective global leaders often blend elements from multiple styles, adapting their approach to specific situations and the needs of their teams and stakeholders. They recognize the importance of cultural intelligence, emotional intelligence, and a global mindset in successfully navigating the complexities of our interconnected world.

The leadership styles effective in a global context differ from traditional leadership approaches in several key ways:

1. **Emphasis on Cultural Sensitivity:** Global leadership styles prioritize cultural sensitivity, recognizing and respecting diverse cultural norms, values, and communication styles. Traditional leadership often assumes a one-size-fits-all approach and may not be attuned to cultural nuances.

2. **Collaboration Over Hierarchy:** Global leadership encourages collaboration and teamwork, often favoring flatter organizational structures where input from team members is valued. Traditional leadership may be more hierarchical, with decision-making concentrated at the top.

3. **Adaptability and Flexibility:** Global leadership styles emphasize adaptability to changing circumstances, rapid decision-making, and the ability to pivot in dynamic environments. Traditional leadership may be more resistant to change and focused on maintaining stability.

4. **Cross-Cultural Competence:** Global leaders possess cross-cultural competence and the ability to bridge cultural gaps. Traditional leadership may lack the skills and awareness needed to navigate diverse, multicultural teams effectively.

5. **Inclusivity and Diversity:** Global leadership promotes inclusivity and diversity, valuing the contributions of team members from various backgrounds. Traditional leadership may not prioritize diversity to the same extent.

6. **Ethical and Sustainable Practices:** Global leadership places a strong emphasis on ethical and sustainable practices, aligning business decisions with broader societal and environmental goals. Traditional leadership may

prioritize short-term profitability over ethical considerations.

7. **Virtual Leadership Skills:** With the rise of remote work and global teams, global leadership styles often include virtual leadership skills, such as proficiency in digital communication tools and the ability to manage geographically dispersed teams. Traditional leadership may lack these virtual competencies.

8. **Transformational Leadership Qualities:** Global leadership often incorporates transformational leadership qualities, such as inspiring vision, innovation, and empowerment of team members. Traditional leadership may rely more on transactional management practices.

9. **Complex Problem-Solving:** Global leadership involves complex problem-solving skills, as leaders must navigate multifaceted global challenges. Traditional leadership may focus on more straightforward, localized issues.

10. **Cross-Boundary Thinking:** Global leaders engage in cross-boundary thinking, transcending organizational and geographical boundaries to collaborate with a broader network of stakeholders. Traditional leadership may have a narrower focus within organizational boundaries.

Global leadership styles are characterized by their adaptability, cultural sensitivity, and emphasis on collaboration, ethics, and inclusivity, reflecting the demands of an interconnected world. Traditional leadership approaches, on the other hand, may be rooted in more hierarchical and localized structures, potentially making them less suitable for addressing the complexities and opportunities of the global landscape. Global leaders must embrace these differences to effectively lead in diverse, rapidly changing environments.

Technology and Digital Leadership

Technology and Digital Leadership refers to a leadership approach that centers on effectively harnessing and leveraging technology and digital tools to drive innovation, transformation, and organizational success. This leadership style involves not only understanding the latest technological trends and advancements but also fostering a digital-first mindset throughout an organization. Technology and Digital Leaders are responsible for aligning technology strategies with broader business goals, promoting digital literacy, and creating an environment that encourages innovation and agility. They play a critical role in navigating the ever-evolving digital landscape, ensuring that their organizations remain competitive and adaptable in an increasingly technology-driven world.

Leadership Adaptation in the Digital Ages

Leadership adaptation in the digital age is crucial for effectively navigating the complexities of the modern world. This adaptation involves acquiring and refining specific digital leadership skills, efficiently managing remote teams, and making data-driven decisions.

Digital Leadership Skills

Digital leadership skills are essential for leaders to excel in the digital age. They encompass a range of competencies, including:

1. **Technological Literacy:** Leaders need a solid understanding of the latest technologies, trends, and emerging tools relevant to their industry. This knowledge helps leaders make informed decisions about technology adoption and integration.

2. **Digital Strategy:** Crafting a clear digital strategy that aligns with organizational goals is critical. Digital leaders must identify opportunities, assess risks, and develop a roadmap for digital transformation.

3. **Adaptability:** The digital landscape evolves rapidly. Leaders must be adaptable and open to change, willing to pivot strategies when necessary to capitalize on emerging opportunities or address new challenges.

4. **Innovation:** Encouraging innovation within the organization is a key role of digital leaders. They create an environment where employees feel empowered to propose and implement digital solutions that enhance efficiency and effectiveness.

5. **Cybersecurity Awareness:** In an era of increasing cyber threats, leaders must prioritize cybersecurity. They should understand cybersecurity risks and promote best practices to protect sensitive data and systems.

Remote Team Management

The digital age has brought about a significant shift towards remote work and distributed teams. Effective remote team management is vital for maintaining productivity and cohesion. Key considerations include:

1. **Effective Communication:** Leaders must be adept at various digital communication tools, ensuring that teams stay connected, informed, and engaged. Clear and consistent communication helps mitigate the challenges of remote work.

2. **Remote Team Building:** Building a sense of community and trust among remote team members is crucial. Leaders can organize virtual team-building activities and create opportunities for social interaction.

3. **Outcome-Based Performance Management:** Focusing on outcomes rather than micromanagement is essential for remote teams. Leaders should set clear objectives, establish key performance indicators, and provide regular feedback.

4. **Technology Infrastructure:** Ensure that remote team members have the necessary technology and infrastructure to work effectively. Leaders must be prepared to address technical issues promptly.

Data-Driven Decision-Making

Data-driven decision-making involves using data and analytics to inform and guide leadership choices. In the digital age, organizations generate vast amounts of data, making data-driven leadership imperative. Key considerations include:

1. **Data Collection and Analysis:** Leaders should establish processes for collecting, analyzing, and interpreting relevant data. This includes both internal data, such as performance metrics, and external data, like market trends.

2. **Data Literacy:** Leaders need to be data-literate to understand the significance and limitations of data. They should be able to ask the right questions and draw meaningful insights from data.

3. **Strategic Insights:** Data-driven leaders use data to identify opportunities, predict future trends, and make informed strategic decisions. They can spot patterns and outliers, allowing them to adapt strategies as needed.

4. **Ethical Considerations:** Data privacy and ethical data use are critical. Leaders must ensure that data collection and analysis adhere to legal and ethical standards, respecting the privacy and rights of individuals.

Case Studies

Leadership adaptation in the digital age involves honing digital leadership skills, effectively managing remote teams, and embracing data-driven decision-making. Leaders who excel in these areas can leverage the opportunities presented by the digital landscape while addressing the challenges of a rapidly evolving world. Here are two case studies of leaders who have successfully adapted to the digital landscape:

Satya Nadella - Microsoft

- **Background:** Satya Nadella became the CEO of Microsoft in 2014, at a time when the company was facing challenges in adapting to the digital era.

- **Adaptation Strategies:**
  - **Cloud Services:** Nadella recognized the importance of cloud computing and shifted Microsoft's focus towards Azure, their cloud platform. Under his leadership, Microsoft became a major player in cloud services, competing with Amazon Web Services.
  - **Openness to Collaboration:** Nadella embraced open-source software and fostered collaboration with other tech companies, marking a departure from Microsoft's historically closed approach.
  - **Acquisitions:** He made strategic acquisitions like LinkedIn and GitHub to expand Microsoft's offerings and strengthen its position in the digital landscape.

- **Outcomes:** Microsoft's market value under Nadella's leadership surpassed $2 trillion in 2021. The company's successful adaptation to cloud computing and digital collaboration tools has made it a dominant force in the tech industry.

Jeff Bezos - Amazon

- **Background:** Jeff Bezos founded Amazon in 1994 as an online bookstore but rapidly adapted to become a global e-commerce and technology giant.

- **Adaptation Strategies:**

  - **E-commerce Dominance:** Bezos recognized the potential of e-commerce and invested heavily in building Amazon's online retail platform.

  - **Cloud Computing:** He launched Amazon Web Services (AWS) in 2006, pioneering the cloud computing industry.

  - **Expanding Services:** Amazon expanded into various sectors, including streaming media (Amazon Prime Video), smart home technology (Amazon Echo), and AI-driven personal assistant (Alexa).

- **Outcomes:** Amazon transformed from a small online bookstore into one of the world's largest tech conglomerates, with diverse revenue streams and a significant global presence. Bezos's visionary leadership and willingness to disrupt traditional business models contributed to Amazon's success in the digital landscape.

These case studies highlight how leaders like Satya Nadella and Jeff Bezos adapted to the digital landscape by embracing technology, fostering innovation, and making strategic decisions that positioned their organizations for growth and relevance in the digital age. Their visionary leadership and adaptability serve as inspirational examples of how leaders can successfully navigate the challenges and opportunities of the digital era.

Cultural Competency and Diversity

Cultural competence refers to an individual's or organization's ability to effectively understand, interact with, and navigate diverse cultures and belief systems. It involves not only awareness and respect for different cultural norms, values, and behaviors but also the capability to communicate and collaborate sensitively across cultural boundaries. Culturally competent individuals and organizations recognize the importance of diversity and actively seek to bridge cultural gaps, fostering inclusivity and mutual understanding.

Diversity pertains to the presence of a wide range of individual differences, including but not limited to race, ethnicity, gender, age, religion, sexual orientation, and physical abilities, within a group, organization, or society. Embracing diversity means acknowledging and valuing these differences, creating an environment where all individuals are welcomed, respected, and given equal opportunities. Diversity is not only a moral imperative but also a source of strength, as it can lead to a richer exchange of perspectives, creativity, and innovation when properly managed and celebrated.

Importance of Cultural Competency and Diversity

Cultural competence and diversity play pivotal roles in leadership adaptation, especially in the context of an ever-evolving global landscape.

1. **Enhancing Global Perspective:**
    - **Cultural Competence:** Leaders who possess cultural competence are better equipped to navigate the complexities of global markets and diverse workforces. They understand the cultural nuances

that influence business practices, communication styles, and consumer behaviors in different regions.

- **Diversity:** A diverse leadership team brings a range of perspectives, experiences, and cultural insights to the decision-making process. This diversity helps leaders make informed choices that consider a broader global context.

2. **Effective Cross-Cultural Communication:**

    - **Cultural Competence:** Leaders with cultural competence can communicate more effectively across cultural boundaries. They can adapt their communication styles and language to be more inclusive and respectful of diverse cultural norms.

    - **Diversity:** Having a diverse team with members from various cultural backgrounds fosters an environment where different communication styles are acknowledged and valued. This can lead to more effective cross-cultural communication within the organization and in international interactions.

3. **Talent Attraction and Retention:**

    - **Cultural Competence:** Leaders who prioritize cultural competence create inclusive workplaces that attract talent from diverse backgrounds. Employees feel valued and respected, which enhances retention rates.

    - **Diversity:** Diverse leadership teams are more likely to attract and retain a wider range of talent. People from underrepresented groups often seek organizations with diverse leadership, where they believe their voices will be heard and their perspectives valued.

4. **Innovation and Problem-Solving:**
    - **Cultural Competence:** Leaders who understand different cultural perspectives can leverage these insights to drive innovation. They can identify new market opportunities, design products that cater to diverse consumer needs, and solve complex problems more creatively.
    - **Diversity:** Diverse teams tend to generate a broader array of ideas and solutions. The fusion of different perspectives can lead to innovative breakthroughs and more effective problem-solving.

5. **Ethical and Inclusive Leadership:**
    - **Cultural Competence:** Culturally competent leaders are often more attuned to ethical considerations related to diversity, such as combating discrimination and promoting fairness. They can create an ethical framework that respects cultural differences.
    - **Diversity:** Demonstrating commitment to diversity by having a diverse leadership team is a visible sign of ethical leadership. It sends a message to the organization that inclusivity and fairness are core values.

6. **Global Market Expansion:**
    - **Cultural Competence:** Understanding cultural nuances is essential when expanding into new global markets. Leaders with cultural competence can adapt their business strategies to fit local contexts, enhancing the chances of market success.

- **Diversity:** Diverse teams can provide insights into the specific needs and preferences of different customer segments. This information is invaluable for tailoring products and services to diverse markets.

Cultural competence and diversity are integral components of effective leadership adaptation in an evolving global landscape. Leaders who prioritize these aspects create more inclusive, innovative, and ethical organizations that are better equipped to thrive in the complex and interconnected world of today.

Strategies for Leader

Navigating cultural differences and fostering inclusive environments is essential for effective leadership in today's diverse world. Here are strategies for leaders to achieve these goals:

1. **Develop Cultural Competence**

    - **Cultural Awareness:** Leaders should actively seek to understand different cultures, including norms, values, and communication styles. This awareness enables them to recognize and respect cultural differences.

    - **Education and Training:** Invest in cultural competence training for yourself and your team. This can include workshops, cross-cultural communication courses, and diversity training programs.

2. **Lead by Example**

    - **Inclusive Behavior:** Demonstrate inclusive behavior by actively listening to diverse perspectives, valuing input from all team members, and avoiding biases or stereotypes.

- **Cultural Sensitivity:** Model cultural sensitivity in your interactions. Show respect for cultural differences and encourage your team to do the same.

3. **Foster Open Communication**
   - **Create Safe Spaces:** Establish an environment where team members feel safe discussing cultural differences and sharing their experiences. Encourage open and honest dialogue.
   - **Active Listening:** Practice active listening by giving your full attention to what others are saying. Ask clarifying questions and seek to understand their viewpoints.

4. **Build Diverse Teams**
   - **Inclusive Hiring:** When forming teams, prioritize diversity in recruitment and hiring processes. Ensure that job postings, interviews, and evaluations are free from bias.
   - **Diversity of Thought:** Recognize that diversity extends beyond visible differences like race or gender. Value diverse perspectives, experiences, and ways of thinking.

5. **Establish Inclusive Policies:**
   - **Inclusive Policies:** Implement policies that promote diversity and inclusion within the organization. This can include flexible work arrangements, anti-discrimination policies, and diversity initiatives.

- **Equal Opportunities:** Ensure that all team members have equal opportunities for advancement, development, and recognition.

6. **Cultural Competence Development**

    - **Cross-Cultural Training:** Provide cross-cultural training and resources to help team members understand and appreciate each other's cultures.

    - **Mentoring and Coaching:** Encourage mentoring relationships between team members from different cultural backgrounds, fostering mutual learning and growth.

7. **Celebrate Differences**

    - **Cultural Celebrations:** Celebrate cultural events and holidays from various backgrounds within the organization. This promotes cultural appreciation and inclusivity.

    - **Recognition:** Acknowledge and reward contributions from diverse team members to demonstrate the value placed on their unique perspectives.

8. **Address Bias and Discrimination**

    - **Zero Tolerance:** Clearly communicate a zero-tolerance policy for discrimination, harassment, and bias within the organization. Implement effective reporting and resolution procedures.

    - **Implicit Bias Training:** Offer training on recognizing and mitigating unconscious biases to help team members become more self-aware.

9. **Engage in Community Outreach**

- **Community Involvement:** Encourage participation in community events and initiatives that promote diversity and inclusion. This demonstrates the organization's commitment to these principles beyond its walls.

10. **Measure Progress**
    - **Data Collection:** Collect data on diversity and inclusion metrics within the organization. Regularly assess progress and adjust strategies as needed to meet inclusion goals.

Effective leadership in navigating cultural differences and fostering inclusive environments requires ongoing commitment, education, and proactive efforts to create a workplace where everyone feels valued and respected, regardless of their background.

Sustainability and Ethical Leadership

Sustainability and Ethical Leadership refers to a leadership approach that prioritizes environmentally and socially responsible practices while guiding organizations toward long-term viability and ethical decision-making. Sustainability in leadership involves strategies and actions aimed at minimizing negative impacts on the environment, conserving resources, and promoting sustainable business practices. Ethical leadership, on the other hand, centers on principles of integrity, fairness, and ethical decision-making. Ethical leaders act with honesty and transparency, making choices that align with moral and societal values. Together, sustainability and ethical leadership emphasize the importance of responsible and sustainable business conduct that benefits not only the organization but also society and the planet at large.

The growing importance of sustainability and ethics in leadership is a response to the complex challenges of the modern world. Here's an examination of why these aspects have become increasingly crucial in leadership:

1. **Global Awareness of Environmental Issues:** The escalating threats of climate change, resource depletion, and environmental degradation have raised global awareness of the need for sustainable practices. Leaders are now expected to address these issues in their strategies and decisions.
2. **Stakeholder Expectations:** Stakeholders, including customers, investors, and employees, are increasingly concerned about the ethical and sustainable practices of organizations. They demand transparency, accountability, and ethical behavior from their leaders.
3. **Regulatory and Legal Pressures:** Governments and regulatory bodies have enacted stricter environmental and ethical regulations, imposing legal obligations on organizations to comply with sustainability standards and ethical guidelines.
4. **Competitive Advantage:** Sustainability and ethics can provide a competitive edge. Organizations that embrace sustainable practices often reduce costs, improve efficiency, and enhance their brand image, attracting environmentally and ethically conscious consumers.
5. **Long-Term Viability:** Sustainability and ethical leadership contribute to an organization's long-term viability. By addressing environmental and ethical concerns, leaders can mitigate risks, build trust, and ensure the sustainability of their businesses.
6. **Employee Attraction and Retention:** Today's workforce, particularly younger generations, values working for organizations with a strong commitment to sustainability and ethics. Ethical leadership and sustainability initiatives can attract and retain top talent.
7. **Reputational Impact:** High-profile ethical lapses or unsustainable practices can lead to severe damage to an

organization's reputation. Leaders who prioritize ethics and sustainability protect their brand's integrity.
8. **Innovation and Adaptation:** Sustainability and ethical leadership encourage innovation. Leaders who seek sustainable solutions often find new opportunities for growth and adapt to changing market demands.
9. **Social Responsibility:** Ethical leaders recognize their role in addressing social issues beyond profit. They engage in corporate social responsibility (CSR) activities, making a positive impact on communities and society.
10. **Mitigating Risk:** Leaders who prioritize sustainability and ethics are better equipped to identify and mitigate risks associated with environmental, social, and governance (ESG) factors. This reduces the likelihood of crises.

Sustainability and ethical leadership have evolved from being optional to becoming imperative in the modern business landscape. Leaders who integrate these principles into their decision-making processes not only contribute to the well-being of the planet and society but also position their organizations for long-term success and resilience in an increasingly complex and interconnected world.

How Leaders can Incorporate Sustainability

Incorporating sustainability practices and ethical considerations into decision-making is essential for responsible and effective leadership. Here's how leaders can do it:

1. **Educate Themselves and Their Teams:** Leaders should stay informed about sustainability trends, ethical frameworks, and industry-specific best practices. They should also provide training and resources to help their teams understand these concepts.
2. **Align with Organizational Values:** Ensure that sustainability and ethics align with the core values and

mission of the organization. Leaders must lead by example in demonstrating a commitment to these principles.
3. **Integrate Sustainability into Strategy:** Embed sustainability into the organization's strategic planning process. This involves setting clear sustainability goals, outlining action plans, and assigning responsibilities for implementation.
4. **Establish Ethical Guidelines:** Develop a code of ethics or conduct that outlines expected ethical behavior within the organization. Communicate these guidelines clearly to all employees and stakeholders.
5. **Evaluate the Triple Bottom Line:** Leaders should consider the triple bottom line—economic, social, and environmental impacts—when making decisions. Assess how decisions affect profitability, people, and the planet.
6. **Conduct Ethical Risk Assessments:** Before making important decisions, leaders should conduct ethical risk assessments to identify potential ethical dilemmas and develop strategies for mitigating them.
7. **Promote Ethical Discussions:** Create a culture where ethical discussions are encouraged. Leaders should be open to feedback and foster an environment where team members feel safe discussing ethical concerns.
8. **Measure and Report Progress:** Implement key performance indicators (KPIs) to measure sustainability and ethical performance. Regularly report on progress and share this information with stakeholders.
9. **Encourage Innovation:** Promote innovation by encouraging employees to find sustainable and ethical solutions to challenges. Recognize and reward innovative approaches that align with these principles.
5. **Collaborate with Stakeholders:** Engage with external stakeholders, including suppliers, customers, NGOs, and regulatory bodies, to collaborate on sustainability initiatives and ethical standards.

6. **Support Employee Engagement:** Involve employees in decision-making related to sustainability and ethics. Encourage their input and ideas for improving sustainability practices.
7. **Review and Revise Policies:** Regularly review and update sustainability and ethical policies to ensure they remain relevant and effective in a changing environment.
8. **Lead by Example:** Demonstrate ethical behavior and sustainability practices in all aspects of leadership. Your actions set the tone for the entire organization.
9. **Seek External Expertise:** In complex ethical or sustainability matters, consider seeking advice from external experts or consultants who specialize in these areas.
10. **Learn from Mistakes:** When ethical lapses or sustainability challenges occur, leaders should acknowledge them, learn from them, and take corrective action to prevent similar issues in the future.

By incorporating sustainability practices and ethical considerations into decision-making, leaders not only enhance the reputation and long-term success of their organizations but also contribute positively to the broader community and environment. These principles align with the evolving expectations of stakeholders and promote responsible leadership in an interconnected world.

Leadership Development and Future Trends

Leadership Development and Future Trends refers to the ongoing process of preparing individuals to assume leadership roles effectively while taking into account emerging trends and changes in leadership dynamics. Leadership development involves cultivating leadership skills, competencies, and qualities that align with the evolving needs of organizations and society. It also encompasses staying ahead of future leadership trends, such as digital leadership, diversity and inclusion, and ethical leadership, to proactively address the challenges and opportunities that leaders will encounter in the ever-changing landscape of the future. In essence, it's about equipping leaders with the knowledge, skills, and adaptability to lead in a rapidly evolving world.

Examination of the Leadership Development Program

Leadership development programs and initiatives designed to prepare leaders for future challenges reveal a range of strategies and approaches aimed at equipping individuals with the skills and qualities needed to excel in leadership roles in an evolving world. Here's a detailed examination:

1. **Executive Education Programs:** Leading academic institutions offer executive education programs that focus on leadership development. These programs often cover topics such as strategic leadership, innovation, and change management, providing leaders with up-to-date knowledge and skills.
2. **Mentorship and Coaching:** Mentorship and coaching programs pair emerging leaders with experienced mentors or coaches. This one-on-one guidance helps individuals develop leadership skills, gain insights, and navigate career challenges.
3. **Leadership Workshops and Seminars:** Organizations frequently host workshops and seminars that focus on leadership development. These events provide opportunities for leaders to learn from experts, engage in hands-on exercises, and network with peers.
4. **Online Learning and E-Learning Platforms:** Digital platforms offer a wide array of leadership development courses and resources. These can be accessed remotely, allowing leaders to learn at their own pace and on their schedule.

5. **Leadership Assessments and Feedback:** Leadership assessments, including 360-degree feedback, help leaders gain insights into their strengths and areas for improvement. This feedback informs personalized development plans.
6. **Diversity and Inclusion Training:** Given the importance of diversity and inclusion in modern leadership, many development programs now incorporate training on cultural competence, equity, and inclusion to prepare leaders for diverse workforces and global contexts.
7. **Emotional Intelligence (EI) Training:** EI is recognized as a critical leadership skill. Training programs focus on enhancing self-awareness, empathy, and interpersonal skills, which are essential for effective leadership.
8. **Ethical Leadership Training:** With a growing emphasis on ethics and corporate social responsibility, programs on ethical leadership help leaders make principled decisions and cultivate an ethical organizational culture.
9. **Digital Leadership and Technology Training:** As technology continues to shape the business landscape, leadership development programs may include training on digital leadership, data analytics, cybersecurity, and other technology-related topics.
10. **Experiential Learning and Action Learning Projects:** Many programs emphasize experiential learning through projects and real-world challenges. These initiatives provide leaders with hands-on experience and the opportunity to apply newly acquired skills.
11. **Leadership Retreats and Conferences:** Retreats and conferences bring leaders together for immersive experiences, networking, and exposure to thought leaders. These events often cover emerging leadership trends and best practices.
12. **Cross-Cultural Experiences:** Some leadership development programs incorporate international experiences, such as cross-cultural exchanges or global assignments, to prepare leaders for diverse global contexts.

13. **Continuous Learning Culture:** In forward-thinking organizations, a culture of continuous learning is cultivated, where leaders are encouraged to seek development opportunities throughout their careers.
14. **Resilience and Change Management Training:** Given the rapid pace of change, leaders are often trained in resilience and change management, enabling them to adapt to unforeseen challenges and lead organizations through transformations.
15. **Customized Development Plans:** Effective leadership development programs create tailored development plans for each participant, addressing their unique strengths, weaknesses, and career goals.

Leadership development initiatives are evolving to meet the dynamic demands of the future. By providing leaders with the right knowledge, skills, and experiences, these programs aim to ensure that organizations are well-prepared to address the complexities and opportunities that lie ahead.

How Organizations Design and Implement Effective Leadership Program

Designing and implementing effective leadership development programs requires careful planning and consideration of best practices. Here are some key steps and practices to ensure the success of such programs:

1. **Define Clear Objectives:** Start by clearly defining the objectives of the leadership development program. What specific skills, competencies, or leadership qualities do you want participants to acquire or enhance?
2. **Assess Individual Needs:** Conduct assessments or use tools like 360-degree feedback to identify the development needs of each participant. Tailor the program to address these individual gaps.

3. **Align with Organizational Goals:** Ensure that the leadership development program aligns with the overall goals and strategic priorities of the organization. It should contribute to the success of the organization as a whole.
4. **Involve Top Leadership:** Gain buy-in and support from top leadership, including senior executives and the CEO. Their endorsement demonstrates the program's importance and commitment to leadership development.
5. **Offer a Variety of Learning Experiences:** Incorporate a mix of learning methods, such as workshops, seminars, coaching, mentoring, e-learning, and experiential learning, to accommodate diverse learning preferences.
6. **Provide Real-World Challenges:** Include practical, real-world challenges and projects that allow participants to apply what they've learned to actual leadership situations.
7. **Foster Networking and Collaboration:** Create opportunities for participants to network and collaborate with peers, both within and outside the organization. Peer learning can be highly valuable.
8. **Encourage Self-Reflection:** Incorporate self-assessment, reflection, and journaling as part of the program to encourage participants to gain deeper insights into their leadership styles and growth areas.
9. **Emphasize Inclusivity and Diversity:** Ensure that the program promotes inclusivity and diversity by including participants from various backgrounds and addressing cultural competence and diversity issues.
10. **Measure and Evaluate:** Implement metrics and evaluations to assess the effectiveness of the program. Gather feedback from participants, mentors, and supervisors to make continuous improvements.
11. **Provide Ongoing Support:** Leadership development is a continuous process. Offer ongoing support and resources to program graduates, such as alumni networks and access to further learning opportunities.

12. **Promote Accountability:** Hold participants accountable for their development goals and progress. This can include regular check-ins and milestones to track their growth.
13. **Flexibility and Adaptation:** - Be flexible and adaptable in response to changing needs and circumstances. Leadership development programs should evolve to stay relevant.
14. **Invest in Quality Facilitators and Coaches:** Ensure that program facilitators and coaches are experienced, knowledgeable, and skilled in leadership development. Their expertise is crucial for program success.
15. **Communicate and Market the Program:** Clearly communicate the benefits of the program to potential participants. Effective marketing can help attract the right candidates.
16. **Promote a Culture of Learning:** Encourage a culture of continuous learning throughout the organization, not just within the program. Leadership development should be part of the organizational DNA.
17. **Evaluate ROI:** Assess the return on investment (ROI) of the leadership development program by measuring its impact on organizational performance, employee engagement, and other relevant metrics.

By following these best practices, organizations can design and implement leadership development programs that empower individuals to become effective and adaptable leaders, ultimately contributing to the success and sustainability of the organization.

Predicting Future Trend in Leadership

Predicting future trends in leadership refers to the practice of forecasting and anticipating the evolving dynamics, challenges, and expectations that will shape leadership roles and strategies in the years to come. This proactive approach involves identifying emerging leadership styles, technological advancements, industry shifts, and societal changes that will impact how leaders operate and make decisions. By staying ahead of these trends, organizations and leaders can better prepare for the challenges and opportunities that the future holds, ensuring they remain effective and relevant in an ever-changing landscape.

Emerging Trend and Challenges

Emerging trends and challenges that leaders may face in the future encompass a wide range of dynamic and evolving aspects of leadership. Here's a some key trends and challenges:

1. **AI Integration**
   - *Trend:* Artificial Intelligence (AI) and automation are becoming integral to various industries. Leaders must understand AI's potential and limitations and incorporate it strategically into their operations, from decision support to customer service.
   - *Challenge:* Balancing AI with human decision-making, addressing ethical concerns, and ensuring job displacement is minimized are challenges leaders will face. They must also adapt to managing AI-driven teams.

2. **Climate Change Leadership**
   - *Trend:* Climate change and sustainability are increasingly central to business strategies. Leaders need to incorporate environmental responsibility into their organizations, aligning with global efforts to mitigate climate change.
   - *Challenge:* Navigating the complexities of sustainable practices, adhering to regulations, and engaging stakeholders in sustainability efforts pose

challenges. Leaders must also foster a culture of environmental responsibility.

3. **Crisis Management**

    - *Trend:* With global interconnectivity, crises can escalate rapidly. Leaders must be prepared for various crises, including pandemics, cyberattacks, natural disasters, and social crises.

    - *Challenge:* Effective crisis management requires quick decision-making, clear communication, and adaptability. Leaders must also prioritize employee well-being and organizational resilience.

4. **Remote and Hybrid Work**

    - *Trend:* Remote and hybrid work arrangements have become more common. Leaders need to manage distributed teams effectively and create a cohesive work culture.

    - *Challenge:* Maintaining team cohesion, preventing burnout, and ensuring equitable opportunities for remote and in-office employees are challenges. Leaders must also address technology and communication issues.

5. **Ethical Leadership and Corporate Social Responsibility**

    - *Trend:* Ethical leadership and corporate social responsibility are increasingly important to stakeholders. Leaders are expected to act with transparency, integrity, and a commitment to social and ethical values.

    - *Challenge:* Balancing profit goals with ethical considerations, addressing social justice issues, and making ethical decisions in complex situations require strong ethical leadership.

6. **Digital Leadership**
    - *Trend:* Leadership in the digital age involves harnessing technology, data, and innovation. Leaders need to adapt to digital transformation and ensure their organizations remain competitive.
    - *Challenge:* Leaders must bridge the digital skills gap within their teams, navigate data privacy and security issues, and keep up with rapid technological advancements.

7. **Inclusive Leadership**
    - *Trend:* Inclusion and diversity are critical components of modern leadership. Leaders are expected to foster inclusive workplaces and embrace diverse perspectives.
    - *Challenge:* Creating a truly inclusive culture, addressing unconscious biases, and ensuring equal opportunities for all employees can be challenging. Leaders must champion diversity at all levels.

8. **Geopolitical Uncertainty:**
    - *Trend:* Geopolitical factors, such as trade tensions and political instability, impact global business environments. Leaders must navigate international complexities.
    - *Challenge:* Adapting to changing geopolitical landscapes, managing international teams, and addressing political risks are challenges leaders may face.

Leaders in the future will need to adapt to a complex and rapidly changing landscape characterized by technological advancements, environmental concerns, and evolving societal expectations. Successfully addressing these emerging trends and challenges requires forward-thinking leadership that combines adaptability, ethical decision-making, and a commitment to sustainability and inclusivity.

How Leaders can Anticipate and Prepare

Leaders can anticipate and prepare for emerging trends by adopting a proactive and strategic approach to leadership development. Here are ways leaders can stay ahead of these trends:

1. **Continuous Learning:** Embrace a lifelong learning mindset. Stay informed about industry trends, new technologies, and global developments through courses, workshops, webinars, and industry publications.
2. **Scenario Planning:** Engage in scenario planning exercises to envision various future scenarios and develop strategies to address each one. This helps leaders prepare for unexpected challenges.
3. **Environmental Scanning:** Regularly scan the external environment for emerging trends and market shifts. This includes monitoring industry reports, competitor activities, and global news.
4. **Network and Collaboration:** Build a strong professional network and collaborate with peers, mentors, and industry experts. Discussions and knowledge sharing can provide valuable insights into emerging trends.
5. **Employee Feedback:** Encourage open communication with employees and teams. Actively seek their input and feedback on emerging workplace trends and challenges.
6. **Diversity and Inclusion Initiatives:** Proactively foster diversity and inclusion within the organization. Encourage diverse perspectives, and ensure leadership teams are representative of the workforce.
7. **Innovation Culture:** Foster a culture of innovation within the organization. Encourage employees to propose and test

new ideas and technologies that could address emerging trends.
8. **Sustainability Commitment:** Integrate sustainability practices into the organization's strategy. Establish sustainability goals and initiatives that align with global efforts to combat climate change.
9. **Ethical Leadership Training:** Invest in training and resources that promote ethical leadership. Develop ethical guidelines and policies that guide decision-making at all levels.
10. **Crisis Preparedness:** - Develop robust crisis management plans and conduct regular drills. Ensure that leaders are well-versed in crisis response and communication protocols.
11. **Technology Adoption:** Stay informed about emerging technologies and their potential impact on the industry. Be prepared to invest in and integrate relevant technologies to maintain competitiveness.
12. **Remote Work Policies:** Continuously adapt remote and hybrid work policies to meet evolving workforce expectations. Prioritize employee well-being and engagement in remote work environments.
13. **Geopolitical Analysis:** Monitor geopolitical developments and their potential impact on the organization's global operations. Consider diversifying supply chains and business relationships when necessary.
14. **Talent Development:** Invest in leadership development programs that equip future leaders with the skills and knowledge needed to navigate emerging trends.
15. **Agility and Adaptability:** Foster a culture of agility and adaptability within the organization. Encourage teams to pivot quickly in response to changing circumstances.
16. **Data-Driven Decision-Making:** Develop data analytics capabilities to make informed decisions based on data insights. Utilize data to anticipate market trends and customer preferences.

By taking these proactive steps and staying attuned to emerging trends, leaders can position themselves and their organizations to adapt successfully to the challenges and opportunities that lie ahead in an ever-evolving landscape.

Role of Continuous Learning

The role of continuous learning refers to the ongoing process of acquiring new knowledge, skills, and insights throughout one's life and career. In a rapidly changing world, individuals and organizations must recognize the importance of continuous learning to remain relevant, adaptable, and competitive. It involves seeking opportunities for education, skill development, and personal growth, both formally and informally, to keep up with evolving trends, technologies, and challenges. Continuous learning empowers individuals to enhance their expertise, make informed decisions, and respond effectively to changes in their professional and personal lives.

Continuous learning and adaptation are of paramount importance in leadership for several compelling reasons:

1. **Evolving Knowledge and Skills:** The business landscape is constantly evolving, driven by technological advancements, industry trends, and market shifts. Leaders must continually update their knowledge and skills to remain effective in their roles.
2. **Enhanced Problem-Solving and Innovation:** Continuous learning exposes leaders to new ideas and perspectives, fostering creativity and innovation. This enables them to approach challenges with fresh insights and develop innovative solutions.
3. **Adaptation to Change:** Change is inevitable, whether due to economic fluctuations, industry disruptions, or global crises. Leaders who engage in continuous learning are better

equipped to adapt to change, guide their teams through transitions, and mitigate risks.

4. **Improved Decision-Making:** Informed decision-making is a cornerstone of effective leadership. Continuous learning provides leaders with a broader knowledge base, enabling them to make well-informed, data-driven decisions.
5. **Keeping Pace with Technology:** Technology plays a pivotal role in modern business. Leaders who continually learn about and embrace emerging technologies can leverage them to enhance operational efficiency and competitiveness.
6. **Flexibility and Resilience:** Continuous learning instills a sense of adaptability and resilience in leaders. They become more open to change and can pivot swiftly in response to unforeseen challenges.
7. **Enhanced Communication Skills:** Effective leadership requires strong communication skills. Continuous learning helps leaders refine their communication abilities, making it easier to convey ideas, motivate teams, and build relationships.
8. **Talent Attraction and Retention:** A commitment to continuous learning can make organizations more attractive to top talent. Employees seek environments where they can grow and develop, which in turn aids in talent retention.
9. **Ethical Leadership:** Continuous learning about ethical leadership principles and societal expectations helps leaders make principled decisions and foster ethical cultures within their organizations.
9. **Future-Proofing Leadership:** By staying updated on emerging trends and industry disruptions, leaders can position themselves to anticipate and proactively address future challenges, ensuring their leadership remains relevant.
10. **Personal Growth and Fulfillment:** Continuous learning contributes to personal growth and fulfillment. Leaders who invest in their own development often find greater job satisfaction and a deeper sense of purpose in their roles.

11. **Leading by Example:** Leaders who prioritize continuous learning set a positive example for their teams. This encourages a culture of learning and growth throughout the organization.

Continuous learning and adaptation are fundamental for leadership effectiveness in a rapidly changing world. Leaders who commit to lifelong learning not only stay ahead of the curve but also inspire their teams, foster innovation, and navigate the complexities of leadership with confidence and agility.

Strategies for Life-Long Learning

Embracing lifelong learning and staying ahead of evolving trends is essential for leaders. Here are strategies to help leaders in this pursuit:

1. **Set Learning Goals:** Define specific learning objectives and goals related to your leadership role. What skills or knowledge do you want to acquire or enhance? Having clear goals provides direction.
2. **Allocate Time for Learning:** Dedicate regular time in your schedule for learning activities. Treat learning as a priority, just like meetings and other work responsibilities.
3. **Utilize a Variety of Learning Methods:** Explore diverse learning methods, including workshops, courses, webinars, conferences, podcasts, and books. Mix formal and informal learning experiences to keep it engaging.
4. **Seek Mentorship and Coaching:** Find mentors or coaches who can guide your learning journey. They can offer insights, provide feedback, and share their experiences to accelerate your growth.
5. **Join Professional Associations:** Become a member of professional associations related to your field. Attend their events, webinars, and conferences to stay updated on industry trends and network with peers.

6. **Create a Learning Network:** Build a network of colleagues, both within and outside your organization, who share your commitment to learning. Engaging in knowledge exchange and discussions can be invaluable.
7. **Embrace Online Learning Platforms:** Explore online learning platforms and resources like Coursera, LinkedIn Learning, and edX. These platforms offer a wide range of courses and certifications.
8. **Participate in Workshops and Seminars:** Attend workshops and seminars relevant to your industry and leadership role. These events often provide hands-on learning experiences and opportunities for interaction.
9. **Reflect and Apply Learning:** After acquiring new knowledge or skills, take time to reflect on how to apply them in your leadership role. Practical application reinforces learning.
10. **Set Aside Self-Development Time:** Dedicate a portion of your personal time to self-development. Read industry-related books, research papers, or articles to expand your knowledge.
11. **Collaborate and Share Knowledge:** Collaborate with colleagues on projects or initiatives that encourage knowledge sharing. Peer learning can deepen your understanding of new concepts.
12. **Embrace Feedback and Adaptation:** Be open to feedback and adapt based on what you've learned. Continuous improvement is a hallmark of effective leadership.
13. **Stay Informed About Global Trends:** Stay informed about global trends and developments that may impact your industry. Follow news, subscribe to industry publications, and engage in thought leadership discussions.
14. **Set a Learning Budget:** Allocate resources for your learning journey, which may include course fees, books, or memberships. Consider it an investment in your leadership skills.

15. **Measure Progress:** Periodically assess your learning progress by reviewing your goals and evaluating the impact of your learning initiatives on your leadership effectiveness.
16. **Encourage Learning Among Your Team:** Foster a culture of continuous learning within your team or organization. Encourage your team members to embrace learning opportunities and share knowledge.

By integrating these strategies into your leadership approach, you can make continuous learning a fundamental part of your leadership journey, ensuring that you remain adaptable, informed, and effective in the face of evolving trends and challenges.

*****

CHAPTER TWELVE
Reflection and integration

Reflection is a cognitive process through which an individual consciously thinks about and analyzes their own thoughts, experiences, actions, or behaviors. It involves deep and thoughtful consideration of one's thoughts, feelings, experiences, and the events or situations they have encountered. Reflection can serve several important purposes, including:

1. **Self-awareness:** Reflecting on your experiences and thoughts can help you gain a deeper understanding of yourself. It allows you to recognize your strengths, weaknesses, values, and beliefs.

2. **Learning and Growth:** Reflection is a powerful tool for learning from your experiences. By looking back on past actions or decisions, you can identify what worked well and what didn't, helping you make better choices in the future.

3. **Problem Solving:** Reflecting on a problem or challenge allows you to consider different perspectives and potential solutions. It can lead to innovative problem-solving and decision-making.

4. **Emotional Processing:** Reflecting on your emotions and reactions to situations can help you manage your emotions more effectively. It enables you to gain insight into why you feel a certain way and how to respond constructively.

5. **Continuous Improvement:** In professional settings, reflection is often used as a tool for continuous improvement. It can help individuals and teams assess their

performance, identify areas for growth, and develop strategies for improvement.

6. **Goal Setting:** Reflecting on your goals and aspirations can help you align your actions with your long-term objectives. It allows you to assess progress and adjust your plans accordingly.

There are various methods for engaging in reflection, including journaling, meditation, group discussions, or simply taking time to think deeply about your experiences. Effective reflection typically involves asking yourself open-ended questions, such as:

- What did I learn from this experience?
- How did I feel during this situation, and why?
- What could I have done differently?
- What were the key takeaways or insights from this experience?
- How does this experience relate to my goals and values?

Reflection is a valuable tool for personal and professional development, as it encourages self-awareness, critical thinking, and the ability to make more informed decisions based on past experiences.

Integration

In the context of leadership theories, integration typically refers to the ability of a leader to bring together various components, concepts, or dimensions of leadership to create a unified and effective leadership approach. It involves blending different aspects of leadership to achieve a cohesive and balanced leadership style. Here's a more detailed explanation of integration in leadership theories:

1. **Integration of Leadership Styles:** Leadership theories often describe various leadership styles, such as transformational, transactional, servant, or charismatic leadership. Integrative leadership involves the skill of combining elements from different styles to adapt to specific situations and meet the needs of the team or organization. This means a leader can be both transformational and transactional as the situation requires, rather than rigidly adhering to one style.

2. **Integration of Competencies:** Effective leadership requires a range of competencies, including communication, decision-making, problem-solving, and emotional intelligence. Leaders who excel in integration can leverage these competencies in a balanced and harmonious manner. They know when to use each competency to achieve the best outcomes for their team or organization.

3. **Integration of Values and Ethics:** Ethical leadership is a critical component of effective leadership. Leaders who integrate ethics into their leadership style ensure that their decisions and actions align with their values and the organization's ethical standards. This integration of values and ethics creates trust and credibility.

4. **Integration of Diversity and Inclusion:** In today's diverse workplaces, leaders must integrate principles of diversity and inclusion into their leadership approach. This means actively valuing and leveraging the diverse perspectives, backgrounds, and experiences of team members to drive innovation and inclusivity.

5. **Integration of Feedback:** Effective leaders actively seek and integrate feedback from their team members and peers. They use this feedback to adapt and improve their leadership practices, demonstrating a commitment to ongoing development and growth.

6. **Integration of Change Management:** In dynamic environments, leaders must be skilled at managing change. Integration in this context involves the ability to seamlessly integrate change initiatives into the organization's culture and operations, minimizing disruption and resistance.

7. **Integration of Vision and Execution:** Visionary leaders excel at setting a compelling vision, but they also understand the importance of executing that vision effectively. Integration involves aligning strategic vision with practical implementation, ensuring that the team can translate the vision into action.

8. **Integration of Leadership Levels:** Leaders often operate at multiple levels, from individual leadership to team leadership and organizational leadership. Integration involves the ability to transition smoothly between these levels, understanding how actions at one level impact the others.

9. **Integration of Context:** Effective leaders recognize that leadership approaches should be adapted to the specific context and challenges they face. They integrate context-awareness into their decision-making, avoiding one-size-fits-all leadership.

Integration in leadership theories reflects the flexibility and adaptability of leaders to harmonize and balance various aspects of leadership to achieve optimal results in different situations. Leaders who can effectively integrate these elements are often more successful in inspiring and guiding their teams toward success while navigating the complexities of leadership in today's ever-changing world.

Role of Reflection and Integration in Understanding Leadership Theories

Reflection and integration play crucial roles in understanding leadership theories by helping individuals engage deeply with the concepts and apply them effectively. Here's how reflection and integration contribute to understanding leadership theories:

1. **Clarification of Concepts:** Reflection allows individuals to dissect and analyze leadership theories and concepts. By taking time to think critically about these ideas, individuals can clarify their understanding of key principles, models, and approaches in leadership. They can identify nuances and subtleties within theories that may not be immediately apparent.

2. **Connecting Theory to Practice:** Integration bridges the gap between theory and practice. It involves taking the insights gained from studying leadership theories and applying them to real-world leadership situations. Integration helps individuals see how theoretical concepts can be practically implemented and adapted to address specific leadership challenges.

3. **Development of Personal Leadership Philosophy:** Through reflection, individuals can identify which leadership theories and principles resonate with them personally. They can consider their values, beliefs, and leadership styles in light of different theories, ultimately leading to the development of a personal leadership philosophy. This philosophy serves as a foundation for their leadership approach.

4. **Critical Evaluation:** Reflection encourages critical thinking about leadership theories. Individuals can assess the strengths and weaknesses of different theories, considering their applicability to different contexts. Integration allows

individuals to incorporate the strengths of various theories into their leadership toolbox while addressing their limitations.

5. **Adaptation and Flexibility:** Effective leadership often requires adapting to changing circumstances and contexts. Reflection and integration foster adaptability by helping individuals understand when and how to apply different leadership theories based on the unique needs of a situation. This adaptability is crucial for effective leadership in dynamic environments.

6. **Continuous Learning:** Leadership theories evolve over time as new research and insights emerge. Reflection and integration promote a culture of continuous learning, encouraging individuals to stay updated with the latest developments in leadership theory and practice. This ensures that their leadership knowledge remains relevant and effective.

7. **Problem-Solving and Decision-Making:** Leadership often involves complex problem-solving and decision-making. Reflective practices help leaders analyze situations from different angles and consider multiple perspectives, improving their ability to make informed decisions and solve challenges effectively.

8. **Conflict Resolution:** Reflection and integration can enhance a leader's ability to navigate conflicts and disagreements within a team. By reflecting on the underlying causes of conflicts and integrating conflict resolution strategies from various theories, leaders can work toward constructive solutions.

9. **Team Development:** Understanding leadership theories through reflection and integration allows leaders to identify strategies for team development and motivation. Leaders can

draw from various theories to create a cohesive and high-performing team that aligns with the organization's goals.

10. **Ethical Leadership:** Reflection and integration encourage leaders to consider the ethical dimensions of their decisions and actions. Leaders can evaluate their behavior in light of ethical theories and integrate ethical principles into their leadership practices.

Reflection and integration are essential tools for individuals seeking to understand and apply leadership theories effectively. They enable a deeper and more practical comprehension of leadership concepts, encourage continuous improvement, and help leaders develop a flexible and adaptive approach to leadership in a complex and ever-changing world.

Identification of Personal Insights

Identification of personal insights in the context of leadership theories involves recognizing and understanding how specific leadership theories or principles relate to your own experiences, beliefs, values, and leadership style. It's about gaining a deeper understanding of yourself as a leader by reflecting on how leadership theories resonate with your personal experiences and perspectives. Here's a breakdown of this concept:

1. **Self-Reflection:** Identifying personal insights begins with self-reflection. You take the time to think critically about your own leadership experiences, behaviors, and beliefs. This reflection may involve considering past leadership roles, challenges you've faced, and the leadership approaches you've used.

2. **Understanding Leadership Theories:** To identify personal insights, you must have a solid grasp of various leadership theories and principles. This includes understanding the key concepts, models, and approaches put forth by different

leadership scholars. It's essential to be familiar with the theories you're reflecting upon.

3. **Relating Theory to Experience:** With an understanding of leadership theories, you can start connecting these theories to your personal leadership experiences. For example, you might recognize instances where you applied transformational leadership principles to inspire your team or times when you used situational leadership to adapt to different situations.

4. **Aligning with Values and Beliefs:** Identification of personal insights often involves aligning leadership theories with your own values and beliefs. You may find that certain theories resonate with your core values and align with the kind of leader you aspire to be. Conversely, you may identify theories that conflict with your values, prompting you to critically assess their relevance in your leadership approach.

5. **Recognizing Strengths and Weaknesses:** As you identify personal insights, you can better understand your strengths and weaknesses as a leader. You may discover that you excel in certain leadership areas because they align with your natural tendencies, while other areas require more development.

6. **Adapting and Growing:** Personal insights also involve recognizing areas for growth and development. By identifying where your leadership style aligns with specific theories and where it diverges, you can make informed decisions about how to adapt and grow as a leader. This adaptability is key to becoming a more effective leader.

7. **Building a Leadership Philosophy:** Through this process, you can develop a personal leadership philosophy that incorporates insights from various leadership theories. Your philosophy serves as a guiding framework for your

leadership approach, informed by both your personal experiences and theoretical knowledge.

8. **Enhancing Decision-Making:** Personal insights can improve your decision-making as a leader. By understanding how different theories apply to different situations, you can make more informed choices about which leadership approach is most suitable for a given context.

9. **Improving Communication and Team Dynamics:** Identifying personal insights can enhance your communication skills and your ability to work effectively with teams. It helps you understand how your leadership style and communication preferences may impact team dynamics and how to adapt for better collaboration.

10. **Evolving Leadership Practice:** Finally, personal insights should lead to the evolution of your leadership practice. As you gain a deeper understanding of yourself and how you relate to leadership theories, you can continuously refine your approach to become a more effective and authentic leader.

The identification of personal insights in the context of leadership theories is a reflective process that helps leaders better understand themselves, their leadership style, and how various theories can inform and improve their leadership practice. It's a valuable step toward becoming a more self-aware and effective leader.

Prompts for Self-Reflection

Some prompts for self-reflection that can help leaders connect the insights from leadership theories to their own experiences and aspirations:

1. **Reflect on Your Leadership Journey**
   - What are the key milestones and experiences that have shaped your leadership journey thus far?
   - How have these experiences influenced your leadership style and approach?

2. **Identify Key Leadership Challenges**
   - Think about the most significant leadership challenges you've faced. What theories or concepts presented resonate with those challenges?
   - How did you address these challenges, and what insights from the theories could have improved your approach?

3. **Examine Your Leadership Values and Beliefs**
   - What are your core values as a leader? How do they align with the leadership theories and principles you've encountered?
   - Are there theories that challenge your existing beliefs? How might they impact your leadership philosophy?

4. **Consider Your Leadership Strengths and Weaknesses**
   - Reflect on your leadership strengths. How do they align with the theories you've studied?
   - Conversely, what aspects of your leadership could benefit from further development based on the insights gained from the theories?

5. **Evaluate Team Dynamics:**
   - Think about your experience leading teams. Which leadership theories have had a significant impact on team dynamics and performance?
   - Are there theories that could help you better understand and navigate team challenges or conflicts?

6. **Explore Decision-Making Moments:**
   - Recall critical decisions you've made as a leader. How were these decisions influenced by leadership theories or concepts?
   - Could a deeper understanding of certain theories have led to different, perhaps more effective, decisions?

7. **Consider Your Leadership Aspirations:**
   - What kind of leader do you aspire to become? Which leadership theories align with your aspirations, and which ones might help you reach your goals?
   - How can you integrate these theories into your leadership development plan?

8. **Reflect on Your Impact:**
   - Reflect on the impact you've had as a leader. How do the insights from leadership theories relate to the outcomes you've achieved?
   - Are there theories that could help you amplify your positive impact or address areas where improvement is needed?

9. **Embrace a Growth Mindset:**

    - In what ways can you continue to learn and evolve as a leader? How can you stay open to new insights and adapt your leadership style accordingly?

    - What steps can you take to foster a culture of continuous learning within your team or organization?

    - **Set Personal Leadership Goals:** Based on your reflections, what are some specific leadership goals you can set for yourself? How can you incorporate the insights gained from leadership theories into your goal-setting process?

These prompts for self-reflection can help leaders dive deeper into their own leadership experiences and aspirations, fostering a more profound understanding of how leadership theories can inform and enhance their leadership journey.

Ever-Evolving Tapestry of Leadership in Modern Times

The Ever-Evolving Tapestry of Leadership in Modern Times represents the dynamic and continuously changing nature of leadership concepts and practices in the contemporary world. This concept acknowledges that leadership is not static but rather a fluid and adaptable construct that responds to shifting societal, technological, and organizational dynamics. In modern times, leaders must constantly update their skills, adapt to new challenges, and incorporate diverse perspectives into their leadership approaches. This ever-evolving tapestry emphasizes the need for leaders to be agile, open to innovation, and committed to lifelong learning as they navigate the complexities of today's rapidly changing global landscape. It underscores the importance of staying current with emerging trends and adapting leadership strategies to meet the evolving needs of organizations and society.

Leadership is a Dynamic Journey that encapsulates the idea that leadership is not a fixed destination but an ongoing and evolving process. It emphasizes that effective leadership is a continuous journey of growth, adaptation, and learning. Leaders must be flexible and open to change as they navigate through various challenges, contexts, and stages of their careers. This perspective acknowledges that leadership skills and approaches may need to evolve to meet the demands of different situations and diverse teams. Leadership as a dynamic journey underscores the importance of self-awareness, continuous development, and the ability to embrace new insights and experiences along the way, recognizing that leadership is a lifelong quest rather than a static position to achieve.

The dynamic nature of leadership in modern times is characterized by rapid changes in society, technology, and the business landscape. This dynamism challenges leaders to adapt, innovate, and continuously evolve their leadership approaches. The key aspects of this dynamic nature are:

1. **Globalization and Diversity:** In the modern era, leaders often manage diverse and geographically dispersed teams. Globalization has increased cultural diversity within organizations, demanding culturally sensitive and inclusive leadership styles. Leaders must navigate different time zones, languages, and cultural norms, requiring adaptability and cross-cultural communication skills.

2. **Technological Advancements:** The digital age has transformed how work is done, with the proliferation of remote work, virtual teams, and advanced communication technologies. Leaders must stay current with tech trends, embrace digital tools, and foster a tech-savvy workforce. They also need to address cybersecurity and privacy concerns.

3. **Rapid Change and Uncertainty:** The pace of change in industries is faster than ever. Leaders must be agile and capable of making quick decisions in uncertain environments. The COVID-19 pandemic highlighted the need for crisis leadership and the ability to navigate unexpected disruptions.

4. **Shift in Leadership Models:** The command-and-control leadership model of the past has evolved into more collaborative, participative, and servant leadership styles. Modern leaders often engage in shared decision-making and empower their teams to take ownership of projects.

5. **Emphasis on Emotional Intelligence:** Leaders today recognize the importance of emotional intelligence in building strong relationships and effective communication. Understanding and managing emotions, both in themselves and in others, is a critical leadership skill.

6. **Sustainability and Corporate Responsibility:** There's a growing emphasis on ethical leadership, environmental sustainability, and corporate social responsibility. Leaders are expected to integrate social and environmental considerations into their decision-making processes.

7. **Continuous Learning:** Leaders in modern times must be committed to continuous learning and development. They should seek feedback, engage in reflective practices, and invest in their own growth. Lifelong learning is essential to stay relevant in an ever-changing landscape.

8. **Remote Work and Flexibility:** The COVID-19 pandemic accelerated the adoption of remote work. Leaders must adapt to managing remote teams, balancing flexibility with accountability, and addressing mental health and work-life balance concerns.

9. **Innovation and Creativity:** Encouraging innovation and creativity is vital for organizations to stay competitive. Leaders need to foster a culture that values new ideas, experimentation, and learning from failures.

10. **Ethical and Inclusive Leadership:** Modern leaders are expected to uphold strong ethical standards, promote diversity and inclusion, and champion social justice causes. They must lead by example and create environments where everyone feels valued and included.

Leadership in modern times is marked by its dynamic and ever-evolving nature. Leaders who thrive in this environment are those who embrace change, exhibit adaptability, prioritize continuous learning, and recognize the importance of ethics, diversity, and innovation. The ability to navigate these dynamic challenges is what sets effective modern leaders apart.

Role of Change and Innovation

Change and innovation play pivotal roles in leadership and are closely interconnected. Effective leaders recognize the significance of both change and innovation in driving organizational success.

Change Leadership

- **Navigating Change:** Leaders must be adept at guiding their teams and organizations through periods of change, whether it's due to market shifts, technological advancements, or internal restructuring. They provide clarity, direction, and support during transitions.
- **Change Management:** Successful leaders implement change management strategies to minimize resistance and facilitate a smooth transition. They communicate the need for change, involve employees in the process, and provide the necessary resources and training.

- **Adaptability:** Leaders embrace change as an opportunity for growth and improvement. They are flexible and open to new ideas, recognizing that resisting change can hinder progress.

Innovation Leadership

- **Fostering a Culture of Innovation:** Leaders create an environment where innovation is encouraged and valued. They promote a culture that rewards creative thinking, experimentation, and calculated risk-taking.
- **Setting the Example:** Effective leaders lead by example, demonstrating their commitment to innovation through their own actions and willingness to explore new solutions to problems.
- **Supporting Innovation Teams:** Leaders provide resources, autonomy, and guidance to teams and individuals responsible for innovation. They remove barriers that may hinder creative processes.
- **Customer-Centric Innovation:** Leaders prioritize customer needs and preferences in the innovation process, ensuring that new products, services, or solutions align with market demands.
- **Continuous Improvement:** Leaders understand that innovation is an ongoing process, not a one-time event. They encourage a mindset of continuous improvement, where even small innovations are celebrated and built upon.

Change and Innovation Synergy

- **Change as an Enabler of Innovation:** Effective leaders recognize that change can create opportunities for innovation. When organizations adapt to new circumstances or challenges, it often sparks creativity and the search for innovative solutions.
- **Innovation as a Driver of Change:** Innovation can be a catalyst for change. New products, services, or processes

may require adjustments to existing practices, and leaders must guide these changes effectively.
- **Balancing Stability and Innovation:** Leaders must strike a balance between maintaining stability and promoting innovation. They ensure that core processes are stable while encouraging innovation in areas that can benefit from change.
- **Managing Risks:** Leaders are responsible for managing the risks associated with both change and innovation. They make informed decisions about when and how to implement change or introduce new ideas, considering potential risks and benefits.

Change and innovation are integral to effective leadership. Leaders who navigate change thoughtfully and foster innovation within their organizations are better positioned to adapt to evolving challenges, stay competitive, and drive long-term success. By recognizing the roles of change and innovation and how they complement each other, leaders can create a culture of continuous improvement and forward momentum.

Leaders Role in Driving Change and Fostering Innovation

Leaders play instrumental roles in driving change and fostering innovation in organizations and society. They serve as catalysts for transformation and progress by inspiring, guiding, and facilitating the processes of change and innovation. Here's how leaders fulfill these crucial roles:

1. **Vision and Direction:** Leaders provide a clear vision and direction for their organizations or communities. They articulate a compelling purpose and a future state that motivates and inspires individuals to strive for change and innovation.
2. **Setting Expectations:** Effective leaders establish expectations for change and innovation as core values within

their organizations. They communicate the importance of embracing new ideas and approaches, creating a culture that values innovation.

3. **Building a Culture of Innovation:** Leaders shape organizational cultures that encourage and reward innovative thinking. They create an environment where employees feel safe to propose and experiment with new ideas, knowing their contributions are valued.
4. **Empowering Teams:** Leaders empower teams and individuals by delegating authority and decision-making power. They trust their teams to take calculated risks and make decisions that drive innovation and change.
5. **Resource Allocation:** Leaders allocate resources, including funding, time, and talent, to support innovation initiatives. They prioritize projects that align with the organization's strategic goals and encourage experimentation.
6. **Encouraging Collaboration:** Leaders foster collaboration among diverse teams and departments, recognizing that innovation often arises from the intersection of different perspectives and expertise.
7. **Modeling Behavior:** Leaders lead by example, demonstrating their commitment to change and innovation through their own actions and willingness to embrace new ideas and methods.
8. **Communication and Transparency:** Leaders communicate the rationale behind changes and innovations, providing context and ensuring that everyone understands the reasons for the transformation. They maintain open and transparent channels of communication.
9. **Overcoming Resistance:** Leaders address resistance to change and innovation by listening to concerns, providing support and resources, and highlighting the benefits and opportunities that arise from embracing change.
10. **Celebrating Successes and Learning from Failures:** Leaders celebrate successful innovations and acknowledge the efforts of teams and individuals. They also foster a

culture that views failures as opportunities for learning and improvement.
11. **Strategic Adaptation:** Leaders continuously assess the organization's external environment and adjust strategies in response to changing conditions. They are proactive in identifying emerging trends and technologies that could impact the organization.
12. **Social Responsibility and Impact:** Leaders recognize their role in society and promote innovation that addresses pressing social and environmental challenges. They advocate for responsible business practices and ethical leadership.
13. **Advocacy and Policy Influence:** Leaders engage in advocacy efforts and influence policy decisions that support innovation and change on a broader societal level. They work with government and industry stakeholders to create an environment conducive to innovation.

Leaders serve as drivers of change and innovation by creating a vision, fostering a culture of creativity, and providing the necessary support and resources. They inspire individuals and organizations to adapt, experiment, and evolve in response to evolving challenges and opportunities. Effective leadership is instrumental in propelling organizations and society forward through transformative change and continuous innovation.

Leadership in the Global Context

Leadership in a Global Context signifies the practice of guiding and influencing individuals or organizations within the complex, interconnected, and culturally diverse landscape of today's globalized world. In this context, effective leaders navigate a variety of challenges, such as diverse cultural norms, international markets, and geopolitical factors. They recognize the importance of embracing diversity, cultural sensitivity, and cross-cultural communication while pursuing common goals. Leadership in a global context also requires a deep understanding of global trends, geopolitical dynamics, and the ability to adapt strategies to suit the ever-changing global environment. Ultimately, it involves both the ability to collaborate across borders and the responsibility to make decisions that impact not only a local or national sphere but also the broader global community.

Challenges and Opportunities

Leading in a globalized world presents both significant challenges and numerous opportunities for leaders.

Challenges

1. **Cultural Diversity:** Global leadership demands an understanding of diverse cultures, customs, and norms. Misinterpretations or cultural insensitivity can lead to misunderstandings and conflicts.

2. **Communication Barriers:** Language differences and communication styles can hinder effective interaction among global team members. Leaders must bridge these gaps to ensure clear communication.

3. **Time Zones and Geography:** Managing teams across different time zones and geographical locations can be logistically challenging, affecting collaboration and coordination.

4. **Global Competition:** In a globalized world, businesses face fierce global competition. Leaders must navigate this landscape by continuously innovating and staying ahead of competitors.

5. **Legal and Regulatory Complexity:** Different countries have varying legal and regulatory frameworks. Leaders need

to ensure compliance with these diverse regulations while operating globally.

6. **Geopolitical Instability:** Leaders must monitor and respond to geopolitical shifts and uncertainties that can impact international business operations.

Opportunities

1. **Access to Global Markets:** Globalization opens doors to a vast customer base and diverse markets. Leaders can expand their organizations' reach and growth potential by tapping into these markets.

2. **Talent Pool:** Access to a global talent pool allows leaders to assemble diverse and skilled teams, fostering creativity and innovation.

3. **Diverse Perspectives:** A diverse workforce provides a wide range of perspectives and ideas, contributing to better problem-solving and decision-making.

4. **Technological Advancements:** Technology facilitates global collaboration, enabling remote work, virtual meetings, and real-time information sharing, making global leadership more feasible.

5. **Cultural Exchange:** Leaders can leverage cultural diversity to foster creativity and cross-cultural understanding, which can enhance global relationships and partnerships.

6. **Innovation:** Exposure to different markets and cultures can stimulate innovation by encouraging leaders to adapt products and services to meet diverse needs.

7. **Global Sustainability:** Leaders have the opportunity to contribute to global sustainability efforts by adopting eco-friendly practices and responsible business conduct on a global scale.

Leading in a globalized world presents leaders with the challenge of navigating a complex and diverse landscape. However, it also offers opportunities to expand businesses, access diverse talent, and leverage cultural diversity for innovation and growth. Successful global leaders are those who embrace these challenges and harness the opportunities to drive their organizations to new heights on a global stage.

Navigating Global Complexities

Navigating global complexities and cultural diversity requires leaders to employ specific strategies that foster effective communication, collaboration, and cultural sensitivity. Here are some key strategies for leaders:

1. **Cultural Awareness and Training:** Invest in cultural awareness training for yourself and your team. Develop an understanding of cultural nuances, customs, and communication styles of different regions where your organization operates.

2. **Diverse Hiring and Inclusion:** Build diverse and inclusive teams that represent various cultures and backgrounds. Encourage cross-cultural collaboration to capitalize on diverse perspectives.

3. **Effective Communication:** Foster clear and inclusive communication within the organization. Use language and communication tools that accommodate non-native speakers and ensure everyone's voices are heard.

4. **Cultural Sensitivity:** Approach global challenges with cultural sensitivity. Avoid making assumptions or judgments based on cultural differences and be open to learning from different perspectives.

5. **Localized Leadership:** Consider appointing local leaders or teams in international branches or markets. Local leadership can provide valuable insights and bridge cultural gaps.

6. **Global Mindset:** Cultivate a global mindset within your organization. Encourage employees to think globally, be open to change, and embrace diversity as a source of strength.

7. **Regular Cross-Cultural Training:** Continuously provide cross-cultural training and learning opportunities for your team to build cultural competence and awareness.

8. **Flexible Leadership Styles:** Be adaptable in your leadership style, recognizing that different situations and cultures may require different approaches. A flexible leadership style can help you connect with diverse teams.

9. **Conflict Resolution Skills:** Develop conflict resolution skills that are sensitive to cultural differences. Address conflicts promptly and with respect for diverse viewpoints.

10. **Global Leadership Teams:** Establish cross-functional teams or task forces that bring together individuals from different regions to work on global initiatives. This promotes collaboration and cultural exchange.

11. **Mentoring and Coaching:** Implement mentorship and coaching programs that pair employees from different cultural backgrounds. This can help foster mutual understanding and professional growth.

12. **Technology for Global Collaboration:** Leverage technology for global collaboration. Use video conferencing, collaboration tools, and virtual team-building activities to bridge geographical gaps.

13. **Feedback Culture:** Create a culture of open feedback where employees feel comfortable sharing their perspectives and

concerns related to cultural diversity and global complexities.

14. **Global Corporate Social Responsibility:** Develop a global corporate social responsibility strategy that aligns with diverse cultural and societal expectations. Show commitment to ethical and responsible business conduct worldwide.

15. **Local Partnerships:** Partner with local organizations and stakeholders to gain insights and build relationships within specific regions or markets.

By implementing these strategies, leaders can navigate global complexities and cultural diversity more effectively, fostering an inclusive and culturally sensitive environment that promotes success on the global stage.

The Ethical Imperative of Leadership

The Ethical Imperative of Leadership underscores the fundamental obligation of leaders to operate with integrity, morality, and a strong ethical compass. It signifies that leaders are not only responsible for achieving organizational goals and driving success but also for upholding high ethical standards and principles in their decision-making and actions. Ethical leadership entails making choices that prioritize fairness, transparency, honesty, and the well-being of all stakeholders, including employees, customers, and the broader community. Leaders who embrace the ethical imperative are committed to doing what is right, even when faced with difficult decisions, and they inspire trust, loyalty, and ethical behavior throughout their organizations. Ultimately, ethical leadership is a moral duty that extends beyond profit motives and reflects a commitment to the greater good.

Increasing Importance of Ethical Leadership

The increasing importance of ethical leadership and social responsibility is a reflection of the evolving expectations and demands of stakeholders, including employees, customers, investors, and society at large. This shift has significant implications for organizations and their leaders. Ethical leadership and social responsibility are gaining prominence because:

1. **Trust and Reputation:** Ethical leadership is closely tied to trust. In an era of information transparency, organizations are acutely aware of the value of a positive reputation. Ethical leaders who prioritize honesty and integrity are more likely to build and maintain trust among stakeholders, which can have a direct impact on brand reputation and long-term success.

2. **Consumer Awareness:** Today's consumers are more socially conscious and informed than ever before. They seek out products and services that align with their values, and they are quick to boycott or criticize companies that engage in unethical practices. Ethical leadership and social responsibility are seen as markers of a company's commitment to ethical and sustainable business practices, making them attractive to consumers.

3. **Employee Expectations:** The workforce increasingly values ethical leadership. Employees want to work for organizations that prioritize ethical behavior, fairness, and social responsibility. Ethical leaders attract and retain top talent and foster a positive and engaged workplace culture.

4. **Investor Priorities:** Ethical considerations have become integral to investment decisions. Many investors are factoring in a company's ethical track record and commitment to social responsibility when making investment choices. Ethical leadership can enhance an organization's access to capital and support from investors.

5. **Regulatory Environment:** Governments and regulatory bodies are imposing stricter regulations related to ethics and social responsibility. Organizations that proactively demonstrate ethical leadership are better positioned to comply with evolving regulations and avoid legal and reputational risks.

6. **Sustainability and Environmental Concerns:** Ethical leadership extends to environmental responsibility. As climate change and sustainability concerns grow, leaders are expected to incorporate ethical and environmentally responsible practices into their business strategies.

7. **Social Impact:** Businesses are increasingly expected to contribute positively to society. Ethical leaders are involved in social causes, philanthropy, and community engagement, recognizing that organizations have a role to play in addressing societal issues.

8. **Long-Term Value Creation:** Ethical leadership is associated with long-term value creation. While unethical practices may yield short-term gains, they often lead to long-term negative consequences. Ethical leaders prioritize sustainable and responsible growth that benefits all stakeholders.

9. **Globalization and Transparency:** In a globalized world with instant access to information, unethical behavior can quickly become a global scandal. Ethical leadership is essential for maintaining a positive global reputation and avoiding reputational damage.

10. **Resilience in Crisis:** Ethical leaders are better equipped to navigate crises. When ethical principles guide decision-making, organizations are more likely to respond to crises with transparency, accountability, and a focus on solutions rather than cover-ups.

The increasing importance of ethical leadership and social responsibility reflects a changing business landscape and the growing awareness of the broader impacts of organizational behavior. Ethical leaders not only meet stakeholder expectations but also position their organizations for sustainable success, resilience in the face of challenges, and a positive impact on society as a whole.

How to Lead with Integrity and Make Ethical Decision

Leading with integrity and making ethical decisions is paramount for leaders to build trust, foster a positive organizational culture, and ensure long-term success. Here are strategies and principles that leaders can follow to lead with integrity and make ethical decisions:

1. **Establish Clear Ethical Values:** Define and communicate clear ethical values and principles that align with the organization's mission and vision. Ensure that these values are embedded in the organizational culture.
2. **Lead by Example:** Demonstrate ethical behavior and integrity in your own actions and decisions. Be a role model for your team, embodying the values you expect from others.
3. **Promote Open Communication:** Create an environment where employees feel safe to voice concerns or report unethical behavior. Encourage open and honest communication, and protect whistleblowers from retaliation.
4. **Seek Diverse Perspectives:** Involve diverse voices and perspectives in decision-making processes. Consider the ethical implications of decisions from various angles to avoid bias and tunnel vision.
5. **Set Ethical Expectations:** Clearly define ethical expectations and standards for all employees. Ensure that these expectations are reflected in job descriptions, performance evaluations, and codes of conduct.

6. **Ethical Decision-Making Framework:** Implement a structured ethical decision-making framework within the organization. This could involve assessing the situation, considering alternatives, and evaluating the ethical implications of each choice.
7. **Transparency and Accountability:** Promote transparency in decision-making processes. Clearly communicate the rationale behind decisions, and be willing to be held accountable for those decisions.
8. **Regular Ethics Training:** Provide ongoing ethics training and education to employees at all levels. Equip them with the knowledge and tools to recognize and address ethical dilemmas.
9. **Ethics Committee or Advisor:** Consider establishing an ethics committee or appointing an ethics advisor who can provide guidance and recommendations on ethical matters.
10. **Ethical Risk Assessment:** Conduct regular ethical risk assessments to identify potential ethical challenges and vulnerabilities within the organization. Develop strategies to mitigate these risks.
11. **Ethical Dilemma Resolution:** When facing ethical dilemmas, involve relevant stakeholders in the decision-making process. Seek input from experts or consult industry standards to arrive at ethical solutions.
12. **Consistency and Fairness:** Apply ethical principles consistently across all levels of the organization. Ensure fairness and avoid favoritism in decision-making.
13. **Review and Adapt:** Regularly review and adapt ethical guidelines and policies to address evolving challenges and changing ethical standards in the business environment.
14. **Corporate Social Responsibility (CSR):** Incorporate CSR initiatives that align with the organization's values and contribute positively to society and the environment.
15. **Moral Courage:** Encourage and develop moral courage within the organization. Encourage employees to stand up for ethical principles, even in the face of adversity.

Leading with integrity and making ethical decisions requires a proactive and ongoing commitment to ethical leadership. By embedding ethical values into the organizational culture and decision-making processes, leaders can foster an environment where ethical behavior is not only expected but also celebrated and rewarded.

Integration and Synthesis

Integration and Synthesis refer to the processes of combining, harmonizing, and unifying various elements, ideas, or information into a cohesive and comprehensive whole. Integration involves bringing together diverse components or perspectives to create a unified and interconnected system or concept. It often entails finding commonalities and bridging gaps between different elements. Synthesis, on the other hand, involves the act of amalgamating or blending distinct parts or ideas to generate new insights, theories, or solutions. In both integration and synthesis, the aim is to create a more holistic understanding or solution by considering multiple facets and perspectives, thereby enhancing clarity, coherence, and effectiveness in decision-making, problem-solving, or knowledge development.

Integrating and synthesizing different leadership styles and approaches to suit various situations and contexts is a hallmark of effective leadership. Here's guidance on how leaders can achieve this:

1. **Know Your Leadership Styles:** Begin by understanding your own leadership style and preferences. This self-awareness is crucial as it forms the foundation for integrating other styles.

2. **Situational Leadership:** Embrace the concept of situational leadership, which entails adapting your leadership style to the specific needs of each situation or team. Assess the

situation, the team's capabilities, and the task at hand before deciding on an appropriate leadership approach.

3. **Learn from Diverse Leaders:** Study and learn from leaders who embody different leadership styles. Seek out mentors or role models who can provide insights into styles that differ from your own.

4. **Build a Leadership Toolkit:** Develop a toolkit of leadership approaches that you can draw from when needed. This toolkit may include elements of transformational, servant, democratic, or authoritative leadership, among others.

5. **Flexibility and Adaptability:** Be flexible and willing to adapt your leadership style as circumstances change. Recognize that there is no one-size-fits-all approach to leadership.

6. **Active Listening:** Practice active listening to understand the perspectives and needs of your team members. Tailor your leadership style to address their concerns and preferences.

7. **Team Diversity:** Embrace diversity within your team. Different team members may respond better to varying leadership styles based on their backgrounds, experiences, and roles.

8. **Collaboration:** Encourage collaboration and teamwork. Foster an environment where team members can contribute their unique strengths and ideas, and be open to integrating these diverse inputs into decision-making processes.

9. **Empowerment:** Empower your team members to take on leadership roles themselves when appropriate. Distributed leadership can be effective in complex or dynamic situations.

10. **Continuous Learning:** Stay committed to continuous learning and self-improvement as a leader. Attend leadership

development programs, workshops, and seminars to gain exposure to different leadership philosophies and approaches.

11. **Feedback and Reflection:** Seek feedback from your team and peers to assess the effectiveness of your leadership style in various situations. Reflect on your experiences and identify areas for improvement.

12. **Ethical Considerations:** Always align your leadership approaches with ethical principles and values. Ethical leadership should be the foundation upon which all styles are built.

13. **Risk-Taking:** Be willing to take calculated risks in adapting your leadership style. Innovation often involves stepping out of your comfort zone and experimenting with new approaches.

14. **Cultural Sensitivity:** If operating in a global context, be culturally sensitive and adaptable. Different cultures may have unique expectations and preferences for leadership styles.

15. **Long-Term Perspective:** Keep a long-term perspective on leadership development. Integrating and synthesizing different styles is a journey that requires ongoing practice and refinement.

By integrating and synthesizing diverse leadership styles and approaches, leaders can become more versatile, adaptable, and effective in addressing the complex and ever-changing challenges they encounter in various situations and contexts. This flexibility enhances their ability to lead teams and organizations toward success.

Creating a Personal Leadership Philosophy

Creating a Personal Leadership Philosophy involves developing a set of guiding principles, values, and beliefs that define how an individual approaches leadership and influences their decision-making and actions as a leader. This personal philosophy serves as a compass, providing clarity and direction in leadership roles. It includes core ideals such as integrity, accountability, vision, and empathy, which guide a leader's behavior and interactions with others. A personal leadership philosophy is an essential foundation for effective leadership, helping leaders stay true to their principles and make ethical, consistent, and purpose-driven decisions in various situations and contexts.

How Leaders can Craft their Philosophy

Leaders can craft their personal leadership philosophy by drawing inspiration from various leadership theories and models, incorporating key principles and insights into their own unique approach to leadership. Here's a step-by-step guide on how to do this:

1. **Study Leadership Theories:** Begin by studying a variety of leadership theories and models, including transformational, servant, authentic, situational, and contingency theories, among others. Understand the key concepts, principles, and insights offered by each theory.

2. **Self-Reflection:** Engage in deep self-reflection to identify your core values, beliefs, and principles. Consider your personal leadership experiences, successes, failures, and the values that have guided your actions.

3. **Identify Common Themes:** Look for common themes and principles that resonate with you across different leadership theories. Identify those aspects of leadership that align with your personal values and beliefs.

4. **Define Your Core Values:** Clearly articulate your core values and ethical principles. These should serve as the foundation of your leadership philosophy. For example, you might value honesty, empathy, innovation, or social responsibility.

5. **Clarify Your Vision:** Develop a clear vision of the kind of leader you aspire to be and the impact you want to have on your team, organization, or community. Consider how your leadership can contribute to a greater purpose.

6. **Incorporate Key Concepts:** Integrate key concepts and insights from the leadership theories you've studied into your personal philosophy. For instance, you might embrace the transformational leadership idea of inspiring and motivating others toward a shared vision.

7. **Adaptability and Context:** Recognize that your leadership philosophy should be adaptable to different contexts and situations. Consider how you can flex your approach based on the needs of your team, the organization, or the challenges at hand.

8. **Embrace Lifelong Learning:** Commit to continuous learning and growth as a leader. Stay open to new ideas and leadership theories that may evolve or complement your philosophy over time.

9. **Seek Feedback:** Invite feedback from mentors, colleagues, and team members. They can offer valuable insights into how well your leadership philosophy aligns with your actions and behaviors.

10. **Put It into Practice:** Live out your leadership philosophy through your actions, decisions, and interactions. Be consistent in applying your values and principles in both routine and challenging situations.

11. **Reflect and Refine:** Continuously reflect on your leadership experiences and assess whether your personal philosophy is achieving the desired outcomes. Be open to refinement and adaptation as you learn and grow as a leader.

12. **Communicate Your Philosophy:** Communicate your leadership philosophy to your team and colleagues. Transparency about your values and principles can foster trust and alignment within the organization.

By crafting a personal leadership philosophy informed by various leadership theories, leaders can create a guiding framework that reflects their unique values and beliefs while benefiting from the wisdom and insights of established leadership models. This approach helps leaders make more informed and principled decisions, inspire others, and create a positive impact within their sphere of influence.

How Personalized Philosophy Can Serve as Guidance?

A well-crafted personal leadership philosophy can serve as a guiding compass for a leader's entire leadership journey in several ways:

1. **Clarity of Purpose:** It provides a clear sense of purpose and direction. Leaders can refer to their philosophy to remind themselves why they lead and what they aim to achieve, helping them stay focused on their long-term goals.

2. **Consistency:** A leadership philosophy establishes a consistent framework for decision-making and action. Leaders can use it as a reference point to ensure that their choices align with their values and principles, promoting consistency and integrity in their leadership.

3. **Ethical Decision-Making:** It serves as an ethical foundation. Leaders can use their philosophy to make ethical

decisions, even in challenging or ambiguous situations, as it provides a moral compass to navigate ethical dilemmas.

4. **Guidance in Complexity:** In complex or uncertain situations, a leadership philosophy offers guidance. Leaders can turn to it for insight and direction when facing tough decisions or when they encounter unfamiliar challenges.

5. **Alignment with Teams:** Communicating the leadership philosophy to team members fosters alignment and trust. Team members can better understand the leader's approach and expectations, which promotes a sense of purpose and unity within the team.

6. **Resilience in Adversity:** During challenging times, a leadership philosophy provides resilience. It reminds leaders of their values and principles, helping them stay grounded and focused on their mission when facing adversity.

7. **Learning and Growth:** Leaders can use their philosophy as a tool for personal and professional growth. They can reflect on their experiences, identify areas for improvement, and adapt their philosophy as they learn and evolve as leaders.

8. **Inspiration for Others:** A well-defined leadership philosophy can inspire others. When team members see their leader consistently living out their values and principles, it can motivate and encourage them to do the same.

9. **Alignment with Organizational Goals:** Leaders can align their personal philosophy with the goals and values of the organization they lead. This ensures that their leadership is not only personally meaningful but also contributes to the success of the organization.

10. **Long-Term Impact:** Over the course of a leadership career, a philosophy can lead to a lasting legacy. It shapes the leader's reputation and the impact they have on their organization, team members, and the broader community.

A well-crafted personal leadership philosophy serves as a guiding compass throughout a leader's journey by providing clarity, consistency, ethics, and resilience. It not only helps leaders make principled decisions but also inspires and aligns their teams, contributing to their long-term success and impact as leaders.

*****

APPENDIX ONE
Leadership Theories

Great Man Theory (1840s): Key Researcher: Thomas Carlyle.

Laissez-faire Leadership (1920s): Origin: French, means letting people do as they choose.

Charismatic Leadership (1922): Key Researcher: Max Weber.

Autocratic Leadership (1930s): Key Researcher: Kurt Lewin.

Participative Leadership (1930): Key Researcher: Kurt Lewin.

Trait Theory (1936): Key Researcher: Gordon Allport.

Management or Transactional Leadership (1947): Key Researcher: Max Weber.

Behavioral Leadership (1950s): Key Researcher: Dr. Rensis Likert.

Psychological Leadership (1953): Key Researcher: Albert Bandura.

Relationship Leadership (1958): Key Researcher: Hollander

Power and Influence Leadership (1959): Key Researcher: Bertram Raven.

Contingency Leadership (1960s): Key Researcher: Austrian psychologist Professor Fred Fiedler.

Coaching Leadership (1960): Key Researchers: Paul Hersey and Kenneth Blanchard.

Situational Leadership (1969): Key Researchers: Ken Blanchard and Paul Hersey.

Path-Goal Leadership (1970): Key Researcher: Martin G. Evans.

Transformational Leadership (1973): Key Researcher: James V. Downton.

Vroom-Yetton Decision-Making Model (1973): Key Researchers: Victor Vroom and Phillip Yetton.

Leader-Member Exchange (LMX) (1975): Key Researchers: Dansereau, Graen, and Haga.

Functional Leadership (1986): Key Researchers: Heckman and Walton.

Distributive Leadership (1990s): Key Researcher: Edwin Hutchins.

Authentic Leadership (2003): Key Researcher: Bill George.

*****

APPENDIX TWO
Leadership Theories

Trait Theory

- Key Idea: Leadership is based on inherent traits and qualities.
- Characteristics: Focuses on identifying specific traits such as intelligence, confidence, charisma, and decisiveness.
- Strengths: Simple and intuitive; helps identify potential leaders.
- Weaknesses: Lacks empirical evidence; ignores situational factors.

Great Man Theory:

- Key Idea: Leaders are born, not made.
- Characteristics: Assumes that great leaders possess innate qualities.
- Strengths: Historical perspective; highlights the importance of innate leadership traits.
- Weaknesses: Ignores the role of nurture and situational factors.

Behavioral Theory

- Key Idea: Leadership is learned through behavior.
- Characteristics: Focuses on observable behaviors like task-oriented and relationship-oriented leadership.
- Strengths: Provides actionable insights for leadership development.
- Weaknesses: Doesn't consider individual differences; can be overly simplistic.

Contingency Theory:

- Key Idea: Effective leadership depends on the situation.
- Characteristics: Different situations require different leadership styles.
- Strengths: Recognizes the importance of context; offers flexibility.
- Weaknesses: Complex to apply; the optimal style may vary.

Transformational Leadership:

- Key Idea: Leaders inspire and transform their followers.
- Characteristics: Emphasizes vision, charisma, and motivation.
- Strengths: Motivates and empowers followers; can lead to organizational change.
- Weaknesses: Requires charisma and may be manipulative if misused.

Transactional Leadership:

- Key Idea: Leaders use rewards and punishments to motivate.
- Characteristics: Transactional leaders set clear expectations and offer rewards or consequences.
- Strengths: Clarity in expectations and rewards.
- Weaknesses: Can lead to compliance rather than commitment.

Servant Leadership:

- Key Idea: Leaders serve their followers' needs.
- Characteristics: Focuses on humility, empathy, and ethical behavior.
- Strengths: Builds trust and ethical leadership.
- Weaknesses: May be perceived as weak by some.

Situational Leadership

- Key Idea: Leadership style should adapt to follower readiness.
- Characteristics: Leaders assess follower readiness and adjust their style.
- Strengths: Adaptable and flexible leadership.
- Weaknesses: Requires frequent assessment.

Path-Goal Theory

- Key Idea: Leaders clarify paths to goals.
- Characteristics: Focuses on support, directive, participative, and achievement-oriented leadership.
- Strengths: Enhances motivation by aligning goals.
- Weaknesses: Lacks attention to individual traits.

Laissez-Faire Leadership

- Key Idea: Leaders take a hands-off approach.
- Characteristics: Leaders delegate authority and decision-making to their team members, allowing them to work independently.
- Strengths: Encourages autonomy and creativity; suitable for expert teams.
- Weaknesses: May result in a lack of direction and control, leading to inefficiencies and confusion.

Authentic Leadership

- Key Idea: Authentic leaders are genuine and self-aware.
- Characteristics: Emphasizes self-awareness, transparency, and ethical behavior.
- Strengths: Builds trust and strong relationships.
- Weaknesses: Subjective and difficult to measure.

Charismatic Leadership

- Key Idea: Leaders have charismatic appeal.

- Characteristics: Focuses on personal magnetism and inspiration.
- Strengths: Inspires devotion and enthusiasm.
- Weaknesses: Potential for abuse and cult-like followings.

Leader-Member Exchange (LMX)

- Key Idea: Leadership quality varies between leaders and followers.
- Characteristics: Emphasizes high-quality exchanges and personalized relationships.
- Strengths: Fosters loyalty and individualized leadership.
- Weaknesses: Can lead to in-group/out-group dynamics.

Contingent Reward Leadership

- Key Idea: Leaders reward performance.
- Characteristics: Clarifies expectations and provides rewards.
- Strengths: Motivates through rewards.
- Weaknesses: Can be transactional in nature.

Adaptive Leadership

- Key Idea: Leaders adapt to challenges.
- Characteristics: Tackles complex problems and fosters innovation.
- Strengths: Addresses dynamic environments.
- Weaknesses: Requires high tolerance for ambiguity.

*****